A
Daily Devotion That is
More Than Milk Toast

Marj Rossing

Tri M Graphics
Owatonna, Minnesota

The majority of the Bible references are taken from the King James version of the Bible. References are also taken from the Contemporary English Version (CEV) , the Amplified version and the New English Bible and are identified. In some cases I have used italics and underlining for emphasis.

A Daily Devotion that is More Than Milk Toast
ISBN 0-9777843-0-4
Copyright © 2006 Marjorie Rossing

Printed by Tri M Graphics
625 East Main Street
Owatonna, MN 55060

Acknowledgments

Without the encouragement from my two sons, Mike and Martin, I doubt that I would have ever stepped into the computer age. It was very hard to be divorced from my trusty old typewriter, but with the constant urging and help from them I finally conquered the touchy temperamental computer, without which this job would have been much harder.

I also thank my granddaughter, Mindi Klein who spent many hours going over Grandma's work. I also have close friends who spent time on this book as well. They are Barb Mrotz, Cindy Christensen, Jo Moore and especially Jerry Neitzell whose computer knowledge finally brought this book into completion. Without these people this book may have never become a reality.

JANUARY 1st

I believe a good place to start out the year is to talk about God's love for His human race. When Adam and Eve sinned way back in Genesis, that disobedience to God's command resulted in bringing the whole human race under the penalty and the curse of sin, which means mankind would die physically.

In Romans 6:23, we see that the penalty of sin is death, *"For the wages of sin is death; but the gift of God is eternal life through Jesus Christ our Lord."* Please notice that in this verse God gives both the negative truth (death) and the positive truth (eternal life), and how each of those truths is attained. Sin brings death, Jesus Christ brings eternal life! God warned them that disobedience would result in death in Genesis 2:16-17 which reads, *"And God commanded the man, saying, 'Of every tree of the garden thou may freely eat: But of the tree of the knowledge of good and evil, thou shall not eat of it: for in the day that thou eat thereof thou shall surely die.' "*

But Adam and Eve disobeyed God, as we see in Genesis 3:6, *"And when the woman saw that the tree was good for food, and that it was pleasant to the eyes, and a tree to be desired to make one wise, she took of the fruit thereof, and did eat, and gave also unto her husband with her and he did eat."*

Now God had a problem. He still loved man and woman, whom He had created, and did not want them separated from Himself. But how could restoration take place and God remain God? God cannot compromise with sin. It must be dealt with. God did not hate Adam and Eve, but rather He hated the sin that they committed, and it was that sin that separated them from God.

God did not move. They had moved away from God when they disobeyed Him. So God, because of His *love* for us, began a restoration process into the lives of the human race. In order for us to really understand God's great love for us, we have to see the depth to which we have fallen. Tomorrow we will begin our upward journey with God's *love*, in our lives.

1

PRAYER: Dear Lord God, thank you for loving me enough to want to restore me to fellowship with you on a one-to-one basis. In Jesus' name, Amen.

JANUARY 2nd

Look at Hebrews 9:22, which states *"And almost all things are by the law purged with blood; and without shedding of blood is no remission (of sin)."* God provided a way to bring a sacrifice of blood that covered the sin and restored a relationship with God not a permanent relationship, that will come later, but a day-by-day relationship with God. He gave them a system of sacrifices for sin that required the animal sacrifice of blood to cover (notice I said *cover*) the sin of that day.

It was *God's love* that provided that method of restoration. Sin still reigned in the thoughts and deeds of mankind, and death also reigned, but they could draw near to God and not run away from Him. Genesis 3:6-11 reads: *"And when the woman saw that the tree was good for food, and that it was pleasant to the eyes, and a tree to be desired to make one wise, she took of the fruit thereof, and did eat, and gave also unto her husband with her; and he did eat. And the eyes of them both were opened, and they knew that they were naked; and they sewed fig leaves together, and made themselves aprons. And they heard the voice of the Lord God walking in the garden in the cool of the day: and Adam* (the man) *and his wife hid themselves from the presence of the Lord God amongst the trees of the garden. And the Lord God called unto Adam, and said unto him, 'Where art thou?' And he said, 'I heard thy voice in the garden, and I was afraid, because I was naked; and I hid myself.' And He* (God) *said, 'Who told thee that thou wast naked? Hast thou eaten of the tree, whereof I commanded thee that thou shouldest not eat?' "*

Let's trace God's love through these verses. We see that Adam and Eve directly disobeyed God (verse 6) and the result, that they were no longer innocent, but knew they were naked and tried to

2

cover themselves (verse 7). Then God came to fellowship with Adam, and Adam hid (verse 8)! God called to Adam! Imagine that! Adam was disobedient, and yet God came hunting for him (verse 9). God first move toward reconciliation after Adam and Eve sinned. Why? Because He *loves* His creation.

Adam claimed that he was afraid because he was naked (verse 10), but God put His finger on the real reason for Adam's fear in verse 11, *"And God said, 'Who told thee that thou was naked? Has thou eaten of the tree, whereof I commanded thee that thou should not eat?' "* God asked Adam two very pointed questions, and the sin of disobedience was revealed right then and there. God is always reaching out to us in *love*.

PRAYER: Heavenly Father, thank you for not giving up on us when we fail you, and thank you for the example of Adam and Eve and how you reached out to them in the midst of their mess, so that I may know that you will reach out to me in my messes also. Amen.

JANUARY 3rd

Before we go any further into the year, I want to describe the word, "love," as we find it in the Bible. The New Testament is written in the Greek language and they have three words for love. One word is eros, which means a sensual type of love, the type we see between lovers. The next word for love is phileo, which means to have ardent affection for another, like love for family members. The other word for love is agape, and that means an unconditional, limitless love.

Agape love is the kind of love that God has for us, and the kind He wants us to have for Him and for one another. John 3:16 states, *"For God so loved* (agape) *the world, that He gave His only begotten Son, that whosoever believes in Him shall not perish but have everlasting life."*

God's love is not dependent upon our performance, although He cares about how each of us lives our Christian life here on this earth. When we accept Jesus as our Lord and Savior, we become a member of the family of God. We come under that unconditional love of God the Father, God the Son, and God the Holy Spirit who are all at work on our behalf to help us grow in grace and holiness.

PRAYER: Help me, Heavenly Father, to see your love for me in my life today, and help me to be more loving to those around me. In Jesus' name, Amen.

JANUARY 4th

In Leviticus 4:1-5, God instructed Moses how to offer up an offering for sin (which was, in this case, a bullock) and how the offering's blood was to be presented to God. All the way through the Old Testament, God's family, the Jews, had the privilege of drawing close to God through the sacrifices of animals, the shedding of blood. But that kind of sacrifice could only cover sin.

God had a plan, but it would have to wait for perfect timing. We can see that explained in Galatians 4:4-5, which states, *"But when the fullness of time was come, God sent forth His Son, made of a woman* (which means He had a human birth), *born under the law* (which means He was under the curse of death and would have to comply to the laws of God like every other person), *To redeem them that were under the law* (the curse of death), *that we* (all of us) *might receive the adoption of sons."*

God had a plan to restore mankind to the position of sonship. We were under the curse of sin, but now could find our way back to God because God loved us so much. I do not believe that we can truly love God until we know just how much God loves us. You will only discover the depth of His love from reading His Word, the Bible. Tomorrow we will consider the word *redeem* in Galatians 4:5.

PRAYER: Lord God, I am beginning to see how much you loved me, and how willing you are to reach out to me. I thank you for taking me, step by step, into an understanding of that love. Help me to not miss one point as I journey with you this year. In Jesus' name, Amen.

JANUARY 5th

Galatians 4:5 explains why God sent His son, *"To redeem them that were under the law* (of sin and death)*, that we might receive the adoption of sons."* That word, *"redeem,"* is important. It means to "buy back."

If you take a watch to a pawn shop, you get paid a certain price for it. Later, when you can afford it, you go back to *redeem* your watch. However, you will have to pay more to get it back than what you received for it in the first place. Otherwise, why would that pawn shop owner be in business?

Well, God is going to carry out His plan to rescue, redeem, buy back, His creation. We see that in John 3:16, which reads, *"For God so loved the world that He gave His only begotten Son, that whosoever believes in Him shall not perish but have everlasting life."*
Just as God reached out to Adam after he had disobeyed God, so also God has reached out to all of us, who are under the curse of sin and cannot help ourselves. God sent His own Son whom He loved, to live a sinless life, shed His blood, suffer and die in our place, in order to satisfy God's holy standard and to redeem us from the curse of sin.

Jesus was the complete answer to the sin question, because He took our sins away. Animal blood could only cover sin, but in John 1:29, John said, *"...Behold, the Lamb of God that takes away the sin of the world."*

Anyone who subscribes to God's plan can be assured of eternal life in heaven with God, just the place God wants us all to be because He loves us that much! Jesus did not just cover sin, He took it away forever!

PRAYER: Heavenly Father, how can I thank you enough for such a free gift as eternal life? I lift my voice to you in thanksgiving and worship for all you have done and will continue to do for me each day of my life. Give me eyes to see your hand in my life today. In Jesus' name, Amen.

JANUARY 6th

 There are some references to love that I believe are vitally important for us to grasp. They are found in I John 4. I suggest that you read all of chapter 4, but there are some verses I want to point out specifically.

John 4:19 reads, *"We love Him* (God), *because He first loved us."* Love originated with God, and the first steps of love in the universe came out from God toward us. It is that fact that gives us the ability to love at all.

Compare that to Romans 5:8, which states, ***"But God commanded His love toward us, that while we were yet sinners, Christ died for us."*** Let's really look at that verse. First of all, God ordered His love to look our way and see our pitiful condition of sin, and to do something about it. He did not order us to clean ourselves up to get ready to meet with Him, because God knew we were not able to do that. We needed help to come to Him.

While we were in that terrible debilitating state of sin, God's Son, Jesus Christ, agreed to come to be the final sacrifice for sin, and to set us free from the curse of sin and death. Oh, yes, we still die physically, but I will deal with what Jesus did about that later on in the year.

PRAYER: Dear God, I am beginning to see how the love you have for me cost you dearly, and how you were willing to pay all that for me. Is there anything you wouldn't do for me? You have my best interests at heart, so I can trust you completely. I want to please you in all I think and do, but I need your help to live that way. In Jesus' precious name, Amen.

JANUARY 7th

I find it very interesting that God performed the first sacrifice for sin in Genesis 3:21, which reads, *"Unto Adam and to his wife did the Lord God make coats of skins and clothed them."* The animal had to shed its blood, lose its life, and give up its coat to make a covering for sin.

God also performed the last sacrifice for sin. He gave His own Son as a sacrifice for sins. But Christ did not just cover our sins, He took them away. Jesus, too, had to shed His blood and experience death. He has given us His coat of righteousness. When we accept Jesus into our hearts He brings with Him His own righteousness and it becomes ours too.

Also look at I John 4:7-8, which states, *"Beloved, let us love one another: for love is of God; and every one that loves is born of God, and knows God, He that loves not, knows not God; for God is love."*

Please understand that the world systems cannot understand real love. They think they do, but it is really only selfish passion that they understand. The love that God is talking about is unconditional, without measure, constant, and pure. It has no selfish motive behind it. It is that kind of love that He calls us to display.

John 4:10 further explains, *"Herein is love, not that we loved God, but that He loved us, and sent His Son to be the propitiation* (sacrifice) *for our sins."* God is forever reaching out to us, to help us walk in step with Him each day. If we need to take baby steps, He will walk baby steps until we can walk adult steps. He teaches us the same way. His desire is for us to *want* to know Him better and better, a little more each day. He does not push and rush us. He is gentle and kind, but He will not compromise with sin. He wants us to love Him back enough so that we do not compromise with sin either. He wants us to hate what He hates and love what He loves. Can you do that?

PRAYER: Dear God, I feel so inadequate when it comes to following you in such a love relationship, but I am willing to try and I ask you to come alongside of me to help me carry it out on a day-to-day basis. Put your love

7

into my heart, and reshape my inner desires toward you and the people around me. In Jesus' name, Amen.

JANUARY 8th

 Today, I want you to turn to Ephesians 3:14-21, but I will be concentrating on verse 17. This whole scripture is a prayer that the Apostle Paul prayed for the church at Ephesus. Look at it this way: it is written by a Christian to a congregation of Christians, and I am a Christian, therefore it is also being prayed for me as I read it. This way, you are able to apply it to your own spiritual life right now.

First, we will look at Ephesians 3:17, which reads, *"That Christ may dwell in your hearts by faith; that you, being rooted and grounded in love."* The word "dwell" means literally to take up permanent residence, and Christ dwells in our hearts by faith. When you invite Jesus into your heart, He brings His own kind of faith into your heart with Him.

Faith is a gift from God, as we see in Romans 12:3, which states, *"...God has dealt to every man the measure of faith."* We put our faith into many things in the world and think nothing of it. We have faith that our food will not have poison in it, a pilot will not crash the plane, elevators will function safely, doctors will perform surgery correctly, and on and on. We live by faith in the world all the time. How much more should we be able to trust and have faith in God, who made us and redeemed us all because He loved us more than tongue can tell?

In Ephesians 3:17, Paul is praying *"...that we be rooted and grounded in love."* What does that mean? A fruit-bearing tree's ability to produce good fruit is measured by its root system and the fertile ground in which it is rooted. In this verse, Paul is praying that we be rooted and grounded in the fertile love of God. Are your roots of faith sinking deeper and deeper into God's love?

PRAYER: Dear Lord, I am beginning to see how my faith and trust in your love is of the utmost value if I am going to live a life of victory. I want to learn all I can about your love for me and for those around me, especially those who do not know you. I pray that every person may come to the truth about your love for them. In Jesus' name, Amen.

January 9th

In Ephesians 3:17-18, *"That Christ may dwell in your hearts by faith: that ye, being rooted and grounded in love, May be able to comprehend with all saints what is the breadth, and length, and depth, and height"* Paul wants us to be able (please notice that word able) *"...to comprehend with all the saints..."* That means to understand, to grasp the truth of all this. What does he want us to comprehend? Paul sort of leaves us hanging ... the breadth, length, depth, and height of what?

Think now, what is he talking about? Ephesians 3:17, isn't it God's love? So what is the breadth, length, depth, and height of God's love? Well, that is simple. Just follow it in John 3:16:

The breadth: *"For God so loved the world"* That includes everyone.

The length: *"that He gave His only begotten Son"* How far are you willing to go to save someone? God gave His only Son to save a world, with many who would ignore His gift of salvation and scoff at it.

The depth: *"that whosoever believes shall not perish"* Even the worst of sinners who would turn to God is welcome. God reached down into the very depths of humanity, the worst of sinners, and invites us to come unto Him. How far are you willing to reach down to bring someone into a saving relationship with Jesus?

The height: *"but have eternal life."* God is willing to put us on the same level with Himself through Jesus.

In Ephesians 2:6 we see that God *"...has raised us up together, and made us sit together in heavenly places in Christ Jesus."* When God does a job, it is not half way, but rather it is total and complete. He planned our salvation, He carried it out, and He works day and night to get our attention to see and understand what He has done for us. Then He helps us

9

to accept and follow the plan, and that all out of His *unconditional love* for us.

PRAYER: Heavenly Father, such love as you have for me is way beyond my comprehension, but I can see that you want me to be able to experience it in my life. I ask you to give me the eyes to see your love in a day-to-day revelation as I live out my life. I want to love as you loved, so help me see the opportunities to do that, and then give me the grace to do it. In Jesus' name, Amen.

JANUARY 10th

 There is another characteristic of God that we are to love, and we find that in II Thessalonians 2:10-12. Here, Paul has been discussing the devil and how he deceives God's people. In II Thessalonians 2:10, Paul continues, *"And with all deceivableness of unrighteousness in them that perish; because they received not the love of the truth, that they might be saved."*

Let me remind you that Jesus said in John 14:6, *"I am the way, the truth and the life. No one comes to the Father, but by me."* Jesus here declares that He always was, is, and always will be, the way (to God), the truth (about everything pertaining to God) and the life (outside of Jesus there is only death, physically, spiritually and eternally). So, when we see in II Thessalonians 2:10 just how dangerous it is not to love the truth, we know that it is referring to Jesus who *is* the truth.

For a person to not love the truth means that person is outside the protection of Jesus' blood-covering for sin and stands naked spiritually before God. Satan, on the other hand, does not want anyone to know or understand the truth, so he will try to lure Christians away from the truth by deceiving them. If they succumb to that lure and begin to doubt God's love for them, or that God even cares for them, they are losing their love of the truth. That is a dangerous place to allow ourselves to be.

Notice, verse 11 states, *"And for that cause God shall send them strong delusion, that they should believe the lie."* God will even allow that doubt to continue and get worse, to the point where they will willfully believe a lie. You see, God gave all of us the freedom of choice. We can choose to believe the lie, or we can choose to love the truth.

The devil is not in charge of your choices, but never forget, he will do everything he can to cause you to doubt God's love, his purpose for you ,and whether he even cares about you at all. When that happens, you have allowed your circumstances, or your ignorance of the Word of Truth, to enter into your thinking and you are on your way to not loving the truth anymore. We will continue with this message tomorrow.

PRAYER: Father, thank you for leaving your truth with me to search and to study. Give me the power to receive your truth into my heart that I might be blessed by it. In Jesus' name, Amen.

JANUARY 11th

 Now, we will look at II Thessalonians 2:12, where we left off yesterday, which states, *"That they all might be damned who believed not the truth, but had pleasure in unrighteousness."*

Think back to Adam and Eve. First the devil planted a thought of doubt in Eve's mind in Genesis 3:1, when he said, *"Yea, has God said, you shall not eat of every tree of the garden?"*

In essence, the devil is saying, "You mean to tell me that God won't let you eat of every tree in the garden? Why in the world would He hold anything back from you anyhow?" It placed a thought of doubt in Eve's mind. In verse 3, she had told the devil that they could eat of every tree except the one tree, and that they would die if they ate of that tree.

Now get this! In verse 4, the devil out and out lies to Eve, and she believes it. He declared to her that she would *not* surely die, but instead would be blessed with the knowledge of good and evil like the gods (note the small "g" in "gods"). There are many false gods out there who want our

11

attention and adoration. But Eve believed the lie, and that threw the whole human race into an inherited sin nature.

So, we see in II Thessalonians 2:12 that to believe the lie brings condemnation. We can vividly see how we can choose to believe a lie, or we can choose to believe and love the truth. Search for the truth. It will be your best friend in the end.

We will talk more about truth at a later time. I want to leave you with a thought: When all was life (when they did not even know what death was), Satan made void God's warning concerning death (Genesis 3:4-5). Now when all is death (vegetation, animals, birds, and humans all die), Satan makes void God's words offering life and life eternal. In Romans 6:11, Paul says, *"Reckon you also yourselves to be dead indeed unto sin, but alive unto God through Jesus our Lord."* What is your choice? Is it to believe Satan's lies or God's truth?

PRAYER: Heavenly Father, I can plainly see that I need you every hour of the day, so I ask for your Holy Spirit to protect me from believing the lies of the enemy of God, namely Satan, and to have a love affair with the truth that I find in your Holy Word. Create in my heart a hunger and a thirst for your Word, so I will recognize the lies of the enemy, and recognize the Truth of God. In Jesus' name, Amen.

JANUARY 12th

I believe it is time to take a look at what love is and what it is not. Turn to I Corinthians 13. This is known as the "love" chapter of the Bible and is often quoted at weddings. I wonder, however, how many people really look at what it says. In some translations it is called "charity," but I will call it "love," which is what most translations call it.

Paul wrote the books of Corinthians, and he says in 13:1-3 that no matter what spiritual gifts you have, if you do not exercise them with love, you have nothing. Love is the glue that holds everything together spiritually. In verses 4 through 8, we see what love is and what it is not. Let us look at them one by one.

Verse 4 reads, *"Love suffereth long, and is kind."* Love will suffer rather than retaliate. Now I am sure this can be stretched in the wrong direction, and that is not what God intended. We are not to be a doormat, but we are to have a tolerance and patience for those around us. If not, how will they ever see Jesus in us, or know His love, if they cannot see it in us? However, because we are made in the image of God, I do not think it is love to allow someone to walk all over us, and to treat us like second-class citizens.

God will help you walk that fine line, if you ask for His help. You would never see someone wipe their muddy shoes off on a pure white rug, but they would not hesitate to wipe the mud off on a dirty, filthy rug. You have been washed white in the blood of the Lamb, and He has given you His righteousness. I believe we need to have enough respect for who God has made us to be (we who are in Christ Jesus), that we will not allow others to wipe their dirty feet on us. I believe that if you ask God to help you to *be* the person He has made you to be, you will not have to be haughty, belligerent, or cruel to gain the respect that a white rug has. It is God's Word that says *"Charity (Love) suffereth long and is kind..."* (I Corinthians 13:4).

PRAYER: This looks like an impossible task, but I want that peace that comes from loving relationships. Help me to grasp the truth in this day's devotion. In Jesus' name, Amen.

JANUARY 13th

 We will continue in the "love" chapter, I Corinthians 13:4, which states that *"...love envieth not."* Love does not envy other people. Envy can eat away at your insides, and actually make you sick.

Look at it this way, God knows what you need and what you want, and He would be only too happy to give you the insight into what is most important.

Many times, what we want is far out of line of what we need. Look at what God's Word says in Philippians 4:19, *"But my God shall supply all your need according to his riches in glory by Christ Jesus."* All your needs will be covered by our loving Heavenly Father.

Do you realize that there may be others who envy you for what you have? Begin to be thankful for what you do have and pray for others who have less than you, and you will begin to dig yourself out of a rut of envy. Why? Because you will be showing love when you pray for those less fortunate than you are, and that love will lift the burden of envy.

Yes, indeed, love does not envy. Verse 4 also explains that *"...love vaunteth not itself, is not puffed up."* That does not mean we do not take some pride in who and what we are. It means that we do not rub someone else's nose in our accomplishments. Let your life of love speak for itself. Reach out to others instead of drawing attention to yourself. If you are half as good as you think you are, it will show in your life and you will not need to draw anyone's attention to it.

PRAYER: Lord, put a guard on my mouth that I do not practice exalting myself before others. I find my pleasure in knowing that you will exalt me when I am obedient to you, and that is the best exaltation I can have. I do not want to bring a reproach to the name of Christ, by which I am called, a Christian. Guard my mouth from boasting in anything, except your love for me and for everyone else in this world. In Jesus' mighty name, Amen.

JANUARY 14th

I Corinthians 13:5 states, *"Love does not behave itself unseemly seeketh not her own, is not easily provoked, thinketh no evil."* Let me remind you that the love I am talking about here is God's love *in* us, being displayed *through* us. We have that love because Jesus, who brought God's love to earth, is the One who is living in and through us. It is that love that the world will see in us, and it will bring either honor to God (if we have that love) or reproach to God (if we do not show that love), for God's name.

Which of those you display in your life is up to you. We are seeing, in this chapter on love, that it is a choice that we make day after day, and many times a day.

Verse 5 continues in the Amplified Bible; *"...it is not rude (unmannerly) and does not act unbecomingly."* I find some of the lose talk among family members very dangerous. It borders on rude, but is considered acceptable in our society today. So, where does the normal conversation go from there? It can only get worse and worse until there is no sense of love in that family at all anymore. Real love nurtures relationships, builds them up, fosters good will, and so on.

Verse 5 of the Amplified reads; *"Love does not insist on its own rights or on its own way."* It is not a "me first" mentality, but rather it is a "we /us" attitude. In this world, we are living in relationship all the time. It is child and parent, student and teacher, employee and employer, husband and wife, nursing home staff, etc. The point is that we live in relationship all the time. It is a trip, a journey through life, and God is watching our love walk in each relationship. It will not be an easy, gentle, enjoyable life if we always insist on our own way. Check your love walk in your relationships to see what it registers: poor, good, better, or excellent. Always, the choice is ours.

PRAYER: Lord, I desire to walk in love, but my old nature is at work in me trying to put me off course most of the time. I ask your Holy Spirit to see ahead of time the places where I fail you and help me to be ready to make the right choice to stand firm in love no matter how I feel about it. In Jesus' name, Amen.

15

JANUARY 15th

 I Corinthians 13:6 states that *"Rejoiceth not in iniquity (unrighteousness), but rejoices in the truth."* When Jesus' love lives in us, we will find that we do not have a satisfied feeling when other people get what we think they deserve. Instead, we would hope that their situation would bring them to a point of truth that would rescue them from their pain.

John 8:32 says, *"You shall know the truth and the truth shall make you free."* The opposite of "free" is "bondage," or "slavery." Many times we need a circumstance in our life to show us that we are in a bondage and need to be set free. The circumstance is designed to cause us to turn to God and seek His help in our times of need. If someone came along to make our circumstances worse (because he was upset, and therefore delighted in our pain) it would make our circumstances worse, but if he came along side of us to give us moral support, it would make our circumstances tolerable and we would come to the truth quicker. Therefore, if we have love in our hearts, we will not rejoice when someone else is hurting. We can respond to that circumstance in others' lives by coming along side of them, either in prayer or in a personal manner, with a visit of support. That will show them we are not rejoicing in their dire circumstances, but that we would rather rejoice in truth, which is, they are hurting right now. One day, it may be my turn or your turn to hurt, and I would want someone to treat me with kindness. Wouldn't you?

PRAYER: Lord God, forgive me for ever rejoicing over someone's hard time or difficulty. Help me put such unrighteousness out of my mind and help me to concentrate on your truth and your love for me and for others. In Jesus' name, Amen.

JANUARY 16th

I Corinthians 13:7 reads, *"Love bears all things, believes all things, hopes all things, endures all things."* The Amplified Bible puts it this way, *"Loves bears up under anything and everything that comes, is ever ready to believe the best of every person, its hopes are fadeless under all circumstances and it endures everything* (without weakening). *"*

Again, I must remind you that the love you have in you, Jesus' love, is able to carry out and fulfill that verse. We, in our own effort are not able to do all this. But if you depend on Jesus' love to work its work through you, then you will be able to do all this.

Jesus has the power to change people and circumstances that you would think are impossible to change, but He needs our cooperation to do this. We give Him our cooperation when we decide to love as He loved. When we do that, Jesus is able to change people and circumstances.

I must warn you, however, that Jesus' way of changing people or circumstances may not be what we think it ought to be. We must not have a preconceived idea of how Jesus will do the changing. If we do, we might find ourselves very disappointed. But His way of doing something is always the *best* for us. We have to know that Jesus is for us, has only our good in mind, and has a lot of time to work it out. We may want it all done yesterday, but Jesus has a time schedule with the knowledge of the truth. Decide to walk in tune to His drumbeat each and every day.

PRAYER: Lord God, I give myself into your game plan for my life. I want your love to shine through me, and your patience to show through me, so that others will want what I have in you. You become more precious to me every day. Thank you for loving me into your Kingdom. Amen.

JANUARY 17th

I Corinthians 13:8 states, *"Love never fails."* This is an awesome statement, almost a scary statement! But, you see, we do not take into consideration that people fail, which may look like love has failed. When we put God first in our lives, and allow His love to manifest itself through us, it will not fail. But our old nature gets in the way when we want things to go our way, and that is when it would appear that love has failed.

17

Many times, a personal desire gets in the way of God's love showing through us. I believe it all boils down to just how much we want to be in tune with God and His ways in our lives. Is it enough so that you will put your own personal feelings on notice that they do not rule the throne of your heart, but that God and His love rules? Isn't it, therefore, a wonderful thing to realize that *"love never fails"*? It is something we can depend on, in fact, God's love for us is always there, no matter what is happening in our lives. God will always love us. Just step out in faith and believe that in your life "love will not fail." Go forward and live your life with that attitude.

PRAYER: Father God, thank you for such a promise that "love will not fail." It is like a rock upon which I can stand firm, but it is plain I cannot do it on my own. I pray that your Holy Spirit will prompt me whenever my old nature wants to shove you out and not allow you to rule in my heart. In Jesus' precious name, Amen.

JANUARY 18th

We are going to skip over a few verses, and finish with the last verse of the "love" chapter. I Corinthians 13:13 reads, *"And now abide faith, hope, love, these three; but the greatest of these is love."* I think this is an awesome statement. Think about it. Hope is very important.

In the Bible, "hope" is not like we think of hope in the world. In the world, it is used as a wishful desire for something in the future. But in the Bible, a confidence is expressed in the word. Where it says "hope," you can almost substitute the word "assurance" or "confidence."

"Faith" is also an awesome word. We live by faith and cannot please God without it, as we read in Hebrew 11:6, *"But without faith it is impossible to please God."* And yet, as important as these two aspects of our walk with God are, *love* is ranked above them all. I believe we need to make a determination in our walk with God to put into practice a life of

18

love. Think of ways you can show love to your fellow men and women. That is God's kind of love, a love that puts others first and yourself last, that does not keep a record of wrongs done to you, that is quick to forgive those who hurt you, accidentally or on purpose. Then, that kind of love will rank way above both hope and faith in your walk with God.

PRAYER: Heavenly Father, the desire to live a life of love, your kind of love, is in me, but I know that I cannot do this on my own. Guide me by your Holy Spirit, that I become sensitive to my actions and the words that come out of my mouth, so that, over time, I will automatically practice the love walk that pleases you. In Jesus' name, Amen.

JANUARY 19th

Today, I want to talk about love as it relates to fruit. Matthew 7:16-20 reads: *"You shall know them by their fruits. Do men gather grapes of thorns, or figs of thistles? Even so, every good tree brings forth good fruit; but a corrupt tree brings forth evil fruit. A good tree cannot bring forth evil fruit, neither can a corrupt tree bring forth good fruit. Every tree that brings not forth good fruit is hewn down and cast into the fire. Wherefore by their fruits you shall know them."*

When you see apples on a tree, you know it is an apple tree. When you see oranges on a tree, you know it is an orange tree. This verse tells us that a tree is known by its fruit, and we are like trees in that we too are known by our fruit. What does that mean? What kind of fruit are they talking about?

Look at I Corinthians 6:19, which reads, *"What? Know you not that your body is the temple of the Holy Spirit which is in you, which you have of God and you are not our own?"*

The Holy Spirit abides (or lives) within you. It is His permanent residence. Now look at Galatians 5:22-23 which reads, *"The fruit of the Spirit* (the Holy Spirit that abides in you and bears fruit like a fruit tree) *is love, joy, peace, long suffering, gentleness, goodness, faith, meekness, temperance* (another word for self control), *against such there is no law."*

What does that mean? It means that there is no law that says "You can only love so much, or you will be arrested," or "You can only have so much peace, or you will go to jail." There is no law prohibiting any of the things on the list of the fruit of the Spirit. But, do you see what God feels He has a right to expect from you, since His Holy Spirit dwells *within* you and His fruit needs to be seen through you? Matthew 7:20 reads; *"By their fruit you shall know them* (us). *"*

One of those fruit listed is *love*, and that is the agape kind of love. Is it really possible for God's kind of love to flow through us? I believe God thinks it is. Why else would He have told us all these things?

I also believe that it is a process, or a growth. Just as a baby cannot walk, talk, or take care of himself and needs time to accomplish all that, so too must we realize that it will take time to love as God loves. It will be by practicing loving unconditionally day by day. Are you ready to begin that journey? It will be you who will benefit from practicing love the most.

PRAYER: Lord God, I can see I will need a lot of help to walk that path of love, but I am willing to begin today with your help. Remind me when I stray off that path so I can form a habit of loving as you love. In Jesus' name, Amen.

JANUARY 20th

Another fruit of the Spirit is "peace." Since God's Holy Spirit lives in you, then it should be just as natural to expect to see peace in you as it is to expect to find apples on an apple tree. So, how is your level of peace? You may think, "How can anyone have peace in such a troubled world as this?" God expects us to have peace in the midst of the storms of life simply because His Spirit lives in us and the Spirit's fruit is *peace*.

So, I want to spend a few days talking to you about peace. I have found that there are three aspects of peace spoken of in the Bible, and I see that you cannot have one without first having the other. They come in three steps. Let's look at all three and then sort them out.

I Corinthians 1:7 states, ***"To all that be in Rome, beloved of God, called to be saints: Grace to you and peace FROM God our Father, and the Lord Jesus Christ."*** In this verse, we see that there is peace *from* God.

Now, let's look at Philippians 4:7, which reads, ***"And the peace OF God, which passes all understanding, shall keep your hearts and minds through Christ Jesus."*** Here we see the peace *of* God. When I read this, I wondered, "Is there a difference?"

Then I found another aspect of peace in Romans 5:1, which explains, ***"Therefore, being justified by faith, we have peace WITH God through our Lord Jesus Christ."*** When I wonder about God's truths in the Bible, I always ask in prayer to be shown the truth. You can know that you *know* the truth also. God is only too willing to reveal His truth to an honest seeker.

PRAYER: Lord God, I desire to know and understand your truth about peace, so that I can experience that kind of peace that passes all understanding. Lead me, step by step, in this daily devotion to that truth and then help me to receive that kind of peace in my life. I want your peace to occupy my heart in such a way that I might go through the storms of life and stay in peace. In Jesus' name, Amen.

Suggestion: Spend this day pondering what you have just read. Here are some added references to ponder: John 16:33; John 14:27 (peace *with* God); I Corinthians 1:3; Galatians 1:3 (peace *from* God); and Colossians 3:15 (peace *of* God). We will spend time in these verses in the next few days, but for now please ponder each one of the references in today's devotion.

JANUARY 21st

 Today, I want to talk to you about Peace *with* God. Romans 5:1 tells us exactly how this is done, all of God and none of self. All we have to do is accept what it says in this verse as true, which is, *"Therefore, being justified by faith, we have peace with God through our Lord Jesus Christ."*

To be justified means that God's justice is satisfied in regard to our sin-debt, the debt caused by sin was settled when Jesus took our sins, which God had placed on Him (look at Isaiah 53:6 and II Corinthians 5:21). That is why the word "therefore" is in Romans 5:1. We can be justified in God's sight because of what God had done on our behalf to bring us into fellowship with Himself. Our part is to receive that gift by faith, a term also found in that verse.

There is God's part, and then there is our part. When it all comes together, *then* we can have peace *with* God. It is then a settled issue as far as God is concerned, and it needs to be a settled issue as far as we are concerned also. Is it a settled issue with you? Do you know in your heart that peace with God is available to you? If so, have you received it and made it your own? Jesus Himself said in John 14:27, *"Peace I leave with you, my peace I give unto you: not as the world gives, give I unto you. Let not your hearts be troubled, neither let it be afraid."* Could it be more plain?

PRAYER: Heavenly Father, thank you so much for doing all this for me. Help me to receive the gift of peace that I might benefit from such a wonderful gift in my life. In Jesus' name, Amen.

JANUARY 22nd

 Yesterday, we saw that we can have "peace with God." That is most important because it paves the way for us to have "peace from God" and "peace of God." Today, we will talk about "peace from God."

22

In most of Paul's Epistles, you will find that statement at the beginning of letters. For example, Galatians 1:3 reads, *"Grace be to you and peace __from__ God the Father and __from__ our Lord Jesus Christ."*

We have already looked at what Jesus said in John 14:27, *"Peace I leave with you, my peace I give unto you: not as the world gives, give I unto you."*

The world tries to tell you that if you have enough insurance policies, a good job, lots of money, or children that are doing well, then you will have peace. That is the world's view of peace. God wants us to have peace even when the storms of life rage around us, which is what the peace *from* God is all about.

When we begin to feel confusion and turmoil mounting up in our hearts and minds, we can call on God to give us that peace that comes from Him, because it is available to us. I believe He will not force it upon us, but that we have to ask Him for it. He has given us the freedom of choice, and He has told us in His word that His peace is available to us. If we are living in strife and turmoil, could it be that it is our fault because we have not asked Him to give us that peace He said we can have?

PRAYER: Lord God, thank you for giving me such peace. I pray that I will hasten to call upon that peace when I need it. Quiet my nerves and emotions, and minister to me your kind of peace. In Jesus' name, Amen.

JANUARY 23rd

We come to the third aspect of peace in Philippians 4:7 which reads, *"And the peace OF God, which passes all understanding, shall keep your hearts and minds through Christ Jesus."* This kind of peace is so beyond describing that Paul says it is *beyond understanding.*

I wondered why this peace was so huge, and just what kind of peace it was? But remember, it says, *"the peace of God."* God's very own

23

kind of peace is available to us. Just allow yourself to rise up to a whole new level when thinking about peace.

You do not think of God as pacing across the heavens wringing His hands in dismay, do you? He is not worried sick, or in a state of confusion wondering just what in the world He is going to do over this or that situation, is He? No! He is in absolute peace at all times.

Everything is on schedule in His date book, and He has everything in control. It may not look that way to us down here, but from His perspective every thing is on schedule. How would you like to have that kind of peace? Well, that is what Paul is talking about in the verse for today.

Colossians 3:15 also addresses peace. It reads, *"Let the peace OF God rule in your hearts, to which also you are called in one body: and be you thankful."* When he uses the word "let", it would imply that we usually do not allow His peace to rule. Instead, we allow something else to rule. I am afraid that something else is our own old nature that wants to figure out what to do to help ourselves out whatever problems we are having. Just as Adam and Eve sewed fig leaves together to try to hide their nakedness, we too try to figure out a way to restore our peace, all the while God's own peace is available to us, if we will would only ask for it.

PRAYER: Father, forgive me for the many times I have not allowed your very own kind of peace to rule in my heart. Give me insight and understanding so that I will not try to solve all my own problems, which surely will steal my peace of mind and emotions. Help me to remember to lean on you when the storm clouds gather in my life. In Jesus' name, Amen

JANUARY 24th

 I believe we need to look at another fruit of the Spirit before we go on to other things. In Galatians 5:22-23, we have already listed the fruit of the Spirit. Remember, the Holy Spirit lives in you, therefore

you should be able to bear fruit; the fruit of the spirit, such as joy, peace, long suffering gentleness, goodness, faith, meekness and faithfulness.

You cannot see the wind, only the manifestations of the wind, such as the leaves vigorously moving on the tree. When you see that, you know it is windy outside. In that same way, others should be able to see that the Holy Spirit lives in you, and that is shown when they see (Galatians 15:22-23 reads;) *"love, joy, peace, long suffering* (which is patience), *gentleness* (which is kindness), *goodness, faithfulness, meekness, and temperance* (which is balance or self control)."

The fruit of the Spirit I want to talk about today is joy. Satan likes nothing better than to steal our joy. According to God's Word, joy is very important. Look at Nehemiah 8:10, which reads, *"Then he said unto them, 'Go your way, eat the fat and drink the sweet, and send portions* (gifts) *unto them for whom nothing is prepared: for this day is holy unto our Lord: neither be you sorry; for the joy of the Lord is your strength.' "*

Here, Nehemiah was encouraging the people of God that it was time to stop feeling so depressed and dejected, and instead set in motion an attitude of celebration. This was done by eating the fat (the best of the meat), drinking the sweet (the best of the wine), and giving gifts to the less fortunate, and deciding not to mourn or weep. They had just finished rebuilding the walls of the ruined city of Jerusalem when God's law was read to them and they realized how far from the law they had fallen, so they had wept.

Sin in our lives can make us so depressed and dejected that we almost lose sight of the wonderful mercy and grace of God. There is a time to stop mourning and decide to rejoice and be happy.

Verse 10 ends by saying, *"...for the joy OF the Lord is our strength."* Just exactly what does that mean? When we subscribe to God's joy, He also gives us a strength to defeat the enemy, Satan. God's joy gives us the strength to put down our old nature and to allow our new nature, the nature of Christ Jesus in us, to reign and bring victory over depression, sorrow and the hard knocks of life. Lay claim to the joy *of* the Lord, because it is yours to claim. The only way you will know that it is yours is to try it when you are down.

25

PRAYER: Heavenly Father, I see that I have allowed myself to wallow in despair when things have overwhelmed me. Please forgive me for not coming to you first and laying down my burden of the sin of not trusting you with my problems. Help me to lay claim to your joy that I might know and experience your strength in my life. In Jesus' name, Amen.

JANUARY 25th

God not only wants us to have joy, but He wants us to have joy in full. Psalm 16:11 reads, *"Thou wilt show me the path of life: in thy presence is fullness of joy; at thy right hand there are pleasures for ever more."* God has invited us into His presence through His Son Jesus Christ, and that is where we find fullness of joy. In His presence we have peace, assurance, strength, and, yes, fullness of joy.

There is also joy in heaven, and Luke 15:7 tells us what brings joy into heaven, *"I say unto you, that likewise joy shall be in heaven over one sinner that repents, more than over ninety and nine just persons, which need no repentance."* God wants us to be mindful of the things we do, think, and say that displease Him, and to turn away doing those things.

That is repentance, when we turn away from the things that do not bring honor to the name of Jesus. When we repent, all of heaven rejoices. Just imagine that! Did you ever think you could bring joy into heaven? Well, I believe the Bible teaches us that we can. I am sure there are those who would say that only means the people who have turned their life over to God and become a Christian, but I think that is limiting the joy in heaven. I believe the angels watch us to see the Christian's life lived out in and through us who have taken Jesus as Lord and Savior. Consider it a type of repentance to live closer and more intone with God's plan for our life.

To repent means to turn around, or turn away from. We do that on a daily basis as we allow the Holy Spirit to guide us through the mazes of life. All day long, we have choices to make. They are either for God or against Him. The choices we make for Him bring joy to heaven.

PRAYER: It makes me so humbled to realize that I can bring joy into heaven. Thank you for the gift of the Holy Spirit who guides me in the choices of life. Help me have sensitive ears to hear the Holy Spirit speak to me. In Jesus' name, Amen.

JANUARY 26th

There are three unusual sacrifices God asks us to bring to Him. Let's look at them now. First, Psalm 27:6 reads, *"And now shall mine head be lifted up above mine enemies round about me, therefore will I offer in his tabernacle <u>sacrifices of joy</u>. I will sing, yea, I will sing praises unto the Lord."* Second, Psalm 107:22 states, *"And let them sacrifice the <u>sacrifices of thanksgiving</u>, and declare his works with rejoicing"* Third, Jeremiah 17:26 reads, *"And they shall come bringing burnt offerings, and sacrifices, and meat offerings, and incense, and bringing <u>sacrifices of praise</u>, unto the house of the Lord."*

God asks us to bring sacrifices of joy, thanksgiving, and praise. What does this mean? Is it a sacrifice to praise God, to have joy toward God, or to thank God? How could that be a sacrifice? To bring a sacrifice, something had to die. But what died when I brought a sacrifice of praise, thanksgiving, or joy?

I pondered that for a long time, and then it was as though a light bulb went on. I was to bring my despair and let it die, and to be thankful instead. I was to bring my sorrow and lay it down, let it die, and praise God for His goodness. I was to deny my old nature, which was to be unhappy, dejected, a "poor me" attitude, and instead show God's strength in joy. Yes indeed, my old nature was the road block to my victorious living. My old nature had to die, and I proved that it was dying by bringing a sacrifice of thanksgiving, praise, and joy, even when *I did not feel like it*! That was the sacrifice!

PRAYER: Lord God, this is a hard lesson, but I see the truth in it and I want to subscribe to that truth. Please give me the strength to put it into practice when I am down, when I feel hurt and do not know where to turn. Let praise and thanksgiving flow from my mouth and may my heart and soul be bathed in joy. In Jesus' name, Amen.

JANUARY 27th

Have you noticed that we have turned a corner in our devotions? For days, we talked about what God had done for us. Yesterday, we talked about something we are to do for God, bring sacrifices of joy, thanksgiving, and praise.

Today, I want to talk about another thing we can do to show God we are on His side and want to be in His good graces. Proverbs 3:5-6 says it best, *"Trust in the Lord with all thine heart; and lean not unto thine own understanding. In all thy ways acknowledge Him, and He shall direct thy paths."*

It is hard to trust in God when things are all going contrary to our plans, or a deadline is coming up and we know we cannot make it (in the natural). But God promises to be there for us when we put our full *trust* in Him. In fact, I believe He delights in showing His children what He can do in impossible situations.

Notice the steps in today's verse. 1) Trust in God and 2) lean not on your own understanding. We seem to understand only what we can see with our naked eyes. With that, "impossibility and understanding" go out the window. But God advises us to not lean on our own understanding, but, in other words, lean and trust in His understanding of the situation. He also, in step three, asks us to 3) acknowledge Him in His ways, or make His ways our ways.

Look at Isaiah 55:8-9, which reads, *"For my thoughts are not your thoughts, neither are your ways my way says the Lord. For as the heavens are higher than the earth, so are my ways higher than your ways and my thoughts than your thoughts."* We should be able to trust a God like that, should we not?

PRAYER: Heavenly Father, to let go and completely trust in you is not so easy. But, I see that you are on my side, and you are not a failure. Therefore, it becomes easier to begin trusting in you with all of my life. Just hold my hand as I step into this new relationship with you, so I can stay steady on that path in life. Thank you for hearing me. In Jesus' name, Amen.

JANUARY 28th

 Today, we will look again at Proverbs 3:5-6, "**Trust in the Lord with all thine heart; and lean not unto thine own understanding. In all thy ways acknowledge him, and he shall direct thy paths.**" When we step up to the plate, God is always there to *"direct our paths,"* as He said in verse 6. When we invest in Him, He is right there to invest time and effort in us also.

How does God direct our paths, and how do we know He is directing our paths? Our paths, I believe, means our daily walk with Him. Children need to learn the value of prayer, and how to believe that God will give them insight and understanding into His ways for them. Their walk as a child will be directed mostly by the parents, but they need to experience God in their lives too. As your life progresses, your walk becomes more and more independent from your parents, but if you have not learned to be dependent upon God, you will try to walk the walk of life independent of God, and that will bring countless problems to you.

I believe our conscience touches our hearts to help us realize when we are stepping over the line. God does not yell at us, but instead He speaks in a still, small voice, and we need to learn to hear that voice within us. I believe He will direct our paths with that small voice, or even by changing or moving our circumstances to make us stop and think about what to do next.

I have seen a calamity come into a man's life, but, in the end, it caused a career change in his life and was the best thing that had happened to him. Just remember, God is well able to direct your path. All you have to do is to ask Him to show you His hand in your life, and to guide you in a way that you will understand.

A good verse for us today is I Thessalonians 5:18, which reads, *"In everything give thanks, for this is the will of God in Christ Jesus concerning you."* That word, "everything," is the key. When things have really gone sour, can you say, "Thank you, Lord"? Remember, that is your personal sacrifice right then. At that point, God will step into your life in such a way you will know He is directing your path. You will only really *know* this when you experience it. God wants you to be ready beforehand for such time. If you are not ready beforehand, it will catch you off guard.

PRAYER: Lord God, I believe you will direct my path, and I want you to direct it. Help me to hear your still, small voice, and then help me to act according to your direction. In Jesus' name, Amen.

JANUARY 29th

Yesterday, we talked briefly about being ready for God's direction beforehand. An example of that is found in Proverbs 3:25-26, which reads, *"Be not afraid of sudden fear, neither of the desolation of the wicked, when it comes. For the Lord shall be your confidence, and shall keep your foot from being taken."*

The Amplified Bible translates it, *"Be not afraid of sudden terror and panic, nor of the stormy blast or the storm and ruin of the wicked when it comes (for you are guiltless). For the Lord shall be your confidence, firm and strong, and shall keep your foot from being caught (in a trap or hidden danger)."*

You see, if you decide ahead of time to not succumb to fear or terror, then when it suddenly happens, God will be right there to fill you with a confidence and trust in Him. Right then and there, fear and terror will melt away and a calm (the peace and joy that God says is yours) will kick in, and you will be amazed at what God can do for you in that situation. I personally have experienced this many times since I found out I could claim that kind of peace beforehand and have a victory over fear and terror.

PRAYER: Lord, you are such an awesome God, so ready to be there for me when I really need you. Thank you for the truth I found out today. Help me to put it into practice. Life is full of sudden surprises, some of them not so welcome, and I want to rise above them and maintain a serenity of peace. Help me store this verse up in my heart for just such a time. In Jesus' precious name, Amen.

JANUARY 30th

I believe there is another word we need to examine, and that is "obey." God wants us to *want to* obey Him. That is why we are not robots programmed to act on command. God gave us the freedom of choice.

Let's look at Deuteronomy 30:19-20, where God says: *"I call Heaven and earth to witness this day against you, that I have set before you life and death, the blessing and the curse; therefore choose life, that you and your descendants may live. To love the Lord your God, to obey His voice, and to cling to Him; for He is your life, and the length of your days, that you may dwell in the land which the Lord swore to give to your fathers, to Abraham, Isaac, and Jacob."*

The Christian is faced with choice after choice. Satan is our enemy and the enemy of God, and he will seek to give you a reason to make the wrong choice as he did to Adam and Eve in the Garden of Eden. Our choice is always to obey or not to obey our heavenly Father. Our lives will depend on the choices we make. The choice you make today is the life you live tomorrow. God knew that way back in Old Testament times, and it is still true today. Choose to obey, and thereby you choose life.

PRAYER: I see the truth in all this with my mind, but my heart is having trouble processing it all. Lord, I want to obey you, and I want to please

31

you. Lord, please give me the strength to carry out this "want to." I will need your strength on a regular basis in this walk of obedience. In Jesus' name, Amen.

JANUARY 31ˢᵗ

I think we shall close out this month talking about the words "bless" and "blessing." In Numbers 6:22-27, God tells Moses: *"Speak unto Aaron and unto his sons saying, 'In this way, you shall bless the children of Israel, saying unto them, 'The Lord bless thee, and keep thee: The Lord make his face shine upon thee, and be gracious unto thee: The Lord lift up his countenance upon thee, and give thee peace.' And they shall put my name upon the children of Israel and I will bless them.'"*

Here we see the *blessing* going from God *toward* man. We see all the things God is doing in these verses. It is a picture of God at work on behalf of you and me. God blesses and keeps us. His face shines in our direction, He gives us peace, and puts His name on us. It all begins with God blessing us, and ends with God blessing us. That is so typical of who God is, what He is about, and we would ask why? Think about it. We were created in God's image. He has given us His name and we are a part of His family. God sent His only begotten Son to die on our behalf.

Is it any wonder He does all this for us? How grateful we ought to be and how quickly we ought to respond to a God like that. We will think more on that tomorrow.

PRAYER: Father, thank you for loving me that you wish to bless me so much. It makes me wonder, "How can I be a blessing to you?" Is it possible for me to be a blessing to you? Thank you for gathering me under the shadow of your wing and giving me the safety of that place. In Jesus' name, Amen.

Ponder on Deuteronomy 1:11, Deuteronomy 7:12-14, and Deuteronomy 24:19.

32

FEBRUARY 1st

When we see how much God is blessing us, what should our attitude or response be? I believe King David says it for all of us in Psalms 103:1-2, which reads, *"Bless the Lord, oh my soul: and all that is within me, bless his holy name. Bless the Lord, oh my soul, and forget not all his benefits."*

David told his soul, commanded his soul, to bless the Lord. It is an act of the will, a free choice. You see, our old nature does not want to bless God or to praise His goodness. Our new nature, our spiritual or born-again side, wants to bless God and praise Him. We need to take authority over that old nature and give our new nature the freedom to bless God.

Not only are we to bless God, but we are also to love our enemies. In Matthew 5:44-45, Jesus explains: *"But I say unto you, Love your enemies, bless them that curse you, do good to them that hate you, and pray for them which despitefully use you, and persecute you; That you may be the children of your Father which is in heaven: for he makes His sun to shine on the evil and on the good, and sends rain on the just and on the unjust."*

God is our example, and since He does not unjustly hold back the blessing of rain and sunshine from the unjust, but blesses them, we too should be willing to bless rather than to curse our fellow man. This is contrary to our willful selves (our old nature), but using our free choice, we can decide to obey God and bless rather than curse.

I have heard it said that the quickest way to break a curse is to bless the one who is cursing. Think about it. What do you have to lose by asking God to bless so and so, to forgive them, and bring them to the knowledge of the truth of the Word? You have nothing to loose, and that person has everything to gain from your prayer.

PRAYER: Thank you, Father, for this lesson. Again, I see the truth of this lesson and know I have a long way to go to measure up to your standard. But now I at least know what your standard is. In the future, as the situation arises, may the Holy Spirit prompt me to put this into practice, so that the pathway of blessing from you to me and from me to you will not become dammed up. I want that pathway of blessing to remain open. In Jesus' name, Amen.

FEBRUARY 2nd

Are you ready to go a rung up on the ladder of knowledge? We have talked about how God wants to bless us and how we can bless God. It is a two-way street, not a one-way street. So, with that thought in mind, let's look at another aspect of the two-way street running between you and God.

In Ephesians 2:8, we read, *"For by grace you have been saved through faith; and that not of yourselves: it is the gift of God."* Our salvation is totally a gift of God's grace. Remember, grace is God's unconditional love (agape love) poured out for you and me, without reservation. It is unlimited. Therefore, when we stand up and are counted for God, and willing to say what He has done for us, then we show that grace to the world around us. We become an evidence to the grace of God. People will see the changes in us and realize something has happened in our lives. Then, when we say that it was God's love for us that brought about the peace and security we have, we are evidence of who God is and what His grace is like.

The first way on that two-way street is God's grace being poured out toward us. Tomorrow, we will look at the other part of that two-way street. In the mean time, ponder Romans 5:15, I Corinthians. 1:4, I Corinthians 15:10, and II Corinthians 6:1.

PRAYER: Abba, Father, thank you for the grace that you have shown me through your Word, that you should count me worthy of your grace. I receive that gift into my spirit by faith and I pray that I may be a reflection to those around me of that grace. In Jesus' name, Amen.

FEBRUARY 3rd

Today, we will look at the other part of the two-way street of grace. (Amplified Bible) Ephesians 1:6 reads, *"So that we might be to the praise and the commendation of His glorious grace—favor and mercy—which He so freely bestowed on us in the Beloved (Jesus)."* In this verse, we see clearly we are to be such an example of God's grace that, in turn, grace is returned to God through us.

People who have lived a life of sin and then found the truth about salvation and turned their lives over to Christ often have such a change of lifestyle even those who knew them before are amazed at the change. It becomes evident that only God could bring about that kind of change. It was by God's grace the change took place.

Those people are an example of what God's grace is like, so attention is given to God, who is then a recipient of the praise of grace. In other words, God gets all the glory. This knowledge should put a desire in your heart to live a life that displays God's grace to the world around you. The two-way street of grace is God's grace showered upon us, and we, in turn, live out that grace so it radiates back to God.

PRAYER: Lord God, your grace is so big it is almost impossible for me to comprehend it. Teach me, step by step, more and more about your grace, so that I can be the example of your grace that you desire me to be. Lift me up when I fall, set me back on the right path, and encourage me to continue on that path. In Jesus' precious name, Amen.

FEBRUARY 4th

Justice is getting what we deserve. We have sinned, and we deserve death. *Mercy* is not getting what we deserve. We deserve death, but God has a plan whereby we can have mercy and receive eternal life instead. *Grace* is getting what we do not deserve. We deserve death, but instead, through God's grace, we have (right now) eternal life and life more abundant.

We deserve to be condemned in God's judicial court of law. We have sinned, and we continue to sin every day. Sin separates us from God. That is our dilemma as sinners. God designed a way that He could be totally just (as a Judge), forgive our sins, and remove the due penalty of sin, which was death. He sent His own Son (Jesus) to live a perfect, sinless life as the law prescribes, and then to carry our sins on His own body to the cross and there die our death. He shed His blood for the penalty and payment of sin.

That act of redemption, by both the Father and Son, bought our salvation from sin and its penalty. That act is called *grace*! In Titus 3:7, we read, ***"That being justified by His Grace, we should be made heirs according to the hope of eternal life."***

We are completely justified in the eyes of God when we accept His plan of salvation and redemption. Remember, redemption is like buying back something from the pawn shop. You redeem an article you left there for money. We were sold under, sin and God Himself paid the price the law required, which was the shedding of blood, the sacrifice of blood and life. That justified us in the eyes of God and it is done by grace.

That also made us heirs to eternal life. In other words, we inherit eternal life. We inherit it right now, not when we die. We need to live and act like it is ours right now. When we do, we please God. We bring glory to His name when we live and act like saved sinners right now. It took me a long time searching God's Word before I could see that truth for myself. I hope you can see it in this verse in Titus. It is all spelled out for you there, *"being justified by His grace."* That was a finished act on the cross 2,000 years ago. When that was finished, you were *"made an heir to eternal life,"* right then and there. It was all done by grace.

PRAYER: Heavenly Father, thank you for such a great inheritance. It is hard to comprehend such grace, as this. Are you telling me, Lord, that I can be assured of eternal life? If that is true, then help me to grasp that truth and make it a part of my faith walk. In Jesus' name, Amen.

FEBRUARY 5th

Another blessing we receive and are supposed to pass on is reconciliation. It flows from God to us, and then it is to flow through us to others. We find it in II Corinthians 5:17-18, which reads, *"Therefore, if any man be in Christ, he is a new creature: old things are passed away; behold all things are become new. And all things are of God, who has reconciled us to himself by* (through) *Jesus Christ, and has given to us the ministry of reconciliation."*

The slate was wiped clean when you were born again, which means you were planted into Jesus through baptism (Romans 6:3-6) and Jesus came into you by invitation (Revelation 3:20). So, you are a new creature, and you were reconciled to God. According to Webster's dictionary "reconcile" means to "return to harmony, make compatible, settle amicably, make acquiescent." That is the picture of what God has done between you and Him. Once that was accomplished, right then and there, you had an obligation to "the ministry of reconciliation." You are now able to tell someone what has taken place in your life between you and God, and how God did it all. Your only obligation was to receive it and pass it on. How do you rate yourself on that?

PRAYER: Gracious Father, I understand with my mind what you are asking of me, and my heart is in agreement. But there is a hint of timidity within me that wants to say it cannot be done. If I am to be bold and speak out on your behalf, then give me the strength and wisdom to do that when the situation arises. In Jesus' name, Amen.

FEBRUARY 6th

We need to be Christians who know that we have eternal life right now. Many Christians think they have to wait for a future judgment before they will know whether they will spend eternity in heaven or hell. I thought that for many years, and then a kind Christian lady began to show me how

37

wrong I was, that it was God's will for me to know that I would spend eternity with Him.

I hope to help you see that truth also. Let's begin by reading some verses from Hebrews. Hebrews 5:8-9 reads, *"Though He were a Son, yet learned He obedience by the things which He suffered; And being made perfect, He became the author of eternal salvation unto all them that obey Him."* There is no book without an author, and our eternal salvation begins with Jesus. Our eternal salvation was in God's mind for us before we were even born. It is His most inward desire that we spend eternity with Him.

Also, in Hebrews 9:12, we read, *"Neither by the blood of goats and calves, but by His own blood He entered in once into the holy place, having obtained eternal redemption for us."* Redemption means the price has been paid in full. Not only do we have eternal salvation, but we also have eternal redemption. That means even the sins we will commit in the future are paid for! Do you get the picture of how much God wants you to spend eternity with Him?

PRAYER: Father, you are stretching my mind today. You mean Jesus paid the price for all my past, present, and future sins when He died on the cross? The answer to that is a resounding "Yes." All I can say is that I am humbled, grateful, and thankful all at once. I feel a weight lift off my shoulders, Lord, and I have you to thank for that. Yes, Lord, thank you again and again. In Jesus' name, Amen.

FEBRUARY 7th

We are not done with the topic of "assurance of eternal life." Hebrews 9:15 states, *"And for this cause He is the mediator of the new testament* (covenant)*, that by means of death, for the transgressions that were under the first Testament, they which are called might receive the promise of eternal inheritance."*

A covenant is an agreement. The Old Testament is the first one, and the New Testament is the new one. God had made an agreement with the people in the Old Testament, and when Jesus came, God made an agreement in the New Testament. A mediator is a "go between," and Jesus is that go between. Just as the Jews inherited a land (the Holy Land) and it was to be theirs forever, so also we see an inheritance in the New Testament, an eternal inheritance, salvation and eternal life.

Now, look at some references in I John. I John 2:25 states, *"And this is the promise that He has promised us, even eternal life."* God keeps all His promises, He does not break even one. Can you claim that promise?

Now, look at I John 5:13, which reads, *"These things have I written unto you that believe on the name of the Son of God: that you know that you have eternal life, and that you may believe on the name of the Son of God."* If that does not convince you that God wants you to know, without a doubt, that you have eternal life right now, not that you have to wait until you die to find out where you land for eternity, then I do not believe anything will convince you!

A lady once told me that for those people who do not know they have eternal life, Jesus died for nothing. I tell you, that opened my eyes to a whole new way of thinking. Was it right for me to be so bold as to think I could be sure of eternal life with God? After searching the scriptures, I found that it is God's wish for me to have that assurance and to have it right now. Allow yourself the privilege of that assurance and just be thankful.

PRAYER: Thank you, Father, for this great truth you have shared with me today. Help me to lay hold of that truth in my life, and thank you for the peace of mind that truth gives to me. In Jesus' mighty name, Amen.

FEBRUARY 8th

We are going to shift gears for awhile and tackle another topic that will be a great help in your Christian growth. We often see the words "wisdom," "knowledge," and "understanding" in the Bible. Those three go together like the "knife," "fork," and "spoon."

Wisdom is the wise use of what you know and understand. Some people have very little knowledge or education but they make great use of what they do know (wisdom), and they would appear to be highly educated. On the other hand, there are those who have much education, but make such poor use of what they know, they would appear to not have the level education they have attained. So, we want to look at knowledge, understanding, and wisdom.

We will begin with knowledge. Hosea 4:6 warns, *"My people are destroyed for lack of KNOWLEDGE: because thou has rejected KNOWLEDGE, I will also reject thee, that thou shall be no priest to me, seeing thou has forgotten the law of thy God, I will also forget thy children."* These are strong words, and we need to reassess our *desire* for knowledge.

Jesus also hinted at this in Matthew 22:29. (Read the whole story in verses 23 through 29.) The religious leaders who did not believe in the resurrection, nor in angels, posed a ridiculous question in verse 28, *"Therefore in the resurrection* (in which they did not believe) *whose wife shall she be of the seven? For they all had her* (for a wife)*."*

Jesus did not answer their silly question, but put his finger right on the problem when He said, *"You do greatly err,* (let me paraphrase this, *"You make a huge mistake.")* *not knowing the Scripture, nor the power of God"* (Matt. 22:29). One of the problems was that they lacked knowledge. The other problem was they did not know the power of God.

It would appear that we are responsible for what we do know and for what we do not know. We are expected to know the Scriptures, and, if we do not, it is our own fault, not God's. Today, is the first day of the rest of your life. Begin to study the Scripture so you can come to know the power of God in your life.

PRAYER: Heavenly Father, I am sorry I do not know your Word as I ought, but I do want to know it better. Provide a teacher or material that I can begin to study, to know your word better, and experience your power in my life. In Jesus' name, Amen.

FEBRUARY 9th

In Philippians 3:4-7, Paul lists all of the things he had before he knew Christ. He had thought it was a lot, but he sees all that as loss since he came to know Christ Jesus. Philippians 8-10 reads: *"Yea, doubtless, and I count all things but loss for the excellency of the <u>knowledge</u> of Christ Jesus my Lord: for whom I have suffered the loss of all things, and do count them but dung* (manure)*, that I may win Christ, And be found in Him, not having mine own righteousness, which is of the law, but that which is through the faith of Christ, the righteousness which is of God by faith. That I may <u>know</u> him, and the power of His resurrection, and the fellowship of His sufferings, being made conformable unto His death."*

Paul had prestige under the law, but once he came to know, really know, Jesus Christ, he saw that everything he had before was nothing in comparison to what he had as a believer in Christ. That is a *knowledge* that God wants us all to attain, to really know God and His love for us, how He longs to see us grow in our knowledge of Him, and that can only happen as we study and meditate on His Word, the Bible.

Think about it, and determine for yourself that you will begin to meditate on what you read in the Bible. Ask God to show you what you are to learn in these verses today, and how to apply them to your own life. Make the Word of God personal to you.

PRAYER: Heavenly Father, I want to get to know you better and better each day. I am beginning to see just how much I do not know and I also see that it is what I do not know that gets me into trouble. Open up the Scripture for me that you and I can become better acquainted. In Jesus' name, Amen.

FEBRUARY 10th

In John 5:39, Jesus advises, *"Search the scriptures; for in them ye think ye have eternal life: and they are they which testify of me."* The Old Testament pointed ahead to a Savior from sin, and the New Testament shows us the Savior who came to save us from our own sins and the penalty of sin (which is death). If you really want to know Jesus, the only way to get that knowledge is through the Word of God, the Bible.

Let's look at Romans 10:1-3, where Paul says: *"Brethren, my heart's desire and prayer to God for Israel is that they might be saved. For I bear them record that they have a zeal of God, but not according to knowledge. For they being ignorant of God's righteousness, and going about to establish their own righteousness, have not submitted themselves unto the righteousness of God."*

Paul's desire for the Jews, his brethren, was that they be saved. Paul acknowledged that the Jews were zealous for God, but their zeal lacked *knowledge.* They did not understand God's standard of righteousness.

The only people who could have righteous standing before God were those who had been washed in the blood of the Lamb of God. That Lamb is Jesus, according to John 1:29, which reads, *"...Behold the lamb of God that taketh away the sin of the world."* The Jews did not understand that Jesus came to pay the price of sin on their behalf. They believed keeping the law would put them in right standing before God.

We also see that there are two kinds of righteousness: God's righteousness and our own righteousness. In order to have God's righteousness, we have to submit to that. Remember, verse 3 says, *"For they being ignorant of God's righteousness, and going about to establish their own righteousness, have not submitted themselves unto the righteousness of God."* Study that verse carefully. God's righteousness is all wrapped up in the person and work of Jesus Christ. He came to live the law perfectly, so that it was fulfilled in Christ. He came to give Himself as a ransom for sin and to die our death for us. By those acts, He purchased for us a righteousness that only God can give.

42

We owe it all to God the Father and God the Son. It is God the Holy Spirit that gives us the eyes to see and the heart to receive that truth. Our own righteousness is when we think we can earn it by our works, our so-called, good works. But Ephesians 2:8-9 states, *"For by grace are you saved through faith; and that not of yourselves: it is the gift of God: Not of works, lest any man should boast."* No works on our part can *ever* buy our salvation. Jesus gives us His righteousness freely, and all we need do is receive it. Can that be so hard? Paul wants us to have that knowledge.

PRAYER: Gracious Lord, thank you for this knowledge about righteousness. Help me to absorb the full meaning of it. The picture you are painting of your love for me is enormous, and now more has been added, that I can have a standing before you of being completely righteous! Forgive me for not knowing this before. Give me the courage to come before you wrapped up in the knowledge that, in Christ Jesus, I am the righteousness of God. In Jesus' name, Amen.

FEBRUARY 11th

Colossians 1:9 reads, *"For this cause we also, since the day we heard it, do not cease to pray for you, and to desire that you might be filled with the knowledge of His will in all wisdom and spiritual understanding."* Paul also wrote this letter to the Colossians, and his prayer is as fresh for us today as it was the day the they read it. It explains that we should have the knowledge of God's will in all wisdom and understanding.

Remember, I said some days ago that knowledge, understanding, and wisdom go together like a knife, fork and spoon. We now see them together in one verse. Did you ever think that God wanted you to know His will? I believe Paul means His will for your life. I believe that God wants us to know a whole lot more than we are willing to try to find out.

In Romans 12:1-2, Paul says, *"I beseech you therefore, brethren, by the mercies of God, that you present your bodies a living sacrifice, holy acceptable unto God, which is your reasonable* (spiritual) *service. And be not conformed* (fashioned according) *to this world: but be you transformed by the renewing of your mind, that you may prove what is that good, and acceptable, and perfect, will of God."*

I believe that when we live our lives in harmony with God, it will prove to the world around us what God's good, acceptable, and perfect will is for us. I believe that if we ask God's Holy Spirit to direct our steps, open the right doors in our lives, and close the doors that lead us down the wrong paths, then God's will for our lives will be attainable and understandable to us.

PRAYER: I always believed that I could not know your will for my life, but now I am changing my mind. May your Holy Spirit guide my thoughts and actions, so I do not stray either to the left or to the right as I walk out your will in my life. In Jesus' name, Amen.

FEBRUARY 12th

In II Peter 3:18, we read, *"But grow in grace, and in the knowledge of our Lord and Savior Jesus Christ."* There are no "ifs," "ands," or "buts" about this. We are to grow. Just as you expect a baby to grow continually, so also are we expected to grow in grace. As we receive grace freely from God, we are to become instruments of that grace in direct relationship to what we receive. That is how we grow in grace.

We are also to grow in our knowledge of our: Lord, Savior, Jesus, and Christ. To many people Jesus is Savior, but not Lord. I think I have presented Him as Savior so far in this daily devotion. There is no other Savior in the world, or in the universe. But is Jesus Lord of your life? Have you grown in your knowledge of what it means to take Him as Lord in your life?

He wants you to give your *all* to Him to manage. You cannot possible manage your life better than He can. Consider your time. Is He Lord of your time? How about your abilities? Are you a teacher, a singer, a leader, a prayer? Is He Lord in those areas? What about your money, goals, hopes, and dreams? He wants us to grow in our knowledge of the *Lord* Jesus.

He also wants us to grow in our knowledge of Jesus. Jesus was born a baby, and, like any other human baby, Jesus was his given name. God named Him Jesus in Luke 1:31, the name "Jesus" means "Jehovah" is salvation. Christ is an official title, which means "the anointed one" and points to the promised Messiah of the Old Testament. Another name ascribed to Jesus is "Immanuel," which means "God with us."

God wants us to grow in our knowledge of Jesus as the Christ, the One God has anointed to be that fulfillment of the promised Messiah. His work is not done yet. The work of salvation and redemption is done, and the work of our sanctification (which means our growth as Christians) is going on, but one day Jesus will come as Lord of Lords and King of Kings, and set up His rule on this earth. He will rule this earth for 1,000 years, putting down every evil and cleansing this world of all that opposes God. He'll bring in a new heaven and new earth. He came as a babe the first time, but when He comes again, He will come as a lion. He wants us to grow in our knowledge of all that.

PRAYER: Gracious God Almighty, you have enormous goals and plans for this world. To think that I am included in those plans of yours just blows my mind. I am growing in my knowledge of your Word, and your character of love, grace, mercy, and peace. I desire to continually grow in those areas and look to you to accomplish that in my life. In Jesus' name, Amen.

FEBRUARY 13th

In Luke 11:52, Jesus says, *"Woe unto you, lawyers! For you have taken away the key of knowledge; you entered not in yourselves, and them that were entering in you hindered."* "Woe" is a strong word of warning. The CEV reads, *"You teachers of the Law of Moses are really in for*

45

trouble! You carry the <u>keys to the door of knowledge about God.</u> But you never go in, and you keep others from going in. "

There is an enemy called the devil who does not want us to know anything about Jesus and will use anything or anyone to hold back that knowledge from us. I believe the key to the door of knowledge is the Bible. It is the only book on earth that tells us all there is to know about Jesus as Christ, Lord, and Savior. Notice that many people will talk about God, but few will talk about Jesus. They just cannot seem to say His name. It is embarrassing to them somehow. The word "God" does not seem to offend anyone, but often people are offended by the name of Jesus.

Now I want you to look at Acts 4:12, which states, *"Neither is there salvation in any other: for there is none other name under heaven given among men, whereby we must be* **saved."** The devil does not want anyone to speak the name of Jesus, because there is such power in that name, and the devil knows that.

Also read Philippians 2:9-11, which says *"Wherefore God also has highly exalted Him, and given Him a name which is above every name: That at the name of Jesus, every knee should bow, of things in heaven, and things in earth, and things under the earth; And that every tongue should confess that Jesus Christ is Lord, to the glory of God the Father. "* There are three realms of space spoken of here: Heaven, earth, and under the earth. In all these realms, the name of Jesus is all powerful. Also notice that *every knee* will bow and *every tongue* confess that name. Some will bow in dreadful fear and trembling, but the saved will bow in reverence, awe, humility, and thanksgiving. Those who refused God's plan of salvation (His gift of righteousness, grace, and peace) will bow in terror, but they will bow! So, why fight it? Why not bow and confess it now rather than later? The benefits are beyond description, life abundant; peace with, from and of God; mercy; grace; joy; and happiness daily. I could go on and on.

PRAYER: Heavenly Father, yes, I bow my knee to you in the name of Jesus who died for me. I confess that you are the Christ, the Messiah, the Savior and Lord, and all that I am, I owe to you. I praise your name. I give my life to you to shape and to mold and to use to your glory. In Jesus' precious name, Amen.

FEBRUARY 14th

When it comes to knowledge, understanding, and wisdom, I often use a blueprint as an example. If I held up a blueprint and asked an audience of men and women how many *knew* what it was, many would probably raise their hands. Then, if I asked how many *understood* what it was and could explain it so that someone else would understand it, several hands would go down. Then, if I asked how many of those who *knew* and *understood* the blueprint could take it and build the design, very few hands would remain raised.

You see, *wisdom* is the wise use of what you *know* and *understand*. The blueprint is like the Word of God. You can read it, and still not understand it. You can read and understand it, and still not make wise use of it. God wants us to be able to do all three, know, understand, and make wise use of the Bible. So, let's look at a reference or two for today.

Proverbs 3:5-6 reads, ***"Trust in the Lord with all your heart; and lean not unto*** (on) ***your own understanding. In all your ways acknowledge Him, and He shall direct thy paths."*** Our natural understanding does not lean toward God at all. It is our natural bent to try to figure things out for ourselves. You have heard the saying, "When all else fails, read the directions." That is the way we are with our old nature, waiting until other attempts fail to look at the directions.

God does not always make sense, but if we submit to Him, trust in Him, and do not waver, the end result will be that He will direct our paths. The decisions we make today will determine how we live with tomorrow. Webster says "understanding" is "to perceive or comprehend the meaning of." With some children, the only way they comprehend that the stove is hot is to get burned. Often times, Christians are no different, not until they feel the result of not trusting in God will they comprehend that it would be best to trust Him.

Proverbs 1:1-3 begins with these instructions, *"The proverbs of Solomon, the son of David, king of Israel. To know wisdom and instruction; to perceive the words of understanding; to receive the instructions of wisdom* (in wise dealing)*, justice and judgment, and equity."* And verse 5 states, *"A wise man will hear, and will increase learning; and a man of understanding shall attain unto wise counsels."*

PRAYER: Father, I am beginning to see my need for both knowledge and understanding, so I will look to you for the answer to my need. Life is too complicated for me to live without your guidance day by day, so I look to you to teach me and lead me, so that I may attain a firm grip on your truths. In Jesus' name, Amen.

FEBRUARY 15th

In Proverbs 2:6, we read *,"For the Lord gives wisdom: out of His mouth comes knowledge and understanding."* As I read that verse, I came to believe that there is no place in the world to get knowledge, understanding and wisdom, except from God. Anyone who would try to acquire those three principles in the world will come far short compared to those who would seek those principles from the Word of God. One reason is that they originate with God, but He is more than happy to bestow them on anyone who seeks them.

Proverbs 4:5- 7 states, *"Get wisdom, get understanding: forget it not; neither decline from the words of my mouth Wisdom is the principle thing; therefore get wisdom: and with all your getting get understanding."* In those verses, we see that our responsibility is to "get." How do we get wisdom and understanding? Look at Proverbs 23:23, which says, *"Buy the truth, and sell it not; also wisdom and instruction, and understanding."* I think the clue to understanding that verse is found in Isaiah 55:1, which instructs, *"Ho, every one that thirsts, come you to the waters, and he that has no money; come you, buy, and eat; yes, come, buy wine and milk without money and without price."*

As I pondered what this all meant, I thought, "How do we buy without money?" Then I remembered how farmers, years ago, used the barter system. They brought eggs to the grocery store and trade to buy groceries. There was no money exchanged. So, if I was to buy "wine and milk," how would I get those things? I would have to lay aside my pride and receive as a humble pauper, admitting that I could never have enough money to fully pay for what I was getting. So it is with knowledge, understanding, and wisdom. I come humbly before God, admitting that I need these three principles in order to live a life pleasing to Him. Tomorrow, we will talk about how that is done.

PRAYER: Thank you, Father, for showing me how I can come to you and receive the priceless gifts of knowledge, understanding, and wisdom. I willingly put aside my own pride and natural will to do and get things on my own. It is presumptuous of me to think for one moment that I could be able to do that. Forgive me, Lord, for that presumption. In Jesus' name, Amen.

FEBRUARY 16th

We see that there are seven spirits who stand before God in Heaven in Revelation 1:4, which reads, *"John to the seven churches which are in Asia : Grace be unto you, and peace, from him which is, and which was, and which is to come* (that speaks of Jesus who was, and is, and is to come), *and from the seven spirits which are before the throne."*

I believe those seven spirits are listed in Isaiah11:1-2, which states, *"And there shall come forth a rod out of the stem of Jesse, and a Branch shall grow out of his roots* (shall bear fruit, i.e., Jesus, who would be born a descendant of Jesse). *And the spirit of the Lord shall rest upon him, the spirit of wisdom, and understanding, the spirit of counsel and might, the*

49

spirit of knowledge and of the fear of the Lord. " (There are the seven spirits.)

Now we are ready to see how we get wisdom, knowledge, and understanding. Turn to James 1:5-6, which reads, *"If any of you lack wisdom, let him ask of God, that gives to all men liberally, and upbraideth not,* (without fault finding)*; and it shall be given him. But let him ask in faith, nothing wavering (doubting). For he that wavers is like a wave of the sea driven with the wind and tossed. "* There it is, all we need to do is *ask* God for wisdom, and if that is how we get wisdom, then that must be how we also get knowledge and understanding, because they were also listed as one of the seven spirits like wisdom.

In fact, we can ask for all of those spirits to be given to us. Satan is only too anxious to give us of his spirits, which have only our harm in mind. God has only our good in mind. You will never know how wonderful it is to have the spirit of knowledge, understanding and wisdom until you ask and realize you have been gifted with those principles.

PRAYER: From the bottom of my heart, Lord, I thank you for this revelation of your truth. I had no idea I could pray for, and receive, wisdom or understanding. So many times in my life I have said, "I just don't understand what is happening." Now, I can ask you to show me these things by your Spirit. My desire is to live a life pleasing to you, but my old nature will rear its ugly head and try to hinder me. I ask for wisdom to overcome in those times. In Jesus' name, Amen.

FEBRUARY 17th

I believe we need to look at a few more verses about knowledge, understanding, and wisdom before we move on to something else. Proverbs 9:10 states," *The fear of the Lord is the beginning of wisdom: and the knowledge of the Holy One is understanding.*

Remember, *wisdom* is an *action,* the wise use of what you know and understand. To have a reverential fear of God Almighty is what John is talking about here, not a terror fear of coming to God. God does not want

50

us to fear Him that way. He does, however, want us to have a reverential fear of disappointing Him, of rejecting Him for other gods, like the god of money or security, or even other people to whom we give more honor than God by paying them more respect and giving them more of our time than we give to God. Once we have that kind of reverential fear of God, it will show that we are wise and have wisdom.

Understanding is to *know* there is a God who loves you, cares about you, meets you on the level of your need, and encourages you to grow spiritually. The wise use of that knowledge and understanding is to read a portion of Scripture each and every day, take time to ponder what you have read, ask God to give you the insight into what you have read, and rely on its truthfulness for you.

PRAYER: Lord God, I almost feel like I am being stretched spiritually. I suppose it is like exercising my spiritual muscles. I have to admit that they have not been stretched like this for a long time. But I am learning to go with the flow, and it feels good. Help me to keep going, growing, stretching, and learning. In Jesus' name, Amen.

FEBRUARY 18th

In Proverbs 14:29 we read, *"He that is slow to wrath is of great understanding: but he that is hasty of spirit exalts folly."* God will help those who have a problem with anger and wrath. He will give them the understanding needed to put those emotions in check. Bursts of anger or wrath never make a person look wise, but foolish. The Word says it *"exalts folly,"* which means that foolishness is lifted up and magnified.

Wisdom will be a big help in managing anger and wrath. Usually nothing good is accomplished by a burst of anger or wrath, and once that is really understood, then that person can use wisdom to control the anger or wrath. Proverbs 10:13 states, *"In the lips of him that has understanding, wisdom is found: but a rod is for the back of him that is void of understanding."* These three principles, knowledge, understanding and wisdom are like the legs on a three-legged stool. It would not be of much use with only two legs.

I believe we underestimate the importance of good understanding. Many people have to experience the results of poor understanding and wisdom in order to "get it," understanding that is. Much of our out-of-control emotions, which give us no end of trouble, can be healed or corrected by the proper use of these three principles. I encourage you to claim them for yourself and then listen to the still, small voice of the Holy Spirit, whose work it is to guide you into all the truth.

As we end today, think about Philippians 4:7, which reads, *"And the Peace of God that passes all <u>understanding</u> shall keep* (guard) *your hearts and mind* (thoughts) *through Christ Jesus."*

PRAYER: Heavenly Father, I am ready for that kind of peace, I do not want my emotions dancing around like a yo-yo any longer. I am gaining insight into your ways and, with baby steps, am moving in that direction to lay hold of your plan for my life, using knowledge of your Word, understanding of your ways through your Word, and the wisdom given by your Spirit to put it all to wise use. I give you all the praise and thanks for these truths. In Jesus' name, Amen.

FEBRUARY 19th

I believe there are a few more verses on the subject of understanding that we need to address, which are found in the New Testament. Take a look at Luke 24:13-53. Let me paint a picture of what is happening here. Two men were walking to Emmaus after hearing that the tomb was empty and that Jesus was not there. They also remembered how He had said He would rise from the dead, and they are discussing all these happenings. Jesus appeared to them on that road, and, bit by bit, revealed Himself to them. First, He listened to their view of what had happened.

Jesus responded in Luke 24:25-27, which reads, *"Then He said unto them, 'O fools, and slow of heart to believe all that the prophets have spoken: Ought not Christ to have suffered these things, and to enter into His glory? 'And beginning at Moses* (in the first five books of the Bible), *and all the prophets, He expounded unto them in all the Scriptures the things concerning Himself."*

Jesus proved to them by Scripture that He was to come as a servant to pay the price for sin and to give the choice of eternal life back to the human race. They were getting knowledge of the Word of God, the truth of the Word of God, from Jesus Himself!

Then, in Luke 24:30-31, we read, *"And it came to pass, as He sat at meat with them, He took bread, and blessed it ,and brake and gave it to them. And their eyes were opened, and they knew Him; and He vanished out of their sight."* Suddenly something clicked, and they really knew who He was. Their understanding was beginning to grow in them. First, they saw in the Scripture just exactly who God intended Jesus to be to the whole human race, and *then* (when they saw the risen Lord and really knew it was Him in resurrection power), understanding came to life within them.

From verses 32 through 35, they could talk of nothing else and hurried back to the rest of the disciples to tell them about their experience with the risen Lord Jesus. Lo and behold, Jesus appeared to them back in Jerusalem. We will continue with this tomorrow.

PRAYER: Dear Jesus, I am beginning to see how the Old Testament and the New Testament are closely linked together. Help me, Lord, to understand those links and how they are to affect my life right now. I know the Bible says you are the same yesterday, today, and tomorrow, so help me to see the Jesus of the Old Testament, as well as the Jesus of the New Testament. In your precious name, Amen.

FEBRUARY 20th

Today, we will continue in Luke 24. Fear gripped the disciples, but Jesus showed them that He was the same person, nail prints and all, and they were filled with joy. But they still had a hard time believing it all. He ate some fish and honeycomb before them to show them He was the same Jesus, only now a risen Lord.

Look at Luke 24:44-48, which states: *"And He said unto them, these are the words which I spoke unto you, while I was yet with you, that all things must be fulfilled, which were written in the law of Moses, and in the prophets and in the Psalms, concerning me. Then opened He their understanding ,that they might understand the Scriptures, and said unto them, 'Thus it is written, and thus it behooved Christ to suffer and to rise from the dead the third day: And that repentance and remission of sins should be preached in His name among all nations, beginning at Jerusalem. And you are witnesses of these things.' "*

Again, He showed them how the Old Testament pointed to Him and His work of forgiveness of sins and redemption. He gave them knowledge. Then, in verse 45, we see that *"He opened their understanding that they might understand the Scripture,"* which they now know. Do you get the picture of how important it is to *understand* what you *know*? Your knowledge will be like milk toast if you do not have understanding to go with it.

Remember that in the Old Testament we read, *"Get wisdom, get understanding"* (Proverbs 4:5), and *"Wisdom is the principle thing, therefore get wisdom: and with all your getting get understanding"* (Proverbs 4:7). Who has the responsibility here? You do! You know how to get it. You pray and ask God to give it to you, and believe that He will! Is that so hard?

When you have understanding to go with your knowledge, then you can make use of wisdom. The goal of knowledge and understanding is to bring forth the proper actions, which is *wisdom*. That is the action word in this whole equation, wise use of what you know and understand. Have a good journey!

PRAYER: Dear Lord Jesus, yes, I want a good journey through this life, and I thank you for the truth I am finding out day by day. Shower your mercy and grace upon me as I struggle to find that path you have laid out

54

for me, let me not stray to the right or to the left. Help me to listen to the Holy Spirit directing my choices. In Jesus' name, Amen.

FEBRUARY 21st

One of the things I have learned in my walk with God is that there is a bitter enemy out there who is determined to undermine everything I learn, and every desire of my heart to stay close to God and His plan for my life. I had not known that in my early walk with God, and I wondered why it was all such a struggle.

I want to help you to see what took me years to find out. One day, my six-year-old son asked me, "Did God make everything?" I assured him that indeed, God had made everything. I was not at all prepared for the next question, "Even the devil?" I stood there before my six-year-old son, completely at a loss for what to say. I did not know who the devil was, where he came from, what he was up to, or why! In other words, I did not know anything about the enemy of God, and that is just the way the devil wants it.

So, in the next few days, I want to try to help you get acquainted with your most bitter enemy and God's enemy also. That is who he is, the enemy! There is a battle going on, a battle to control your mind, your choices, your actions based on those choices, and, finally, your life, both here on earth and for eternity. That is *who* the devil is.

We also need to know by what names he is called. Revelation 12:9-10 reads; *"And the great dragon was cast out, that old serpent, called the Devil, and Satan, which deceives the whole world; he was cast out into the earth and his angels were cast out with him. And I heard a loud voice saying in heaven, 'Now is come salvation, and strength, and the kingdom of our God, and the power of His Christ: for the <u>accuser</u> of our brethren is cast down, which accused them before our God day and night.' "*

Here we see the names by which the devil is known. The dragon has great strength, and so does the devil. The serpent is subtle, sneaky, and deceptive, just like the devil. "Devil" means "slanderer" and "accuser," and in these two verses we see that he accuses us before God day and night. Is that an enemy, or what? Satan means "adversary, the great opposer." He opposes everything that God will try to do for you in your life. Now you know the devil's names and what they mean, which gives you an idea of how he operates.

PRAYER: Is there any hope to overcome the devil in my life, Lord? I pray that your Word will lead me to know just what and how much you have done so that I can take back control from the enemy. In Jesus' holy name, Amen.

FEBRUARY 22nd

You also need to know the devil's origins. In Luke 10:18, Jesus says, *"...I beheld Satan as lightening fall from heaven!"* We just saw that he was cast out into the earth, and now we hear Jesus say he fell from heaven. So, did he originate in heaven? Did God make everything, even the devil?

In Isaiah 14:12-15, we read: *"How are you fallen from heaven, O Lucifer* (day star)*, son of the morning! How are you cut down to the ground, which did weaken the nations! For you have said in your heart, I will ascend into heaven, I will exalt my throne above the stars of God: I will sit also upon the mount of the congregation, in the sides of the north: I will ascend above the heights of the clouds, I will be like the most High."*

Oh boy, does Satan have great aspirations about his future position! He thinks he can push God off His throne and take over the universe! No wonder he is an enemy! Did you notice the "I wills" that he said in that verse? He really believes that he can do it. In fact, he is determined to do it, and he does not care who he uses to get it done.

The devil seeks to undermine everything God is doing in your life, so he can gain a foothold, one person at a time. No one is off limits to him.

Every Christian is a target, simply because each is too dangerous for him to let alone to grow in grace and holiness. He must try, again and again, to persuade Christians that God does not love them, does not care about them, and would send them to hell. (God does not send anyone to hell, but rather people choose to go there by refusing God's salvation. But Satan deceives them to believe that God puts people in hell.) Do not let the devil deceive you about your salvation, or about God's love for you. He is a liar, which we will talk more about that later.

PRAYER: Lord Jesus, I want to live a life of victory, so stay close by me to help me recognize Satan's tactics and subtleties so that I can be a step ahead of him and can say "no" when no is needed and "yes" when yes is needed. In your mighty name, Amen.

FEBRUARY 23rd

Yesterday, we saw that Isaiah called the devil "Lucifer," which means, "morning star." A star that shines in the morning has to be a very bright star. In order for a star to out-shine the sun, it has to be very brilliant.

We know the devil was a high angel, because he was cast out of heaven, and *his* angels with him. Turn to Ezekiel 28:12-13, which reads: *"Son of man, take up a lamentation* (dirge of sorrow) *upon the king of Tyrus, and say unto him, 'Thus says the Lord God: Thou sealed up the sum, full of wisdom, and perfect in beauty. Thou has been in Eden, the garden of God; every precious stone was thy covering, the sardius, topaz, and the diamond, the beryl, the onyx, and the jasper, the sapphire, the emerald, and the carbuncle, and gold: the workmanship of thy tabrets and of thy pipes was prepared in thee in the day that thou was created* (so, he was in fact created), *thou art the anointed cherub that covers and I have set thee so.' "*

Let me explain some things here. There are those who believe that this is addressed to the King of Tyrus, but others believe it refers to Lucifer, Satan, the devil. We need to remember that behind every evil ruler there is the devil influencing him against God. But also notice that it cannot possibly be the king of Tyrus, because it says, *"...Thou has been in Eden."*

The verses also speak of "tabrets" and "pipes," which were musical instruments, leading some to think the devil had been in charge of the choirs of heaven before he fell to earth. Look at the direction music is going today and ask yourself who is behind its influence and whether the devil would have the ability to do that.

The devil was identified as an "anointed cherub." A cherub is a winged angelic being that is often associated with worship and praise of God. I do not think this would be a description of the King of Tyrus, do you? Furthermore, to be anointed means to have a specific job or work to do (that of covering). I am not sure what the devil was to cover, although some have suggested that since he was so bright he was to cover God's Shekinah Glory as a protection for the creation. Remember how Moses shone when he came down from meeting with God on the mountain? Moses shone so bright that he had to cover his face.

We will continue in Ezekiel 28:14-15, which states, *"Thou was upon the holy mountain of God; thou has walked up and down in the midst of the stones of fire. Thou was perfect in thy ways from the day that thou was created, till iniquity was found in thee."* After Adam and Eve sinned, there had not been a perfect person because of the sin nature, so how could this refer to the King of Tyrus? I firmly believe it is talking about our adversary, the devil, Satan, Lucifer, whom Jesus saw fall from heaven. He fell because of iniquity. He wanted to be God, to be worshipped as God. For that to happen, there had to be someone who would do the worshipping. He wanted other angels to worship him, and when Adam and Eve came along, he wanted them to worship him. That is still true today, he wants you to worship him instead of God. You choose.

PRAYER: Heavenly Father, I choose to worship you. You are worthy of worship. As Peter said in John 6:68, *"Lord, to whom shall we go, you have the words of eternal life."* Satan can only offer misery, sickness and death, but you offer us abundant life. I choose abundant life in Christ Jesus. In Jesus' name, Amen.

FEBRUARY 24th

Now that we know who Satan is and from where he came, we also need to know what tactics he uses to beckon us to follow him. John 8:43-45 reads: *"Why do you not understand my speech? Even because you cannot hear my word. You are of your father the devil, and the lusts of your father you will do. He was a murderer from the beginning, and abode not in the truth, because there is no truth in him. When he speaks a lie, he speaks of his own: for he is a liar, and the father of it. And because I tell you the truth, you believe me not."*

Wow, this is Jesus' own words about the devil. Let us really learn a lesson from this. First of all, notice that in verse 43 Jesus gives the reason why people do not understand His speech, because they cannot hear it! Then Jesus goes on to tell them why they cannot hear it. They are connected at the hip to their fathers who had lied, and lied so much that they cannot hear the truth.

If you hear a lie long enough, you will believe it as the truth. And the "father" of all lies is the devil, plain and simple. God can speak nothing but the truth!

Remember what Jesus said in John 14:6, *"I am the way, the truth and the life: no one comes to the Father but by me."* Jesus said, *"I AM the truth,"* so He cannot lie. When we lie, we do so because there is a lying spirit influencing our old nature to follow the devil rather than God and the truth.

We also see, in today's verses, that Satan was a murderer from the beginning. Think about it. When Adam and Eve allowed Satan's lies to deceive them into disobeying God, they did not believe a word about death, but then the first death they saw in their lives was the death of Abel who had been murdered by their other son Cain. So Satan's lies lead to murder. You have heard the saying, "Don't kill the messenger." But "kill the messenger" is exactly what they did to Jesus, just as they had done to many of the prophets in the Old Testament. Tomorrow, we will look at some other tactics of the devil spoken of in the Bible.

PRAYER: Dear Heavenly Father, I am glad you are my Father. I do not want to think of Satan as my father, so help me with my choices, help me to not speak lies, but stick with the truth. Neither do I want a spirit of murder in my heart. Let me be willing to put the most charitable thoughts on what others do, and not succumb to a spirit of jealousy, bitterness, or envy. I want my desires to be in harmony with your character of being "the way, the truth, and the life." May your Holy Spirit direct my steps in my journey of life. In Jesus' name, Amen.

FEBRUARY 25th

In John 10, Jesus talks about sheep and the sheepfold (the enclosure for the sheep), the shepherd, the thief, and the robber. Sheep are put in a sheepfold for safety and the shepherd will enter that sheepfold by the door, but a thief or robber will climb over the fencing to get in to do his dirty work. His objective is to take what is not his for his own gain. He is a thief in every sense of the word.

The shepherd here is Jesus, the sheep are you and me, and the thief is the devil. I would encourage you to read the whole chapter, but right now we will look at John 10:9-11, which reads: *"I am the door: by me if any man enter in, he shall be saved, and shall go in and out and find pasture. The thief comes not, but for to steal, and to kill, and to destroy: I am come that they might have life, and that they might have it more abundantly. I am the good shepherd: the good shepherd lays down his life for the sheep."*

Here we see plainly what Satan's goals are (to steal, kill, and destroy), and we also see what Jesus' goals are (to give life and to give it more abundantly). What does it mean to steal, kill, and destroy? I see that as meaning a step-by-step plan to take you away from the protection of the sheepfold and the good shepherd. What would the devil try to steal? I believe he will try to steal your joy, peace, assurance of salvation, and belief that God loves you, so he can establish a foothold in your heart to go to the next phase of his plan, which is to kill!

So, what can he kill? I must remind you that he cannot do a thing unless you give him the permission to do so. He prompts those choices by lying to you about God and His love for you. He cannot kill anything without your permission, but he will try everything, try to steal your peace and security, to lead you to make bad choices.

He wants to kill your relationship with Jesus, because if he can accomplish that, then he can destroy God's whole plan for salvation in your life. And he will do it all with your permission. Remember, he is very subtle and sly. So do not let him steal your peace and security in Jesus, or steal your righteous standing before God either. You have on Jesus' coat of righteousness as you stand before God! Stop the devil dead in his tracks as he comes at you with disasters, trials, and troubles. Tell him to get back where he came from, hell!

Tell him that you belong to God, first, because you were created in God's image; second by the life, death, and resurrection of Jesus Christ that was secured 2,000 years ago; and, thirdly, by being baptized into Christ. Romans 6:3-4 says, *"Know you not, that so many of us as were baptized into Jesus Christ were baptized into his death? Therefore we were buried with him by baptism into death: that as Christ was raised up from the dead by the glory of the Father, even so we also should walk in newness of life."*

Today, we are to live a resurrected life, with all the benefits of that resurrection of Jesus, including the power over the devil. When Jesus died and rose again, He defeated all the power of the devil, <u>all</u> his <u>power</u> and <u>all</u> his <u>authority</u>. The abundant life Jesus is prepared to give us is ours as soon as we rely on Him in all things and will not listen to Satan and his lies.

I must add one more thing. I also believe that the devil's goals are to <u>steal our soul</u>, <u>kill our body</u>, and <u>destroy our spirit</u>, which God had intended to live eternally with Him. Remember how Satan had all of Job's children killed? Satan heckles God all the time to allow him to destroy us. He begins all this strategy by deceiving us, then planting doubt about God in our minds and hearts. We choose who to listen to, and our future life depends on our choices. Choose life!

PRAYER: Lord God, I am beginning to see where my trouble has been. I did not realize that Satan was behind all the hard times in my life. I did not realize, either, that I was giving him permission to mess up my life. Help me, now, to apply your victory over sin, death, and the power of the devil in my life, so that I can attain that abundant life. In Jesus' name, Amen.

FEBRUARY 26th

Today, we will look at some ways that Satan gets at us. In I Thessalonians 2:18, we read, *"Wherefore we would have come unto you, even I, Paul, once and again; but Satan hindered us."* Satan will do everything he can to hinder the work of the Christian, so the gospel will be hindered from reaching the ears of those who need to hear it.

In I Timothy 3:7, Paul is talking to Timothy who is a young man following in Paul's footsteps to do the work of a Christian. Here, Paul explains that *"he* (the young worker in God's Kingdom work) *must have a good report of them which are without; lest he fall into reproach and the snare of the devil."* The devil will use any tactic he can devise to cast a shadow of doubt on your reputation as a follower of Jesus. Paul calls that a "snare." A snare is a trap that is hidden from sight, but right in the path to suddenly stop the work of the Christian, and not just stop him, but render him unfit.

Have you ever seen an animal in a snare? Usually, the creature has a broken leg, or is so maimed that it could not even flee if it were set free. That is what Satan wants to do to you in your life, so your witness of a changed life will be so muddied up it will not serve God's intended purpose.

Matthew 24:24 states, *"For there shall arise false Christ's and false prophets, and shall shew great signs and wonders; in so much that, if it were possible, they shall deceive (lead astray) the very elect."* Satan is able to use people to pose as a Christ, or prophet, who are actually counterfeit, but look so much like the real thing, it will deceive people into following the false rather than the true Christ. Satan is the father of lies and a master at deception (which is a lie that looks like truth).

PRAYER: Lord God, help me to see the snares of the devil, and help me to recognize the false and the true Christ or prophet in my life. In Jesus' name, Amen.

FEBRUARY 27th

In Matthew 13:38-39, Jesus explains the meaning of a parable he just told to his disciples, *"The field is the world; the good seed are the children of the kingdom; but the tares are the children of the wicked one. The enemy that sowed them is the devil; the harvest is the end of the world; and the reapers are the angels."* Jesus had said, in Matthew 13:25, *"But while men slept, his enemy came and sowed tares among the wheat, and went his way."*

So, we see that it was Satan who sowed tares (children of the wicked one) among the children of God. He will plant just the kind of person at our elbow, at work, at play, anywhere and everywhere he can, to give us grief and struggles. We need to also be aware of the fact that Satan does this when we are asleep, at night, under the cover of darkness.

There are people who bring out the worst in us and there are people who bring out the best in us. Satan knows just who he can use to bring out the worst in us, and he uses them to the fullest. When we learn not to let that person get under our skin or to ruin our day by some unkind word or action, then we will gain the victory Jesus wants us to have in a situation like that.

Those people are like the tares among the wheat in our lives. They enjoy our reaction to what they have just said or done to us. It gives them pleasure to see us hurt, whether it be a little or a lot. Those things steal our peace and security It is Satan's first step in establishing a foothold in our hearts and souls so he can move on from there.

I will use an object lesson to show how we are to react in such situations. It is a matter of action and reaction. If I held a ball five feet above the floor and dropped it (the action), it would bounce (the reaction) in direct relationship to the height from which it was dropped. The ball would bounce back and forth until it had worn itself out. That is how we tend to react to an offensive word or action, according to our old nature.

However, if I put a pillow on the floor, when I drop the ball (same action), and it hits the pillow what will happen? What will be the reaction? It would not bounce at all (different reaction) the typical reaction falls dead. We need to learn how to be like that pillow, giving no reaction at all. Then Satan will not even try anymore, because he will not be successful. In the meantime, we will keep our peace and joy, and live abundant lives. Do not allow Satan to use you to bring out the worst in someone else. Such behavior is not becoming for a Christian, and Satan knows it.

PRAYER: Thank you, Father, for this lesson. I understand the principle of reaction here, and I want to put it into practice. Help me to remember this the next time Satan sets me up for such a snare. In Jesus' name, Amen.

FEBRUARY 28th

Fear is another one of Satan's tools. God's Word says over and over to "fear not." FEAR stands for False Evidence Appearing Real. In Luke 12:4-5, Jesus says, *"And I say unto you my friends, 'Be not afraid of them that kill the body, and after that have no more that they can do.' But I will forewarn you whom you shall fear: Fear him, which after he has killed has power to cast into hell. Yes, I say unto you, 'Fear him.' "*

Jesus is saying not to fear Satan, who can kill the body, but rather, fear God who has the power to cast into hell. We see murders in the news all the time, and the Bible says Satan is a murderer. But when we are completely in the hands of God, God will not let anything happen to us that would be against His directive will.

We are stepping into touchy territory here, because we know that there are Christians who have been killed for their testimony and witness to the Word of God. We call them martyrs. There have also been innocent people killed in car accidents by drunk drivers. You may ask, "Where was God, then?" Believe me when I say that God was there, and He will use this death for His honor and glory. Satan is not the winner, not ever, unless we let him be the winner.

I will talk later this year about how Jesus defeated even death on our behalf, but, for now, believe me when I say that there is no death that comes into our life but what God did not have the final say in it. It will touch every human being at one time or another and to lay the blame at the feet of God, who never wanted death to reign at all, is a great insult to God. All God ever wanted was for us to have life, and that more abundantly. Sin and death go hand in hand, and we live in a sinful world. Sin is all around us, and so is death. But Jesus has conquered death, and we will talk more about that later this year.

In the meantime, we are not to fear death. Hebrew 2:14-15 reads, *"For as much then as the children are partakers of flesh and blood, He also Himself likewise took part of the same; that through death he might destroy him that had the power of death, that is, the devil; And deliver them who through fear of death were all their lifetime subject to bondage."* We will talk more about this tomorrow. This is enough to think about in one day.

PRAYER: Heavenly Father, there are so many things to fear out there. How do I take hold of a fear-free life? Help me to address the fears in my life, and to gain victory over them all. Give me the understanding, and then the wisdom to make wise choices about the things I fear. In Jesus' precious name, Amen.

FEBRUARY 29th (Leap Year)

I want to take time to explain the reference we had yesterday. The children in Hebrew 2:14, those with flesh and blood, represent the human race. Jesus *"...took part of the same"* when he became human, being born of the Virgin Mary. He became flesh and blood like you and me. He knew what it was to be tired, cold, and hungry, and to bleed when He was hurt. He even had to die a physical death, like we all will die one day.

There was a reason for His becoming human. He did it so He could *destroy* the one who *had* (past tense) the *power* of death, the devil. Jesus destroyed the devil's power over death. When we understand that, then we will be free from the fear of death. We have been *delivered* from the *fear of death*.

For the time being, I am going to ask you to just believe the Word of God concerning this. My objective at this time is to show you that fear is one of Satan's tools to hinder us in our walk with God, to throw us off guard and into a snare, or whatever else he can do through fear to cause us not to believe God, just like he did with Adam and Eve. If they would have just believed what God said, and not believed what Satan had said, none of this would have been an issue. But are we any different? Can we believe that Jesus has destroyed the power of Satan over death as we read in Hebrews 2:14, or will Satan have the power to take that truth and make it into a lie for us as well? The choice of who to believe is yours.

PRAYER: Lord Jesus, you have done so much for me, and I want to believe all that you have done, you destroyed Satan's power over death on my behalf. How ever my instinct is to say, "There is still so much death all around me" Help me to fasten my eyes on your Word of truth and get my eyes off what I see in the world. In Jesus' name, Amen.

MARCH 1ˢᵗ

What is the antidote for fear? In I John 4:18, we read, *"There is no fear in love; but perfect love casts out fear: because fear has torment* (punishment). *He that fears is not made perfect in love."* Fear of punishment will be a deterrent. However, when we have that perfect love for God and live like we have it, then fear will disappear.

We will know at all times that God is for us, and *"…if God is for us, who can be against us?"* (Romans 8:31). If you have fears, you need to identify them. Then bring those fears to God and confess that you have them. Ask God to forgive you for the fear of _____, and name it. Then ask God to help you overcome that fear so it cannot cripple you again, or be a burden on you that you do not deserve to carry.

Notice the promise given to us in II Timothy 1:7, which reads, *"For God has not given us the spirit of fear* (fearfulness); *but of power, and of love, and of a sound mind."* That is what God is prepared to give us. But again, like wisdom and understanding, we have to *go* after it. We have to ask God for the spirit of power, love, and a sound mind.

Philippians 2:5 says, *"Let this mind be in you which was also in Christ Jesus."* You mean we can have a mind like Christ? That is what it says there! Notice that it says, "let," which would indicate a free choice. God never forces anything on us, we always have the free choice.

Having a free choice is a tremendous blessing from God. We are not a programmed robot, but instead have been given the awesome privilege of choice. Imagine entrusting the freedom of choice into the hands of sinful mankind, knowing full well how easy it would be for us to make bad choices every day. Yet God gave us that gift, because God did not want people worshipping Him by force. He wants our worship because we *choose* to worship Him.

PRAYER: Gracious Heavenly Father, thank you for the freedom of choice. Help me make those right choices day by day. Help me subscribe to the spirit of power, love, and sound mind, rather than succumb to the spirit of fear. Calm my heart when those choices are in front of me and I must suddenly choose which one I will follow. Let it be the right one. In Jesus' name, Amen.

MARCH 2nd

Does Satan and his coworkers believe in God? You may say, "What kind of a question is that?" But I think it is a very good question. If he believes in the God that created him, then he must surely know he will never reach that goal of being worshipped that he is seeking. If he does not believe in God, then why does he want to be worshipped as God? He could be satisfied right now as things are. He can get humans to worship him, which he has done for years and years. Isn't that enough?

Let's see what the Bible says about it. In James 2:19, we read, *"Thou believes that there is one God. thou does well: the devils* (plural!) *also believe, and shudder."* Yes indeed, they know beyond a shadow of a doubt that there is a God who is in full control even of them, and they shudder because they also know their destiny, which is hell. You may ask, "Aren't they in hell right now?" Some of them are, but not all. Many are still free to roam this earth and to resist God's work.

Look at Ephesians 6:12, which states, *"For we wrestle not with flesh and blood* (that means our troubles are not with other human beings made up of flesh and blood)*, but against principalities, against powers, against the rulers* (world rulers) *of this darkness of this world, against spiritual host of wickedness in high* (heavenly) *places."* We can see here clearly that <u>our warfare is with spiritual beings</u>, the devil being the CEO of the organization. Those devils are highly organized and they do have a certain amount of freedom in the heavenly realm. No, they are not all in hell yet. That will come later.

But we who are in Christ Jesus need not fear, because of I John 4:4, which reads ,*"You are of God, little children, and have overcome them* (the devils in this world)*, because greater is he that is within you, than he that is in the world."* Jesus is in you if you have asked him into your heart. The one in the world is Satan and he is a completely defeated

68

enemy. Jesus defeated Satan by paying for our sins when he shed His blood. By His death, he paid the penalty of sin, which was death. We need not fear any devil, trials, or tribulation, because it is Jesus who lives in you to direct your life and guide you in your choices to protect you from the evil one.

Please notice what Jesus prayed for His disciples before He was crucified in John 17. Jesus knew that when He was crucified, Satan would try to attack His disciples, the ones He depended on to carry on His work. They would be left very vulnerable, like an open target for Satan. As we read in John 17:13-15, Jesus prayed to His Father: *"And now I come to thee; and these things I speak in the world, that they might have my joy fulfilled in themselves. I have given them thy word; and the world has hated them, because they are not of the world. I pray not that thou should take them out of the world, but that thou should keep them from the evil one."*

Do you even for a moment think that God would not answer that prayer? That prayer also covers us because of verse 20, which reads, *"Neither pray I for these alone, but for them also which shall believe on me through their word."* That is us!

PRAYER: Dear Jesus, thank you for such a prayer on my behalf. Yes, I want to be kept from the evil one. Thank you also for the gift of salvation you purchased for me with your blood and death. No wonder you can offer abundant life to us as we walk out our life on this earth. Redemption is a settled fact, and Satan is defeated thoroughly. You asked God to keep me from the evil one. It has all been done for me, all I have to do is to receive it and believe it. Thank you, Father God, for such a gift as that. In Jesus' name, Amen.

MARCH 3rd

The subject of Satan is a big one and I do not want to beat it to death, but I also do not want you to be only partially informed. There are some more details we need to cover. Today, we will look at a few verses that also explain who he is, according to God's Word. In John 12:31, we see that the day of Jesus' crucifixion is drawing close and He tells His disciples, *"Now is the judgment of this world: now shall the prince of this world be cast out."* A prince is royalty, and Satan goes about acting like he is royalty, in charge of things with power and authority.

Ephesians 2:1-2 reads, *"And you hath He quickened* (made spiritually alive) *who were dead in trespasses and sins; Wherein in times past ye walked according to the course of this world, according to the prince of the power of the air, the spirit that now works in the children of disobedience."*

In this verse, Paul called Satan "the prince of the power of the air." Again, he is called a prince or power in the heavenly realm. It is hard to even realize that he has the right to travel into the heavenly realm, but that is what the Bible says.

There is one more reference for today. II Corinthians 4:3-4 reads, *"But if our gospel is hid, it is hid to them that are lost; In whom the god of this world has blinded the minds of them which believe not, lest the light of the glorious gospel of Christ, who is the image of God, should shine unto them."* In these verses, Satan is called "the god of this world." Notice it is not a capital G, but a small g. Satan will use any tactic, any person, or situation to cause us to turn our back on the one true God and follow the god of this world. He makes us depend on money, position, friends and so on for our security in life. God the Father wants us to depend on Him for our livelihood, for security. If we do not, then we make Satan the god of our lives.

PRAYER: Dear Lord, I see how easy it is to depend on the things of this world, insurance policies, savings accounts, and so on, for my security without even realizing it. Forgive me, Lord. I do not want Satan to be god in my life. Help me to understand my actions and thoughts that lead me into that sort of situation. In Jesus' name, Amen.

MARCH 4th

Today, we will address a couple more verses on Satan's nature. I Peter 5:8-9 reads: *"Be sober, be vigilant; because your adversary, the devil, as a roaring lion, walketh about, seeking whom he may devour. Whom resist steadfast in the faith, knowing that the same afflictions are accomplished in your brethren that are in the world."*

When a lion is old and no longer has teeth, he will roar an ear-splitting roar to scare his prey so much that it will freeze in fright, and then the lion can pounce and kill it. Satan has lost his teeth. His power is gone, because Jesus defeated him completely. Satan will make a lot of noise to frighten us, distract us, cause us to freeze and become immobile.

His objective is to devour us, to make us useless to the kingdom of God. Wise up to that tactic. Face him head on and declare that you will not be frightened or distracted by his roar. He has more nerve than you can imagine.

Look at Zechariah 3:1-2, which reads: *"And he showed me Joshua the high priest standing before the angel of the Lord, and Satan standing at his right hand to resist him. And the Lord said unto Satan, The Lord rebuke thee, O Satan; even the Lord that has chosen Jerusalem rebuke you: is not this a branch plucked out of the fire?"*

Satan has the guts to stand up and accuse right in God's face. We must never underestimate the nerve of our adversary, the devil. He will try every avenue and sneak under any fence to get at Christians trying to live a life for God. Do not let his roar unnerve you, not ever!

PRAYER: Heavenly Father, I begin to see that I need to deal with my fear of Satan and his roar, and I really need to see in my spirit how completely he is defeated. I need to see that Jesus' blood is the thing that took Satan's power away. It paid the price for my sins, all of them. Help me, Lord, to live in that victory, and to not give a glance or notice to Satan at all. In Jesus' name, Amen.

MARCH 5th

There is one more settled fact we need to touch on before we close the door on the subject of Satan. What is in store for him? I believe we need to start with I Corinthians 6:2-3, which reads: *"Do ye not know that the saints* (that refers to all believers) *shall judge the world? And if the world shall be judged by you, are ye unworthy to judge the smallest matters? Know ye not that we shall judge angels? How much more things that pertain to this life?"*

Paul is writing this letter to the Christians at Corinth. Those angels who did not rebel against God surely will not need any judging, but those angels who listened to Satan and rebelled against God's authority will need to be judged and sentenced for punishment. Of those angels, Satan is the chief.

Imagine us of the human race actually sitting in judgment of Satan himself. You also need to see another dimension of this whole affair. Angels were created a higher creation than man. They are not flesh and blood like we are. We are of the earth, made from the earth. Angels are heavenly host and do not die, nor were they born, but were created.

Now look at Hebrew 2:6-8, which reads: *"But one in a certain place testified, saying, 'What is man, that thou art mindful of him? Or the son of man* (Jesus)*, that thou visited him? Thou made him a little lower than the angels; thou crowned him with glory and honor, and did set him over the works of your hands. Thou has put all things in subjection under his feet...' "* Get the picture here? Jesus became human, flesh and blood. He left His heavenly realm and became earthly like us. Then Jesus, when He had purchased our redemption, also descended into hell and defeated Satan, who is a higher creation than mankind. But judgment of this higher creation will be given to us who have struggled against his wiles all these years on this earth. In the end, Satan will be judged by a lower creation. What a blow to his pride.

PRAYER: Heavenly Father, it amazes me that everything is spelled out so clearly in Scripture. I cannot imagine being a judge of the world and of

Satan, but who better than those who have had to withstand all his fiery darts and devilish tactics? Lord God, I am beginning to see even more clearly how much you have done for mankind, how much you have trusted us, how much you have given of yourself to us, and I cannot help but stand in awe of such trust, such trust in such a fragile unpredictable human race. Is there hope for us to measure up to your standard, even a little bit? I pray that I will get a little closer to your standard for me each day, so that there is progress, even if it is slow. Thank you for creating me just the way I am. In Jesus' name, Amen.

MARCH 6th

Satan will surely come to his final end. But before that, he will want to rule the world. He will have two helpers toward the time of the end. They are found in Revelation 13 and are called the "beast" and "another beast," later known as "the Beast and the False Prophet." In this way, Satan will attempt to counterfeit the Trinity of God the Father, Son, and Holy Spirit.

Please notice the message in Matthew 28:18, *"And Jesus came and spoke unto them* (the disciples)*, saying, 'All power and authority is given unto me in heaven and earth.' "* Who had given Jesus all that power and authority? God had. Then we read in Ephesians 1:19-20, *"And what is the exceeding greatness of his power to us-ward who believe, according to the working of his mighty power, which he wrought in Christ, when he raised Him from the dead and set Him at His own right hand in the heavenly places."*

Who gave Jesus the right to sit in that seat of honor? God did! So God gave Jesus His power and great authority and His seat. Do you remember that Satan is also called the dragon? Now look at Revelation 13:2, which states, *"And the beast* (the anti-Christ) *which I saw was like a leopard, and his feet were as the feet of a bear, and his mouth as the mouth of a lion: and the dragon gave him his <u>power</u>, and his <u>seat,</u> and great <u>authority</u>."*

Satan will counterfeit the Trinity toward the end of his days. Then, in Revelation 13:11, we read, *"And I beheld another beast coming up out of the earth; and he had two horns like a lamb, and he spoke as a dragon."* This is the "false prophet" who will represent both the beast and the dragon, just as the Holy Spirit represents both Jesus and God the Father. They will all three do their dirty work here on this earth for an appointed time, but they will meet their end as you can see in Revelation 19:20, which states: *"And the beast was taken, and with him the false prophet that wrought miracles before him, with which he <u>deceived</u> them that had received the mark of the beast, and them that worshipped his image. These both were cast alive into a lake of fire burning with brimstone."*

In Revelation 20:10, we also read, *"And the devil that deceived them was cast into the lake of fire and brimstone, where the beast and the false prophet are, and shall be tormented day and night for ever and ever."*

Did you notice that their entire work was one of deception? That is Satan's main trump card, he will do everything he can to deceive you. You can also see that their destiny is determined. Satan and all his hosts are defeated already, and we need to live and act like we know that.

PRAYER: Heavenly Father, thank you for revealing to me the truth of Satan's end, it helps me to see that he has been judged already, maybe not sentenced, but at least judged. It is only a matter of time before that judgment will be carried out. I pray, Father, that I will make the right choices in my life so that I defeat Satan by my choices on a daily basis. In Jesus' name, Amen.

MARCH 7th

Today, we will look at John 16:23-24, which reads: *"And in that day ye shall ask me nothing. Verily, verily, I say unto you, what so ever ye shall ask the Father, in my name, He will give it you. Hitherto have ye asked nothing in my name: ask, and ye shall receive, that your joy may be full."* The name of Jesus is our weapon against Satan's onslaughts against us. It was the blood, the death and resurrection that secured the victory for us and Jesus' name was given to us as a badge of authority over the evil one who accuses, deceives, lays a snare, and plans situations against us day and night.

We should never be defeated with such a power given into our lives! Yet we as Christians crumble in times of adversity, when Satan has succeeded in finding a little crack in our foundation to sneak in. But even then, God will be there to lift you up if you will only admit your weakness and determine to live as a winner no matter what.

It is a choice we make. It is not always easy, but I believe the alternative is even more disastrous and hard. The alternative is to deny there is a loving God around to help you get through the adversity, to believe that you are alone, without any help at all, and wallow in your condition. It is my prayer that I will not succumb to such self pity, but will stick with God and expect Him to *be there* for me even when it looks impossible! I believe I have everything to gain if I keep that attitude and everything to lose if I do not.

Jesus began John 16: verse 23 by saying "in *that* day." What day do you think He was talking about? I believe it was the day that He had finished defeating sin, death, and the power of the devil, after He had descended into hell, rose from the dead, ascended into heaven, and sat down at God's right hand. I believe it was *that* day that He had the perfect right to tell His disciples (and us as well) that His name was the all-powerful tool in the whole universe to go with us to the Father to secure favor with God and victory over all of Satan's wiles. Please read for yourselves Philippians 2:10. Every knee, including Satan's, shall bow.

PRAYER: Dear God, we live in a world full of sin, sickness, and death. Nothing in that looks beautiful and kind. But you offer hope even in the midst of such evil. I pray that you will help me keep my eyes on that hope, and that I will be blind to the evil around me that spoils your beautiful world. I know that you have prepared a place for me in eternity, a place that is full of kindness, love, purity, peace, joy, goodness, and justice, where no evil exists, no sickness, contention, fear, or death. Thank you for creating such a place to spend eternity with you. A place that you have prepared specially for me. Thank you for loving me so much that you were willing to suffer and die for me. It is my desire to be with you throughout all eternity. In Jesus' name, Amen.

MARCH 8th

I believe we need to talk about God's justice for a few days. If you went before a court of law in our country you would want a judge presiding whom you knew to be a just man, one with just discernment and just ways. If the God we worship appeared to be unjust, how could we ever have faith in Him or His work on our behalf? If He used favoritism in any of His dealings, we could not have a real factual trust in him, now could we?

How do you perceive the God of the whole creation? What is your concept of the God that created you and all that exists? Let's see if we can find references to settle this issue. I will begin in Genesis 18. I would suggest you read the whole chapter because I am going to quote verses here and there.

Abraham had such a strong faith in God that it stands out as a lighthouse to all of us. There was no Scripture for him to read, as there is for us today. Abraham was the Scripture of the future, and he was living it. But his perspective of God was so on target it is amazing. God had called him to leave his country, kindred, and father's house (siblings, etc.) and go to a country God would show him. Believe it or not, he obeyed God with one exception, his nephew Lot went with him. Lot's father (Abraham's brother) was dead, so Abraham took him on this journey. After some time, Lot's herdsmen and Abraham's herdsmen began to argue about the pasture land. There was not enough for them all, so Abraham gave Lot the choice of land. Lot went toward the best land, near the cities of Sodom and Gomorrah, and Abraham took the second-best land.

After some time, some heavenly messengers met with Abraham to tell him that Sodom and Gomorrah were very sinful, as we see in Genesis 18:20-21, *"And the Lord said, 'Because the cry of Sodom and Gomorrah is great, and because their sin is grievous I will go down now, and see whether they have done altogether according to the cry of it, which come unto me; and if not I will know it.' "* Today, we see that God will have evidence before pronouncing any kind of judgment Abraham's thoughts immediately go to Lot, that nephew who took the best land. Is he in danger of any kind?

PRAYER: Heavenly Father, it is comforting to know that you are a God who needs evidence before destroying people. Thank you for including this in your Word for me to read and understand. Build my confidence and trust in you through this Word. In Jesus' name, Amen.

MARCH 9th

In Genesis 18, we see that after a discussion with the three messengers, (two messengers left to go to Sodom and Gomorrah), then Abraham had "the Lord" to himself. Abraham got right to the point in verses 23-25: *"And Abraham drew near, and said, 'Wilt thou also destroy the righteous with the wicked? Peradventure there be fifty righteous within the city: wilt thou also destroy and not spare the place for the fifty righteous that are therein? That be far from thee to do after this manner, to slay the righteous with the wicked: and that the righteous should be as the wicked, that be far from thee: Shall not the Judge of all the earth do right?' "*

Here is Abraham standing before God and confronting Him with such an issue of justice! He did it for all of us who wonder if God *is* a just God! I see Abraham believing that in order for God to be God of the universe, He would have to be a just God in everything. That certainly would be a reasonable conclusion, would it not?

But Abraham is not done yet. He whittles that ratio from 50 righteous down to 10 in verses 26 to 32. Abraham was not afraid to confront God on hard issues. It was finally decided that God would not destroy the whole city for the sake of 10 righteous people within that city. Now I will ask you, *"Is God a just God in your eyes?"*

PRAYER: Lord God, I am grateful to Abraham for asking and confronting you on this hard question, and for including it in your Word for me to read today. I am also grateful to know that you do not shrink from such hard questions, but are ready to help us in our weaknesses to see that you can be approached by us with questions such as these. I also see you are a God of great patience with us sinful human beings. Often times we deserve a stern look, but you give us a loving smile instead, and also you give us your time for discussion. Thank you Lord God. In Jesus' name, Amen.

MARCH 10th

We are not done with Abraham and God's justice yet. In Genesis 19, there is an account of the visit of the two angels to Sodom and Gomorrah, and how they tried to convince Lot and his family, all who were righteous; to get out of the city before God destroyed the city and all who were unrighteous in it. Please note here that God is giving the family of Lot a free choice. That is also a part of God's justice. He will not force us to choose right over wrong. He gave us a free choice as a gift, so we are responsible for our choices. Genesis19:12-13 reads: *"And the men* (the angels) *said unto Lot, 'Hast thou here any besides? Son in law, and thy sons, and thy daughters, and whatsoever thou hast in the city, bring them out of this place. For we will destroy this place, because the cry of them is waxen great before the face of the Lord; and the Lord hath sent us to destroy it.' "*

Notice how hard God is working to get the righteous out of the city, those whom Abraham had reasoned about with God. In verse 14 we read, *"And Lot went out and spoke unto his sons in law, which married*

78

his daughters, and said, 'Up, get you out of this place; for the Lord will destroy this city.' But he seemed as one that mocked unto his sons in law."

Lot's witness within that city, within his family, was not strong enough for them to be believed in Abraham's God. Had Lot made Abraham's God his God? Keep in mind we are looking at God's justice here! Verses 15 through 16 state: *"And when the morning arose, then the angels hastened Lot, saying, 'Arise, take thy wife, and thy two daughters, which are here; lest thou be consumed in the iniquity of the city.' And while he lingered, the men laid hold upon his hand, and upon the hand of his wife and upon the hand of his two daughters; the Lord being merciful unto him; and they brought him forth, and set him without the city."* Imagine that, Lot was still dragging his feet! How much warning did he have to have before he would believe God meant what He said, "Get out of the city, it will be destroyed!"

The Lord was not only merciful, but long suffering, which is another word for patient. If you keep on reading you will see the resistance does not stop yet, but we will leave that for you to discover on your own.

PRAYER: Heavenly Father, help me to never be this reluctant to obey your Word. In Jesus' name, Amen.

MARCH 11th

I want to take you to Genesis 19:23-24,26 which reads: *"The sun was risen upon the earth when Lot entered intoZoar. Then the Lord rained upon Sodom and upon Gomorrah brimstone and fire from the Lord out of heaven, ...but his wife looked back from behind him, and she became a pillar of salt."*

In verse 17 they had been told not to look back. The lesson in this is that when God sends us in a new direction, if we keep looking back we will never do what we could do where we are going. His wife could not leave what she had back there. The angels had laid hold of her hand and pulled her out. Her feet went but her heart was back in the city. She was engulfed in the brimstone and fire and became a pillar of salt.

I am sure that when Lot chose the best land, he never dreamt that it would strip him of almost every thing he had. He was left only with his two daughters. We need to look at the rest of the story in verses 27 through 29: *"And Abraham gat up early in the morning to the place where he stood before the Lord.* (Abraham had a place he retreated to every morning to communicate with God. Do you make it a practice to communicate with God *early* in the morning?) *And he looked toward Sodom and Gomorrah, and toward all the land of the plain* (the fertile part of the land that Lot had taken for himself)*, and beheld, and, lo, the smoke of the country went up as the smoke of a furnace. And it came to pass, when God destroyed the cities of the plain, that God remembered Abraham, and sent Lot out of the midst of the overthrow, when he overthrew the cities in the which Lot dwelt."*

God remembered Abraham! Remember, Abraham had stood before the Lord on Lot's behalf, and that was why Lot was saved from the fierce anger of God over the sins of the cities of Sodom and Gomorrah. That tells me that our prayers have a place in the justice system of God's laws! How can we ever be a useful instrument in God's behalf in regards to the lives of those we know and love, like Abraham loved and knew Lot. We need to be we aware of how important a prayer is in the eyes of God.

Today, I have told you how important your prayers are according to the story of Abraham and Lot. What are you going to do about that? That choice and privilege is yours.

PRAYER: Dear Heavenly Father, I am amazed to learn that I can pray as an intercessor and expect you to move so mightily as you did for Abraham. I feel too weak spiritually right now to grasp the full strength of this lesson, but I come to you for the help I will need to put this into practice. Open my eyes to see myself as a candidate for such strong intercession, so that I can pray like that and feel confident that I am not stepping over the boundary lines and come into a place of twisting your arm, to get my way. In other words, I want to know it is all right for me to pray such a prayer as

Abraham did, and thank you for answering this prayer. In Jesus' name, Amen.

MARCH 12th

A just God cannot wink at sin. Sin is to God's justice what mud is on a pure white wedding dress, or a scratch is on a brand new car. It is no longer without blemish, but is marred and less than what it was intended to be. You will either try to dry clean the dress or discard it, and you will either try to get the scratch buffed out and repainted or leave it and be reminded of the fact it is no longer perfect.

We are that spoiled dream of a perfect wedding dress or new car to God. He could not leave us the way we were, anymore than we would leave the dress or car that way, without trying to do something about it.

But God's problem was that if He did do something about it, it would have to be within the confines of His own perfect justice system. He needed to be perfectly justified in forgiving sin, and putting it out of the way. How could this all be done and God still be perfectly just?

Romans 3:23 states, *"For all have sinned and fallen short of the glory of God."* That word *"all"* does not leave out one human being. We are born with the inclination to sin. We all are in need of a just plan of salvation from sin and the wages sin brings with it. No one is exempt! So, we are going to try to hurdle that subject in such a way that you can understand it. It is very simple really, but to explain it simply, is not easy.

PRAYER: Dear Lord God, thank you for being a just and fair Heavenly Father and judge. I do not want to lose sight of that fact, so help me fasten my eyes on you when trouble comes and I feel it is unfair or unjust, so that I do not place blame on you in any way. In Jesus' name, Amen.

MARCH 13th

I left off yesterday talking about a *just* plan for God to deal with our sin and still remain a *just* God. In I Corinthians 15:21-22, we read, *"For since by man* (Adam) *came death, by man* (Jesus) *came also resurrection from the dead. For as in Adam all die, even so in Christ shall all be made alive."*

I see God's reasoning here like this: If Satan can use one man to bring sin and death to the entire human race, why can not God use one man (Jesus, His own son) to bring a resurrection life into the human race. I also want us to look at Romans 8:1-2. I may have used these verses early in the year, but I need to use it here in the context of God's justice. These verses state, *"There is therefore now no condemnation to them which are in Christ Jesus, who walk not after the flesh, but after the Spirit. For the law of the Spirit of life in Christ Jesus hath made me free from the law of sin and death."*

Why would the Word say *"now no condemnation"*? The Word could say that because ever since Jesus came, shed his precious blood for our sins, and died our death on the cross of shame and suffering, all that was needed to satisfy God's justice in regard to forgiving sin had been accomplished. From that moment on, there was "no condemnation."

That is only good for those who are *in* Christ Jesus, however, Romans 6:3 tells us how that is accomplished, *"Know ye not that so many of us as were baptized INTO Christ Jesus were baptized INTO His death."* And Roman 8:1 goes on to say that they are those *"...who walk not after the flesh, but after the Spirit."* That word "walk" refers to our daily life. If there is no change in your life after Jesus takes over, then how can anyone say that He, Jesus lives in you? Well, when you are *in* Him, then you have to make the choice to have Him *in* you.

Revelation 3:20 reads, *"Behold, I stand at the door* (of your heart*) and knock: if any man hears my voice, and opens the door, I will come into him, and will sup with him and he with me."* You will have a fellowship after you have invited Him into your heart, and then you will walk your daily life in a different way than when you followed your old

82

sinful nature. So "now" includes all the above, and there is no condemnation. God's just system was fully satisfied and complete by that one man, Jesus.

PRAYER: Dear Lord Jesus, I am so grateful for what you did for me on the cross, all your suffering and actually dying my death, just so that God the Father could deem me justified in His sight. Help me to live a life that shows that I am grateful. In Jesus' name, Amen.

MARCH 14th

In Romans 8:2, we read , *"For the law of the Spirit of life in Christ Jesus has made me free from the law of sin and death."* Here, God speaks of two laws, with one in complete opposition to the other. We are born under the *law of sin and death,* which was brought into the world by one man. But there is a higher law, now. God's one man, Jesus, came and did for man's good what the law of sin and death could never do. The *law of the Spirit of life* (abundant life now, and eternal life when we die!) in Christ Jesus has set me *free* from the law of sin and death. There is no other place to find that life, it is exclusive.

If you visualized two freight trains racing down a track, one going north named "The Love of God For the Sinner" and the other going south named "The Wrath of God Over Sin." They do not see each other, so they crash. When the dust settles, all you see is a man hanging there, on a cross, battered, beaten, and dead. That would be a picture of God's intense hatred and disgust for sin, and God's total and complete love for mankind being resolved in a way that only God could design and carry out.

The sinner that came racing down the track and hit head onto the Son of a loving Father was the crash, the explosion that took place at the cross. Jesus, who took on the force of all the sins of the world, and came out the victorious winner, had to do that by being beaten, humiliated, and crucified. I believe that is what the cross would look like. God's hate and wrath for sin, and God's love and mercy for mankind, had to meet if that

83

issue was ever going to be resolved. I believe they met at the cross of Jesus Christ. That is what God's justice required in order for Him to forgive our sins and accept us into His family. All this because God is a *just* God. The *justice* of God wrapped His loving arms around you to include you in the equation.

PRAYER: Father, I am so humbled to think that Jesus agreed to become that sacrifice for me, so that you could forgive me my sins and accept me as a child into your family. How can I show you my gratitude for what you did for me? Help me to live a life that will reflect that sacrifice you made on my behalf, so I will be able to walk according to the Spirit of life in Christ Jesus. In Jesus' name, Amen.

MARCH 15th

God's justice is displayed vividly in another reference in Genesis. Genesis 15:13-16 states: ***"And He said unto Abram, know of a surety that thy seed shall be a stranger in a land that is not theirs, and shall serve them; and they shall afflict them four hundred years; And also that nation, whom they shall serve, will I judge: and afterward shall they come out with great substance. And thou shall go to thy fathers in peace; thou shall be buried in a good old age. But in the fourth generation they shall come hither again: for the iniquity of the Amorites is not yet full."*** God had been telling Abram what was going to happen to his people the Jews. They would live as strangers in a land that was not theirs (Egypt) and be afflicted there for over 400 years. Abram would live to be an old man and be buried, but in the fourth generation his people would come out of that land because the "iniquity of the Amorites" would not yet be full.

The Israelites encountered the Amorites on their way back to their promised land, but God had a perfect timing here to accommodate His justice system, and they could not return until He could justly judge the nation of the Amorites. You see, not until their iniquity was complete could they be judged. God will make sure all the evidence is in before He pronounces judgment. I believe this is why the devil is not in eternity hell yet. His cup of iniquity is not yet full.

Without thinking, we have a tendency to lay blame at the feet of God for our trouble, wondering why He does not put Satan the deceiver and trouble maker in hell where he belongs right now! But do you know what? Even after Jesus has ruled this earth for a thousand years, and Satan had been bound in the bottomless pit, Satan will be let loose again and do the same thing he has always done, deceive the nations. There will be many people ready for a change, so the number that will follow Satan will be "as the sands of the sea" in number! You can read all about this in Revelation 20.

After that, Satan will be cast into the lake of fire and brimstone, which is eternity hell. But God will not even judge Satan until all the evidence is in. He is a perfectly *just* God. You can depend on it. Consider I Peter 2:23, which reads, *"Who, (Jesus) when He was reviled, reviled not again; when He suffered, He threatened not; but committed Himself to Him (God) that judges righteously."*

PRAYER: Heavenly Father, the more I read about your love, mercy, grace, justice, and righteousness, the more I realize how much you love us sinful beings, and how far you stretch out your arm towards us, to enclose us in your loving arms. Forgive me, Lord, for even thinking you are far from me and my trouble, that you don't care for me, and that if you did you would cast Satan out of my life. Help me in my choices to follow you instead of following Satan. In Jesus' name, Amen.

MARCH 16th

Today, we will look again at I Peter 2:23. I want to talk some more about God's righteousness. He is not only a *just* judge, but He is a *righteous* judge as well. Jesus satisfied God's *standard* of righteousness when He suffered, died, and rose again from the dead. God applies that

85

righteousness to us when we are in Christ Jesus. What a winner that makes us!

And just think about this: Jesus did this for _every_ person, but only those who accept it will reap the benefits. Those who are too proud, or full of fear, or whatever it is that holds them back from accepting this terrific gift of salvation, will not have that coat of righteousness when the day comes that they must answer to God the Father for their lives on earth.

I think Philippians 3:9 explains it well, _"And be found in Him_ (Jesus), _not having my own righteousness, which is of the law_ (keeping the law to the letter), _but that which is through the faith of Christ, the righteousness which is of God by faith."_ You see, it is God's righteousness that we receive. Jesus, by faith in His Heavenly Father, did the work that needed to be done. Then the Father gave that righteousness to all who have Jesus as their savior. How simple it is to just accept it now and know that you are on the winning side.

PRAYER: Lord, I do not want to be on the losing side, but rather on the winning side. Thank you for what you have done for me. Help me to stick to your side all the days of my life. In Jesus' name, Amen.

MARCH 17th

It is important that we practice righteousness, since we have been made the righteousness of Christ as we learned yesterday. I John 3:9-10 states, _"Whosoever is born of God does not commit sin; for his seed remains in him and he cannot sin, because he is born of God. In this the children of God are manifest_ (which means that their lifestyle will be the evidence of their faith as a believer in Christ), _and the children of the devil_ (the same is true of them, their lifestyle will be the evidence of who they follow); _whosoever does not righteousness is not of God, neither he that loveth not his brother."_

If Jesus lives in us, then our lives ought to be a reflection of the One who lives in us. Jesus _is_ righteous, _is_ love, _is_ faithful, and so on,

86

therefore, we ought to practice those things also. If we do not practice righteousness, love, faith, mercy, justice, grace, and peace, then how can we say we are a follower of the One who lives in us?

Also look at I Timothy 6:11-12, which reads: *"But thou, O man of God, flee these things* (greed, pride, lust, etc.) *and follow after righteousness, godliness, faith, love, patience, meekness. Fight the good fight of faith, lay hold of eternal life, whereunto thou art also called and has professed a good profession before many witnesses."*

The Apostle Paul wrote this letter to a young man named Timothy, whom Paul was mentoring. This is also good advice to us . When he says *"follow after righteousness, godliness, faith, love, patience, meekness,"* he means we are to practice those things in our daily life. We should address each day with the attitude that we will practice those qualities and virtues like it would be the last day we would have the opportunity to do so.

PRAYER: Lord God, I give you my days to honor you. Help me to live a life that will speak of you and your righteousness, love, meekness, grace, mercy, and godliness. I want to be the person who lifts you up, but I also know my weaknesses that slow me down and hold me back, so I ask you to strengthen me in each of these areas so that I can be victorious over the wiles of the devil who will try to keep me from fulfilling my desire to be all that you created me to be. In Jesus' name, Amen.

MARCH 18th

I believe that God has an individual plan for each of us, a national plan for the nations, and a global plan for this earth. I would like to attempt to address this subject for a few days. Since we have discussed God's justice, righteousness, how much God loves us, wants us to have His peace, and assurance of salvation, I think we can now talk about God's overall plan in the area of us as individuals, nations, and as a planet.

His plan for us as individuals is probably three-fold: He wants us to, 1) be saved, 2) live with Him in eternity, and 3) grow into the likeness of Christ. Let's address God's desire and plan to save us first of all. John 3:16 reads, *"For God so loved the world* (that includes you) *that whosoever believes in Him shall not perish but have eternal life."*

I believe that is plain enough to understand God's plan for us. But remember, He must work within the boundaries of our freedom of choice, so He does not stop us from practicing sin. He will even come to find us after we have sinned to help us get back on track with Him, but His whole desire for us is to *want* to follow Him and His ways, so that we do not lose fellowship with God the Father, not ever. Eternity is a long time, and He wants us all, you included, to spend that time with Him. John 14:1-3 states: *"Let not your hearts be troubled: you believe in God, believe also in me* (Jesus). *In my Father's house are many mansions: if it were not so, I would have told you. I go to prepare a place for you. And if I go and prepare a place for you, I will come again, and receive you unto myself, that where I am, there you may be also."*

Now, can that be more clear? He is definitely talking about heaven and eternity. It is God's desire and plan that you should spend eternity there with Him. He did not just create you to live a miserable life here on this sin-ridden earth. You bet not! God wants you with Him throughout eternity to fellowship with Him, learn more about Him, and enjoy eternity. But what about the meantime, the time between salvation and eternity? Is there a plan for this time on earth also? You bet! We will begin to address that in the next few days.

PRAYER: I guess I had not thought of you as a "planning" God before. It is comforting to know that you have been planning for me, and are planning for me, and will continue to plan for me. To think that even in eternity there is a plan in place for me (a mansion no less), a place that you prepared just for me! This puts it all on such a personal level. All I can say in response to this is a great big THANK YOU, FATHER. In Jesus' name, Amen.

88

MARCH 19th

We will start with God's complete plan first, and then fill in the blanks as we go forward. God's complete plan for this time on earth, between salvation and eternity, is found in Ephesians 4:11-14. Verse 11 reads, *"And He* (Jesus) *gave some to be apostles; and some, prophets, and some, evangelists; and some, pastors and teachers."* After Jesus descended into hell and defeated Satan on his own turf, Jesus gave gifts to men, gifts to be apostles, prophets, evangelists, pastors, and teachers.

They were called and appointed for a reason, and we see that in verses 12 through 13: *"For the perfecting of the saints* (i.e., you and I, we are called saints since we believe in Jesus as the Son of God who died to bring us eternal life), *for unto the work of the ministry, for the edifying* (building up) *of the body of Christ: Till we all come in the unity of the faith, and of the knowledge of the Son of God, unto a perfect* (full grown) *man, unto the measure of the stature of the fullness of Christ."*

In these verses, we see the reason for the apostles, prophets, evangelists, pastors, and teachers, to perfect the saints. God wants us to reach a plateau where we will be like Him in every way. He calls that the full stature of Christ, a full grown man or woman of God.

That, in a nut shell, is God's plan for you and me as we live out our lives here on earth. God has provided men and women who can aid us on our way as we grow, and practice a Christ-like life a little more each day. We can see the results we will enjoy in verse 14, which reads, *"That we henceforth be no more children, tossed to and fro, and carried about with every wind of doctrine, by the sleight of men, and cunning craftiness, whereby they lie in wait to deceive* (after the wiles of error);*"* In other words, we will not be swayed by false doctrines that would deceive us and lead us astray, neither spend years vacillating, first hot, but then cold, or zealous, and then lazy, which are all tricks of the devil to slow our spiritual growth. So God's three-fold plan is 1) to save us, 2) have us live with Him in eternity, and 3) help us grow into the likeness of Christ as we make that journey through life on earth.

PRAYER: Heavenly Father, thank you for the mentors in my life who have helped me to grow and get spiritual roots sunk deep into the love of Christ Jesus. Also, help me to give to others what they have taken time to give to me. It is comforting to know that you have a plan in place for my life right now. Give me eyes to see that plan as it unfolds before me. In Jesus' name, Amen.

MARCH 20th

How do we grow up into the full stature of Christ? We will talk about that for a day or two now, since we have established that it is God's overall plan for us to become like Christ. I Peter 2:1-2 reads: *"Wherefore laying aside* (notice the free choice here, you decide to lay aside something or to not lay it aside), *all malice* (wickedness)*, and all guile, and hypocrisies, and envies, and all evil speaking, as new born babes, desire* (long for) *the sincere milk of the Word* (the spiritual milk, which is without guile)*, that ye may <u>grow</u> thereby* (unto Salvation)*."*

Just as a newborn baby desires the mother's milk, so also are we to desire the Word of God. Just as a baby grows as a result of that good milk, we too will grow spiritually from reading, studying, and assimilating the Word of God. When we study that Word, and actually drink it in, we will want to lay aside all malice, guile, hypocrisy, envies, and evil speaking. Our "want to" will change right before our very eyes. But I do not believe it will ever happen unless we get into the Word of God.

The Word has a power in that it is a mystery, but anyone who has taken it seriously will attest to the fact that it is the power of God unto Salvation. Romans 1:16 states, *"For I am not ashamed of the Gospel of Christ: for it is the power of God unto salvation to every man who believes; to the Jew first, and also to the Greek* (Gentiles)." So, we see it is from reading the Word that we grow.

Now look at II Peter 3:18, which reads, *"But grow in grace, and in the knowledge of our Lord and Savior Jesus Christ. To Him be glory both now and for ever. Amen."* We are to grow as a new born baby grows, which means a balanced growth, not just one part of the body, but the whole body is to grow together at the same time. That is done as we study the Word of God. In this verse, God wants us to grow in grace and in the knowledge of Jesus Christ as both Savior and Lord. That is God's plan for us during this time between salvation and eternity.

PRAYER: Heavenly Father, I am so grateful for the teachers I have had in my life. Forgive me for being preoccupied with the mundane things of life to neglect the reading of your Word and neglecting to grow. Remind me from time to time not to neglect it even now, but to diligently purpose in my heart and will to read and meditate on your word each day. In Jesus' name, Amen.

MARCH 21ˢᵗ

We'll read of one more place for growth before we move on. In II Thessalonians 1:3, which reads, *"We are bound to thank God always for you, brethren, as it is meet* (fitting), *because that your faith groweth exceedingly, and the charity of every one of you all toward each other aboundeth."* You see, our faith needs to grow, and it grows in two ways: first, as we read and study the Word of God, and secondly, as we step out in faith to obey the Word. This is how we test and strengthen our faith muscles.

An airplane is not ready for use until it has been taken for a test ride. Our faith is much like that, and it needs to be tested. The same is true of our muscles, if they are not used, they will wither and soon be useless.

There is also a lesson that you need to learn about temptation and testing: Satan tempts, God tests. God never tempts us, never! James 1:13 states, *"Let no man say when he is tempted, 'I am tempted of God,' for God cannot be tempted with evil, neither tempts He any man."* We see that God is not the tempter, but rather Satan is the one who tempts us.

Then the Scripture goes on to say in James 14-15 just how that temptation goes, step by step, *"But every man is tempted, when he is drawn away of his own lust, and enticed.* **Then when lust has conceived,** **it brings forth sin, when it is finished** (full grown, you see, sin can grow also)**, brings forth death.** *"* God uses the word "conceived" here, which is like the conception of a child. The union between the egg and the sperm brings forth a child.

So, what union brings forth sin? I believe *lust* is like the egg, and Satan's *temptations* and *enticements* are like the sperm. Put the two together, and they will produce sin. And when sin is allowed to flourish, the result is death. It can be death of a dream, marriage, plan, hope, and, finally, where you will spend eternity, heaven or hell.

So, we know for sure from these verses that God does not tempt us. What then is a test? We will consider that tomorrow.

PRAYER: Heavenly Father, it looks like I must be on my guard at all times to recognize Satan's plans and schemes of temptations. Help me see the traps he sets for me to fall into, and give me the strength spiritually to resist him. Help me recognize enticements in my life, so that I can overcome them and be a victorious Christian. In Jesus' name, Amen.

MARCH 22nd

God will test us to strengthen our faith muscles. How can we ever put our faith to the test if we never have any trials and tribulations? It is during those times that we turn to God with all our hearts and trust Him when everything looks hopeless. It is at those times that God is there to walk through the trial with us.

I believe that for every temptation, if we would turn it into a time of testing our faith, we will look at the whole picture from a more positive point of view. Let's look at some of God's advice in this. James 1:2 reads, *"...Count it all joy when you fall into divers temptations."* Let's stop right here and analyze what is being said. To be tempted is *not* a sin. Only when we succumb to a temptation does it become a sin. So, when the enemy comes with his hidden schemes and temptations (and we have grown

92

spiritually enough to see what is happening), we are to count it a great challenge to go through the time of tempting. We are to see it as a chance to stand the test of our faith in the One True God who loves us, is always there for us, and will see us through it all, so that we can come out victorious on the other side.

Now let's look at James 1:3-4, which reads, *"Knowing this, that the trying* (testing) *of your faith works patience* (a virtue of God the Father, Son, and Holy Spirit)*, but let* (remember, it is your choice) *patience have her perfect work, that you may be perfect and entire* (complete)*, wanting nothing* (meaning lacking nothing)*."* If you ever had doubts about God's protection or love for you, going through a test like this will chase doubts away.

Let us also look at I Peter 1:5-7, which states: *"Who are kept* (guarded) *by the power of God through faith unto salvation ready to be revealed in the last time. Where in ye greatly rejoice, though now for a season, if need be, ye are in heaviness through manifold temptations: That the trial of your faith, being much more precious than of gold that perishes, though it be tried with fire, might be found unto the praise and honor and glory at the appearing of Jesus Christ:"*

Here it is very obvious that temptations are opportunities for our faith to be tried, or, in other words, tested. Our faith is as precious as gold, and just as gold is tried by fire, so too is our faith tried by the fires of temptation. When gold is refined, it is put into the hot furnace, the dross comes to the top, and it is taken out of the furnace and scraped off. Then the refiner would look into the gold, and if he could not see his image in the gold, as in a mirror, it had to go back into the furnace to go through the process again. This would continue until the refiner could no longer see his image in the gold, (the gold was pure when his image was reflected back to him like a mirror) then it was pure gold, without any sign of dross.

It is that way with us, as well. We go into the fires of temptation, and when we go through it, God will look to see if we reflect His character. Each time, we should be able to reflect His character more and more. If we do, we are using temptations to strengthen our faith and trust in the God, who loved us enough to send His Son to die for us and pay the price and penalty of sin for us.

So, "count it all joy when you fall into divers temptations" as you journey through this life. It is your opportunity to reflect God's character and to win the victory over the devil who wanted to use that very temptation to put you over the edge. This is God's three-fold plan for you: 1) to be saved from the penalty of sin, 2) spend eternity with Him, and 3) conquer the sin in your life as you live the journey, so that you can reflect the character of God and strengthen your faith. In that way, you have the abundant life Jesus wants you to have as you journey through this life to heaven.

PRAYER: Heavenly Father, I begin to see some sense in this maze of life one lives down here on this earth. Nothing happens without a reason. You are in the midst of each thing that comes into my life. Now, it is up to me to turn every trial into an opportunity for growth and victory. Help me to choose victory and claim victory each day. In Jesus' name, Amen.

MARCH 23rd

Now, we will turn our attention to God's national plan. God wants to be the ruler of the nations, especially the nation of Israel. The first mention of a specific nation in the Bible is found in Genesis 12:1:3, which reads: *"Now the Lord had said unto Abram, 'Get thee out of thy country, and from thy kindred, and from thy father's house, unto a land that I will show thee: And I will make of thee a great nation, and I will bless thee, and make thy name great; and thou shall be a blessing: And I will bless them that bless thee, and curse him that curses thee and in thee shall all the families of the earth be blessed.' "*

This was the call God gave to Abraham (his name was Abram at first, but God changed it later to Abraham). There are three points to this call: God would 1) give him land, 2) make of him a great nation (that means there had to be a vast number of descendants, because a nation is made up of people), and 3) bless him and make him a blessing to the whole world. (That blessing was Jesus the Messiah.) But here we see God's first move to bring about a special nation upon this earth.

It is not hard at all to figure out what God was up to. The sin nature was prevalent in the earth and God wanted someone to represent Him, His love, mercy, and grace to the world. He not only needed individuals to do that, but He also needed a nation. Israel was to be that nation, but they failed because they were a stubborn and stiff-necked people, even rejecting their blessing (Jesus Himself was God's blessing to Israel, Gen 12:1-3) when they rejected Jesus as their Messiah. All other blessings (plural) come out of Jesus, God's Blessing (singular) to Israel.

God's plan was to display His character to the world through that nation. I believe that, before all is said and done, Israel will yet finish the job God had laid out for them. I also believe that God helped America to become the nation it is today, so we can reflect God's character to the world. But we, too, are miserably failing in that work. God will bring nations to their knees, if they do not allow Him to use them to His glory and honor. Israel is an example of that, and I am afraid that America will also be an example of God's wrath if we do not go to Him on behalf of our country and pray for the forgiveness of our sins, which are many.

PRAYER: Lord God, I do pray for our country, that you would raise up men and women that will speak out about the loose morals of our country. Forgive the sins of our country, Lord. We name them in our hearts before you. Help each one of us to make a difference right where we are, in our part of this world. We want our nation to be a reflection of your love, mercy, and grace, that the world, (the other nations), would begin to see you as the God of all gods, Lord of lords, and sovereign God that you are. In Jesus' name, Amen.

MARCH 24th

Today, we will look at Psalm 2:1-5, which reads: *"Why do the nations rage, and the people imagine a vain thing? The kings of the earth set themselves, and the rulers take counsel together, against the Lord, and against His anointed, saying, 'Let us break their bands asunder, and cast away their cords from us.' He who sits in the heavens shall laugh: the Lord shall have them in derision. Then shall He speak unto them in His wrath, and vex them in His sore displeasure.' "*

Nations scheme and plan without any thought of what God wants, and God just laughs at them. One day, God's nation of Israel will be the notable nation God intended it to be. Also, Jerusalem, the city where God chose to put His name, will be Israel's capitol city. II Chronicles 6:5-6 reads: *"Since the day that I brought forth my people out of the land of Egypt, I chose no city among all the tribes of Israel to build a house in, that my name might be there; neither chose I any man to be a ruler over my people Israel: But I have chosen Jerusalem, that my name might be there; and have chosen David to be over my people Israel."*

Just because we do not see Jerusalem as the city where God's name is right now does not mean that God has forgotten what He said in those verses. How do you think God feels when He looks down upon this earth and His name is not residing in His city of Jerusalem, in His land called the Holy Land? It will all be put right one day, simply because it is God's national plan, and nothing will be able to stop it from happening.

Deuteronomy 14:2 states, *"For thou* (Israel) *art a holy people unto the Lord thy God, and the Lord has chosen thee to be a peculiar people unto Himself, above __all the nations__ that are upon the earth."* Do you think this is just some idle talk? God means what He says. Not only does He mean it, but He will carry it all out as well. Israel will be that nation through whom God will reveal Himself to the whole world. When that happens, every devil in earth and under the earth will shudder and be filled with fear. We will also look at God's justice in regard to the nations of the earth. We are not done yet.

96

PRAYER: Heavenly Father, I am beginning to see that God is at work on many fronts at the same time. Not only in us as individuals, but also in families, communities, villages, towns, cities, and nations. It presents to me a God so huge it causes me to marvel that I am so important to Him. It also shows me that my witness, small as it may seem, is of great importance to you, simply because nations are made up of people like me, and we can make a major difference right where we are. Help me to make a difference right where I am, Lord. In Jesus' name, Amen.

MARCH 25th

Jeremiah 25:31-32 states: *"A noise shall come even to the ends of the earth; for the Lord has a controversy with the nations* (plural), *He will plead with all flesh; He will give them that are wicked to the sword, saith the Lord. Thus saith the Lord of hosts, Behold evil shall go forth from nation to nation, and a great whirlwind shall be raised up from the coasts of the earth."* We see here that God has a controversy with the nations. God is not just interested in individuals, families, and so on, but also in nations on this earth. It has been said that every nation that has come against Israel eventually ceases to be a powerful nation. With that thought in mind, let us look at Joel 3:1-2, which reads; *"For, behold, in those days, and in that time, when I shall bring again the captivity of Judah and Jerusalem* (I believe this refers to what we see today, Israel, a nation among nations for the first time for at least 2,000 years or more), *I will also gather all nations, and will bring them down into the valley of Jehoshaphat, and will plead with them there for my people and for my heritage, Israel, whom they have scattered among the nations, and parted my land."*

When God says, "I will plead with them there," He means He will examine and judge them there. Some translations call the place "Judgment Valley." Part of the problem is that the nations have been instrumental in scattering the Jews all over the world. They are God's inheritance, even

97

though they have been stubborn and rebellious. They are still God's people, chosen for a purpose in God's scheme of things.

The other reason God will plead with them there is that the nations have parted God's land. So you see, it is not Israel's land, and it is not any other nation's land either. It is God's land for God's people and for God's purpose. God's *will* will be done, no matter how Satan tries to usurp it or use kings and nations to interfere with His plan. His *will* will be done. No one can stop it. It is a national plan.

PRAYER: Lord God, I believe my understanding of the scope of what you are doing in the world is beginning to get bigger and bigger. World affairs take on a whole new dimension, now that I see your national plan. I do pray for our nation that we will never make the mistake to come against Israel, but that we will pray for the peace of Jerusalem as your Word tells us to do. And I also pray that the people of Israel will have the blinders taken off their eyes so that they can know and understand that Jesus, the Christ, is their long looked for Messiah. In Jesus' name, Amen.

MARCH 26th

We have one more scripture that we need to look at before we move on to the global plan. We are not done with the plan for the nations yet. Matthew 25:31-33 reads; *"When the Son of man shall come in His glory, and all the holy angels with Him, then shall He sit upon the throne of His glory; And before Him shall be gathered all nations: and He shall separate them one from another, as a shepherd divides His sheep from the goats: And He shall set the sheep on His right hand, but the goats on the left."*

Here we see that there will be a judgment day for the nations of the world. Not one thing, be it good or evil, will be overlooked, but rather will either be rewarded or judged for punishment. I often think of a county fair when various entries are judged and ribbons are distributed to those who entered flowers, sewing items, vegetables, cattle, poultry, rabbits, and so on.

Some get a prize, but some receive no ribbon at all. However, each article or animal has been put through the test of judgment, and so will the nations of the earth be examined before Jesus.

In Matthew 25:34 and 41, we learn what happens to the sheep and goats. Verse 34 explains, *"Then shall the King say unto them on His right hand, 'Come, ye blessed of my Father, inherit the kingdom prepared for you from the foundation of the world.' "* And verse 41 continues, *"Then shall He say also unto them on the left hand, 'Depart from me, you cursed, into everlasting fire, prepared for the devil and his angels.' "* That is the outcome of the judgment. And what was the standard put forth for such a judgment?

We see the standard in verses 35-36, which read, *"For I was hungry, and ye gave me meat: I was thirsty, and ye gave me drink: I was a stranger, and ye took me in: Naked, and ye clothed me: I was sick and ye visited me: I was in prison, and ye came unto me."* Both groups are judged by the same standard. However, the rebuked group did *not* tend to those in need. The groups reacted to the final sentence in a very different way, which I believe tells us a lot about the character of each. But let's leave that for tomorrow.

PRAYER: Dear Lord, since you are a righteous and just God, I feel that I can trust you completely. I know that your judgments are pure, without any partiality. Open the eyes of the rulers of the nations that they may understand that their behavior will influence their nation, either for or against your over all plan for the nations of the world. I also pray for those nations who have evil rulers over them, that they could be set free from that kind of bondage and live peaceable lives. In Jesus' name, Amen.

MARCH 27th

Today, we will continue with Matthew 25:37-40, which reads: *"Then shall the righteous answer Him, saying, 'Lord, <u>when</u> saw we thee an hungered and fed the?, or thirsty, and gave thee drink? <u>When</u> saw we* *thee a stranger, and took thee in? or naked, and clothed thee? Or when saw we thee sick, or in prison, and cam unto thee, And the King* (Jesus is the King of kings at this point in time) *shall answer and say unto them, 'Verily I say unto you, inasmuch as ye have done it unto one of the least of these my brethren, ye have done it unto me.' "*

What I want you to see here is that the righteous had been doing the right thing all along, and were not even aware of it. They actually had to ask Jesus *when* they had done such good deeds. It had just been a natural thing to them.

Now, look at the question the wicked asked Jesus in verses 44-45, *"Then shall they also answer Him, saying, 'Lord, <u>when</u> saw we thee hungred, or athirst, or a stranger, or naked, or sick, or in prison, and <u>did not</u> minister unto thee?' "* They thought they had done it the right thing all the time. They no doubt had gone about doing their own things in their own time and in their own way, and did not follow the Holy Spirit. They were so sure of themselves that they were shocked not to be among the blessed or righteous.

Then, in verse 46, we see in that wicked *"...shall go away into everlasting punishment: but the righteous into life eternal."* Only nations who follow the Spirit of God will survive that judgment. And at that time, Israel will have seen the truth about who Jesus is, and will accept Him as their Messiah and be the nation God had planned for them to be all the time. Those nations who survive the judgment will not have a problem treating the nation of Israel with the kindness and respect God wants Israel to receive.

Deuteronomy 32:9-10 states, *"For the Lord's portion is His people; Jacob* (God later changed Jacob's name to Israel), *is the lot of His inheritance. He found him in a desert land, and in the waste howling wilderness; He led him about, He instructed him, He kept him as the <u>apple of His eye</u>."* Lamentations 2:18, also reads, *"Their heart cried unto the Lord, O wall of the daughter of Zion, let tears run down like a river day and night: give thyself no rest; let not the <u>apple of thine eye</u> cease."* Israel is the apple of God's eye, and we must be careful that we do not mistreat them.

God is not done with Israel yet, and all that God had planned for her will be realized, either with her cooperation or without it. The same is true in our lives as well. God is sovereign. No one tells God what to do or how to do it. His *will* will prevail. We need to realize that the sooner we get in step with His will for our lives, the sooner He can pour out His blessing upon us.

PRAYER: Jesus, I am so thankful for all you have done for me so that I can get in step with God the Father and walk in His ways. I ask you for the Holy Spirit to prompt me whenever it is needful for me to get back in step with you and keep walking according to your will. I yearn for your blessings to pour down upon me like you blessed the righteous nations who ministered to your people on your behalf. In Jesus' precious name, Amen.

MARCH 28th

Now, we will talk about God's global plan. God does not like the fact that there is evil in His world. God wants all evil done away with, and behind all the evil is Satan and all his henchmen. We see a list of them in Ephesians 6:12, which reads, *"For we wrestle not against flesh and blood, but against principalities, against powers, against the rulers of the darkness of this world, against the spiritual host* (angels) *of wickedness in high (heavenly) places."* There are also the demons, which are Satan's henchmen. All of that evil will need to be taken out of the way, once and for all.

How is that all going to be done? It began when Jesus, whose blood was holy blood from God the Holy Spirit, not human blood that carried the sin-factor, was willing to shed His blood and give up His life to begin that process of destroying the evil in this world. When Jesus descended into hell, He took the next step to defeat all evil.

I Peter 3:18-20 explains: *"For Christ also hath once suffered for sins, the just for the unjust, that He might bring us to God, being put to death in the flesh, but quickened by the Spirit: By which also He went and preached unto the spirits in prison; Which sometimes* (before) *were disobedient, when once the long suffering of God waited in the days of Noah, while the ark was a preparing, where in few, that is, eight souls were saved by water."*

Hell is also called Sheol (Hebrew), Hades (Greek), and Gehenna (Greek). It was the "place of the dead." This place had a division, or gulf, through it, and no one could pass from one side to the other. Jesus explains this in Luke 16:19-26, which states: *"There was a certain rich man, who was clothed in purple and fine linen, and fared sumptuously every day: And there was a certain beggar named Lazarus, which was laid at his gate full of sores, and desiring to be fed with the crumbs which fell from the rich man's table: moreover the dogs came and licked his sores. And it came to pass that the beggar died, and was carried by the angels into Abraham's bosom'. The rich man also died and was buried; And in hell* (Hades) *he lift up his eyes, being in torments, and seeth Abraham afar off and Lazarus in his bosom. And he cried and said, 'Father Abraham, have mercy on me and send Lazarus, that he may dip the tip of his finger in water, and cool my tongue; for I am tormented in this flame.' But Abraham said, 'Son, remember that thou in thy lifetime receivedst thy good things, and likewise Lazarus evil things: but now he is comforted, and thou art tormented. And beside all this, between us and you there is a great gulf fixed: so that they which would pass from hence to you cannot; neither can they pass to us, that would come from thence.' "*

One side was a comfort side, but the other was a torment side. This place was *not* the paradise that Jesus talked about as He hung on the cross and said to thief on the cross beside him, *"Today you will be with me in paradise."* So, when Jesus descended into hell, it was to this place that he went. He preached to those disobedient spirits in torment, showing them that He, Jesus, had conquered sin and death, and that the whole Bible was true. They could have heard the message Noah was preaching and been saved through the water trial, but they had no doubt laughed at Noah instead. But in Hades, they were not laughing. They were in torment.

In Ephesians 4:8 we read, *"Wherefore he saith, 'When He ascended up on high, he led captivity captive, and gave gifts unto men.' "*

102

We have already talked about the gifts given to men. This time around, we want to talk about the captives that were led out of captivity.

Another verse I want to quote before we go on is found in Psalms 49:15, which reads, *"But God will redeem* (buy back) *my soul from the power of the grave* (Shoel), *for He shall receive me..."* Please notice that it was not from the grave that he would be redeemed, but from the *power* of the grave. This is an Old Testament promise to the Psalmist, which was to take place many years in the future. In fact, it took place when Jesus went down there and led captivity (those under the power of the grave) captive. Jesus was their captor and He led them to paradise, the place He had prepared, as He told His disciples in John 14:2-3, saying, *"In my Father's house are many mansions: if it were not so, I would have told you. I go to prepare a place for you. And if I go and prepare a place for you, I will come again, and receive you unto myself; that where I am, there ye might be also."*

When Jesus led captivity captive, this verse was fulfilled, and also the one in Psalms 49:15. We see, step by step and little by little, Jesus is destroying the power of the enemy in the world. You might not think so as you look at our world today, but trust the Word of God, it is being done. Also, remember that God cannot justly judge the enemy until all the evidence is in. Therefore, God will have to let him do his dirty work in order to pile up the evidence needed to convict him and destroy him. We will continue on this theme for a day or two.

PRAYER: Heavenly Father, it is a pleasant thought to think of a time when we no longer have an enemy biting at our heels all the time. But, in the meantime, give me the discernment and insight so I may be able to withstand the evil the enemy hurls in my direction so that I can walk in that victory that Jesus died to purchase for me. In Jesus' name, Amen.

MARCH 29th

In I Corinthians 15, we see the whole picture of God's global plan. I Corinthians 15:20-28 reads; *"But now is Christ risen from the dead, and become the first fruits of them that slept* (were dead)*. For since by man* (Adam) *came death, by man* (Jesus) *came also the resurrection of the dead. For as in Adam all die, even so in Christ shall all be made alive. But every man in his own order: Christ the first fruits; afterward they that are Christ's at His coming."*

If the enemy had the right and power to bring sin and death into the world by one man, could not God also do the same thing and remain just by bringing *life* and *resurrection* into the world by one man, Jesus? Another interesting point is that death came into the world through a tree (the fruit of a tree), and life came by a tree (the cross) and the fruit of the tree (Jesus).

We also see in verse 23 that there is an order to all of this. Christ was the first fruit of the resurrection. He rose first, and we will follow in a resurrection like His when He comes back for us at "His coming." Let's continue with verses 24-26, which read; *"Then cometh the end, when He shall have delivered up the kingdom to God, even the Father; when He shall have put down __all__ rule and __all__ authority and power. For __He must__ __reign till__* (that period of time has a time limit, until) *He has put __all__ enemies under His feet* (global plan)*. The last enemy that shall be destroyed is death."*

Imagine this world without death. God calls death an enemy right here. Death was never God's plan for us, and God wants it completely destroyed. Not only do humans die, but all vegetation and animals dies as well. Our planet is a planet of death. God wants it to be a planet of life, like He had intended it to be all the time. Therefore, little by little, He is moving in that direction. We will look at a few more verses on this topic tomorrow.

PRAYER: Thank you, Father, for giving me a glimpse into the future you have planned for this earth. Thank you, too, for giving me the right to choose eternal life and resurrection, and the promise that I will spend eternity with you. I tell my soul to bless you for your great love, mercy, and grace towards me. In Jesus' name, Amen.

MARCH 30th

Addressing again God's global plan, let's look at I Corinthians 15:27-28, which states; *"For He* (God) *has put all things under His* (Jesus') *feet. But when He* (God) *saith, all things are put under Him* (put under Jesus in subjection)*, it is manifest that He* (God) *is expected, which did put all things under Him. And when all things shall be subdued unto Him, then shall the Son also Himself be subject unto Him* (God the Father) *that put all things under Him, that God may be all in all."*

Let me explain what I believe is being said here. Jesus will reign on this earth for a time, and during that time, He will overrule all evil powers. When everything evil has been destroyed, Jesus will hand the reigns back to God, and God will be "all in all." I believe this is the overall plan of the Trinity, God the Father, God the Son, and God the Holy Spirit.

God is not a God of confusion, but a God of order. This planet is out of order, and God wants it back in order as He had intended it to be. Jesus is working to bring back that order, and once that has been accomplished, then God can be all in all once again.

Let's turn to Revelation for a few verses. Revelation 19:20 reads, *"And the beast was taken, and with him, the false prophet that wrought miracles before him, with which he deceived them that had received the mark of the beast, and them that worshipped his image, these both were cast alive into the lake of fire burning with brimstone."* We see that the beast (who is the anti-Christ) and the false prophet (who is the counterfeit of the Holy Spirit) will be thrown alive into the lake of fire burning with brimstone.

Revelation 20:2-3 also states, *"And he laid hold on the dragon, that old serpent, which is the Devil, and Satan, and bound him a thousand year, And cast him into the bottomless pit* (abyss), *and shut him up, and set a seal upon him, that he should deceive the nations no more, till the thousand years should be fulfilled: and after that he must be loosed a little season."*

PRAYER: Lord God, as I see your plan unfold, I am amazed that you can bring any order out of the chaos of this world. I also am getting a glimpse of your tremendous patience. Help me to exercise more and more of that kind of long suffering patience. If you can wait for the right timing, then so should I? In Jesus' name, Amen.

MARCH 31st

Today, we will look more at Revelation 20:7-10, which reads: *"And when the thousand years are expired, Satan shall be loosed out of his prison, and shall go out to deceive the nations which are in the four quarters of the earth, Gog and Magog, to gather them together to battle: the number of whom is as the sand of the sea. And they went up on the breadth of the earth, and compassed the camp of the saints about, and the beloved city* (Jerusalem)*: and fire came down from God out of heaven, and devoured them. And the devil that deceived them was cast into the lake of fire and brimstone, where the beast and the false prophet are, and shall be tormented day and night for ever and ever."*

This then is the end of Satan and his two main henchmen. But what is Jesus doing during these thousand years? Revelation 20:4 explains: *"And I saw thrones, and they sat upon them, and judgment was given unto them: and I saw the souls of them that were beheaded for the witness of Jesus, and for the word of God, and which had not worshipped the beast, neither his image, neither had received his mark upon their foreheads, or in their hands: and they lived and reigned with Christ a thousand years."* Jesus and those who had lived a life pleasing unto God will reign with Jesus on this earth for a thousand years, during which time all evil will have been put down, so love, mercy, and grace will prevail during that rule.

But the world itself will not have changed, and people will want all the evil, rather than the good, and will follow Satan once again. God will reign down fire to destroy the evil, but the evidence for judgment will have been gathered. There will be a judgment of the wicked dead.

Revelation 20:12-14 reads; *"And I saw the dead, small and great, stand before God; And the books were opened: and another book was opened, which is the book of life: and the dead were judged out of those things which were written in the books, according to their works. And the sea gave up the dead which were in it', and death and hell* (Hades) *delivered up the dead which were in them: and they were judged every man according to their works. And death and hell* (Hades) *were cast into the lake of fire. This is the second death. And whosoever was not found written in the book of life was cast into the lake of fire."*

Let me explain something here: Christians will not stand before God to be judged. Jesus will judge us, and those who stand before God will not have anyone to plead for them, like Jesus. All those who were in Hades, after Jesus took the captivity out, will stand before God and be judged. This resurrection will be after Jesus has ruled the earth for a thousand years. Their works will be examined, and I believe that will determine their punishment in hell. But never get your eyes off the fact that God is working to rid this world of all that is evil, so He can have this planet back the way He wanted it in the first place. Death and hell itself will all be put away.

Revelation ends with two chapters telling about the new heaven and earth. I will not comment on those chapters, but you can read that yourself and ask God to reveal His truth to you as you read about the new heaven and new earth God has planned for Himself and us.

PRAYER: Lord God, I look forward to that new heaven and new earth, a time when you are in full control. This world is so full of conflict and harm and pain. No family is immune to it. How pleasant to think that you have a plan to remove all that from the environment one day, and to restore your plan for this earth. In the meantime, Lord, help me to live this life to the fullest, with peace and joy in my heart, with contentment a rule in my life, rather than a chance in passing. I determine to lay hold of your power to make the right choices that I may maintain a level of consistency from day to day. In Jesus' name, Amen.

APRIL 1st

I believe we have one loose end to address before we can move on to another topic. If the wicked dead are going to be judge by God, what about the believing dead when they are raised? Will they be judged? If so, by whom? And why will they be judged, since all our sins have been paid for and we have been given victory over all that is evil and sinful, even victory over death itself? We will address those issues today.

Yes, our sins are paid for, and that is not a penalty we have to face, nor is death. Turn to II Corinthians 5:10, which will set the stage for the next one we will look at. Here we read, "*For we* (we believers, *we* are the ones reading and believing the Word of God, so *we* are the ones saved by the blood of the Lamb) *must all appear before the judgment seat of Christ* (Can it be more clear who you will stand before, to be judged and examined?) *That every one may <u>receive</u> the things done in his body, according to that he has done, whether it be good or bad*" Yes indeed, a day is coming when we will have our lives examined by Jesus, and our motives for the choices we made will also be revealed to us. Hebrews 4:12 states, *"For the word of God is quick, and powerful* (living and active), *and sharper than any two edged sword, piercing even to the dividing asunder of soul and spirit, and of the joints and marrow, and is a discerner of the thoughts and intents of the heart."* In I Corinthians 4:5, we also read, *"<u>Therefore, judge nothing before the time, until the Lord come</u>, who both will bring to light the hidden things of darkness, and will make manifest the counsels of the hearts: and then shall every man have praise of God."*

Jesus lived on this earth and knows what it is to be tempted, to be cold and hot, hungry and tired, pushed around and attacked, rejected and wounded, tortured and killed. He will be able to understand our trials and tribulations better than anyone. Not only that, but He also will have a heart of compassion toward us. He knows that He has paid the price for our sins.

So, what is this judgment all about? Did you notice the word "receive" in that verse? This is "awards day," and we will receive recompense (another word for payment) for the good things we did. Remember the hungry, naked, thirsty, imprisoned, etc.? Even a cup of cold water, the Bible says, will receive a reward or recompense. Luke 14:13-14 states, *"But when you makest a feast, call the poor, the maimed, the lame, the blind: And thou shalt be blessed: for they cannot recompense thee: for thou shalt be recompensed at the resurrection of the just."* Yes, indeed, you will be recompensed for your good work. Tomorrow we will put the frosting on this cake.

PRAYER: This is better than I had ever thought. You mean there will be no punishment for me when I stand before Jesus to have my life examined? It is not at all like I thought it was going to be. It will take some time for me to really absorb all this. All I can say at this point is a great big THANK YOU FATHER, THANK YOU JESUS, for what you have done for me. I want more than ever to live a life pleasing unto you. Give me the inner strength to live up to my "want to" right now. You have done so much for me, all *I want to* do is live a life pleasing to you. *I want to* be that shining light you have said believers are. Help me make the right choices so that I do not fail you. In Jesus' name, Amen.

APRIL 2nd

I Corinthians 3:10-15 we read; *"According to the grace of God which is given unto me, as a wise masterbuilder, I have laid the foundation, and another builds thereon. But let every man take heed how he builds thereupon. For other foundation can no man lay than that is laid, which is Jesus Christ. Now, if any man build upon this foundation gold, silver, precious stones, wood, hay, stubble; every man's work shall be made manifest* (evident): *for the day shall declare it, because it shall be revealed by fire: and the fire shall try every man's work* (prove each work) *of what sort it is. If any man's work abide which he has built thereupon, he shall <u>receive a reward</u>. If any man's work shall be burned, he shall suffer loss: but he himself shall be saved; yet so as by fire."*

I shall try to explain this to you. Remember, I said that this judgment before Jesus will be one where you will receive a recompense. This scripture explains that process. Paul uses a building as a way to explain how it all works. There must be a good solid foundation to build a building, and the foundation is Jesus Christ. Then there are six kinds of material that can be used to build on this foundation. But keep in mind that those materials will be tried by fire.

So, it is not hard to figure out that you do not want to use wood, hay, or stubble. Wood would last longer than hay or stubble. Hay is inferior to wood, and stubble is even more inferior, but if you put a torch to them, they would all burn. What kinds of deeds would fall into these categories? Where would *busy work* fall, or *social events*? Consider a social event to raise money to pay for something that the tithe should have paid for. Why not put on a play that tells about God's mercy or great love, something from which people would gain something spiritually instead. Wood, hay and stubble do not last and have no eternal value.

What do gold, silver, and precious stones stand for? I believe gold stands for God the Father, silver stands for God the Son, and precious stones are the people in whom God the Holy Spirit dwells and whom we deal with in our every day lives all the time. What is your relationship to God the Father? To God the son? To God the Holy Spirit? Every time we have an opportunity, we need to reveal to God by our actions what our relationship is to the Trinity. Those kinds of things will have an eternal value and will not be burned by the fire of trial. But, if everything is burned up and there is nothing but ashes left, you will not lose your salvation. That is what is meant by, verse 15 *"If any man's work should be burned, he shall suffer loss* (loss of recompense), *but he himself shall be saved, yet so as by fire."* Our salvation is not dependent upon our works, but our recompense is.

110

PRAYER: Heavenly Father, thank you for making all this so clear to me. I have often had bad thoughts about judgment day. I can see now that I did not know the truth about it. You have given us so much leeway in which we can serve you that we should not have any trouble doing what is right and good and pure. You put opportunity before us again and again, to respond to your Spirit to do good unto our fellow man. Even to speak good of him or her instead of speaking negative or evil. Give me eyes to see and ears to hear what your Spirit is telling me to do at each opportunity you present me. In Jesus' name, Amen.

APRIL 3ʳᵈ

 I believe there is an object lesson in the Old Testament that would be a good thing to look at right about now. It is found in Exodus 20:25, which reads, *"And if thou wilt make me an altar of stone, thou shalt not build it of hewn stone: for if thou lift up thy tool upon it, thou hast polluted it."* The first time I read that, I thought, "What has that got to do with anything?" I always turn to God in prayer at a time like that, and ask God to give me the understanding of the verse.

As I pondered it, I began to realize believers, God's people, are often likened to stones. For instance, Aaron, the first High Priest chosen by God to fill that office, had on his dress a breast plate with twelve stones in it representing the twelve tribes of Israel. Exodus 28:17-21 explains: *"And thou shalt set in it settings of stones, even four rows of stones: the first row shall be a sardius, a topaz, and a carbuncle: this shall be the first row. And the second row shall be an emerald, a sapphire, and a diamond. And the third row a ligure [jacinth], an agate, and an amethyst. And the fourth row a beryl, and an onyx, and a jasper: they shall be set in gold in their inclosings. And the stones shall be with the names of the children of Israel, twelve, according to their names like the engravings of a signet; every one with his name shall they be according to the twelve tribes."*

111

And when you look at the New Jerusalem, the foundations are also of precious stones and represent the twelve apostles of the Lamb. Revelation 21:14,19-20 states: *"And the wall of the city had twelve foundations, and in them the names of the twelve apostles of the Lamb. And the foundations of the wall of the city were garnished with all manner of precious stones. The first foundation was of jasper; the second, sapphire; the third, a chalcedony; the fourth, an emerald. The fifth, sardonyz; the sixth, sardius; seventh, chrysolite; the eighth, beryl; the ninth, a topaz; the tenth, a chrysoprasus; the eleventh, a jacinth; the twelfth, an amethyst."*

In the New Testament, we are also called "living stones," as in I Peter 2:5, which reads, *"Ye also, as living stones, are built up a spiritual house, an holy priesthood, to offer up spiritual sacrifices, acceptable to God by Jesus Christ."* Jesus Himself is called a "chief corner stone." So, we can conclude that the stones that are built up into that altar are a picture of people just like you and me. It is so much easier to make a nice square altar if the stones are nice and rectangular themselves, but we are not to treat one another that way. We are to be able to take each other just the way we are and work side by side together without any difficulty. Therefore, they were told not to lift up a tool against the stone. In other words, do not shave off that lump over here on this stone and that lump over there on that stone so that they will fit together in that altar.

Then I had to figure out what tool was used to hew the stones. It says, *"...if thou lift up thy tool upon it, thou hast polluted it."* No doubt each individual has a special tool for hewing. And then it hit me, we use our tongues to cut people up, reshape them, and tell them how they need to change. It is the tongue that pollutes the stone, which in turn pollutes the altar at which we worship God.

So, I believe the lesson here is to be very careful what we say about other people. God is in charge of their lives, not you or me. Only God can change people, and that includes each of us. Kids want to change their parents, parents want to change their kids, spouses want to change each other, employers change employees, and on and on. Stop it! You are polluting those around you, and I am sure that you pollute yourself in the

112

meantime. Make sure that you hear what God wants you to change about *yourself*. Who knows … maybe when you change yourself, things around you will change as well.

PRAYER: Lord Jesus, I had no idea my words can do so much damage in the eyes of God. Forgive me, Lord, for not paying attention to what I say about others. Open my eyes to this sinful action in my life and prompt me to stop it. I can remember being told as a child, "If you can't say something nice about someone, don't say anything at all." Help me practice that. In Jesus' name, Amen.

APRIL 4th

 As we are approaching Easter, I believe this is a good time to talk about what Jesus' life and death have to do with our own death. The Bible says that *"…old things have passed away and all things have become new"* (II Corinthians 5:17). Does that mean death has become new as well?

I can recall a clergyman saying that to sit at the bedside of a dying person who is a Christian is completely different than attending the death of an unbeliever. I often wondered what he meant by that. I later found out that there is no fear for the one who is a Christian, and again I wondered what Jesus would do to bring peace in the face of death. I hounded my pastor about it, asking him if he knew anything about it, whether he had been taught anything in seminary concerning it. He suggested that, since I had all the questions, maybe God was telling me to search the Bible and find it out. That sent me on a three-year journey in the Word.

I first had to be assured that it was all right for someone like me, who did not have a college education, to even think I could have the right to do that. God led me to Isaiah 1:18, which states, *" 'Come now, and let us reason together,' saith the Lord: 'Though your sins be as scarlet, they shall be as white as snow; though they be red like crimson, they shall be as wool.' "* As I pondered that verse, I took special notice of the words

113

"now" and "reason together." I could see that God was giving the invitation to debate, reason, and discuss the issue of our sins and how they look to Him and how He wants them to look. He sees them as red, scarlet, crimson (very, very red in fact), and He wants them to look white to Him.

So, if I could reason about such an issue, then there is nothing that would be off limits to reason with Him about, as long as I stuck to the Bible. I had a green light, a go ahead to research my questions. Before I go on, though, let me also explain the red sins and how they are to become white. If you have red cellophane (pure red, not orange red) and hold it up to your eyes and look at something red, such as the chicken on the Corn Flakes box, you will see that the red on the chicken turns pure white. Red cancels out red. It is the only color that does that. You see, the red blood of Jesus that covers your sins makes them *turn white* in the eyes of God! That ought to make you stand up and shout "Alleluia."!

Once I had my go ahead, I began to write down every reference I came across that pertained to death, burial, the grave, heaven, etc., as I read the Bible through. Certain truths began to emerge, for example, those who died in the Old Testament went *down* at death, and those who believed in Jesus went *up* at death. That in itself told me that *something changed* when Jesus died. This is enough for today. We will continue on this topic tomorrow.

PRAYER: Dear Lord, since I am in you and you are in me, I believe this is going to be good news for me. Thank you for making me white as snow, covering my red sins from your eyes and making me whiter than the snow. It is hard to comprehend that such a transformation could take place in the life of a sinner, but your Word cannot lie either, so it is up to me to believe it. I choose to believe it. In Jesus' name, Amen.

APRIL 5th

Today, let's look at Psalm 16:10, which reads, *"For thou wilt not leave my soul in hell* (Sheol)*; neither wilt thou suffer thine*

Holy One to see corruption." This is one of David's psalms. He knew his soul would go to that place we talked about earlier, called hell, Shoel, or Hades. That is down, so the souls of mankind went down at death in the Old Testament.

In John 14:2-3, Jesus says: *"In my Father's house are many mansions* (some translations say rooms)*; if it were not so, I would have told you. I go to prepare a place for you, and since* (if) *I go to prepare a place for you, I will come again, and receive you unto myself; that where I am, there ye may be also."* Right here we have a promise of a change in direction. Jesus ascended into heaven, so it must follow that the place He went to prepare had to be in heaven. But did you ever wonder why it was not prepared from the beginning of time? Apparently those who died under the Old Testament covenant did not have that place to go to. Something had to happen so that a new and better place could be made available for those who believed in Jesus, God's only Son, who came and paid the price and penalty of sin for us. Are you beginning to get the picture?

There was a war that had to be won before that place could be prepared. Jesus won that war over sin, death, and the power of the devil. I believe Jesus had to go to the third Heaven, which is also called Paradise, and sweep it clean of anything satanic, so that Jesus could bring the captives He led from the comfort side of Sheol to that place He had prepared for the New Testament believers. He said that He would receive us unto Himself, so we could be with Him where He was.

Remember what He said to the thief on the cross in Luke 23:43, *"...verily I say unto thee, 'To day shalt thou be with me in paradise.' "* So that is where the New Testament believers, who are called "saints," go when they die. That is not down, but up. And Jesus Himself will receive you, the Bible says.

To finish the thought for today, turn to II Corinthians 12:2-4. Here, Paul is retelling an experience he had, an out of body experience: *"I knew a man in Christ above 14 years ago,* (he is speaking of himself here), *(whether in the body, I cannot tell; or whether out of the body, I cannot tell: God knoweth;) such an one caught up to the third heaven. And I knew such a man, (whether in the body, or out of the body, I cannot tell:*

God knoweth;) How that he was caught up into paradise, and heard unspeakable words, which it is not lawful for a man to utter. "

Paul calls that place by two names: the third heaven and paradise. That was the same place that Jesus referred to when He told the thief on the cross, "Today you shall be with me in paradise." It is a *real* place, it is where those who believe in Jesus go when they die, not down to Sheol. So, we see some of what changed in regard to death when Jesus finished His work here on earth. But there is more, much more.

PRAYER: Dear Lord, it is so comforting to know that you have interrupted and changed the direction we take at death. The more I learn about you, Lord Jesus, and your work on my behalf, the more grateful I become, and the more humbled I am to think you did it all just for me, as I am included in the "whosoever wills." Yes, Lord, I *will* believe in you. I *will* trust you. I *will* try to walk a life that reflects your love, mercy, grace, peace, and patience. Fill me with your Holy Spirit so that I may be empowered to live a life that is pleasing to you. In Jesus' precious name, Amen.

APRIL 6th

Today, we will start with Hebrews 2:6-9, which reads; *"But one in a certain place testified, saying, 'What is man, that thou art mindful of him? or the son of man, that thou visitest him? Thou madest <u>him a little</u> lower than the angels; thou crownedst him with glory and honor, and didst set him over the works of thy hands: Thou has put all things in subjection under his feet.' For in that he put all in subjection under him, he left nothing that is not put under him. But now we see not yet all things put under him. But we see Jesus, who was made a little lower than the angels for the suffering of death, crowned with glory and honor; that He, by the grace of God, should taste death for every man."*

116

We need to pick this all apart to understand what is being said. When God created man in God's image, God also made him of flesh and blood. Angels were not born, but were created, and they do not procreate like mankind does. So, we are a lower creation than the angels, yet God chose to put mankind in authority over the creation of earth. Jesus is also included in this because He was made man with flesh and blood.

We also see that not everything is in subjection to mankind, and I believe that is referring to the fact that Satan is still roaming around and stands before God to accuse us for all our shortcomings and sinful ways. One day, that will all be taken care of as part of God's global plan. So, what I want you to see here is that Jesus died our death already.

It plainly says in Hebrews 2:9 *"...that he by the grace of God, should taste death for every man."* Now, you can chose to believe that He tasted death for you, or you can chose not to believe it. I believe what the Bible says, that when Jesus died on the cross, He actually died my death and the death of every man, woman, and child on the face of the earth ever since. I believe Jesus died even for those who do not believe in Him. How sad that they would chose not to believe and be set free from the fear of death.

I also want you to notice that Jesus was made lower than the angels so He could suffer death. You see, angels do not die, but mankind dies. Jesus could not pay the penalty for our sin by dying if He were an angel, since angels do not die. Therefore, He had to take upon Himself the form of a man. Jesus chose to come as a man, to suffer and die *in order* to satisfy the Father's requirement of payment for sin.

PRAYER: Thank you, Lord Jesus, for all you did for me, and for showing me the truth of your Word concerning death. You thought of everything when it came to saving me from sin, death, and the power of the devil. You did it all. My problem is making the right choices in this sinful world. Help me to believe your Word of encouragement, comfort, and truth, and to believe that it is for even me. In Jesus' name, Amen.

APRIL 7th

Today, we will look at Hebrew 2:14-15, which states, *"Forasmuch then as the children are partakers of flesh and blood, He also Himself likewise took part of the same; that through death He might destroy him that had the power of death, that is the devil; And deliver them who through fear of death were all their lifetime subject to bondage."*

Jesus was flesh and blood, like all the rest of us. He came to save, so that *through* death He could do what? He came to *destroy* the one who had (past tense) the power of death, and that one was even named. It is none other than the devil. God never intended death for His children, but the devil wants us all dead. But the devil's power over death has been broken, destroyed, so that we can be delivered from the fear of death.

Can you allow yourself to believe all this? It is God's Word, which cannot lie. It is God's truth to us. Another verse we need to look at, Revelation 2:10, which reads, *"...Be thou faithful <u>unto</u> death and I will give thee the crown of life."* We are not asked to be faithful *through* death. And why not? Because we are only asked to be faithful *unto* death. If Jesus tasted our death, then surely we will not taste it, or else Jesus did not taste it good enough for us, did He? While we are looking at Revelation, we see there will be a reward for being faithful unto death. We will receive a crown named "life." There are five crowns to be given to the faithful believers, but we will address that much later. Right now, we are talking about what Jesus did in regard to death and dying. Allow yourself to believe God's Word, and to believe that it includes even you.

PRAYER: I feel like I am being drawn into a deeper and deeper relationship with God the Father, Son, and Holy Spirit, and I wonder how much deeper I can go. I ask you, Father, to increase my ability to exercise the faith you have given me to grasp all of this that has been done for me. I do not want to miss a point, not even a small segment of all the truth that you are able to give to me though your Word. In Jesus' name, Amen.

APRIL 8th

The first scripture I want to take you to today is found in John 8:51-52, which reads: *"Verily, verily, I say unto you, If a man keep my saying, he shall never see death. Then said the Jews unto Him, 'Now we know that thou hast a devil. Abraham is dead, and the prophets; and thou sayest, 'If a man keep my saying, he shall never taste of death.'"*

The Amplified Bible presents it this way; *"I assure you, most solemnly I tell you, if any one observes My teaching, lives in accordance with My message, keeps My word, he will by no means ever see or experience death. The Jews said to Him, 'Now we know that You are under the power of a demon* (insane). *Abraham died and also the prophets; yet You say, if a man keeps My word he will never taste of death to all eternity.'"*

And the New English Bible puts it this way; *"In very truth I tell you, if anyone obeys my teaching he shall never know what it is to die."* It is perfectly clear that when Jesus died on the cross, He not only paid the price and penalty for sin, but He completely destroyed Satan's power over death. The Word has tried to tell us as clearly as possible that we will not experience death, nor know what it is to die.

I want to give you two more verses to put an exclamation point to all this. John 5:24 reads, *"Verily, verily, I say unto you, He that heareth my word, and believeth on Him that sent me, hath everlasting life, and shall not come into condemnation* (judgment); *but is passed from death unto life."* Here, we see that it is a done deal. We have passed from death unto life, as far as God is concerned. God knows we will not experience death, and He wants us to know it too. Can you lay hold of that truth for yourself?

In II Timothy 1:9-10 we read: *"Who hath saved us, and called us with an holy calling, not according to our works, but according to His own purpose and grace which was given us in Christ Jesus before the world began* (times eternal), *But is now made manifest by the appearing of*

119

our Savior Jesus Christ, who <u>hath</u> abolished death, and <u>hath</u> brought life and immortality to light through the gospel;."

The Gospel of John was written long before the Book of Timothy, so I believe that when Paul wrote to his friend Timothy, he had determined that Jesus had completely abolished death for the believers. If the believer is not even going to know what it is to die, then is not death a done deal for the believer? And if Jesus tasted our death, then why would we have to taste it? If He went through death for us, then why would we go *beyond*, unto death? It all adds up to the fact that Jesus did indeed abolish death for us.

PRAYER: Again, I am so thankful for what you have done for me. Keep me under the protection of your mighty arm throughout this life on earth. Let wisdom reign in my everyday dealings with whatever comes along. I want to live a life pleasing onto you. In Jesus' name, Amen.

APRIL 9th

 Today, I want to bring you into a wider view of what Jesus did for us in regard to death. I know that my eyes were opened wide when this was first revealed to me. Let us look at I Corinthians 15:54 which reads, *"So when this corruptible shall have put on incorruption, and this mortal shall have put on immortality, then shall be brought to pass the saying that is written, 'Death is swallowed up in victory.' "* And Isaiah 25:8 states, *"He will swallow up death in victory* (forever)*; and the Lord God will wipe away tears from off all faces; and the rebuke of His people shall He take away from off all the earth: for the Lord has spoken it."*

If something has been swallowed, it is gone. It will go through the digestive system and will either become a part of the body or discarded as waste. I want to take you to a place in the Old Testament where Moses also used this very idea to make sure that the gold his people had used to make a false god to worship, (while his back was turned), would never be used in that way again. You can read the whole story in Exodus 32, but let us look at verse 20, which states, *"And he* (Moses) *took the calf which they had made, and burnt it in the fire, and ground it to powder, and strawed* (scattered) *it upon the water, and made the children of Israel to drink* (swallow) *of it."*

Do you see Moses' reasoning here? Even if the gold had been sprinkled on the water, the people would have tried to retrieve it. Moses wanted none of that. It was a defiled metal to God now, and could not be used to build the Tabernacle which God had instructed Moses to tell the people to build. Yes, indeed, that gold had to be destroyed completely.

Now look at Exodus 7. I would like to suggest you read the whole chapter to get the feel of what is happening. In Exodus 7:9-13, the Lord instructed Moses and Aaron: *"When Pharaoh shall speak unto you, saying, 'Shew a miracle for you,' then thou shall say unto Aaron, 'Take thy rod, and cast it before Pharaoh, and it shall become a serpent.' And Moses and Aaron went in unto Pharaoh, and they did so as the Lord had commanded; and Aaron cast down his rod before Pharaoh, and before his servants, and it became a serpent. Then Pharaoh also called the wise men and the sorcerers; now the magicians of Egypt, they also did in like manner with their enchantments. For they cast down every man his rod, and they became serpents; but Aaron's rod swallowed up their rods. And he hardened Pharaoh's heart, that he hearkened not unto them; as the Lord had said."*

Here is the point I want to make: the rod in Aaron's hand represented *all* the Power of God, and the rods in the hands of the wise men represented *all* the power of the enemy, namely Satan. So when Aaron's serpent swallowed up the serpents of the wise men, and when Aaron took up his serpent and it became a rod again, where was the power of the wise men? It was gone, never to be retrieved again. God Almighty had proven His power over the enemy. So when we read in I Corinthians 15:54 that *"...death is swallowed up in victory,"* We can understand how that happened. When Jesus died on the cross and went through death for us, He indeed swallowed up death in the victory. It is a done deal.

As I studied the subject of death recorded in the Bible, and found out the truths that laid hidden just waiting to be discovered, I was amazed that I had not heard a thing about it before!

The Bible so clearly teaches that "we have passed from death to life, we will not know what it is to die, we will not know or experience death, death has been swallowed up in victory, death has been abolished etc". Can it get more clear? Jesus died, was buried, descended into hell, rose again on the third day and by so doing He forever changed the face of death for all who believe in Him?

I believe it is a sad fact that believers, who hear the accounts of those who have had near-death experiences, place their faith in their testimony more than they do in the word of God which teaches the same truth. I am grateful for the testimony of those who have had near-death experiences however, because they are living proof of the truth of the Bible, but I am even more grateful that the word of God, the Bible, is the eternal truth of the great news that Jesus died our death and we will go unto death and not through death like Jesus did.

PRAYER: Lord, I thank you for such a truth as this. I pray that I can grasp the depth of its meaning and live with this assurance that belongs to me, that you tasted death for me and have abolished death, delivering me from the bondage of the fear of death. I give you all the glory for your victory, bought for me on the cross and bestowed unto me by the resurrection. In Jesus' name, Amen.

APRIL 10th

 It is time to talk about choices. We make many choices all day long, and without thinking, I might add. God wants us to *think* about our choices. They are vitally important to our Christian walk with God. Joshua 24:15 reads; *"And if it seem evil unto you to serve the Lord, choose you this day whom you will serve; whether the gods which your fathers served that were on the other side of the flood, or the*

gods of the Amorites, in whose land you dwell: but as for me and my house, we will serve the Lord."

Joshua was saying that if everyone else chose to serve other gods, he would still choose to serve the Lord himself and be willing to stand alone. How determined are you to follow God Almighty? Would you be willing to stand alone?

Let's look at Mark 14:27, which states, *"And Jesus saith unto them, 'All ye shall be offended because of me this night: for it is written, 'I will smite the shepherd, and the sheep shall be scattered.' "* Also see verses 29-31, which reads: *"But Peter said unto him, 'Although all shall be offended, yet will not I.' And Jesus saith unto him, 'Verily I say unto thee, That this day, even in this night, before the cock crow twice, thou shalt deny me thrice.' But he* (Peter) *spake the more vehemently, 'If I should die with thee, I will not deny thee in any wise.' Likewise also said they all."*

Peter was so sure of himself, but he did not reckon on an attack by Satan. In fact, Peter gave Satan a challenge here by saying, "I will never deny you." Satan took on that challenge, and in short order Peter had denied *ever knowing* Jesus. Let us read in Mark 14:66-72, about his denial and the cock crowed: *"And as Peter was beneath in the palace, there cometh one of the maids of the high priest: And when she saw Peter warming himself, she looked upon him, and said, 'And thou also wast with Jesus of Nazareth.' But he denied, saying, 'I know not neither understand I what thou sayest.' And he went out into the porch and the cock crew. And a maid saw him again, and began to say to them that stood by, 'This is one of them.' And he denied it again. And a little after, they that stood by said again to Peter, 'Surely thou art one of them: for thou art a Galilaean, and thy speech agreeth thereto.' But he began to curse and to swear, saying, 'I know not this man of whom you speak.' And the second time the cock crew. And Peter called to mind the word that Jesus said unto him, 'Before the cock crow twice, thou shalt deny me thrice.' And when he thought thereon, he wept."*

We need to have our faith firmly rooted in the Word of God in order to follow through with our choices to follow Jesus. If we are not, we

123

will be caught off guard when Satan attempts to challenge our choices, and we may stumble and fall.

PRAYER: Lord God, I plainly see how easy it is to give you lip service, and to make a poor choice without thinking it through. I pray that you will help me to be so rooted in your Word that I will not make the mistake that Peter made. As much as I want to follow you completely, I also know that I have an old nature, contrary to my new nature, that wishes to pull me down. So I humbly ask for your ever-watchful eye to help me stay on course with you, even in the small details of my life. In Jesus' name, Amen.

APRIL 11th

Before we go any further, here is a word of advice; a scripture to follow to help you keep on course. James 4:7 says, *"Submit yourself therefore to God. Resist the devil, and he will flee from you."*

Here is a three step order to follow, 1) submit 2) resist 3) he will flee. This is like, "Put key in lock, turn key, open door." It is not, "Turn key, open door, put key in lock." Unless we are submitted to the Lord, we are not able to resist the devil, and the devil knows it! He will not flee from us.

The only way to really be submitted to the Lord is to *know*, really know, the Word of God, the scripture! This is one reason I have typed in all scripture references, so you will read them for yourself. You cannot base your faith on what I know about the scripture. You have to know what it says for yourself. When push comes to shove, can you stand firm in what you believe about God according to what the Bible says?

Joshua was sure of the God he worshipped, and could boldly proclaim that he and his household would serve the Lord. We see a similar verse in I Peter 5:6, which reads, *"Humble yourselves therefore under the mighty hand of God, that he may exalt you in due time."*

When you have chosen to follow God, tests and temptations will come your way. Can you stand firm and humble yourself under God's mighty hand? Standing firm in your conviction that God will not ever give you more than you are able to bear? Remember, God tests our faith to strengthen it. Satan tempts our old nature to give up, to try to solve problems ourselves, to lie, cheat, and do whatever it takes to change the circumstance. Satan delights when we fail to let God help us through our troubles. To enjoy victory in the Lord and be exalted by God, rather than defeated by Satan, will require making *good choices* on our part.

PRAYER: Heavenly Father, how will I know when I am fully submitted to you? Is it a day-by-day replacement that takes place? Is it more of you in my heart and mind, and less of the world, myself, and Satan in charge? My "want to" is ready to charge ahead and take hold of all your promises; promises to forgive, guide, keep victorious the abundant life, resurrection power, the whole nine yards. But am I submitted and grounded in the Word of God sufficiently to hold on when the tough times come? I choose to depend on your Holy Spirit to stand by me to carry out my choice to be submitted to you. You know only too well my weaknesses, and I will depend on you to strengthen my weak points and guide me through each test and temptation. Thank you, Father, for hearing this prayer. In Jesus' name, Amen.

APRIL 12th

I believe it is time for us to look at some people in the Bible and how the choices they made and affected their lives. I want to set the stage before we go on, though. We will be talking about Joseph, and how his life mirrors the life of Jesus in many ways. Joseph had many hard choices to make, but he reached a point in life where he had passed a tests and temptations over and over again.

I must give you some background in order for you to get a complete picture of what is happening. Abraham, the father of the Hebrew

125

nation of Israel, had a son in his old age named Isaac. Isaac had twin sons, Esau and Jacob. Esau became the father of the Arab nations, and Jacob carried on the blessing of God from Abraham and Isaac. God later changed Jacob's name to Israel.

Jacob had two wives: Rachel, who was barren, and Leah. Jacob loved Rachel, but when he asked for her hand in marriage, her father tricked him into marrying her older sister, Leah, instead. Not until after the ceremony did Jacob realize he had the wrong wife. He had worked for her father for seven years, and then got the wrong daughter. He was told he could work seven more years and have Rachel also, which he did.

These daughters also came with handmaids. While Leah had one son after the other, Rachel was barren, so she (Rachel) gave her maid to Jacob to raise up a child for her. This was common practice in that day and age. Leah did the same thing.

Finally, after Leah, her hand maid, and Rachel's hand maid had ten sons, Rachel had a son named Joseph. Some time later Rachel had another son, Benjamin, but Rachel died in childbirth. These were the twelve sons of Jacob, the twelve tribes of Israel. Remember Israel was the name given to Jacob by God.

There was much jealousy among the sons, especially against Joseph. He was a special son to Jacob since he was the child of his love, Rachel. You need to keep this background in mind as we progress, because it will help you to understand the family dynamics behind Joseph's choices. You can find all this in Genesis 29 through 35. Genesis 37:2-4 reads: *"These are the generations of Jacob. Joseph, being seventeen years old, was feeding the flock with his brethren; and the lad was with the sons of Bilhah and with the sons of Zilpah, his father's wives* (hand maids of both Leah and Rachel)*: And Joseph brought unto his father their evil report. Now Israel* (Jacob) *loved Joseph more than all his children, because he was the son of his old age; and he made him a coat of many colors. And when his brethren saw that their father loved him more than all his brethren, they hated him, and could not speak peaceably with him."*

Joseph was "daddy's pet" so to speak, and he was naïve. He may have delighted to bring an evil report to his father, we don't know, but he did tell the truth you can be sure. None of this helped his situation however, his father had set him up for trouble, and trouble is about to happen, as we will see tomorrow.

PRAYER: Lord God, I can see that, as a parent, one has a tremendous responsibility to not foster jealousy among my children. To pick and choose favorites is like having a bomb ready to explode. I pray that I never take that path as a parent. Each child is precious to you, Lord. Help me to see my children's potential through your eyes. In Jesus' name, Amen.

APRIL 13th

Genesis 37:5-8 reads: *"And Joseph dreamed a dream, and he told it his brethren: and they hated him yet the more. And he said unto them, 'Hear, I pray you, this dream which I have dreamed: For, behold, we were binding sheaves* (stalks of grain in a bundle to dry) *in the field, and, lo, my sheaf arose, and also stood upright; and, behold, your sheaves stood round about, and made obeisance to my sheaf.' And his brothers said to him, 'Shalt thou indeed reign over us? Or shalt thou indeed have dominion over us?' And they hated him yet the more for his dreams, and for his words."* I have often wondered why Joseph told his brothers such a dream, which could only incite greater hatred toward him. It was a choice he made, and as I see it.

Joseph was open to God and being in close fellowship with Him. Joseph's brothers, I believe, did not begin to understand such a relationship with God. So, to me, Joseph was doing what Jesus advises us <u>not</u> to do in Matthew 7:6, which states, *"Give not that which is holy unto the dogs, neither cast ye your pearls before swine, lest they trample them under their feet, and turn again and rend you."*

This is exactly what is going to happen to Joseph. I believe it is a bad choice to share some of the intimate things God does in your life with

127

those who cannot understand that there can be such an intimacy in spiritual things. Something so precious as that needs to be kept pure and holy. Those who cannot understand trample on what God meant to be pure and holy, when they learn of it. It is then God who is diminished in their sight.

The lesson for us, here, is to *be careful* with whom we share such deep things of God, like Joseph's dream. The dream was a truth for Joseph, not for his brothers. However, the day came when the brother's had to admit the dream had been true. God allowed this to happen.

You can also see the struggle between Satan and God here. Satan will do everything he can to thwart God's plan for His children's lives. We need to keep in mind that God will have His way no matter what, either with our cooperation, or without it. God had a plan, to save the nation of Israel from starvation and grow them into a nation comprising as many people as there are stars in the sky.

PRAYER: Heavenly Father, I pray that your Holy Spirit keeps me from throwing the holy and pure things of God before those who are unable as yet to understand them. May my witness in the world be one that will relate to people on the level of their *need*, and no further. Joseph did not have an evil intent in his heart, his life proves that. It is no wonder he was a delight to his father. It is easy to understand that he felt others should also have that kind of a heart rather than a jealous, evil heart of hate. Help me to be careful where I put my trust. Satan can not be trusted. Only God can be trusted. Give me discernment, Lord. In Jesus' name, Amen.

APRIL 14th

In Genesis 37:9-11, we learn of another one of Joseph's dreams: *"And he dreamed yet another dream, and told it his brethrens and said, 'Behold, I have dreamed a dream more; and, behold, the sun and the moon and the eleven stars made obeisance* (pay honor) *to me.' And he told it to his father, and to his brethrens: and his father rebuked him, and said unto him, 'What is this dream that thou have dreamed? Shall I and thy mother and thy brethren indeed come to bow down to thee to the earth?' And his brethrens envied him; but his father observed the saying."*

Here is more of the same, a picture of something to happen in the future. This time, however, it is not only Joseph's brothers who bow down to him, but his father and mother as well. That a man's parents would bow down to him was unheard of in that day! I believe God wanted them to get a message of what was going to happen, so that when it did, they would know that it was from God, that God was in charge all the time and that He had a plan for their safety and future.

God is the same today. He wants us to *know* what is to come and that He is in charge and will keep us safe through it all. Joseph made the choice to share this news from God. However, the brothers were so full of jealousy that they could not receive the message at all, but his father did at least observe and think about it. Joseph must have been given a signal from God to share this news, not just once, but *twice*.

The brothers are about to make a terrible choice as a result of these dreams. Have you ever shared something intimate you know about God, only to have it made fun of? If so, then you can pray that the people you shared it with may have their eyes opened by the Holy Spirit, so that they can see the things of God and understand that God is an intimate God who wants to bless us with such knowledge. Maybe they had never heard or knew that such words or dreams from God were even possible, and when you shared that knowledge with them it was the first time they even thought along such lines. However, I still feel it is very important to be careful what you share with an unbeliever or a "lukewarm" Christian. It may drive them away instead of bless them.

PRAYER: Dear Lord Jesus, help me to discern your will in my life. My desire is to be faithful to you, to share with others what you are doing in my life. However, I do not want to go beyond your will in my enthusiasm to be a witness of your love, mercy, and grace. In Jesus' name, Amen.

129

APRIL 15ᵗʰ

We continue in Genesis with verses 37:12-14, which reads; *"And his brethrens went to feed their father's flock in Shechem. And Israel* (Jacob) *said unto Joseph, 'Do not thy brethrens feed the flock in Shechem? Come, and I will send thee unto them.' And he said to him, 'Here am I.' And he said to him, 'Go, I pray thee, see whether it be well with thy brethrens, and well with the flocks; and bring me word again.' So he sent him out of the vale of Hebron, and he came to Shechem."*

In the next few verses Joseph finds out they were gone from Shechem to Dothan, so Joseph goes there to find his brothers. Incidentally, Dothan is about 65 miles from Hebron where Israel (Jacob) is. This is no small feat for Joseph. There were no road maps at that time. Joseph could be a half a mile from his brothers and miss them entirely. We pick up the story again at Genesis 37:18-22, which reads, *"And when they saw him afar off, even before he came near unto them, they conspired against him to slay him. And they said one to another, 'Behold, this dreamer cometh.' "*

There is mischief in the camp, and what is to become of Joseph? We discover what the brothers are planning in verse 20, *"Come now therefore, and let us slay him, and cast him into some pit, and we will say, 'Some evil beast has devoured him and we shall see what will become of his dreams.' "* Now, it is plain to see that the brothers did not believe those dreams were given to Joseph from God. In fact, they are not fighting Joseph, but rather they are fighting God, which is not a good idea at all!

Verses 21-22 go on to explain; *"And Reuben* (the eldest son, half brother to Joseph) *heard it, and he delivered him* (Joseph) *out of their hands; and said, 'Let us not kill him.' And Reuben said unto them, 'Shed no blood, but cast him into this pit that is in the wilderness, and lay no hand upon him;' that he might rid him out of their hands, to deliver him to his father again."*

Reuben wanted to save Joseph from the wicked brothers who wanted him dead. There is a struggle between God and Satan here. God

130

had a big plan to use Joseph to save this Abrahamic covenant family from starvation, and Satan did not want this family to be saved, especially Judah, through whose line Jesus would come. Remember, Jesus is the promised seed of the woman who would one day "bruise Satan's head." In Genesis 3:15, God gave Adam the first promise of a savior to come, *"And I* (God) *will put enmity* (hostility) *between thee* (Satan) *and the woman, and between thy seed and her seed; it shall bruise thy head, and thou shall bruise his heel."*

So yes, indeed, Satan does not want Joseph to survive if Satan can at all accomplish his evil scheme by using the jealous, envious brothers to kill Joseph. It all boils down to *choices*. The brother's are making choices (very bad choices). As we get into Joseph's story we will see the choices Joseph makes. I believe we can learn some great lessons from it all.

PRAYER: Father God, how easily it is to succumb to jealousy and strife when we allow our emotions to rule in our hearts. Help me to give my emotions to you to control, so that I can display your kind of love, mercy, and grace, and not be lead by Satan into areas that create strife, confusion, and hardship for others. Help me also to listen to your Spirit and not to other people as I ponder my choices in life. In Jesus' name, Amen.

APRIL 16th

Genesis 37:23-25 reads: *"And it came to pass when Joseph was come unto his brethren, that they stripped Joseph out of his coat, his coat of many colours that was on him; And they took him, and cast him into a pit: and the pit was empty, there was no water in it. And they sat down to eat bread: and they lifted up their eyes and looked, and, behold, a company of Ishmeelites came from Gilead with their camels bearing spicery and balm and myrrh, going to carry it down to Egypt."*

I want to point out something here. They put him in the pit and sat down to eat. Now, compare that to Matthew 27:35-36 which reads, *"And*

131

they crucified him, and parted his garments, casting lots: that it might be fulfilled which was spoken by the prophet, 'They parted my garments among them, and upon my vesture did they cast lots. And sitting down they watched him there; " Sitting down, they watched Him there on the cross. Joseph was in the pit and they sat down and ate, a mirror picture of Jesus and his conspirators.

Genesis 37:26-28 continues; *"And Judah said unto his brethren, 'What profit is it if we slay our brother, and conceal his blood? Come, let us sell him to the Ishmeelites, and let not our hand be upon him; for he is our brother and our flesh.' And his brethren were content (hearkened unto him). Then there passed by Midianites merchantmen; and they drew and lifted up Joseph out of the pit, and sold Joseph to the Ishmeelites for twenty pieces of silver: and they brought Joseph unto Egypt."*

Jesus was sold for thirty pieces of silver, the price of a slave man. Joseph was sold for twenty pieces of silver, the price of a slave boy. This is another mirror picture of Jesus.

PRAYER: Heavenly Father, it seems like you do not miss a beat. You are in such control it amazes me. If you are that much in control of Joseph's life, then you must be that much in control of my life, too. Help me to see your hand in my day-to-day life, and to see that it is for my good and the good of those around me. In Jesus' mighty name, Amen.

APRIL 17th

In Genesis 37:21-22, Reuben saved Joseph from being killed and had him put into a pit, a dry pit where he would be safe. In verses 26-27, Judah had the bright idea to sell him to merchants on their way to Egypt, which they did. Now look at Genesis 37:29-36, which reads, *"And Reuben returned unto the pit; and, behold Joseph was not in the pit; and he* (Reuben) *rent his clothes."*

To rent ones clothes meant to tear them from yourself, a sign of great distress, horror, grief, and despair. You might say it was an outward sign of an inward condition of sorrow over sin. What were they to do now? Joseph was gone. How would this affect their old father?

We continue in verse 30, where we read that Reuben *"returned unto his brethren, and said, 'The child is not; and I, whither shall I go?'"* I believe that Reuben, since he was the eldest son, felt responsible for Joseph, who was special to his father, a son longed for by both Jacob and Rachel. Are you beginning to see how *choices*, especially those made in haste, can affect all those around you? This act on their part will affect every member of that family. And usually one bad choice will only lead to another bad choice to cover up the first one and so on.

But, as we progress in this account in Joseph's life, we will also be made aware of the fact that despite horrible decisions made by the sons of Jacob, God is in full charge and has a plan, a major plan. Not, that it will excuse those sons, not at all. But God can take ashes and bring forth gold, only if we will turn it all over to God, which is what Joseph will be doing.

Choices shape our lives. They either bring us and those around us joy and peace, or they bring distress and sorrow. This point is prominent in Proverbs 18:21, which states, *"Death and life are in the power of the tongue: and they that love it shall eat the fruit thereof."* Everything that comes out of our mouths flows from what is in our hearts, which was in our minds first of all. We *choose* what *thoughts* to entertain, and when we have entertained them for some time, they settle into our hearts and become an *attitude*. It is from this attitude that our mouths *speak*. In Matthew 12:34, Jesus says to the Pharisees, *"O generation of vipers, how can ye, being evil, speak good things? for out of the abundance of the heart the mouth speaketh."*

The same is true for us today. Our choices have the power of life or death spiritually, and we better start paying attention to what we think, what we allow our hearts to harbor, and what we say. Tomorrow we will see what the brothers said to their father. Will it be the truth or a lie?

PRAYER: Lord God, I see there is so much room for improvement in my life. I pray that the Holy Spirit will give me that check in my spirit when I am about to harbor a thought, or say an unkind, distasteful word. I have a

133

lifetime of bad habits that need to be broken, and that is a major overhaul, so let's start today, Lord. In Jesus' name, Amen.

APRIL 18th

Genesis 37:31-36 reads; *"And they took Joseph's coat, and killed a kid of the goats, and dipped the coat in the blood; And they sent the coat of many colours, and they brought it to their father; and said, 'This have we found: know now whether it be thy son's coat or no.' And he knew it, and said, 'It is my son's coat; an evil beast has devoured him; Joseph is without doubt rent in pieces.' And Jacob rent his clothes, and put sackcloth upon his loins, and mourned for his son many days."* To wear sackcloth was a sign of great sorrow and a broken heart. Sackcloth was a rough, course cloth, a symbol of mourning. They often put on ashes with the sackcloth at a time of mourning. How would you like to stand by and watch your father go through this sorrow, all the while you knew your own evil heart in the matter? All of this pain was the result of jealousy harbored in the hearts of Joseph's brothers. Was it worth the sorrow they brought upon their father? I doubt it!

Verses 35-36 state: *"And all his sons and all his daughters rose up to comfort him; but he refused to be comforted; and he said, 'For I will go down into the grave* (Shoel) *unto my son mourning.' Thus his father wept for him. And the Midianites sold him into Egypt unto Potiphar, an officer of Pharaoh's, and captain of the guard."*

So then Joseph was in Egypt, about to face many new trials, but his father cannot be comforted. A dark cloud hung over the whole family. Would it ever go away? How about God's justice system? Will this whole mess ever be made right? We will continue to follow this account of Joseph and watch God's hand in the plan, and the *choices* everyone continues to make. It should teach us a few lessons also.

PRAYER: Dear Heavenly Father, do you mourn over our sins and foolish choices like Jacob mourned over his son Joseph? Sometimes I feel like I ought to sit in sackcloth and ashes, and then I am reminded that you died to cleanse me from all sin, pay the price of my salvation, and all I need to do is come to you and receive it all, a free gift. You want me to have life, even life abundant. You tell me that I am more than a conqueror, and that no one can pluck me out of your hand. You must rejoice for every step of faith I take in the right direction. Help me, Lord, to live a life pleasing unto you, so that you can rejoice, and I can speak words of life rather than words of death. In Jesus' name, Amen.

APRIL 19th

We will jump over chapter 38 and pick up the account of Joseph in Genesis 39:1-6, which reads; *"And Joseph was brought down to Egypt; and Potiphar, an officer of Pharaoh, captain of the guard, an Egyptian, bought him of the hands of the Ishmeelites, which had brought him down thither. And the Lord was with Joseph, and he was a prosperous man; and he was in the house of his master the Egyptian. And his master saw that the Lord was with him, and that the Lord made all that he did to prosper in his hand. And Joseph found grace in his sight, and he served him: and he made him overseer over his house, and all that he had he put into his hand. And it came to pass from the time that he had made him overseer in his house, and over all that he had, that the Lord blessed the Egyptian's house for Joseph's sake; and the blessing of the Lord was upon all that he had in the house, and in the field. And he left all that he had in Joseph's hand, and he knew not ought he had, save the bread which he did eat. And Joseph was a goodily* (attractive and good looking) *person, and well favored."*

I am sure that Joseph did not change his attitude toward God just because of his circumstances. I can just imagine he kept that dream stored up in his heart, knowing that God is faithful, even if men (like his brothers) are not. If we do not guard our attitudes, then Satan can use circumstances to create in our hearts a bitter attitude toward God. God blessed Joseph to such a degree that even the man who owned him was blessed.

135

Do you know that one determined Christian in a household can bring the blessings of God into it? Joseph must have had a pleasant attitude toward his work. He must have done it "as unto the Lord." What a lesson for us in our everyday lives. We are where we are because it is where God *wants* us. He knows exactly what is happening to us at all times and He has good in mind for us, but we have to cooperate with God, and maintain a good attitude toward our circumstances. This is a free choice on our part. It was a free choice on Joseph's part, and God could not have blessed him and the household if Josephs life had not been a good witness of the Love of God.

PRAYER: Gracious Heavenly Father, I surely can see how important it is to have the right attitude in my heart, but, oh, how the enemy wants me to complain, and criticize, and display self pity again and again. I also see and understand that, when I do that, I am diminishing you and your love for me, not acknowledging your presence in my life and circumstances. I feel like I am being turned around like a big ship in the ocean, and being steered in a new direction spiritually. I need your help, Lord, to make the *choices* to lay aside old habits and to take on new and better attitudes. In Jesus' name, Amen.

APRIL 20th

 Genesis 39:7-9 reads; *"And it came to pass after these things, that his master's wife cast her eyes upon Joseph, and she said, 'Lie with me.' But he refused, and said unto his master's wife, 'Behold, my master wotteth not* (has concern about nothing) *what is with me in the house, and he hath, committed all that he hath to my hand: There is none greater in this house than I; neither has he kept back anything from me but thee, because thou art his wife: how then can I do this great wickedness, and sin against God?' "*

Think of the choice he made here! He refused to sin against God even though there was every reason to do so. He was invited by the woman herself, so no one else should ever need to know. Satan had it all set up for Joseph to sin, yet he kept himself pure in the eyes of God. He had a *heart attitude* not to sin against his God. Is it any wonder his father had a really soft spot in his heart for Joseph? Parents know their children, know their potential, how they think, what is in their heart, whether it be for good or for evil. Joseph also knew that even if no one else on earth would know what he had done, God would know, and that made all the difference in the world to Joseph. We shall see what this choice did for him!

PRAYER: Dear Lord, I am beginning to see the importance of watching what *attitudes* are stored up in my heart. It is too late to make a decision to stay pure and close to you when the temptations and tests come crashing down upon me. That is a decision I need to make today, when there is no temptation or test nipping at my heels. I also realize that if I make the decision (or choice) to follow you and stay close to you, then you will help me to carry out that decision. I realize it gives you a legal right to defend me during that time of temptation when I have given my life over to you to handle and protect. Thank you, Father, for such assurance of help. In Jesus' name, Amen.

APRIL 21st

Genesis 39:10-16 reads: *"And it came to pass, as she spake to Joseph day by day, that he hearkened not unto her, to lie by her or to be with her. And it came to pass about this time, that Joseph went into the house to do his business; and there was none of the men of the house there within. And she caught him by his garment, saying, 'Lie with me.' and he left his garment in her hand, and fled, and got him out. And it came to pass, when she saw that he had left his garment in her hand, and was fled forth, that she called unto the men of her house, and spake unto them, saying, 'See, he has brought in an Hebrew unto us to mock us; he came in unto me to lie with me, and I cried with a loud voice: And it came to pass, when he heard that I lifted up my voice and cried, that he left his garment with me, and fled, and got him out.' And she laid up his garment by her, until his lord came home."*

Do you see the setup that Satan had made? He used the woman to try to trick Joseph into sinning against his God, and to make such a terrible mistake that he could be killed. For that is what Satan wants, to have Joseph killed. Satan is no dummy. He knows that God has a plan and that Joseph is a part of that plan. God has a plan for all of us and Satan tries hard to tempt us into something so that we are of *no use to God.* It is so important to have given our life over to God for Him to run, direct, guide, and protect.

Never forget that God is in the forgiveness business, also. Since Jesus came and paid the price and penalty for sin, we can always go to God for forgiveness. So never allow a sin in your life separate you from God. Just ask God to forgive you and it will be done. We see Satan's schemes against Joseph all over the place here. I wonder if Potiphar's wife had told all the men to have a day off in verse 11 to ensure there would be no men in the house. It would be her word against Joseph's. Not only that, the master was gone away, so she was free to make mischief. Never underestimate Satan's schemes. But, also remember, we have the powerful name of Jesus, and we can take authority over Satan and put him to flight. Joseph did not have that edge over the enemy back in his day.

PRAYER: Dear Lord Jesus, I lift up my voice in thanksgiving for what you accomplished on the cross for me. I can turn to you and know that the enemy is a defeated foe, that he cannot do any more than you will allow him to and that you will strengthen me through every test in life. Help me to have eyes to see the temptation for what it is: Satan's desire to put me down, defeat me, and make me believe that you have left me alone and helpless. Also help me to see the test and what you want to accomplish through that test, like strengthen my faith in you, and to have an attitude to, *"In everything give thanks; for this is the will of God in Christ Jesus concerning you,"* (I Thessalonians 5:18). In Jesus' name, Amen.

APRIL 22ⁿᵈ

 Genesis 39:16-20 reads; *"And she laid up his garment by her, until his lord came home, And she spoke unto him according to these words, saying, 'The Hebrew servant, which you have brought unto us, came in unto me to mock me: And it came to pass, as I lifted up my voice and cried, that he left his garment with me, and fled out.' And it came to pass, when his master heard the words of his wife, which she spoke unto him, saying, 'After this manner did thy servant to me; that his wrath was kindled.' And Joseph's master took him, and put him into the prison, a place where the king's prisoners were bound: and he was there in the prison."*

Innocent Joseph was in prison! Where was God in all of this? God knows exactly what He is doing, but we have a hard time accepting God's hand in things of this nature. Pay attention to the fact that the prison Joseph was in was "where the king's prisoners were bound." Later on this will be an important fact. In the Bible, it often looks like Satan is getting the upper hand, but we discover that what Satan planned for evil was the very thing God will use for good for his people. In fact, Satan had actually helped God's plan take shape right under the devil's nose.

How well do you know your God? Joseph knew his God very well, and the devil was no match for him. Joseph must have also known the enemy, but most importantly, one must know God, know how He operates, what His goals are, how you fit into His plan in your life, why He sometimes answers, "no" or "wait awhile," to your prayers, etc.

That is why one studies the Bible, to learn these things about God. And one must always keep in mind that God is completely just. If He were not just, He could not be God. God has given every human being the freedom of choice, and God will not violate that freedom. Potiphar's wife chose to falsely accuse Joseph, and Potiphar chose to believe her and not even ask Joseph about the accusation. God allowed all this, and Joseph did not complain to God about it either.

PRAYER: Dear Heavenly Father, I can feel anger rise up in me as I see how Joseph was falsely accused and there was no one to stand up for him. How lonely he must have felt, in a strange land, and that not by his choosing, either. It is such a lesson for me to see how he kept his eyes and mind on you. Help me in my hour of trial to feast my eyes on you and to stay my mind on you, so I can stand up to the tests in life, knowing also that you have something better in mind down the road. Your desire to bless in the midst of trials is also evident in this account of Joseph. Help me to see your blessings in the midst of my trials. In Jesus' name, Amen.

APRIL 23rd

Genesis 39:21-23 explains; *"But the Lord was with Joseph, and shewed him mercy, and gave him favour in the sight of the keeper of the prison. And the keeper of the prison committed to Joseph's hand all the prisoners that were in the prison; and whatsoever they did there, he was the doer of it. The keeper of the prison looked not to any thing that was under his hand; because the Lord was with him, and that which he did, the Lord made it to prosper."*

God is not limited by prisons, or unkind masters, or Satan himself. Always remember that fact when you face a trial. Choose to keep your eyes on God, and you will see God stand up for you. Joseph kept his eyes on God. We know that because of God's continued favor upon him.

If we give God half a chance, He will chase us down to bless us. But it may not come easy. Joseph was in prison, after all. But he was also free, free to choose to stick close to God. That was a freedom Satan could not take away from him. If there is anything to be said for Joseph, it is that he did not forsake his God. He must have also kept the dream God gave him stored up in his heart, knowing that one day it would all come true.

PRAYER: Lord God, there is no wall too high, no dungeon too deep, no man too evil, but you are able to overcome any obstacle. Help me keep that in mind when things look bleak and impossible. I thank you for Joseph and the lessons I am learning from him. Thank you for revealing yourself to me, in and through his life. In Jesus' name, Amen.

APRIL 24th

 Genesis 40: 1-4 reads: *"And it came to pass after these things, that the butler of the king of Egypt and his baker had offended their lord the king of Egypt. And Pharaoh was wroth against two of his officers, against the chief of the butlers, and against the chief of the bakers. And he put them in ward in the house of the captain of the guard, into the prison, the place where Joseph was bound. And the captain of the guard charged Joseph with them, and he served them: and they continued a season in ward."* God, not Satan is in charge here, as you watch this scenario play out. These two men are connected to the king of Egypt, the Pharaoh himself! And Joseph was in charge of these two prisoners. The plot thickens.

When you begin to see God's hand in situations, and you begin to see how Satan tries to thwart God's plans, only to be himself tricked over and over again. You will begin to see too how that same scenario plays out in your own life. Just make sure your choices are to follow God and to stick close to Him. That was all Joseph had to do, no matter the circumstances, and God would do all the rest.

God gave Joseph a dream, and he shared it with his family. The very people who should have been for him and not against him. It backfired, and he was hated instead. That brought him into a pit, then into Egypt as a slave. Back at home the brothers had a lie they had to hide, and their father was in great grief. The brothers had no idea what had happened to Joseph, and the father was convinced he was dead, torn apart by a wild beast.

But God! There is always a "But God," in our lives. God is at work behind the scenes, and He has nothing but "good" in mind for us. It may take some time for the good to be made manifest in our lives, just as it was taking time for it to be made manifest in Joseph's life.

There are often times when we despair and give up. That is when we need to be more resolved than ever to look for God's breakthrough. Think of it this way, "I am going to put my hand in yours, Lord, and I will not let go. We will go through this thing together, and there is no other way for it to be done." That kind of determination will get the job done. God is free to work His work and to do it in His timeframe.

Are you familiar with Ecclesiastes 3:1-8? I would advice you to read these verses, but I will quote only a couple verses here. Verse 3 states that there is *"A time to kill, and a time to heal; a time to break down, and a time to build up,"* and verse 6 reads, *"A time to get, and a time to lose; a time to keep, and a time to cast away;"* There was a time for Joseph to be in prison, and there will be a time for him to be out of prison.

Ecclesiastes 3:1 says, *"To everything there is a season, and a time to every purpose under the heaven:"* I believe the "purpose" here is all those things that are in the hands of God, your life and mine, for instance. Joseph's life was surely in the hands of God. As we progress through this whole account, you will see that the brother's lives were also in God's hands.

PRAYER: Dear Lord God, my view of you and your ways are becoming more and more clear all the time. Forgive me, Lord, for having such a small view of you and your ways. Continue to widen my view of your work in the lives of your people in the Bible. It gives me hope for my own life. It helps me to realize that you have many blessing in store for me, and to see that your desire is to bestow those blessing upon me. I open my arms to you, Lord, to give you myself and to be ready to receive your blessings. In Jesus' name, Amen.

APRIL 25th

 In Genesis 40:5-8, we read; *"And they dreamed a dream both of them, each man his dream in one night, each man according to the interpretation of his dream, the butler, and*

the baker of the king of Egypt, which were bound in the prison. And Joseph came in unto them in the morning, and looked upon them, and, behold, they were sad. And he asked Pharaoh's officers that were with him in the ward of his lord's (Potiphar's) *house, saying, 'Wherefore look you so sadly today?' And they said unto him, 'We have dreamed a dream, and there is no interpreter of it.' And Joseph said unto them, 'Do not interpretations belong to God? Tell me them, I pray you.' "*

Do you think God is in charge of dreams? I believe it was God who had given these dreams to those two men, and both on the same night. Joseph knows that it is God who will interpret dreams. Do you suppose Joseph has wondered what happened to the dream he had about his family bowing down to him one day. Did God interpret that dream to him, or did his father and his brothers do it when they were told about the dream? It was obvious what it meant, was it not?

But Joseph is confident that he can interpret these dreams, because he is confident that God will tell him the meaning. How confident are you about God in your life? I do believe that God will reveal every truth we need in our life, and I also believe God wants us to ask Him for the revelation of the truth. God wants us to know Him better and better all the time, day by day. What do you think these dreams have to do with Joseph and his situation? Keep an eye on what is about to happen. Sometimes, when God moves, He will take giant steps. We may think He has forgotten about us, and then it is suddenly all over. Will there be a "suddenly" in Joseph's life?

PRAYER: Heavenly Father, it is so awesome to watch you work in the lives of your people. It gives me an insight behind the scenes, which we would ordinarily miss if we just read the Bible as a story. There is a struggle between Satan and God going on, and there are the choices people make, some bad and harmful, and others right and good. There is your time table ticking away, with perfect timing in spite of mankind's choices. There are dreams with meaning far beyond our wildest thoughts. We have drama, plots, revenge, grief, lies, truths, and a final goal to be reached in spite of all these things. Only a God who knows the end from the beginning could manage all this. It is to that God I put my trust, my hope, and my allegiance. I thank you, Father, for being that kind of a God in my life. I thank you for creating me just the way I am, and giving to me the life that I have. It is perfect in your eyes; therefore I accept it as perfect in my eyes too. In Jesus' name, Amen.

APRIL 26th

 Genesis 40:9-11 reads: *"And the chief butler told his dream to Joseph, and said to him, 'In my dream, behold a vine was before me; And in the vine were three branches: and it was as though it budded, and her blossoms shot forth; and the clusters thereof brought forth ripe grapes: And Pharaoh's cup was in my hand: and I took the grapes, and pressed them into Pharaoh's cup, and I gave the cup into Pharaoh's hand:"* Let's examine this dream a bit. A butler serves all the master's wishes. (In this case, the master is the King of Egypt.) One such wish was to bring him his wine, and to make sure it was not poisoned. Often times, the butler would have to drink a swallow of it first. In the dream, there were three branches and ripe grapes. The butler squeezed the juice from the grapes into Pharaoh's cup and gave the cup to Pharaoh.

Now let's look at the interpretation in Genesis 40:12-13, which states; *"And Joseph said unto him, 'This is the interpretation of it: The three branches are three days: Yet within three days shall Pharaoh lift up thine head, and restore thee unto thy place: and thou shalt deliver Pharaoh's cup into his hand, after the former manner when thou wast his butler.' "*

To Joseph, the interpretation was simple. He could see the meaning right there before him. Think back to the dream he had about his sheaf standing up and his brother's sheaves bowing down to his. He figured that out easily, too. And when the sun, moon and eleven stars made obeisance (bow) to him, he could see what that meant right away, too.

Who are the eleven stars? They are his eleven brothers. Joseph was the twelfth of the twelve tribes of Israel. This is a detail I do not want you to miss. The day would come when, in fact, his whole family would be in subjection to him. It may sound far fetched to everyone in his family, including his father, but that dream was not from Joseph, it was from God.

I want to address one more thing before we move on to the baker's dream. Verses 14 and 15 of chapter 40 showed the first sign that Joseph even thought about what all had happened to him, and the injustice of it all. These verses read; *"But think on me when it shall be well with thee, and shew kindness, I pray thee, unto me, and make mention of me unto Pharaoh, and bring me out of this house: For indeed I was stolen away out of the land of the Hebrews: and here also have I done nothing that they should put me into the dungeon."*

Joseph did not have any feelings about what had happened to him. He knew well and good that he had not done anything to deserve all the evil that had happened to him. All he asked of the butler was to make mention of him to Pharaoh.

PRAYER: Heavenly Father, I have not gone through anything compared to Joseph, yet he kept an attitude of *gratitude* toward you. He could have complained bitterly, instead he suffered silently. One verse jumps out at me, I Peter 5:6, which says, *"Humble yourself therefore under the mighty hand of God, that He will exalt you in due time:"* How hard it is to remember that verse when I am in the midst of a trial that just does not seem to go away or even improve. In times of trial, help me to remember Joseph and his attitude toward his circumstances, so that I too can keep on *keeping on*, and bring honor to your name. In Jesus' name, Amen.

APRIL 27th

Today, we will look at the baker's dream in Genesis 40:16-17, which reads; *"When the chief baker saw that the interpretation was good, he said unto Joseph, 'I also was in my dream, and, behold, I had three white baskets on my head: And in the uppermost basket there was all manner of bakemeats for Pharaoh; and the birds did eat them out of the basket upon my head.'* " What is the dream? There were three baskets full of baked goods on the baker's head, with birds eating out of the top basket. Notice that when the baker heard the butler's dream interpreted, he thought it safe to disclose his dream. You could tell that he was fearful of the interpretation.

Then we see in verses 18 and 19, *"And Joseph answered and said, 'This is the interpretation thereof: The three baskets are three days: Yet within three days shall Pharaoh lift up thy head from off thee , and shall hang thee on a tree; and the birds shall eat thy flesh from off thee.'"* What an unexpected lot for the baker!

But we need to see something beyond that, here. Joseph is a mirror to what will happen to Jesus. Jesus was crucified between two malefactors, one of whom was saved, as we see in Luke 23:43, which states, *"...Today shalt thou shall be with me in Paradise."* The other was not saved.

Then, in Genesis 40:20-23, we read; *"And it came to pass the third day, which was Pharaoh's birthday, that he made a feast unto all his servants: and he lifted up the head of the chief butler and of the chief backer among his servants* (who were in prison), *and he restored the chief butler unto his butlership again; and he gave the cup into Pharaoh's hand: but he hanged the chief baker: as Joseph had interpreted to them. Yet did not the chief butler remember Joseph, but forgat him."*

Believe me, when it happened exactly as Joseph had said it would, even to the three days, it got their attention. I am sure Joseph did not have a clue that it would be the Pharaoh's birthday in three days. He just interpreted the dream as he saw it. But in spite of all that, the butler forgot all about Joseph. Do you see how easy it is to put God aside, or even the servants of God, such as Joseph, when all goes well for us, such as it did for the butler? How quickly we forget that God has a hand in our lives, to protect, guide, comfort, and convict. Oh, yes, it is important that we are convicted of what we do that displeases God. How else would we ever desire to be a better follower of Jesus?

PRAYER: Dear Lord Jesus, remind me, day by day, of your goodness toward me, so that I do not forget, as the butler did. I need to be sensitive to the kindness people show me, and not take it for granted. Help me be kind in return, Help me to be a reflection of your kindness and patience, which stretches out from horizon to horizon. Joseph needed patience to wait it out until his dream would come true. You, Lord, have more patience than us all. This calls to mind II Peter 3:9, which states, *"The Lord is not slack concerning his promise as some men count slackness; but is long suffering* (extremely patient*) towards us, not willing that any perish, but that all should come to repentance."* We need your help to show that kind of patience to the world, like you show it to us in your Word. In Jesus' name, Amen.

APRIL 28th

We are not done with Joseph's story yet. When God takes a giant step, it almost causes mankind to run like crazy to keep up. We will begin to see that happening now in Genesis 41:1-8, which reads: *"And it came to pass at the end of two full years, that Pharaoh dreamed: and, behold, he stood by the river. And, behold, there came up out of the river seven well favoured kine and fatfleshed; and they fed in a meadow. And, behold, seven other kine came up after them out of the river, ill favoured and leanfleshed; and stood by the other kine upon the brink of the river. And the ill favoured and leanfleshed kine did eat up the seven well favoured and fat kine. So Pharaoh awoke. And he slept and dreamed the second time: and, behold, seven ears of corn came up upon one stalk, rank and good. And, behold, seven thin ears and blasted with the east wind sprung up after them. And the seven thin ears devoured the seven rank and full ears. And Pharaoh awoke, and, behold, it was a dream. And it came to pass in the morning that his spirit was troubled; and he sent and called for all the magicians of Egypt, and all the wise men thereof: and Pharaoh told them his dream; but there was none that could interpret them unto Pharaoh."*

147

Something you need to be aware of is that the Egyptians worshipped many false gods. There were gods for everything, the god of the Nile, the sun god, and even a god scribe who was secretary of the pagan gods of Egypt. So, when Pharaoh called for the magicians and wise men, he expected one of them to be able to interpret his dreams. But there was no way those false gods could interpret a dream brought on by the God of heaven and earth, the Creator God. There would be only one man in all of Egypt who could interpret a dream from the Creator God, and that man is Joseph!

How glorious is the hand of God when you see how He works in the lives of His people on earth. There is another side to all this that I believe we need to address. These people of Egypt were in need of seeing a demonstration of the power of the God of creation. Who better to show them that than Joseph, who believed in the God of Abraham, Isaac, and Jacob? Then, once people have come face to face with such a God, it becomes their choice which God or gods they wish to follow. I believe that this concept is truly "killing two birds with one stone," revealing the power of the One True God and exposing the truth of the powerlessness of the false gods.

PRAYER: Heavenly Father, your wisdom is so far reaching, it encompasses every minute detail. And I am supposed to see that kind of wisdom at work in my life? Give me the eyes and ears to see and hear that wisdom as it relates to me, right where I am. Things you do for me one day may be *setting the stage* for something more important even years later. For Joseph, it was two years later. Lest I forget, fix those things in my mind and spirit so that I am aware of them when the time is ripe for you to take a giant step. In Jesus' name, Amen.

APRIL 29th

We left off yesterday with no one able to interpret the Pharaoh's dreams. Genesis 41:9-13 continues; *"Then spake*

the chief butler unto Pharaoh, saying, 'I do remember my faults this day: Pharaoh was wroth with his servants, and put me in ward in the captain of the guard's house, both me and the chief baker: And we dreamed a dream in one night, I and he; we dreamed each man according to the interpretation of his dream. And there was there with us a young man, an Hebrew, servant to the captain of the guard; and we told him, and he interpreted to us our dreams; to each man according to his dream he did interpret. And it came to pass, as he interpreted to us, so it was; me he restored unto mine office, and him he hanged.' " As I read this and saw how God Almighty was bringing Joseph closer and closer to the destiny God had in mind for him, I wondered if this made Satan nervous at all. I have often wondered about something else. Remember how Potiphar's wife lied about Joseph? How do you think she is going to feel when Joseph is elevated to a high position in Egypt, next to Pharaoh? It was lucky for her that Joseph was not into revenge, right?

The truth about Joseph's ability to interpret dreams is now known to Pharaoh, the top man in Egypt. Genesis 41:14-16 state; *"Then Pharaoh sent and called Joseph, and they brought him <u>hastily</u> out of the dungeon: and he shaved himself, and changed his raiment, and came in unto Pharaoh. And Pharaoh said unto Joseph, 'I have dreamed a dream, and there is none that can interpret it: and I have heard say of thee, that thou canst understand a dream to interpret it.' And Joseph answered Pharaoh, saying, 'It is not in me: God shall give Pharaoh an answer of peace.' "*

Joseph refuses to *ever* take credit for what God does in his life. God gets *all* the credit. Not only that, but Pharaoh most likely never heard about Joseph's God before, and since none of his wise men or magicians who served those false gods were able to interpret his dream, it will prove there is a higher God than theirs. Joseph certainly is the man for this hour. God knew that, long before his brother's hated him.

When you begin to see God in your life, in every minute detail of your life, then life gets exciting and you almost get giddy watching the working of God day by day. We need to *expect* great things from God. I think we limit Him by having low expectations. He is a great and awesome

149

God, interested in you and your life, ready to help you, even if it means just interpreting a dream for someone else. Did you notice how quickly Joseph's environment changed? He was hastily taken out of prison, shaved, given new clothes, and then to be invited before the highest authority of the land! A giant step indeed!

PRAYER: Dear Heavenly Father, I hope I never lose my expectation of your work in my life. Do give me eyes to see your hand at work in the little things that I might miss along the way. In Jesus' name, Amen.

APRIL 30th

Genesis 41:17-24 reads: *"And Pharaoh said unto Joseph, 'In my dream, behold, I stood upon the bank of the river: And, behold, there came up out of the river seven kine, fatfleshed and well favoured; and they fed in a meadow: And, behold, seven other kine came up after them, poor and very ill favoured and leanfleshed, such as I never saw in all the land of Egypt for badness: And the lean and the ill favoured kine did eat up the first seven fat kine: And when they had eaten them up, it could not be known that they had eaten them; but they were still ill favoured, as at the beginning. So I awoke. And I saw in my dream, and, behold, seven ears came up in one stalk, full and good: And, behold, seven ears, withered, thin, and blasted with the east wind, sprung up after them: And the thin ears devoured the seven good ears: and I told this unto the magicians; but there was none that could declare it to me'..."*

Did you notice that one detail was added to this retelling of his dream? He said that when the lean cows and the thin ears had eaten up the fat cows and the full ears that they looked no better than they had at the first. Joseph will be tested here by God to tell the story or interpretation just as God wants him to. It will be a hard message to tell the Pharaoh, but it will also be a big warning of what is to come and to help them prepare for it.

It is an awesome blessing from the God of all creation to give this warning to a land that could help the then-known world endure a hardship. Also, be aware of the fact that this is a dream from God. God is in the dream-giving business. I have heard it said that God will help you to interpret a dream that you have if you go to Him in prayer and ask for the interpretation. God wants us to be in the know. Many people are of the opinion that we are not to know this or that, but as I read the Word of God I cannot come to that conclusion at all.

Ephesians 5:17 reads, *"Wherefore be ye not unwise, but understanding what the will of the Lord is."* The foolish do not understand the will of God. Where there is understanding, there must also be knowledge. Knowledge comes first, and then the understanding. I believe there is so much God wants us to know for our own good, but we do not want to do the job of digging into the Word to know God better. If Pharaoh had not wanted to know what the dream meant, he would have chucked it and forgotten it. That would have been a disaster.

PRAYER: Heavenly Father, I want to know and understand your will for my life. I believe it is available to all of us. As I read your Word faithfully every day, reveal to me what you want from me and what you want to do through me. We can all be a "Joseph", right where we are, and bring glory to your name, but not without the help of your Holy Spirit, which you so freely poured out to us so long ago at Pentecost. Fill me, sanctify me, and use me for your glory. In Jesus' name, Amen.

MAY 1ˢᵗ

Genesis 41:25-32 reads: *"And Joseph said unto Pharaoh, The dream of Pharaoh is one: God hath shewed Pharaoh what he is about to do. The seven good kine are seven years; and the seven good ears are seven years: the dream is one. And the seven thin and ill favoured kine that came up after them are seven years; and the*

151

seven empty ears blasted with the east wind shall be seven years of famine. This is the thing which I have spoken unto Pharaoh: What God is about to do he sheweth unto Pharaoh. Behold, there come seven years of great plenty throughout all the land of Egypt: And there shall arise after them seven years of famine; and all the plenty shall be forgotten in the land of Egypt; and the famine shall consume the land; And the plenty shall not be known in the land by reason of that famine following; for it shall be very grievous. And for that the dream was doubled unto Pharaoh twice; it is because the thing is established by God, and God will shortly bring it to pass."

What a dream and what an interpretation. It would appear that Joseph is not a bit afraid to deliver this message from God to Pharaoh! That is because Joseph really knows His God. Pharaoh and the land of Egypt worshipped a number of false gods, but here we see that the God of creation can get his message through to the highest person in the land when He really wants a message to get through. In fact God had been setting up this whole situation a long time before. I wonder if Joseph was beginning to see the hand of God in a positive way in his life at that time. I also see that Joseph is a "take charge" type of person, and he gets the job done. That is why he was recognized by Potiphar and the jailer, and as we continue on tomorrow, you will really see how he takes charge.

So what do we learn from this scripture today? I believe we learn that God is never taken by surprise, and that He wants people, especially His own people, to know what He is about to do. I have always been amazed at how much God is willing to tell us about Himself and how He operates. He is completely *just*, and He is always *right on time*. Also, His Word is completely *true*! In the New Testament, I Peter 5:6 reads, **"Humble yourselves therefore under the mighty hand of God, that He may exalt you in due time."** This was also true in the Old Testament, because we can surely see that truth in the life of Joseph. That is the character of God, and it is true also for us today.

The next time a situation comes up in your life, ask God to open your eyes so you can see what He is trying to do in your life. Are you

152

supposed to just sit back and take it humbly, simply because in the right time God can justly exalt you? Think it over.

PRAYER: Gracious Father, why is it so hard to be humble? It goes against everything we want to do. Help me, Lord, so I can be a fit vessel to be exalted when the time is right. Help me to remain humble when that is what is called for. In Jesus' name, Amen.

MAY 2nd

In Genesis 41:33-36 Joseph advises Pharaoh: *"Now, therefore, let Pharaoh look out a man discreet and wise, and set him over the land of Egypt. Let Pharaoh do this, and let him appoint officers over the land, and take up the fifth part of the land of Egypt in the seven plenteous years. And let them gather all the food of those good years that come, and lay up corn under the hand of Pharaoh, and let them keep food in the cities. And that food shall be for store to the land against the seven years of famine, which shall be in the land of Egypt; that the land perish not through the famine."*

Joseph not only interpreted the dream, he also gave the Pharaoh sound advice. Who do you think gave Joseph that advice in the first place? Yes, of course, it was God. God has a plan, a big plan, and it will be carried out in God's timing! You need to begin to see how God's hand is in the midst of the things that happen on earth. Ask God to open your eyes so you can see how His hand directs your life. It is not hard to see it in the life of Joseph as we follow his life in the pages of the Bible, but we have only started to see great things in regard to God's overall plan here. Remember, the dream that Joseph had still needs to be fulfilled. Nothing is said about how old Joseph is at this point, but I believe he is not a very old man. If we would guess that he was about 15 when he was sent to find his brothers and the sheep, and if we guessed that it had been 10 or 15 years that he was in Egypt, then he would be 25 or 30 years old. But he was mature far beyond his years.

How do you suppose he learned to be so obedient toward God? Ask yourself some questions. How obedient are you toward God? How have you learned to be obedient? What has to die in us for obedience toward God to flourish in our lives? How did Jesus learn to be obedient, or did he have to learn obedience?

In Hebrews 5:8, we read, *"Though He were a Son, yet learned He obedience by what He suffered."* Yes, even Jesus had to learn obedience and He learned it through suffering, all because of sin in the world and in the human race. Jesus was sinless, and yet He suffered because of our sins. God asks obedience from us, too. The thing that must die in us for obedience to be in charge is our self will, the desire to satisfy our old nature.

Our old nature and Satan are partners in crime. They are allies with a desire to overcome our new nature. Our new nature and God the Holy Spirit are also allies, and they are far more powerful than Satan and our old nature. Obedience to God is simply choosing to follow God's plan for our lives. That is what Joseph did, and look what it did for him! Joseph is about to receive a big responsibility from Pharaoh. Can he do the job? Will he continue to be faithful? We shall see.

PRAYER: Heavenly Father, Joseph is an inspiration to me, a good example to follow. I want to be obedient in every area of my life like Joseph was, so I depend on you to hold me up, to guide me day by day to make the right choices that will honor you. Help me to stay close to you. Fill me with your Word for my defense against Satan's attacks. In Jesus' name, Amen.

MAY 3rd

Genesis 41:37-43 reads: *"And the thing was good in the eyes of Pharaoh, and in the eyes of all his servants. And Pharaoh said unto his servants, 'Can we find such a one as this is, a man in whom the Spirit of God is?' And Pharaoh said unto Joseph, 'For as much as God has shown thee all this, there is none so discreet and wise as thou art: Thou shall be over my house, and according unto thy word shall all my people be ruled: only in the throne will I be greater than thou.' And Pharaoh said unto Joseph, 'See, I have set thee over all the land of Egypt.' And Pharaoh took off his ring from his hand, and put it upon Joseph's hand, and arrayed him in vestures of fine linen, and put a gold chain about his neck; And he made him to ride in the second chariot which he had; and they cried before him, 'Bow the knee:' and he made him ruler over all the land of Egypt."*

Joseph would be young to be put in charge of all the land of Egypt for seven years of plenty, and no doubt, seven years of famine. God's hand is not short when it comes to blessing His servants. Prison walls and chains do not hinder God from releasing His servants from their bondage either. Joseph is a great lesson to us all, telling us to keep the faith, never waver, and be willing to help others as you see the need. Remember the verse we have looked at before, Peter 5:6, *"Humble yourself therefore under the mighty hand of God that He may exalt you in due season."*

Can you imagine being exalted to the second highest of a whole country as Joseph was. He went from prison to a place of great authority. Above all things, do not desire to take revenge! I have often thought about how Joseph could have sought out Potiphar and made life miserable for him and his wife. I am sure there are a lot of things that went on behind the scenes that are not recorded in God's Word. What do you think would happen to Potiphar if Pharaoh found out how Joseph had been treated by him and his wife? God is able to turn the tables on those who are unkind to us. He can do a better job than we could ever do ourselves anyway. So, never consider revenge. It is not up to us to do that. Romans 12:19 reads, *"Dearly beloved, avenge not yourselves, but rather give place to wrath: for it is written, 'Vengeance is mine; I will repay,' saith the Lord."*

PRAYER: Heavenly Father, I believe you are in the midst of my life, but there are times when I cannot see it and it does not feel like you are anywhere near me. That is when I need your help to step past my feelings and go right to your Word that tells me you are near. You will never leave

155

me or forsake me. Thank you for the lessons for me in the account of Joseph's life. They are an encouragement to me. Help me hang in there like Joseph did, and keep me from the evil one. Help me recognize vengeance when it wants to surface in my heart, so I do not fall into that trap. In Jesus' name, Amen.

MAY 4th

In Genesis 41:44-52, we read: *"And Pharaoh said unto Joseph, 'I am Pharaoh, and without thee shall no man lift up his hand or foot in all the land of Egypt.' And Pharaoh called Joseph's name Zaphnath-paaneah; and he gave him to wife Asenath the daughter of Potipherah priest of On. And Joseph went out over all the land of Egypt. And Joseph was thirty years old when he stood before Pharaoh king of Egypt. And Joseph went out from the presence of Pharaoh, and went throughout all the land of Egypt. And in the seven plenteous years the earth brought forth by handfuls. And he gathered up all the food of the seven years, which were in the land of Egypt, and laid up the food in the cities: the food of the field, which was round about every city, laid he up in the same. And Joseph gathered corn as the sand of the sea, very much, until he left numbering; for it was without number. And unto Joseph were born two sons before the years of famine came, which Asenath the daughter of Potipherah priest of On bare unto him. And Joseph called the name of the firstborn Manasseh: 'For God,' said he, 'has made me forget all my toil, and all my father's house. And the name of the second called he Ephraim: For God has caused me to be fruitful in the land of my affliction.' "*

In these verses, we see a faint hint of Joseph's struggle as a prisoner and alien in Egypt. God had helped him forget all his toil, and his father's house. Can you imagine the pain of homesickness when he first found himself in Egypt? And he also said God had made him fruitful in the land of his affliction. Think of how you would feel if you had been afflicted as Joseph had been. Just the separation from family would be hard to take, and then to remember how he had been treated by his own brothers would hurt to the core, and to wonder if his father was even still alive to think of him, wondering all these years what had happened to his son whom he loved so much. Yes, indeed, he had been in a place of affliction. But now he had been exalted, highly exalted!

Is he remembering the dream of his parents and brothers bowing down to him? Could I have kept the faith through all that? Joseph's life story helps me to claim his kind of faith while I am not in affliction, so that I might put that kind of faith into action if the need should ever arise. Believe me, it is too late to rely on that kind of faith when the time arrives and you have not decided beforehand to have that faith. It must be a decision you make now.

PRAYER: My dear Heavenly Father, I come to you a humbled person as I compare my faith to that of Joseph, and I place my faith on the God that watched over Joseph, and lay claim to the protection and help that is available to even one like me. In fact, Father, I believe I have even more to lay claim to than Joseph had, since I live in a time when Jesus has defeated the enemy and given me that right to abundant life so I might be "more than a conqueror" during my journey through life. What an exalted position you have given us who belong to Jesus! Thank you for all you have done for me. In Jesus' name, Amen.

MAY 5th

Genesis 41:53-57 states: *"And the seven years of plenteousness that was in the land of Egypt were ended. And the seven years of dearth* (famine) *began to come, according as Joseph had said: and the dearth was in all lands; but in all the land of Egypt there was bread. And when all the land of Egypt was famished, the people cried to Pharaoh for bread: and Pharaoh said unto all the Egyptians, 'Go unto Joseph; what he saith to you, do.' And the famine was over all the face of the earth: and Joseph opened all the storehouses, and sold unto the Egyptians; and the famine waxed sore in the land of Egypt. And all countries came to Egypt to Joseph for to buy corn; because the famine was so sore in the lands."*

Just as the years of plenty were foretold and took place, so too the years of famine came, and by this time, the people knew they too would be fulfilled just as Joseph had interpreted the dream. I think Joseph was also a very shrewd business man. He had the people bring in a portion of their corn in the years of plenty, and then when famine came they had to buy back corn. At least that is what I read here. Look at Genesis 41:34, which reads, *"Let Pharaoh do this, and let him appoint officers over the land, and take up the fifth part of the land of Egypt in the seven plenteous years,"* and also verses 47-48, which say, *"And in the seven plenteous years the earth brought forth by handfuls. And he gathered up all the food of the seven years, which were in the land of Egypt, and laid up the food in the cities; the food of the field, which was round about every city, laid he up in the same."*

It does not say he bought it from the people. Now look at Genesis 41:56-57, which states, *"And the famine was over all the face of the earth: and Joseph opened all the storehouses, and sold unto the Egyptians; and the famine waxed sore in the land of Egypt. And all countries came into Egypt to Joseph for to buy corn; because the famine was so sore in all lands."*

On the surface, this does not look like anything unusual is going to happen because of the famine, Joseph is in a position of great power at this point in his life. But guess what? The famine is also affecting his own brothers and parents. Sooner or later they too will need to come to Egypt to buy corn. Then what? God's hand is not short when it comes to bringing about His plan in the lives of those who *give* their lives to Him.

There is a prophecy given to Abraham that must be fulfilled also. Genesis 15:12-14 reads: *"And when the sun was going down, a deep sleep fell upon Abram; and, lo, an horror of great darkness fell upon him. And He said unto Abram* (his name was later changed to Abraham by God), *'Know of a surety that thy seed shall be a stranger in a land that is not theirs, and shall serve them; and they shall afflict them four hundred*

158

years. And also that nation, whom they shall serve, will I judge: and afterwards shall they come out with great substance.' "

The nation Abraham's descendents served was Egypt, and yes, it was for 400 years, as confirmed in Exodus 12:40, *"Now the sojourning of the children of Israel, who dwelt in Egypt, was four hundred and thirty years."*

They also came out rich, just as God had told Abram they would. When God says He will do something, you can count on it that it will be done. Our job is to make right choices in our lifetime. If we teach our children anything, it should be how to make the right choices. We cannot follow them around and make choices for them at every turn. They will grow up and need to make choices themselves throughout their lifetime.

PRAYER: Lord God, I see that you take your time to carry out your plans, and then, when you want to, you take a giant step and leave us with our mouths hanging open. Help me to keep in step with you. I am sure Joseph had a hard time adjusting to being at the head of such a big undertaking to prepare a whole nation for a deadly famine. Then I remind myself that he knew you in such a way that he could depend on you at all times. Help me, also, to turn it all over to you to handle, and then I will claim that "rest" you tell me I can have. In Jesus' name, Amen.

MAY 6th

Now we come to Genesis 42, where the focus changes back to Joseph's family. Genesis 42:1-4 reads: *"Jacob saw that there was corn in Egypt. Jacob said unto his sons, 'Why do you look one upon another?' And he said, 'Behold, I have heard that there is corn in Egypt: get you down thither, and buy for us from thence; that we may live, and not die.' And Joseph's ten brethren went down to buy corn in Egypt. But Benjamin, Joseph's brother, Jacob sent not with his brethren; for he said, 'Lest preadventure mischief befall him.' "*

159

There is so much we can see here in these verses. Remember the dream? There were eleven brothers who bowed down to Joseph. Jacob did not trust his sons with Benjamin. Did he suspect foul play in regard to Joseph's disappearing? One could almost think so. Yet he could never have produced proof that his sons had dealt treacherously with Joseph, either. But he was not going to give them a chance to do it again if, indeed, they had a hand in Joseph's disappearance. I wonder how many times we go about life never giving it a thought that God knows all. Maybe those brothers thought their dirty plan would always remain a secret, but things are going to begin to heat up, and the day of truth is approaching. Today we can go to God and ask Him to forgive us for all our sins and shortcomings, and He will do that right away. Jesus gave us that right when we accepted Him as our Lord and Savior, because He has paid the price and the penalty of our sin. We do not need to have a heavy heart, as those brothers should have had. Just open up to Jesus and let Him come into your heart and wipe it clean and fill it with His presence.

PRAYER: Heavenly Father, I do want to lay all my burdens down and walk away cleansed and forgiven. It almost seems too easy to be true. The more I read about how you operate and the love you have for me, the more I realize you did it all for me, If I do not tap into that pool of love, then we both loose, you would have died for nothing and I would gain nothing for thinking that way. So I will take a giant step and give myself to you lock, stock, and barrel and say, "Have at it, Lord. I am yours to mold and shape, and hopefully to use." In Jesus' name, Amen.

MAY 7th

Before we look at today's verses, you should know that Canaan was the name of the land that God had given to Abraham, and that is where Jacob and his sons were living. The famine had also reached Canaan. Now, let's turn to Genesis 42:5-10, which reads: *"And the sons of Israel came to buy corn among those that came: for the famine was in the land of Canaan. And Joseph was the governor over the land, and he it was that sold to all the people of the land: and Joseph's brethren came, and bowed down themselves before him with their faces to the earth. And Joseph saw his brethren, and he knew them, but made himself strange unto them, and spake roughly unto them; and he said unto them, 'Whence come ye?' And they said, 'From the land of Canaan to buy food.' And Joseph knew his brethren, but they knew not him. And Joseph remembered the dreams which he dreamed of them, and said unto them, 'Ye are spies; to see the nakedness of the land ye are come.' And they said unto him, 'Nay, my lord, but to buy food are thy servants come.'"*

Remember that Jacob's name was changed to Israel. I believe that when the Bible talks about Jacob, that refers to the man, the man with an old nature, the sinner man. And when the bible addresses him as Israel, that refers to the spiritual man, the God-like man, or that part of him that is in tune with God and God's plan in his life.

Also remember that Joseph is a mirror image of Jesus. John 1:11 states, *"He* (Jesus) *came unto His own, and His own received him not."* Joseph's brothers did not know they were dealing with Joseph, but Joseph knew his brethren, just as Jesus knew His fellow Jews, but they did not know who Jesus was, their Savior!

Another mirror image of Joseph and Jesus is in Philippians 2:10-11, which reads, *"That at the name of Jesus every knee shall bow, of things in heaven, and things in earth, and things under the earth. And that every tongue should confess that Jesus Christ is Lord, to the glory of God the Father."*

Joseph did not make his brethren bow down to him. They did it willingly. One day, the whole realm will bow down to Jesus. In fact, there are three levels that bow down: heaven, earth, and under the earth, which I take to mean hell itself. So far, there were only ten brothers that bowed down before Joseph, but the dream indicated it would be eleven. So there is more to come.

PRAYER: Lord God, what a Book this Bible is! I am beginning to see how it all fits together, more and more as I read and study it. Do you have such an intricate plan for my life, too? I know you want me to grow into the full stature of Christ, but is that really happening Lord? I pray that as I read your Word, and understand it more and more, the growth you want to happen in my life will take place. I see how you exalted Joseph, and how he had to suffer humiliation and learn to be humble. Grant me the grace to be humble before you. Your riches can never be bought with money, and even when I am humble, I am richer than any king of the earth. May I grasp that truth with my whole heart. In Jesus' name, Amen.

MAY 8th

Today we will see it is time for Joseph's brothers to confess what they had done. It has been a long time coming, but it has finally arrived. Their consciences must have been bothering them over the years. They saw how their dealing with Joseph had affected their old father, how he mourned and grew old under the sadness he carried. And there was nothing they could do about it. How could they ever find Joseph after they sold him? Make no mistake, what we sow is what we will reap, and when we reap, it is always much more than what we sow!

Also remember that God is able to bring gold out of ashes. In Genesis 42:11-17, the brothers explain: *"'We are all one man's sons; we are true men, thy servants are no spies.' And he* (Joseph) *said unto them, 'Nay, but to see the nakedness of the land ye are come.' And they said, 'Thy servants are twelve brethren, the sons of one man in the land of Canaan, and behold, the youngest is this day with our father, and one is not* (this was a common saying to mean one was dead).' *And Joseph said unto them, 'That is it that I spake unto you, saying, Ye are spies: Hereby ye shall be proved: By the life of Pharaoh ye shall not go forth hence, except your youngest brother come hither. Send one of you, and let him fetch your brother, and ye shall be kept in prison, that your words may be proved, whether there be any truth in you: or else by the life of Pharaoh*

162

surely you are spies.' And he put them all together into ward (into prison)
three days. "

Joseph's brothers had proven themselves to be a bunch of
scheming trouble makers, so why should Joseph think they had changed?
But Joseph did find out that his father was still alive, and that Benjamin was
too. He also found out that these ten brothers were aware that one brother
was presumed dead. His head must have been whirling. Joseph was not
one to desire revenge, not because he did not have an old nature like we do
and would be able to think in terms of revenge, but because he believed in
and reverenced God. He would not stoop to revenge. We will watch how
Joseph moves on to a solution that is right in the eyes of God.

PRAYER: Heavenly Father, is it possible to have such a pure heart as
Joseph did? I see my old nature just bristle at the memory of what these
brothers did to Joseph, and at how they put their father through so much
grief. That ugly word, "hate," just comes rushing to the surface of my
mind, but I know that you, Lord Jesus, would not entertain that thought.
Therefore, I realize that I need to examine my own heart. Help me, Lord, to
end my own hatred toward those who take an unfair advantage over me in
order to satisfy their own ugly emotions of jealousy. Help me to have a
forgiving heart as Joseph had. In Jesus' name, Amen.

MAY 9th

Genesis 42:18-24 reads: *"And Joseph said unto them the third
day, 'This do, and live; for I fear God: If ye be true men, let
one of your brethren be bound in the house of your prison: go ye, carry
corn for the famine of your houses. But bring your youngest brother
unto me; so shall your words be verified, and ye shall not die.' And they
did so. And they said one to another, 'We are verily guilty concerning our
brother, in that we saw the <u>anguish</u> of his soul, when he besought us, and
we would not hear; therefore is this distress come upon us. And Rueben
answered them saying, Do not sin against the child; and ye would not*

hear? Therefore, behold also his blood is required.' And they knew not that Joseph understood them; for he spake unto them by an interpreter. And he turned himself about from them, and wept; and returned to them again, and communed with them, and took from them Simeon, and bound him before their eyes."

Before we go any further, look at Luke 19:41, which says of Jesus, *"And when He was come near, He beheld the city, and wept over it."* Jesus had come to restore the broken relationship between God and man, to bring salvation and peace for the hearts of men, but when He looked on the city of Jerusalem and saw the teeming population walking in darkness, refusing to see or live in the light of the truth of God, He wept. Similarly, Joseph saw the condition of his brothers, the hidden, unconfessed sin that lay in their hearts, and how they had deceived their father and still harbored hatred in their hearts, and Joseph wept. Both Joseph and Jesus were alone when they wept.

Does Jesus weep over us, over our hardness of heart, our refusal to study His Word in order to know Him better? Do you want to walk closer to God every day, or do you want God to be just close enough to be at your beck and call in case you suddenly need Him for something big? Do you have an attitude of, "I will handle all the little things myself, thank you very much"? God wants your worship, devotion, and commitment because you really love Him. He will not twist your arm to get it.

PRAYER: Heavenly Father, it melts my heart to even think that you might weep over me. I do not want to cause you that kind of grief. Thank you for sending your Son to be a substitute for me, and to bring me the gift of salvation. Help me to bask in that truth and to soak it up so that it becomes a fact and reality in my inward being. I confess that I need you every day, I need your presence, your peace, your joy, your strength, and, yes, your mind also, so I can live a life of victory in Christ Jesus. In His name I pray it, Amen.

MAY 10th

Genesis 42:25-28 reads: *"Then Joseph commanded to fill their sacks with corn, and to restore every man's money into his sack, and to give them provision for the way: and thus did he unto them. And they laded their asses with the corn, and departed thence. And as one of them opened his sack to give his ass provender in the inn, he spied his money; for, behold, it was in the sack's mouth. And he said unto his brethren, 'My money is restored; and, lo, it is even in my sack,' and their heart failed them, and they were afraid, saying one to another, 'What is this that God hath done unto us?' "* The money in the mouth of the sack got their undivided attention! How could this happen? Was it a trick? (After all, they were acquainted with tricks, were they not?) They knew they would have to go back there, because one of the brothers was counting on them to come and get him.

God often speaks to us in a small, still voice, and He wants us to hear Him and obey Him. I see this money as God's still, small voice speaking clearly to them. Notice the brothers' reaction in verse 28,. *"What is this that God has done to us?"* They recognize God in the midst of this dilemma. We, too, need to be sensitive to God's hand in our lives every day. What are the brothers going to tell their father when they get back home? One brother is left in Egypt, and Joseph has demanded they bring Benjamin back with them. And now there is money in their sacks. But they will have more troubles when they get back home. We will look at that tomorrow.

PRAYER: Heavenly Father, I want to be able to see your hand in my life, every day of my life. I know in my head, according to your Word, that you are that close to me, but I also want to know it in my heart and be able to recognize your hand, your interest in my life, as these men did. It should be that much easier for me, since I have the Holy Spirit to lead me into all the truth. John 16:13 says, *"Howbeit when He, the Spirit of truth, is come, He will guide you into all truth: for He shall not speak of Himself, but whatsoever He shall hear, that shall He speak: and He will show you* *things to come."* Thank you, Father, for the truths you have shown me already. I expect to see and hear more truths from this day forward. In Jesus' name, Amen.

MAY 11th

In Genesis 42:30-34, Joseph's brothers return to Canaan and tell their father of their experience, saying: *" 'The man, who is the lord of the land, spake roughly to us, and took us as spies of the country. And we said unto him, 'We are true men; we are no spies: We be twelve brethren, sons of our father; one is not, and the youngest is this day with our father in the land of Canaan.' And the man, the lord of the country, said unto us, 'Hereby shall I know that ye are true men; leave one of your brethren here with me, and take food for the famine of your household, and be gone: And bring your youngest brother unto me: then shall I know that ye are no spies, but that ye are true men: so will I deliver you your brother, and ye shall traffic in the land.' "*

Can you imagine what an impact this had on Jacob, their father? He believed that Joseph was dead, and now one of his sons is in prison in Egypt and the only way to release him from prison is to send Benjamin with the other brothers as a sign of their truthfulness. If they thought that they were in trouble before, imagine the trouble they are in with their father now. Can't he trust them to do anything right?

Also keep in mind that they *know* that Joseph was not killed, but sold by them because of their jealousy. They are also well aware of the fact that God knows all, and just maybe God's hand is in all this. Would God protect both Benjamin and Simeon and keep them from great harm in the mean time, or would God allow harm to come to those two brothers because of the sin of the ones who brought such harm to Joseph?

I also believe Joseph wanted them to suffer a bit, to bring them to a place of repentance. He means no harm to either Benjamin or Simeon, they are safe enough, but the other brothers do not know that. One verse seems

166

particularly appropriate here. Numbers 32:23 warns, *"Be sure your sin will find you out."*

I grew up on a farm, and every spring we would have to go out and pick rocks that had risen to the surface of the ground after the harsh winter. Those rocks were hidden beneath the soil, but year by year they would come to the surface. Sin is like that, it will not lay hidden forever. The day will come when the truth will be evident, as evident as those rocks in the field.

That is what is happening here. One day Jacob will know exactly what happened to Joseph, and exactly who was to blame for it, and those brothers do not look forward to that day. God gave Joseph a dream, and that dream was the truth. Not even ten brothers could stop it from happening, and they needed to learn that they could not mess around with God's plans. His plans will be carried out, either with our cooperation or without it. The choice is up to each one of us.

PRAYER: Heavenly Father, I do not want to hinder your plan in my life. Help me to stay in step with your plan for me. Give me a vision of your plan for my life, and then give me the strength, will, and wisdom to follow that plan. I know you are always *good*, and therefore your plan must be good also. That gives me the courage to subscribe to your plan. All I ask from you is the guidance I will need and the wisdom to stay in step with you. In Jesus' name, Amen.

MAY 12th

Genesis 42:35-38 states: *"And it came to pass as they emptied their sacks, that, behold, every man's bundle of money was in his sack: and when both they and their father saw the bundles of money, they were afraid. And Jacob their father said unto them, 'Me have ye bereaved of my children: Joseph is not, and Simeon is not, and ye will take Benjamin away: all these things are against me.' And Reuben spake unto his father, saying, 'Slay my two sons, if I bring him*

not to thee: deliver him into my hand, and I will bring him to thee again.'
And he said, 'My son shall not go down with you; for his brother is dead,
and he is left alone: if mischief befall him by the way in the which ye go,
then shall ye bring down my gray hairs with sorrow to the grave.' "

I believe there are hints in these verses that Jacob knew, or at least
suspected, that his sons of were responsible for Joseph's demise. In verse
36, he implies that the reason three of his sons are being taken away from
him is their fault, and in verse 38 he uses the word "mischief" in regard to
Benjamin being in their custody.

Nevertheless, Jacob has spoken and Benjamin was not permitted to
be used as a proof of their honesty. Rueben goes so far as to offer his own
two sons as a promise that no mischief would befall Benjamin. Rueben is
ready to do anything to get this whole mess behind him. If you had been
one of Jacob's sons, how would you have felt to hear your father offer such
a bargain? If they had listened to Rueben in the first place, they would not
be in this trouble.

Meanwhile, is Joseph wondering if his brothers will come back
with Benjamin or not? If they would not return, what would he do with
Simeon? It is plain to be seen that he is betting they would come back with
Benjamin. And, maybe, it is not a gamble either. After all, he had a dream
that needs to be fulfilled, a mother, father, and eleven brothers bowing
down to him. Notice it is not ten, but eleven brothers, which means all of
them.

God is faithful, and Joseph knows that, so he is trusting in God to
fulfill the dream that he had about the future. We need to rely on God's
faithfulness too. Here I am reminded of I John 1:9, which reads, ***"If we***
confess our sins (that is our part*), He is faithful and just to forgive us our***
sins, and to cleanse us from all unrighteousness (that is God's part, and
God will keep His part if we will do ours*)."*

See how far God is willing to go? All we need to do is to confess
our sin, be truthful with God, and He will not only forgive us our sins, but
He will also cleanse (wipe you clean) of *all* unrighteousness. In fact, Jesus
will give us His own righteousness in exchange for our sins. Not only is
God faithful to us in regard to forgiveness, but He is able to do that and still

be perfectly just. That is because Jesus has paved the way for God to be *just* as he forgives us, cleans us up, and gives us Jesus' righteousness. It is so important for us to see who we are (children of God) so we can believe we have what God says is our right to have.

Joseph never lost sight of who, and whose, he was. He was God's chosen vessel and he belonged to God by right of creation. So are you! God created you, His Son paid for your sins, and His son died and rose again to give you a new life. That is who you are. Then God sent you out into the world to be a reflection of His love, mercy, and grace, and to be a witness for God. We do not belong to ourselves, but rather we belong to God, to live for Him. Therefore, we are His to use. Joseph knew exactly who and whose he was. He could wait patiently for all of this to play out in God's time and in God's way.

PRAYER: Lord God, it is assuring to know that I belong to you, that you have a plan for my life, and that you intend for that plan to be realized. It is also assuring to know that you are faithful to forgive my sins and to make me clean, inside and out, from unrighteousness. As I watch the story of Joseph's brothers unfold, I wonder whether I am as afraid as they are that my sin will find me out. Help me, Lord, to want to confess my sins, to lay it all out before you, and let you deal with my sins in the best possible way. You are in the restoration business, so I know that you will immediately restore my fellowship with you when I confess my sins. Joseph's brothers are afraid, and that shows me they are not in fellowship with you, just as Adam was afraid when you, God, called to him after he had sinned in the garden of Eden. I do not want sin to make a breach in our fellowship, so help me to immediately confess when I realize I have sinned against you. In Jesus' name, Amen.

MAY 13th

 In Genesis 43: 1-14, we read: *"And the famine was sore in the land. And it came to pass, when they had eaten up the corn*

169

which they had brought out of Egypt, their father said unto them, 'Go again, buy us a little food.' And Judah spake unto him, saying, 'The man did solemnly protest unto us, saying, "Ye shall not see my face, except your brother be with you." If thou wilt send our brother with us, we will go down and buy thee food: But if thou wilt not send him, we will not go down: for the man said unto us, "Ye shall not see my face, except your brother be with you."' And Israel said, 'Wherefore dealt ye so ill with me, as to tell the man whether ye had yet a brother?' And they said, 'The man asked us straightly of our state, and of our kindred, saying, "Is your father yet alive? Have ye another brother?" And we told him according to the tenor of these words: could we certainly know that he would say, "Bring your brother down?"' And Judah said unto Israel his father, 'Send the lad with me, and we will arise and go; that we may live, and not die, both we, and thou, and also our little ones. I will be surety for him; of my hand shalt thou require him: if I bring him not unto thee, and set him before thee, then let me bear the blame for ever: (I shall have sinned against thee for ever) *For except we had lingered, surely now we had returned this second time.' And their father Israel said unto them, 'If it must be so now, do this; take of the best fruits in the land in your vessels, and carry down the man a present, a little balm, and a little honey, spices, and myrrh, nuts and almonds: And take double money in your hand; and the money that was brought again in the mouth of your sacks, carry it again in your hand; peradventure it was an oversight. Take also your brother, and arise, go again unto the man: And God Almighty give you mercy before the man, that he may send away your other brother, and Benjamin. If I be bereaved of my children, I am bereaved.'"*

It is plain to see that Israel had no other choice but to let Benjamin go to Egypt to prove the truthfulness of his brother's words. Joseph did not plan evil for them, but rather good for his own kin, but his family did not know that, especially his father.

I can just imagine the sense of fear they all had as they began this journey back to Egypt. There is no doubt that the man of power in Egypt, namely Joseph, was in complete charge of the whole thing. Don't you wonder what was going through Joseph's mind during this time. Would he see them again? Would they come after Simeon and be a real brother to him? Had they learned anything from their mistakes?

What about us? Do we learn anything from our past experiences? Joseph had learned to see good in everything that happened to him, and we are admonished to; *"In everything give thanks, for this is the will of God in Christ Jesus concerning you"* (I Thessalonians 5:18). If you do not learn anything else, please learn this truth: in everything, we are to give thanks. You would be surprised at how much that one truth will bless you. Start to practice it right now in your life.

PRAYER: Dear Lord, I want to learn that truth and practice it. I know it doesn't necessarily make sense, but I have come to know and understand that your ways are not like our ways, and your thoughts are not like our thoughts, so I will practice self discipline and not let my "old nature" boss me around. Instead, I will offer to you thanks in everything. In Jesus' name, Amen.

May 14th

Genesis 43:15-23 states: *"And the men took that present, and they took double money in their hand and Benjamin; and arose up, and went down to Egypt, and stood before Joseph. And when Joseph saw Benjamin with them, he said to the ruler of his house, 'Bring these men home, and slay, and make ready; for these men shall dine with me at noon.' And the man did as Joseph bade; and the man brought the men into Joseph's house. And the men were afraid, because they were brought into Joseph's house; And they said, 'Because of the money that was returned in our sacks at the first time are we brought in; that he may seek occasion against us, and fall upon us, and take us for bond-men, and our asses.' And they came near to the steward of Joseph's house, and they communed with him at the door of the house, and said, 'O sir, we came indeed down at the first time to buy food: And it came to pass, when we came to the inn, that we opened our sacks, and, behold,*

every man's money was in the mouth of his sack, our money in full
weight: and we have brought it again in our hand. And other money
have we brought down in our hands to buy food: we cannot tell who put
our money in our sacks.' And he said, 'Peace be to you, fear not: your
God, and the God of your father, hath given you treasure in your sacks; I
had your money.' And he brought Simeon out unto them."

This is the first time Joseph has seen his brother Benjamin for
many, many years. Benjamin was a child when Joseph went to Egypt, now
he was probably a teenager. The fulfillment of Joseph's dream had just
come closer to being fulfilled.

What kind of an attitude will Joseph have as it becomes more and
more evident to his brothers just exactly who this ruler in Egypt is. He
could be in a position to take revenge on Reuben and Judah. He could take
full advantage of the distance between them and their father, and make life
miserable for them, use them as slaves or put them all in jail. Maybe a few
months in jail might make them think about what they had done to him so
many years ago.

There are many thoughts of how Joseph could have acted. What
will he be doing next do you think? How can he keep his cool throughout
this scenario? Joseph teaches us many lessons: how to keep our cool when
we suffer injustices; how to not let these events make you bitter, or carry a
grudge until you can give them what they deserve; how to exercise patience
over the long haul; and how to hang onto your faith in God no matter what
happens to you.

I can imagine Joseph would have liked to scoop Benjamin up into
his arms and hug and kiss him, but he didn't do that. He has a plan, most
likely from God, as to how to proceed, and to lead his brothers down a path
that would bring repentance and restoration. Joseph never wanted division
in the family. That was what the enemy, Satan, wanted. Instead, God was
working toward restoration and peace within the family. Joseph was God's
only hope of accomplishing that and I don't think Joseph would disappoint
God.

PRAYER: Dear Lord, I thank you for the lessons Joseph gives us. I hope I can exercise such patience and wholesome attitudes as he did for so many years. I also thank you for showing me that it is possible to wait on your timing in regard to restoration in family matters. I also am thankful for the fact that you, Lord, are faithful, and when it comes to my sinfulness, you want me to confess and be forgiven, even more than I do. Yes, Lord, I am most grateful for the lesson I am learning in the life of Joseph. In Jesus' name, Amen.

MAY 15ᵗʰ

In Genesis 43:24-34, we read: *"And the man brought the men into Joseph's house, and gave them water, and they washed their feet; and he gave their asses provender. And they made ready the present for Joseph's arrival at noon: for they heard that they shall eat bread there. And when Joseph came home, they brought him the present which was in their hand into the house, and bowed themselves to him to the earth* (all eleven of them, I might add). *And he asked them of their welfare, and said, 'Is your father well, the old man of whom ye spake? Is he yet alive?' And they answered, 'Thy servant our father is in good health, he is yet alive.' And they bowed down their heads, and made obeisance. And he lifted up his eyes, and saw his brother Benjamin, his mother's son, and said, 'Is this your younger brother, of whom ye spake unto me?' And he said, 'God be gracious unto thee, my son.' And Joseph made haste; for his bowels did yearn upon his brother: and he sought where to weep; and he entered into his chamber, and wept there. And he washed his face, and went out, and refrained himself, and said, 'Set on bread.' And they set on for him by himself, and for them by themselves, and for the Egyptians, which did eat with him, by themselves: because the Egyptians might not eat bread with the Hebrews; for that is an abomination unto the Egyptians. And they sat before him, the firstborn according to his birthright, and the youngest according to his youth: and the men marveled one at another. And he took and sent*

173

messes unto them from before him: but Benjamin's mess was five times so much as any of theirs. And they drank, and were merry with him."

By this time Joseph was used to refraining himself. He had had a lot of practice. Can you see times in your life when you had to practice refraining yourself? Joseph's main objective was to live a life pleasing to God. When that is uppermost in your life, then it becomes easier and easier to refrain yourself. You need to feel the desire Joseph had to embrace and kiss his brother. This was his true full-blooded brother, all the others were half brothers, but Joseph's mother had only those two sons, Joseph and Benjamin.

Joseph left the room and had himself a "good cry," but he went right back into the situation and was ready to carry on. I wonder if he had any idea how this was all going to play out. The one thing he did know was that God was in charge now, just as surely as He was in charge when Joseph was given that dream so many years before. You can go back even further and remember the promise made to Abraham, that his descendants would be captives in a strange land for 400 years, and then they would be taken out of the land. God is working to bring that prophecy to pass.

What we need to see is that there is no insignificant person in God's family. You cannot look at people like Joseph, or King David, or Moses, and think that they were something extra special. They were just like you or me. They had fears, insecurities, and weaknesses just like the rest of us, but they also had a resolve to follow God, to worship Him and put Him first in their lives. Even if they stumbled and backslid, they always came back to God to do things His way. Joseph will reveal himself to his family at just the right time, also a characteristic of God. God is never a minute early or a minute late, but always right on time. It should not be all that hard to trust a God like that, now should it?

PRAYER: Lord God, the more I read your word, the more I realize what a privilege it is to belong to God's family. You are so true to your Word, you will never leave us or forsake us. You stretch yourself to reach out to be by our side at all times. That prompts us to give you all the praise and glory, and it drives us to worship you above all gods. Help me be a reflection of who you are wherever I am, just as Joseph was. In Jesus' name, Amen.

MAY 16ᵗʰ

Genesis 44:1-13 reads: *"And he commanded the steward of his house, saying, 'Fill the men's sacks with food, as much as they can carry, and put every man's money in his sack's mouth. And put my cup, the silver cup, in the sack's mouth of the youngest, and his corn money.' And he did according to the word that Joseph had spoken. As soon as the morning was light, the men were sent away, they and their asses. And when they were gone out of the city and not yet far off, Joseph said unto his steward, 'Up follow after the men; and when thou dost overtake them, say unto them, "Wherefore have ye rewarded evil for good? Is not this it in which my Lord drinketh, and whereby indeed he divineth? Ye have done evil in so doing." ' And he over took them, and he spake unto them these same words. And they said unto him, 'Wherefore saith my lord these words? God forbid that thy servants should do according to this thing. Behold, the money, which we found in our sack's mouths, we brought again unto thee out of the land of Canaan. How then should he steal out of thy lord's house silver or gold? With whomsoever of thy servants it be found, both let him die, and we also will be my lord's bondmen.' And he said, 'Now also let it be according unto your words: he with whom it is found shall be my servant; and ye shall be blameless.' Then they speedily took down every man his sack to the ground, and opened every man his sack. And he searched, and began at the eldest, and left at the youngest: and the cup was found in Benjamin's sack. Then they rent their clothes, and laded every man his ass, and returned to the city."*

Remember, to rend ones clothes was an expression of grief, despair, and sorrow. That certainly describes how the brothers were feeling in this situation. They realized that Benjamin would not be allowed to go

175

back to his father! And just maybe none of them could go back to their father! Is it any wonder they rent their clothes?

They had no idea they were being set up, but I think that when they bowed down to Joseph the first time, it was not so much in reverence, but a formality to an authority. This time, when they come before Joseph, their attitude will certainly be different, an attitude they should have had in the first place, when he was a son in the family.

God is interested in how we treat one another, and our first place to practice a right attitude is in the family. We need to be aware of the attitude we have toward God, our parents, our siblings, our spouse and our children, as well as our employer, neighbors, and co-workers. Yes, indeed, God is interested in our attitudes.

Not only is He interested in our attitudes, but He is also concerned about our motives as well. Examine your attitudes for a whole week and then determine how they measure up to God's standards. These brothers were jealous of Joseph. He grew up with that attitude day after day, and could do nothing about it. They did not honor God when they dishonored a member of their family either, now did they?

Neither did they honor their old father by being jealous of Joseph. In fact, Genesis 37:4 says *"They hated him and could not speak peaceably unto him."* All of that will come back to haunt them, and well it should. Let us not look down our noses at their behavior, though, but instead examine our own attitudes and motives in the light of God's Word.

PRAYER: Father, I ask you to show me the attitudes I have that displease you. Nudge me by your Holy Spirit so that I can correct myself, and not have to have it shown to me in such a dramatic ways as these brothers did. I know you want harmony in our family relationships, and strife does not please you at all. So, Lord, I ask you to point out to me what I do or say that causes disharmony, strife, and pain so I can make an adjustment in my behavior in your eyes. In Jesus' name, Amen.

MAY 17th

In Genesis 44:14-34, we read: *'And Judah and his brethren came to Joseph's house; for he was yet there: and they fell before him on the ground.* (This is far more than mere bowing, this is nearly groveling.) *And Joseph said unto them, 'What deed is this that ye have done? Know ye not that such a man as I can certainly divine?' And Judah said, 'What shall we say unto my lord? What shall we speak? Or how shall we clear ourselves? God hath found out the iniquity of thy servants: behold, we are my lord's servants, both we, and he also with whom the cup is found.' And he said, 'God forbid that I should do so: but the man in whose hand the cup is found, he shall be my servant; and as for you, get you up in peace unto your father.' Then Judah came near unto him, and said, 'Oh my lord, let thy servant, I pray thee, speak a word in my lord's ears, and let not thine anger burn against thy servant: for thou art even as Pharaoh. My Lord asked his servants, saying, "Have ye a father, or a brother?" And we said unto my lord, "We have a father, an old man, and a child of his old age, a little one; and his brother is dead, and he alone is left of his mother, and his father loveth him." And thou saidst unto thy servants, "Bring him down unto me, that I may set mine eyes upon him." And we said unto my lord, "The lad cannot leave his father: for if he should leave his father, his father would die." And thou saidst unto thy servants, "Except your youngest brother come down with you, ye shall see my face no more." And it came to pass when we came up unto thy servant my father, we told him the words of my lord. And our father said, "Go again, and buy us a little food." And we said, "We cannot go down: if our youngest brother be with us, then will we go down: for we may not see the man's face, except our youngest brother be with us." And thy servant my father said unto us, "Ye know that my wife bare me two sons: And the one went out from me and I said, 'Surely he is torn in pieces,' and I saw him not since. And if ye take this also from me, and mischief befall him, ye shall bring down my gray hairs with sorrow to the grave." Now therefore when I come to thy servant my father, and the lad be not with us; seeing that his life is bound up in the lad's life; It shall come to pass, when he seeth that the lad is not with us, that he will die: and thy servant shall bring down the gray hairs of thy servant our father with sorrow to the grave. For thy servant became surety for the lad unto my father, saying, "If I bring him not unto thee, then I shall bear the blame to my father forever." Now therefore, I pray thee, let thy servant abide instead of the lad a bondman to my lord: and let the lad go up with his brethren. For how shall I go up to my father, and the lad be not with me? Lest, peradventure, I see the evil that shall come on my father?' "*

It all finally came out, and the brothers (especially Judah, who was speaking for them all), were sorry for what they did to Joseph and their father. They did not want to see their father go through such grief again. Judah was willing to take Benjamin's place as a slave, and considering Judah had sons of his own, that was a pretty big bargain he was willing to strike.

God does not like hidden sins. He wants it all out in the open. God does not want to see anyone suffer, but rather He does want sins to be confessed, He wants us to repent and be forgiven. God has his eye on the forgiven part, and the process to that is to admit (confess), repent (be sorry for the sin with the attitude not to do it again), and then to receive forgiveness.

Jesus' death on the cross paid both the penalty and the price of sin, so God is able to freely forgive all of our sins. It is so simple for us, but Satan wants to cause our pride to be a barrier to that forgiveness. Our old nature does not want to bow down before God and simply ask for forgiveness. The choice is ours. Remember, it is a free choice, and we will be the winners, the victorious ones, if we will admit, repent, and ask for forgiveness. Try it. You will be glad you did.

PRAYER: Heaven Father, thank you for this lesson. The importance of confession is vividly displayed in the brother's confession. And who better to confess it to than Joseph? He was the one who needed to hear it after all those years. Help me to never let something eat away at me for a long time. Instead, help me to humble myself, admit my wrong, and seek your forgiveness, and the forgiveness of whoever else I have hurt. I want to live a victorious life, and to live in peace, your kind of peace. Thank you for making it possible for me to *"Let us therefore come boldly unto the throne of grace, that we may obtain mercy, and find grace to help in time of need"* (Hebrews 4:16). In Jesus' name, Amen.

MAY 18th

In Genesis 45:1-15, we read: *"Then Joseph could not refrain himself before all them that stood by him; and he cried, 'Cause every man to go out from me.' And there stood no man with him, while Joseph made himself known unto his brethren. And he wept aloud: and the Egyptians and the house of Pharaoh heard. And Joseph said unto his brethren, 'I am Joseph; doth my father yet live?' And his brethren could not answer him; for they were troubled at his presence. And Joseph said unto his brethren, 'Come near to me, I pray you.' And they came near. And he said, 'I am Joseph your brother, whom ye sold into Egypt. Now therefore be not grieved, nor angry with yourselves, that ye sold me hither, for God did send me before you to preserve life. For these two years hath the famine been in the land: and yet there are five years, in the which there shall neither be earing nor harvest. And God sent me before you to preserve you a posterity* (remnant) *in the earth, and to save your lives by a great deliverance. So now it was not you that sent me hither, but God: and he hath made me a father to Pharaoh, and lord of all his house, and a ruler throughout all the land of Egypt. Haste ye, and go up to my father, and say unto him, "Thus saith thy son Joseph, 'God hath made me lord of all Egypt: come down unto me, tarry not:'"* And thou shalt dwell in the land of Goshen, and thou shalt be near unto me, thou, and thy children, and thy children's children, and thy flocks, and thy herds, and all that thou hast. And there will I nourish thee; for yet there are five years of famine; lest thou, and thy household, and all that thou hast, come to poverty. And, behold, your eyes see, and the eyes of my brother Benjamin, that it is my mouth that speaketh unto you.* (He

179

was speaking to them in Hebrew.) *And ye shall tell my father of all my glory in Egypt, and of all that ye have seen; and ye shall haste and bring down my father hither.' And he fell upon his brother Benjamin's neck and wept; and Benjamin wept upon his neck. Moreover he kissed all his brethren, and wept upon them: and after that his brethren talked with him.* (They talked together in Hebrew, I might add. Before that Joseph talked through an interpreter to his brothers.)"

Only a person who is sold out to God would be able to not have a hint of revenge in his voice. Joseph is that kind of man. He immediately saw God's hand in the whole of his life, the bad and the good. Had he not been in jail and had not the butler and baker had a dream that he was able to interpret, he may never have become the ruler of all of Egypt.

Joseph was able to "see" God in every fine detail of his life. He also kept strong the his faith in the dream he had as a child about his brothers and father bowing down to him. When only ten brothers came to Egypt, he just knew this was not the time to reveal himself to them. There had to be eleven brothers, and they had to really, really want to bow down in complete obeisance, and with humility before him in order for it to be as it was portrayed in his dream.

We are not told about the prayer life Joseph had with God during these days, but I am sure that when his brothers came out of nowhere and entered Joseph's life, he knew in his spirit that God was at work, and all he had to do was walk in step with God's will for this very hour. Joseph did not disappoint his Heavenly Father, he did not display revenge, but instead he showed forgiveness, love, humbleness, and a look toward the future.

There was to be life, not death for his people. We need to look behind the scenes and see that the battle between God and Satan is going on all the time. They are battling over all who belong to God. These people were, and still are, God's chosen nation upon this earth, and the battle still rages. God will not lose this battle, even if it appears that He is losing. He preserved that nation back in the days of Joseph, and He will continue to do so. He will also watch over you and me with the same diligence, if we will just simply determine to walk in His ways and live to please Him.

PRAYER: Dear Lord God, it is so refreshing to see that it is possible to reign over our old nature that wants to keep score, fight back, make others pay for their evil, and become bitter toward you for my unhappiness. Help me to live like Joseph lived, to trust in you no matter what happens in my life. Help me to see that God means it for good, no matter how awful things become. If I can live that kind of a victorious overcoming life, then I believe I can find happiness on a new level. Thank you for showing me it is possible and it is available to us all. In Jesus' name, Amen.

MAY 19th

Genesis 45:16-28 reads: *"And the fame thereof was heard in Pharaoh's house, saying, Joseph's brethren are come: and it pleased Pharaoh well, and his servants. And Pharaoh said unto Joseph, 'Say unto thy brethren, this do ye: lade your beasts, and go, get you unto the land of Canaan; And take your father and your households, and come unto me: and I will give you the good of the land of Egypt, and ye shall eat the fat of the land. Now thou are commanded, this do ye; take you wagons out of the land of Egypt for your little ones, and for your wives, and bring your father, and come. Also regard not your stuff; for the good of all the land of Egypt is yours.' And the children of Israel did so: and Joseph gave them wagons, according to the commandment of Pharaoh, and gave them provisions for the way. To all of them he gave each man changes of raiment: but to Benjamin he gave three hundred pieces of silver, and five changes of raiment. And to his father he sent after this manner; ten asses laden with the good things of Egypt, and ten she asses laden with corn and bread and meat for his father by the way. So he sent his brethren away, and they departed: and he said unto them, 'See that ye fall not out by the way.' And they went up out of Egypt, and came into the land of Canaan unto Jacob their father. And told him, saying, 'Joseph is yet alive, and he is governor over all the land of Egypt.' And Jacob's heart fainted, for he believed them not. And they told him all the words of Joseph, which he had said unto them: and*

181

when he saw the wagons which Joseph had sent to carry him, the spirit of Jacob their father revived: And Israel said, 'It is enough; Joseph my son is yet alive: I will go and see him before I die.' "

There are many things that need to be explained in these verses, and made clear so that you can learn to understand what you read in the Bible. First of all, Joseph felt it was necessary to tell his brothers to behave themselves on the way home. He said, *"See that ye fall not out by the way."* That meant that Joseph knew his brothers through and through. There was great jealousy between them. That often happens in large families. It was jealousy that was at the root of the trouble that sent Joseph away to Egypt in the first place.

No doubt in just watching the goings on between the brothers, Joseph could see that the jealousy was still there. So Joseph made sure that they knew that he knew just how awful they could treat Benjamin on the way home, and Benjamin was old enough to tell Joseph all about it if he was questioned upon their return to Egypt. These brothers need to be aware that they were under Joseph's thumb from now on in. It was either that or die of famine. Joseph did not scold them, he just let them know he was well aware of their evil past.

Another thing we want to look at is the fact that the brothers now have to reveal the truth to their father. They had to explain the evil plan they had devised for Joseph, how they lied to their father and let him think Joseph was dead all those years. What would their father think about them? This will be a hard thing to weather for all of them. Trust is broken, shattered. Joseph will have an even greater place in their father's life. Can these jealous brothers take that without making a strain on the family?

The last thing I want to point out is that their father is called Jacob in verse 27, and Israel in verse 28. Remember, in his early life, God changed his name from Jacob to Israel, as we see in Genesis 32:28, *"Thy name shall be called no more Jacob, but Israel: for as a prince hast thou power with God and with men, and hast prevailed."* After that, when God uses the name Jacob, he is talking about the man (the humanness of man), and when God uses the name Israel, He is talking about the man who is to carry out the promise given to Abraham and passed on to his son, Isaac, and on to his son, Jacob, the spiritual man.

So, in verse 28, when it says, *"And <u>Israel</u> said, 'It is enough; Joseph my son is yet alive: I will go and see him before I die,'* it draws our attention to the spiritual aspect of the situation and to think in terms of God's will being accomplished. God had told Abraham that his descendants would be in a strange land for 400 years, and then would come out with great substance and go to a land of promise. Here, God is beginning to get those descendants into the land of Egypt, and God is right on schedule. *Israel* (not the man, Jacob) is a part of that plan.

PRAYER: Lord God, I know you have a plan for my life, also, and I pray that I may be in your perfect schedule. I know with my head that you do all things perfect and right, but sometimes, Lord, my heart gets in the way and throws up barriers to what I know your Word says. So, I pray that my heart will also know what my mind knows about your words of promise and assurance, assurance that my prayers are all heard and answered by you, and that you and I can have an intimate relationship on a daily basis. When I feel far away from you, remind me that you promised to never leave me or forsake me, and that the Holy Spirit is praying for me also. Help me remember Romans 8:26-27, which reads, *"Likewise the Spirit also helpeth our infirmaties: for we know not what we should pray for as we ought: but the Spirit himself maketh intercession for the saints* (that's us, folks), *with groanings which cannot be uttered. And He that searcheth the hearts knoweth what is the mind of the Spirit, because He maketh intercession for the saints according to the will of God."* Thank you too, Lord, for the work of the Holy Spirit in my life. In Jesus' name, Amen.

MAY 20th

 Genesis 46:1-7states: *"And Israel took his journey with all that he had, and came to Beersheba, and offered sacrifices unto the God of his father Isaac. And God spake unto Israel in the*

183

visions of the night, and said, 'Jacob, Jacob.' And he said, 'Here am I.'
And He said, 'I am God, the God of thy father: fear not to go down into
Egypt; for I will there make of thee a great nation: I will go down with
thee into Egypt, and I will also surely bring thee up again: and Joseph
shall put his hand upon thine eyes.' And Jacob rose up from Beersheba:
and the sons of Israel carried Jacob their father, and their little ones, and
their wives, in the wagons which Pharaoh had sent to carry him. And
they took their cattle, and their goods, which they had gotten in the land
of Canaan, and came into Egypt, Jacob, and all his seed with him: His
son's and his sons' sons with him, his daughters, and his sons' daughters,
and all his seed brought he with him into Egypt."

Verses 46:8-25 describes their genealogy, their family tree so to
speak, but we will skip over that to Genesis 46:26-27, which reads: *"All*
the souls that came with Jacob into Egypt, which came out of his loins,
besides Jacob's sons' wives, all the souls were threescore and six (66).
And the sons of Joseph, which were born him in Egypt, were two souls:
all the souls of the house of Jacob which came into Egypt were threescore
and ten (70). *"*

God's promise to Abraham was to make of him a great nation,
give him a huge and fruitful land, and bring into the world through him a
great blessing. With that, anyone who blessed Abraham, or sat under the
blessing God brought into being through him, would be blessed, and anyone
who cursed him or the blessing would be cursed. That was a powerful
promise and God does not break promises.

Right here, as we watch Jacob move with all his family and
substance into Egypt, we see a part of the fulfillment of that promise. In
verse 3 God told Jacob, *"Fear not to go down into Egypt for I will there*
make of thee a great nation," God does not explain the *how* or *why* of his
plans. He expects us to trust Him enough to not ask, but instead to just
follow His instructions. God did not tell Abraham, nor Isaac, nor Jacob,
how they would get into Egypt. Neither did God explain how they would
be brought out again, but Jacob knew enough, as he was the one traveling
toward Egypt with all his family and substance, that surely if God can

accomplish that, then Jacob could trust that kind of God to also bring them back out.

If God has called you to do something for Him, then God can surely accomplish it, all you need to do is obey His directions. Jacob is in the process of obeying God's directions. Jacob did not plan them, and he did not even have to provide the substance to carry it out. He was traveling in the wagons that Pharaoh had provided.

I could also go into another direction here and point out that Egypt was a land of false gods. The Egyptians did not know the God of Abraham, Isaac, and Jacob, so Jacob's trip to Egypt is like Adam taking the whole world into sin, into a foreign, God-less place. However, God has a special place prepared for this family in the land of Goshen separated from the Egyptian lifestyle and culture.

Just as we are a part of the world and its system, we cannot escape the fact that we are *in* the world but not *of* it. In John 17:11and 14, Jesus prays before He is crucified: *"And now I am no more in the world, but these are in the world, and I come to thee. Holy Father, keep through thine own name those whom thou hast given me, that they may be one, as we are. I have given them thy word; and the world hath hated them, because they are not of the world, even as I am not of the world."*

Yes, indeed, we are not *of* the world, but we are definitely *in* the world. So, too, it will be with Jacob (Israel) and his whole family. They will be *in* Egypt, but they will not be *of* Egypt. God also promised Jacob that Joseph would be with him when he died to close his eyes.

PRAYER: Heavenly Father, just as you are the God of Abraham and all his descendants, and you are the God and Father of my Lord Jesus Christ, you are my God and Father also. Help me, Lord, to truly grasp the gravity, the depth, of this truth. You knew me before the world was made, your Word says, and you had a plan for my life. You have nothing but good in mind for me. How, then, can I fret or be anxious? That old nature of mine wants to rule, to fret and be anxious. So, Father, I deny that old nature of mine the right and privilege to rule over me, and I choose to have calm and rest in the midst of stress and confusion the world throws at me. Thank you, Lord, for providing me with a reason to have peace, rest, and calm in my life. In Jesus' name, Amen.

MAY 21ˢᵗ

As we look at today's verses, notice the use of the name "Jacob" compared to "Israel." Remember, Jacob is a picture of the old natures, the sinful side of us, and Israel is a picture of the new nature, the spiritual side of us. Now, turn to Genesis 46:28-34, which states: *"And he* (Jacob) *sent Judah before him unto Joseph, to direct his face unto Goshen; and they came into the land of Goshen. And Joseph made ready his chariot, and went up to meet Israel his father to Goshen, and present himself unto him; and he fell on his neck, and wept on his neck a good while. And Israel said unto Joseph, 'Now let me die, since I have seen thy face, because thou are yet alive.' And Joseph said unto his brethren, and unto his father's house, 'I will go up, and show Pharaoh, and say unto him, "My brethren, and my father's house, which were in the land of Canaan, are come unto me. And the men are shepherds, for their trade hath been to feed cattle; and they have brought their flocks, and their herds, and all that they have." And it shall come to pass, when Pharaoh shall call you, and shall say, "What is your occupation?" That you shall say, "Thy servants' trade hath been about cattle from our youth even until now, both we, and also our fathers," that ye may dwell in the land of Goshen; for every shepherd is an abomination unto the Egyptians.' "*

Now that Jacob had seen Joseph he could die in peace. But death is not in our hands, it is in God's hands. As Ecclesiastes 3:2 states, *"There is a time to be born and a time to die."* After all these years, Joseph finally was able to embrace his old father and weep for joy! God has done something great here, and in grand style.

Just look for a moment at how Satan's plans had been shattered. He wanted Joseph and his dreams put to death, but God had other, more noble plans. Satan wanted Joseph to become bitter and vengeful, but, again, God had other plans. Satan wanted Joseph to die in jail, but God's plan was for Joseph to interpret and believe in dreams. Satan wanted to kill many people with a famine, but God's plans prevented that from happening. Satan wanted to keep Joseph's family out of Egypt, as had been foretold to Abraham, but God had other plans.

Satan is not done yet, but neither is God. On whose side would you choose to be? I believe the whole Bible is a story of the struggle between God and Satan, and the objects of that struggle are the people God loves unconditionally, that includes you and me. Have you ever asked God to open your eyes to the ways that Satan is trying to trip you up, how he tries to make your life miserable and make you believe God is not there for you. That is when you need to *know* beyond a shadow of a doubt that God is working doubly hard to give you strength and knowledge to know He is right there beside you, to help you stand firm against Satan's attacks against you.

Please notice what God's Word says in Romans 8:31, *"What shall we then say to these things? If God be for us, who can be against us?"* All through the Bible, you see how much God is on your side, wanting, hoping and, yes, praying (the Holy Spirit prays for you, remember), that you will choose to walk in God's ways, study His word, learn from His Word and live according to His Word. You bet, God is for you, so then, who would even dare to be against you?

Satan will not give up so easily, though. He is banking on the fact that your old nature just might cave in and listen to him. We need to make the decision that Satan will not have his way in our lives, and if, by chance, we stumble and fall, we have a Savior who is willing and able to forgive us, because He already paid the price and penalty of sin.

PRAYER: Dear Heavenly Father, my view of you as "my heavenly father" is growing by leaps and bounds, and I find myself learning to trust you more and more. Today I almost feel like I have on my boxing gloves and sleeves rolled up, ready to fight the good fight of faith. I Timothy 6:12 says, *"Fight the good fight of faith; lay hold of the eternal life to which you were summoned, and confessed the good confession of faith before* *many witnesses.*" And in II Timothy 4:7-8, Paul goes on to say more about our Christian life, *"I have fought a good fight, I have finished my course, I have kept the faith. Henceforrth there is laid up for me a crown of righteousness, which the Lord, the righteous judge, shall give me at that day: and not to me only, but unto all them also that love His appearing."* There is a battle going on in the spiritual world over you and me. In order for us to be victorious in that battle, we need to join hands with God the Father, Son, and Holy Spirit, the Trinity, to fight along side of us. So, Lord, please help me to apply these verses when the battle of faith gets heated. In Jesus' name, Amen.

MAY 22nd

Genesis 47:1-6 reads: *"Then Joseph came and told Pharaoh, and said, 'My father and my brethren, and their flocks, and their herds, and all that they have, are come out of the land of Canaan; and, behold, they are in the land of Goshen.' And he took some of his brethren, even five men, and presented them unto Pharaoh. And Pharaoh said unto his brethren, 'What is your occupation?' And they said unto Pharaoh, 'Thy servants are shepherds, both we and also our fathers.' They said moreover unto Pharaoh, 'For to sojourn in the land are we come; for thy servants have no pasture for their flocks; for the famine is sore in the land of Canaan: now therefore, we pray thee, let thy servants dwell in the land of Goshen.' And Pharaoh spake unto Joseph, saying, 'Thy father and thy brethren are come unto thee: The land of Egypt is before thee; in the best of the land make thy father and brethren to dwell: in the land of Goshen let them dwell: and if thou knowest any men of activity among them, then make them rulers over my cattle.' "*

Joseph presented his brethren to Pharaoh, just like Jesus presents us to the Heavenly Father. Joseph was not ashamed to identify with the shepherds who were an abomination to the Egyptians. So also is Jesus willing to identify with sinners, even though sin is an abomination to God.

When God sent His only Son, who was sinless, pure, holy, and undefiled in any way, into this earth that was like a sewer of sin from one end to the other, Jesus came willingly. He came to do the will of His

Father, which was to save us from our sin and its penalty. That work was done nearly 2,000 years ago, and if you do not want the salvation Jesus offers, that is up to you. But, please, do not criticize those of us who do want it and know that we need it.

Humble Joseph also presented his aged father to Pharaoh, and made it perfectly clear that they would be in the land of Goshen, and what Pharaoh may not have known was the fact that God wanted His people separated from Pharaoh's people just as much, if not more so, than they did. There is more going on than we can see at this point, and I will clue you in on that. Later, when Moses is called to bring these people out, and God uses ten plagues to accomplish that, not one plague touched the land of Goshen. Only the land of Egypt suffered from the plagues. You see, God knows the end from the beginning, and He knows what is in your future, every fine detail of what is in store for you.

As you learn these truths you begin to know right off that what is happening in your life is a good thing, even though every outward sign would say it is evil, not fair, horrible, or sad. God is *good*, He is *righteous*, and He is *full of love and kindness* towards His creation, man and woman. Romans 5:8 reads, ***"But God commanded His love toward us, in that, while we were yet sinners, Christ died for us."*** Please get a good hold on what is said in this verse. God told His own *love*, "You better do something for these poor wretched sinners while doing is good, or they will all be lost." God actually commanded His love to obey Him.

He did not ask us to clean ourselves up first, so then Jesus would come and die for us. After learning this truth, how can you ever doubt God's intense love for you ever again? God is looking down the road 400 years to the day when the Egyptians would actually want the descendants of Abraham to leave Egypt. They were the slave labor of that day and they numbered in the millions then, but God had a plan, a long-range plan and they were to live in Goshen.

PRAYER: Lord God Almighty, how can I adequately praise you for your love, mercy, and grace, which you shower on me unconditionally day after day? My simple "thank you" seems so small. How can it cover all that you are, and all you do for me? Please hear my heart cry out to you. I am so grateful for what you have planned and carried out on my behalf. To think that you planned for me to fellowship with you in heaven for eternity, and that Jesus carried it out so that I should have no problem enjoying and receiving that blessing of truth is almost more than my mind can comprehend. I offer to you my grateful thanks. In Jesus' name, Amen.

MAY 23rd

Genesis 47:7-12 states: *"And Joseph brought in Jacob his father and set him before Pharaoh: and Jacob blessed Pharaoh. And Pharaoh said unto Jacob, 'How old art thou?' And Jacob said unto Pharaoh, 'The days of the years of my pilgrimage* (sojournings) *are one hundred and thirty years: few and evil have the days of the years of my life been and have not attained unto the days of the years of the life of my fathers in the days of their pilgrimage.' And Jacob blessed Pharaoh, and went out from Pharaoh. And Joseph placed his father and his brethren, and gave them a possession in the land of Egypt, in the best of the land, in the land of Rameses* (one of the cities in Goshen), *as Pharaoh had commanded. And Joseph nourished his father, and his brethren, and all his father's household, with bread, according to their families."*

And in Genesis 47:23-26, we read: *"Then Joseph said unto the people, 'Behold, I have bought you this day and your land for Pharaoh: lo, here is seed for you, and ye shall sow the land. And it shall come to pass in the increase, that ye shall give the fifth part unto Pharaoh, and four parts shall be your own, for seed of the field, and for your food. And for them of your households, and for food for your little ones.' And they said, 'Thou hast saved our lives: let us find grace in the sight of my lord, and we will be Pharaoh's servants.' And Joseph made it a law over the land of Egypt unto this day, that Pharaoh should have a fifth part; except the land of the priests only, which became not Pharaoh's."*

190

Joseph was a true servant. He watched out for his master, the Pharaoh, and for his master's subjects. Joseph had bought his family for Pharaoh it says, and that meant they were slaves for Pharaoh. Goshen was located in the northeastern part of the Nile delta, and was not valued as highly by the Egyptians as the land along the Nile itself, but it was a very rich land for Israel and their herds and flocks. God was protecting His people from the Egyptians, just as He wants us protected from the evils of the world around us.

Jesus is our protection. This is not to say that bad things never happen to the people of God, but God is always there in the midst of the bad things, and He will help us to get through our bad times. Israel will grow up into a big nation, with many flocks and herds during their time in Egypt. I found it very interesting that Jacob blessed Pharaoh, but it is not surprising either. Pharaoh had given Israel quite a gift of life, all because of Joseph.

Do not lose sight of the fact that God had given Pharaoh the dream about the years of plenty and the years of famine, nor that God had given Joseph the gift of interpreting dreams. God is always in charge, and the sooner we see that truth, the easier it will be for us to live through both good times and bad. One verse that fits well here is Romans 8:28, which reads, *"And we know that all things work together for good to them that love God, to them who are the called according to His purpose."* Also look at I Thessalonians 5:18, which states, *"In everything give thanks: for this is the will of God in Christ Jesus concerning you."*

If we really know and act like we believe that God is always for us, and He has only good in mind for us, then we will know that all things work together for good for us. When we know that, we will be able to say, "Thank you, Lord," for everything that happens in our lives, even if it looks bad at the time. God can bring good out of it. God was prepared to bless all the people of Israel in Egypt, and bless them He did!

PRAYER Dear Father, I can see that I need to adjust my attitude toward those things in my life that would appear bad, and I also know that I will need help in adjusting my attitude. Fill me with your Holy Spirit so that I am able to say, "Thank you," when I don't feel like it. Help me to put my feelings aside and to obey your Word instead. In Jesus' name, Amen.

MAY 24th

Genesis 47:27-31 states: *"And Israel dwelt in the land of Egypt, in the country of Goshen; and they had possessions therein, and grew, and multiplied exceedingly. And Jacob lived in the land of Egypt seventeen years: so the whole age of Jacob was a hundred forty and seven years. And the time drew nigh that Israel must die: and he called his son Joseph, and said unto him, 'If now I have found grace in thy sight, put, I pray thee, thy hand under my thigh, and deal kindly and truly with me; bury me not, I pray thee, in Egypt: But I will lie with my fathers, and thou shalt carry me out of Egypt, and bury me in their burying place.' And he said, 'I will do as thou hast said.' And he said, 'Swear unto me.' And he swore unto him. And Israel bowed himself upon the bed's head."*

Remember that in Genesis 46:4 God said, *"I will go down with thee* (Jacob) *into Egypt, and I will also surely bring thee up again: and Joseph shall put his hand upon thine eyes."* God keeps every promise He ever makes. Jacob knew that one day his people would go back to Canaan, where they came from, and he also knew that Joseph would be with him when he died, Joseph would put his hands upon his eyes and close them in death. Jacob knew death was close at hand, and he did not want to be buried in Egypt with his ancestors buried back in Canaan. So, he made Joseph swear he would see to it that he would be buried with his fathers. I also hope you are watching the places where the names Jacob and Israel are being used. When God says, "I will," then you can be sure He will.

PRAYER: Heavenly Father, there are many "I wills" in the Bible, and I know that you will carry out every one of them. I am also reminded of John 3:16, which reads, *"For God so loved the world, that He gave His only* *begotten Son, that whosoever believeth in Him should not perish, but have everlasting life."* I also lay hold of that promise, and claim it as though it was made for me, and me alone. I have heard it said that if I were the only one living when you died, Lord Jesus, that you would have died for just me. That gives me the right to claim that verse for myself, and lay my trust in its truth. I give you thanks for what you have done for me, something I could not have done for myself, no matter how hard I tried. What a gift! In Jesus' name, Amen.

MAY 25th

We are going to pass over chapter 48 and much of 49 that record the blessings Jacob gave to Joseph's two sons, who were born in Egypt, but were now included in the genealogy and inheritance of Israel, and we will pick up the story as Jacob is about to die. Genesis 49:28-33 explains: *All these are the twelve tribes of Israel: and this is it that their father spake unto them, and blessed them: every one according to his blessing he blessed them. And he charged them, and said unto them, 'I am to be gathered unto my people: bury me with my fathers in the cave that is in the field of Ephron the Hittite, in the cave that is in the field of Machpelah, which is before Mamre, in the land of Canaan, which Abraham bought with the field of Ephron the Hittite for a possession of a burying place. There they buried Abraham and Sarah his wife; there they buried Isaac and Rebekah his wife; and there I buried Leah.' The purchase of the field and of the cave that is therein was from the children of Heth. And when Jacob had made an end of commanding his sons, he gathered up his feet into the bed, and yielded up the ghost, and was gathered unto his people."*

I have often thought that the people of faith in the Old Testament had a better outlook on death than we of the New Testament. And it should be just the opposite, because Jesus came and tasted death for all of us who believe in Him, and, of all people, we should have the most positive outlook. Notice that it says that Jacob *"yielded up the ghost"* and "*was*

193

gathered unto his people. " The emphasis is on the reunion on the other side of the grave. If we would have that attitude, looking forward to the reunion over there, we would not be so sorrowful.

I also want to say a few words about the blessing. Parents need to bless their children, and to let them know that they are being blessed. Jacob blessed each one of his sons, and the two sons of Joseph. God blesses us too, and we can be a blessing to God. Let your children know you are proud of them. Give them a compliment often. That is a blessing. Tell them you recognize their potential, the potential God put into them when He created them. Those things will bless your children. And if you think it is too late to do that, remember, Jacob was 147 years old. Imagine how old his sons were when he blessed them. They were still his children. We never stop being parents, so bless your kids, no matter how old they are.

PRAYER: Heavenly Father, I know I need to bless my children, but I don't even know how to do that! I am grateful for each one of them, for their potential that I am able to see, but how do I get them to see their potential? Guide me with your Holy Spirit. Give me the eyes to see and the insights I need to be the parent I should be to my children. I know my own example is very important for them to learn to follow you, and I pray that is a blessing to them. Can I share the hope for their future that I have for them? Will that be a blessing in your eyes? My hope for them is that they will get to know you on a personal level, and want to obey and follow you, closer and closer each day. I know they have the ability to do that. Open a door for me to share that with them. You plan the opportunity, prepare their hearts to hear those words from me, and then give me the insight to know that is the right timing. In Jesus' name, Amen.

MAY 26th

 Genesis 50:1-6 reads: *And Joseph fell upon his father's face, and wept upon him, and kissed him. And Joseph commanded his servants the physicians to embalm his father: and the*

194

physicians embalmed Israel. And forty days were fulfilled for him; for so are fulfilled the days of those which are embalmed: and the Egyptians mourned for him threescore and ten days (70 days). *And when the days of his mourning were past, Joseph spake unto the house of Pharaoh, saying, 'If now I have found grace in your eyes, speak I pray you, in the ears of Pharaoh, saying, "My father made me swear, saying, 'Lo, I die: in my grave which I have digged for me in the land of Canaan, there shalt thou bury me.' " Now therefore let me go up, I pray thee, and bury my father, and I will come again.' And Pharaoh said, 'Go up and bury thy father, according as he made thee swear.' "*

Joseph had a very high position in Egypt, but not so high that he could just leave and bury his father in Canaan. He needed the Pharaoh's permission to do that. Joseph was a man who knew his place, and he was not so proud that he could not stoop to ask permission from Pharaoh at this time of mourning. Also notice that Egypt mourned his father for 70 days!

It is also interesting that Jacob was embalmed, like the mummies we see today. He would be buried with Abraham, Sarah, Isaac, Rebecca, and Leah, and with Jacob there will be six bodies in that cave, one of which was embalmed. I have often wondered if anyone has tried to find a burial mound or cave with five bodies that are not mummified and one that is. It would be sure proof of whose bodies they were, would it not? There are times when God leaves foot prints that big on the face of the earth.

Joseph promised Pharaoh he would come back again. This is important because the people of Israel were the slave labor of that land. Keep in mind this is not their homeland, and they know that some day they will leave it for Canaan. But Joseph put those fears to rest by saying he would "come again." Joseph was an honest, truthful, trusted man, and Pharaoh knew that, so he simply said, *"Go up and bury thy father according as he made thee swear."*

PRAYER: Heavenly Father, Joseph is such a faithful son to his father, a real picture of what you, God, want to see from me. Help me, Lord, to want to be a trusting faithful child of yours. In Jesus' name, Amen.

MAY 27th

Genesis 50:7-13 states: *And Joseph went up to bury his father: and with him went up all the servants of Pharaoh, the elders of his house,, and all the elders of the land of Egypt, And all the house of Joseph, and his brethren, and his father's house. Only their little ones, and their flocks, and their herds, they left in the land of Goshen. And there went up with him both chariots and horsemen: and it was a very great company. And they came to the threshing floor of Atad, which is beyond Jordan, and there they mourned with a great and very sore lamentation: and he made a mourning for his father seven days. And when the inhabitants of the land, the Canaaites, saw the mourning in the floor of Atad, they said, 'This is a grievous mourning to the Egyptians: wherefore the name of it was called Abelmizraim, which is beyond Jordan. And his sons did unto him according as he commanded them: For his sons carried him into the land of Canaan, and buried him in the cave of the field of Machpelah, which Abraham bought with the field for a possession of a burying place of Ephron the Hittite, before Mamre."*

It was a long distance to travel to bring Jacob back to that burial place, and they must have been quite a scene upon the landscape. Many Egyptians, all of Pharaoh's house, the elders of his house, and of Egypt as well, plus all the sons of Jacob were there. The only ones left in Egypt were the children and their flocks and herds. Leaving those behind in Egypt was insurance that the fathers would come back. It does not say anything about the wives. They may have been left to tend to the little ones. It may not have been considered a woman's place to travel with the men for that distance. The Bible does not shed any light on this, but we can imagine the large company of people, with chariots and horses and horsemen.

They mourned another seven days. I wonder what they did as mourners. Whatever they did, it drew the attention of the curious inhabitants of the land who renamed the place after such lamentations. But, the job had to be done right, and it was.

196

I have wondered whether the sons of Jacob did his will to the letter when he died because they wanted to or because Joseph was in charge. One thing I do know is that God knows the hearts of men and He will judge according to the motives of our hearts.

In (Amplified) I Corinthians 4:5, we read, *"So do not make any hasty or premature judgments before the time when the Lord comes* (again), *for He will both bring to light the secret things that are in darkness* (now hidden), *and disclose and expose the aims* (secret motives and purposes) *of hearts. Then every man will receive his commendation* (due) *from God."*
This is not necessarily a bad thing, because the end result is to receive a commendation, which is a good thing. But for those who harbor evil intentions in their hearts, it may not be so good. Check on the motives of your heart often. Satan likes to creep in unaware, and he is good at that. So give your heart notice that you are watching what its intentions and motives are.

PRAYER: Dear Lord Jesus, your motives were always in line with the will of God, and everything you did, you did for our benefit. Forgive me for being so lazy in watching my motives. Prick my heart when I begin to harbor wrong motives in my heart. Joseph is such a strong example of this, and if he can do it, then so can I. I want to come through this walk of life with the right motives in all that I do and think. In Jesus' mighty name, Amen.

MAY 28th

Genesis 50:14-21 reads: *"And Joseph returned unto Egypt, he, and his brethren, and all that went up with him to bury his father, after he had buried his father. And when Joseph's brethren saw that their father was dead, they said, 'Joseph will peradventure hate us, and will certainly requite us all the evil which we did unto him,' and they sent a messenger unto Joseph, saying, 'Thy father did command before he died, saying. "So shall ye say unto Joseph, 'Forgive, I pray thee now, the trespass of thy brethren, and their sin; for they did unto thee evil:' " and now, we pray thee, forgive the trespass of the servants of the God of thy father.' And Joseph wept when they spake unto him. And his brethren also went and fell down before his face; and they said, 'Behold, we be thy servants.' "*

Not until after their father died did Joseph's brothers ask him to forgive them, or even acknowledge before him that they had done him wrong. I wonder if they had felt a bit safe while their father was living, but now that their father was dead, Joseph was the master in the land, and they were under his authority, things could be different. They are still thinking in an "eye for an eye" attitude, but Joseph did not think like they did. Joseph was in tune to God's way of thinking, as he had been all his life.

And guess what? That is the way God wants us to think also, in terms of forgiveness and love rather than hatred and holding grudges. Just think about it for a minute. God does not hold grudges, and He has patience toward us. However, if we do not ever repent, then God's wrath will be upon us. But He will wait and wait for us to turn away from what is evil, and encourage us to lay hold of what is right and true.

God is not pleased with bitterness, jealousy, nitpicking and back stabbing. These things may not look or seem all that big, but they are symptoms of a bigger problem. They are symptoms of dissatisfaction in life, unhappiness with life's circumstances. Basically, that is pointing a finger at God and, in a back handed way, telling Him it is all His fault. Remember how Adam and Eve pointed the finger when they were exposed by God to the awful sin they committed? It was not their fault at all, they thought. Someone else was to blame.

When we complain, and become jealous and unhappy over our circumstances, it is God we are really blaming. "Why me, Lord? Why me?" Well, why not you? You believe in Jesus as Savior, who will never leave you or forsake you! You are assured that God will never give you more to bear than you can handle, and will provide a way of escape if it gets too tough! God's riches in glory are available to you, all you have to do is apply them.

198

What do you have to complain about? These things were the brother's problems, but not Joseph. He had made the best of a bad situation, and came out the winner. The brother's could have done that themselves. Instead, they had hung onto their lie. Had they ever told their father what they did to Joseph? The Bible does not address that, but I, for one, doubt that they did, or why would they send such a message to Joseph, putting words in their dead father's mouth? We will look at Joseph's response tomorrow.

PRAYER: Dear Lord God, I look at my life and realize how much more I need to learn about taking control of my feelings, and not allowing them to get between you and me. I want to have a life that reflects your kindness, love, and mercy, and not reflect the seedy side of my unbridled fleshly desires. I ask for your Holy Spirit to come into my heart and take control, be my guide and strength to live in tune with the Spirit of God and have fruit of the Spirit to prove it. In Jesus' name, Amen.

MAY 29th

Genesis 50:19-21 states: *"And Joseph said unto them, 'Fear not: for am I in the place of God? But as for you, ye thought evil against me: but God meant it unto good, to bring to pass, as it is this day, to save much people alive. Now therefore fear ye not: I will nourish you, and your little ones.' And he comforted them, and spake kindly unto them."*

Everything that Joseph said is a reflection of God's mercy and grace. Let us look at it bit by bit. The first thing out of Joseph's mouth is "fear not!" Think about it. That is what the angels said in Luke 2:10 to the shepherds when Jesus was born, *"And the angel said unto them, 'Fear not: for, behold, I bring you good tidings of great joy, which shall be to all people.' "*

And isn't that what the angel said to Mary at Christ's empty tomb? Mark 16:5-6 says,

"And entering into the sepulcher, they saw a young man sitting on the right side, clothed in a long white garment; and they were affrighted. And he saith unto them, 'Be not affrighted: Ye seek Jesus of Nazareth, which was crucified: He is risen; He is not here: behold the place where they laid Him." I have read that there are 365 "fear nots" in the Bible, one for every day of the year. The many "fear nots" are meant for us in our time of being afraid, too.

These are the words Joseph spoke to his brothers. He also assured them of having provisions for their families, which included a place to live, a way to make a living, contentment, and happiness. He comforted them. Jesus promised us a "comforter," the Holy Spirit, to comfort us, as well. John 14:16-17 reads, *"And I will pray the Father, and He shall give you another Comforter, that He may abide with you forever; Even the Spirit of truth, whom the world cannot receive, because it seeth Him not, neither knoweth Him: but ye know Him; for He dwelleth with you, and shall be in you."*

Today we have the Holy Spirit who dwells in us to help us live the life God wants us to live, and be the "over comer" in this evil world. Joseph gave that promise to his brothers who had been so hateful toward him. If Joseph can do that, how much more should we be able to do that, since we have the Comforter right out of Heaven to dwell in us and help us be like Joseph in every circumstance? Is it any wonder that Joseph said to his brothers, *"As for you, you thought evil against me: but God meant it unto good, to bring to pass, as it is this day, to save many people alive."*

Joseph did not dwell on what his brothers had done to him. He had his eyes set on God, and His will in his life. He saw everything through God's eyes. That is how we can be winners too, no matter what the circumstance. If we can see that God is in charge of our lives, we will have the battle practically won. I would like to say 100% won, but we do have an old nature who is in hot pursuit to pull us down, and every now and again Satan will find us like a ripe grape ready for picking. It is when we fall or fail to see the devil coming that we need God to pick us up, dust us off, give us a pat on the back and send us on our way.

200

I want you to see, too, that the Holy Spirit is with you to stay. He was given forever, so we do not need to fear. Joseph's brothers did not need to fear either. What comfort that must have been to them.

Also look at what Joseph saw. God had used him to literally save many people from starvation. As he was overseer of all the corn and grain (which fed not only people, but the cows that gave milk, and sheep who gave wool for clothing and meat for food, as well), Joseph was able to see, first hand, the magnitude of what God had done through Pharaoh's dream and Joseph's ability to interpret it. Yes, indeed, it had saved many people, including his own family from Canaan.

PRAYER: Heavenly Father, it is amazing to see the long-reaching effect of the obedience of one person who determines to follow you. And you have created each one of us with the same ability to follow you. That is an awesome thought, but it is also a frightening thought. Yet you say, "Fear not!" How do I follow you like Joseph did? How do I hear from you so I know I am following you? Give me a heart that is open to your bidding, and ears that are sensitive to your voice, so that I will be able to hear and respond like Joseph did. Also help me to starve my old nature so that it cannot rule in my heart. Help me to say "yes" to you and "no" to the flesh that cries out to be satisfied. In Jesus' mighty name, Amen.

May 30th

Genesis 50:22-26 reads: *"And Joseph dwelt in Egypt, he, and his father's house: and Joseph lived a hundred and ten years. And Joseph saw Ephraim's children of the third generation: the children also of Machir the son of Manasseh were brought up upon Joseph's knees. And Joseph said unto his brethren, 'I die: and God will surely visit you, and bring you out of this land unto the land which he swore to Abraham, to Isaac, and to Jacob.' And Joseph took an oath of the children of Israel, saying, 'God will surely visit you, and ye shall carry up my bones from hence.' So Joseph died, being a hundred and ten years old: and they embalmed him, and he was put in a coffin in Egypt."*

So ends the life of Joseph at 110 years of age. He had seen his posterity to the third generation. What a blessing for a man who had been sold into Egypt, hated by his brothers, framed and jailed unjustly, forgotten in jail, and then lifted up to the highest position in a strange land (next to Pharaoh). He had one more longing and request, that his dead body would be taken out of Egypt to that land that had been promised to Abraham, Isaac, and Jacob. Joseph was just sure that they would be taken out of Egypt after he appointed time. He believed the words of his God to his fathers Abraham, Isaac, and Jacob. It had been told to each one of them (that was three times) that they would one day be in that land of promise, flowing with milk and honey.

Joseph was so sure of God's promise that he charged those who were still alive to take his body with them and bury him in Canaan when that appointed time came. That showed more then anything else the depth of his faith in the God of his fathers.

What kind of a relationship do you have with God, the God and Father of our Lord Jesus Christ? We have more reason for strong faith than Joseph had, because we know the account of the life of God's own Son, Jesus Christ, the Messiah, how He came in obedience to His Father, to give His life as a sacrifice for our sins, and rose again on the third day to give us resurrection power to live a life of victory in the midst of a world of evil that is at work to tempt us to stray away from our loving God. Learn lessons of obedience, faithfulness, forgiveness, and restoration from the life of Joseph. Thank your God for a Bible that tells it like it is, so we can learn such lessons.

PRAYER: Lord God Almighty, I do, indeed, thank you for this Book we call our Bible. I thank you for the faithful men who wrote what you told them to write, for the records of those faithful men and women who followed you through thick and thin and did not stop when the going got tough. It helps me to take courage in thinking, "If they can do it, then perhaps so can I." Our lives are so brief on this earth, and eternity is forever. Help me to remember that what I do today may affect my eternal life as well. Jesus surely told us that we would live and be where He is, and we know He is in Paradise, so that is where we are heading also. I want to hear your words,

*"Well done thou good and faithful servant: thou hast been faithful over a few things, I will make thee ruler over many things: enter into the joy of thy Lord" (*Matthew 25:21).

MAY 31st

I believe we have one small detail to look at before wrapping up the account of Joseph. Turn to Exodus 13:19, which states,

"And Moses took the bones of Joseph with him: for he (Joseph) *had straightly sworn the children of Israel, saying, 'God will surely visit you: and ye shall carry up my bones away hence with you."*

Do you recall how long God had told Abraham that the people would be in a strange land? It was 400 years, or four generations. Joseph had told his brothers to take his bones with them when they went out, but that was spoken to the first generation! Just think of how many years that oath had to be handed down. And that oath was kept alive along with the promise that they would one day leave that land for a land of promise.

It is a stretch of our imagination to even think that an oath could be kept alive for that many years. Imagine sitting around the table, or fire place in the evening and hearing old grandpa say, "You know, our people will one day be taken out of this land, and will go to a land that flows with milk and honey. And when that happens, we need to remember to take Joseph's bones with us." Can't you just hear some of the young men say, "Yeah, yeah. We have heard that before. It will never happen." With that response, the oath would die.

But it did not die. Moses remembered hearing about it, and he made sure the oath was kept. Also remember that they wandered in the wilderness under Moses for 40 years. After Moses died, someone else took over that responsibility. Joshua 24:32 reads, *"And the bones of Joseph, which the children of Israel brought up out of Egypt, buried they in Shechem, in a parcel of ground which Jacob bought of the sons of Hamor the father of Shechem for a hundred pieces of silver: and it became the inheritance of the children of Joseph."*

This was many years after they had left Egypt that Joseph's bones were put into their final resting place. He too had been embalmed and placed in a coffin.

I wonder if an archeologist will ever stumble upon that grave and know that they are Joseph's bones, since he was embalmed. What a find that would be! We see in this final episode that God is faithful to His word. He does not make idle promises, and He keeps those promises He makes. God is not like we human beings, who break promises left and right.

We serve and worship an awesome God, a God above all gods. There is none like Him. It is that God that judged all the false gods of Egypt during the days of Moses. As we look at our world today, there are many false gods creeping into our society, and we fickle human beings fall in step with the world and begin to worship those false gods. We need to beware of the false gods in our own lives and I believe that if we ask God to show us the false gods in our lives, He will be more than willing to do that. But He will expect us to turn away from them and worship them no more.

PRAYER: Dear Heavenly Father, give me the eyes to see the false gods in my life. I want to walk in faith as Joseph did, and not serve false gods. The more I read your Word, the more I see your faithfulness to your own promises and to us, your creation, and your handiwork. I think we often times forget that you created us just the way we are for your own purpose. Even that is an awesome thought, Lord. I realize that I belong to you in three ways: first by creation, I was created in your image; secondly by the salvation that Jesus bought with His blood; and thirdly by my own choosing when I invited you, Lord Jesus, into my heart. Thank you, Father, for such a gift as that. In Jesus' name, Amen

JUNE 1ˢᵗ

I believe we need to explore how God is a God of time, and His timing is always perfect. There are times when we feel like He is way too late, or perhaps too early, but that is never the case with God. He is always right on time. We human beings are the ones who have a problem with time and with timing. We are going to spend a few days just looking at God's Word about that very topic, and hopefully you will see how *on time* God always is.

God had promised Abraham that he would have a son, but God did not tell him when. Abraham and his wife, Sarah, were getting older and older, and still had not had their son. They were two human beings who could not wait for God to do things His way or in His time, so Sarah gave her handmaiden to Abraham to have a son in Sarah's stead. With this situation, Sarah would still raise that child as her own. In other words they were going to help God keep his promise, so Ishmael was born to them through Sarah's handmaiden.

Now turn to Genesis 17:15-21, which reads: *"And God said unto Abraham, 'As for Sarai thy wife, thou shalt not call her name Sarai, but Sarah shall her name be. And I will bless her, and give thee a son also of her: yea, I will bless her, and she shall be a mother of nations; kings of people shall be of her.' Then Abraham fell upon his face, and laughed, and said in his heart, 'Shall a child be born unto him that is a hundred years old? And shall Sarah, that is ninety years old bear?' And Abraham said unto God, 'O that Ishmael might live before thee!' And God said, 'Sarah thy wife shall bear thee a son indeed; and thou shalt call his name Isaac: and I will establish my covenant with him for an everlasting covenant, and with his seed after him. And as for Ishmael, I have heard thee: Behold I have blessed him, and will make him fruitful, and will multiply him exceedingly; twelve princes shall he beget, and I will make him a great nation. But my covenant will I establish with Isaac, which Sarah shall bear unto thee at this set time in the next year.' "*

God will have His way in our lives, either with our cooperation or without it. Abraham and Sarah are good examples of that. God's timing is not detoured no matter what we may do to change it. What we need to see here is that God had a set time for the birth of Isaac, just as it says in verse 21, *"at this set time next year."*

We could let go of so much stress, if we would just be willing to let God have His perfect timing, just relax and let God be God in our lives. You see, all logic went out the window as far as Abraham was concerned. He was 100 years old and Sarah was 90! Who had a baby at that age? God is not bound by logic like we are, though. We look at our circumstances and see it as hopeless and we despair. Instead, what we need to do is give it all to God and ask Him to give us the patience to let Him turn our circumstances around. Satan loves it when we focus on the circumstances and give way to doubt and despair. God has perfect timing. We will look at a few more examples in the next few days.

PRAYER: Lord God, I think it will take some time to win the battle of not looking at my circumstances, and instead depending on your perfect timing in my life. It may help me if I remember that you know the future as well as you know the past, and I can depend on you to take care of my future. I also realize, as I look back on Joseph's life, that you, Lord God, were in charge of timing then too. Even as I look at the world around me, I can see your hand of perfect timing in my past, even though I fretted about it at that time. Forgive me for not trusting you more and help me to learn from this experience, to trust you sooner, rather than later. In Jesus' name, Amen.

JUNE 2nd

Ecclesiastes 3:1-8 reads: *"To every thing there is a season, and a time to every purpose under the heavens. A time to be born, and a time to die; a time to plant, and a time to pluck up that which is planted; A time to kill, and a time to heal; a time to break down, and a time to build up; A time to weep, and a time to laugh; a time to mourn, and a time to dance; A time to cast away stones, and a time to gather stones together; a time to embrace, and a time to refrain from embracing;*

A time to get, and a time to lose; a time to keep, and a time to cast away; A time to rend, and a time to sew; a time to keep silence, and a time to speak; A time to love, and a time to hate; a time of war, and a time of peace."

So, here God is telling us that there is a time for everything. If God is telling us there is a time for everything under heaven, then is it so hard to figure out that God Himself would live by the rule He has established?

Just look at our universe. It runs like a well-oiled machine, all perfectly timed. Pay attention to small details in your life for awhile and see God's timing. I even expect God to provide parking places for me when I go shopping, and it is amazing how the timing is so perfect that I can just drive into a "just now" vacated space. That is a very small detail, I know, but God is that gracious if we will but be more sensitive to watching for His perfect timing.

People will say, "God has bigger things to do than plan a parking space for you." Or they may say, "You were just lucky. That's all." But that is denying that God had anything to do with it, and I think God is too big to miss such opportunities to bless us in our lives. Of course, when those things happen in my life, I am quick to thank God for the blessing. You need to do that too. In fact, when I go shopping (which I do not like to do), I ask God to bless my time and to lead me to the right store, to the right article I need to buy, and to provide a good parking place for me.

Why do I do that? I do that because I acknowledge that my time is not my own. My time is God's time. God is in charge of my life from the time I get up in the morning to the time I go to bed at night, and all night long as well. If He is not in charge of my life, then who is? He wants to be in charge of your life too, so invite Him into your time of day and night.

PRAYER: Dear Lord God, it is reassuring to know that you are in charge of my time, that you want to bless me and the time I have on this earth. I thank you for your protection over me, no matter where I am, in my home, in the car on the highway, or in the stores deliberating over purchases, in church at worship, or in bed at night. In Jesus' name, Amen.

JUNE 3rd

Today, we will look at Matthew 8:28-29, which states: *"And when He* (Jesus) *was come to the other side into the country of the Gergesenes, there met Him two possessed with devils, coming out of the tombs, exceeding fierce, so that no man might pass by that way. And, behold, they cried out, saying, 'What have we to do with thee, Jesus, thou Son of God? Art thou come hither to torment us before our time?' "*

Here we have the account of a demonic encounter with Jesus. Notice that the demons knew exactly *who* Jesus was, while the religious leaders of that day did not know who He was, although they should have, because the Old Testament told all about Him and they knew the Old Testament very well.

But today we are talking about timing, and I want you to see that even the demons know there is a day in the future when they will be judged and sent to the place of torment. In these versus, we see that they even feared they would be sent there before the right time. So they know there is a time appointed for that.

If they are aware of such timing, then should it not follow that we, who call ourselves Christians, should also know about God's timing? I believe there is a lot that could be written about God's timing, but I will let someone else go into that in detail. I want to just pose the thoughts about God's timing for our own lives, so we can at least be in tune with God's work in our lives.

PRAYER: Dear Lord Jesus, I do not want to be ignorant regarding the timing of God, so if there is more about it that I should know in order to adjust my lifestyle, or my thought life, then I ask your Holy Spirit to enlighten me, show me in your Word the importance of your timing, and how it can affect my life. Help me also to see your timing in my day-to-day life, so that I can be thankful. In Jesus' name, Amen.

JUNE 4ᵗʰ

Galatians 4:4-5 reads, *"But, when the fullness of the time was come, God sent forth his Son, made of a woman, made under the law, to redeem them that were under the law, that we might receive the adoption of sons."* Here we see that when Jesus was born (fully Son of God and Son of man), it was *in the fullness of time.* I believe His birth was not a minute early or a minute late. I believe it was on precisely the right minute, on the right day of the right year.

But guess what? I believe every one of us are born that way also. I think that until we see how precious we are to God and how precisely He has created us, we will never really appreciate *who* we are, and especially *who we are in Christ Jesus.*

Notice that it says Jesus was born under the law. He lived according to the law to such an extent that He fulfilled the law to the letter so that we can be redeemed from under the law. Remember, to be redeemed means to be bought back. And when we are bought back, we can be called an adopted son or daughter of God. So, yes, I believe our birth is right on time also.

Remember, we saw that there is a time to be born and a time to die. Just as we celebrate a birth, I believe that we should also celebrate a death of a Christian, who is destined to go into the presence of Jesus the Son, God the Father, and the Holy Spirit. What a privilege we have as a Christian!

PRAYER: There is a little song that goes like this, "Thank you God for sending Jesus. Thank you, Jesus, that you came. Holy Spirit, come and help me. Glorify His holy name." I believe that says it all. Dear Lord Jesus, I do thank you for coming to bring eternal life into the world, so I may choose life and live forever with you. Thank you for living the law for me, dying for me, and rising again to give me power to live a life pleasing to you. In Jesus' mighty name, Amen.

JUNE 5th

Today, we will turn to Mark 11:12-14 and 19-23, which read: *"And on the morrow, when they were come from Bethany, He was hungry: And seeing a fig tree afar off having leaves, He came, if haply He might find any thing thereon: and when He came to it, He found nothing but leaves; for the time of figs was not yet. And Jesus answered and said unto it, 'No man eat fruit of thee hereafter for ever. And his disciples heard it." And when evening was come, He went out of the city. And in the morning, as they passed by, they saw the fig tree dried up from the roots. And Peter calling to remembrance saith unto Him, 'Master, behold, the fig tree which thou cursedst is withered away.' And Jesus answering saith unto them, 'Have faith in God. For verily I say unto you, that whosoever shall say unto this mountain, "Be thou removed, and be thou cast into the sea;" and shall not doubt in his heart, but shall believe that those things which he saith shall come to pass; he shall have whatsoever he saith.' "*

This is a very interesting piece of the Bible. For years, I could not make any sense out of it, but then one day I read that when there are leaves on a fig tree, there should also be figs. This particular fig tree had leaves but at the wrong time, for it was not the time for figs.

As Jesus saw it from a distance, and since He was hungry, He expected to find figs on it, simply because there were leaves there. It showed signs of fruit, wonderful inviting signs of fruit, but there was no fruit, and His hunger could not be satisfied after all. Jesus cursed the tree and it withered completely overnight, so much so that Peter was shocked.

The lesson for us here is that Jesus expects fruit from us too, once we know who He is and who we are in Him. When you see an apple tree blossom, then you know there will be apples in due time. The blossoms are the sign that fruit will come, and if no fruit comes year after year, what good is the tree? It may be good for shade, but not for apples.

God will give us time to produce fruit for His name's sake, but what if we do not produce any fruit at all? Then what good are we to His kingdom's work, or to our fellow man, or to ourselves, for that matter?

God will not curse us as He did the tree, but it is a lesson to us that there is a time for us to produce fruit just as there is a time for the fig tree. To only show signs of being a fruit-producing Christian is not good enough any more than it was for the fig tree to have leaves and no fruit. The tree should not have had leaves in the first place. I believe there is a time in our lives when we are to become fruit-bearing Christians.

Let us look at what the fruit of the Spirit is (that is the Holy Spirit that lives within us) according to the Word of God, and ask yourself, "Is this fruit evident in my life?" Galatians 5:22-23 says, *"But the fruit of the Spirit is love, joy, peace, long suffering, gentleness, goodness, faith, meekness, temperance: against such there is no law."* People who are in a dither, anxious, depressed, full of despair, and so on, do not display fruit of the Spirit of peace, long suffering, or faith. If they have no medical problems, then they should be at peace, and filled with patience and faith for today and tomorrow. God is able to take all your hurts and help you to let them go, one by one, and let God handle them for you.

Don't be like the fig tree, giving signs of the full Christian life and having no fruit to back it up. When Jesus is really *in your life*, then fruit is a natural product of your life.

PRAYER: Dear Lord Jesus, I see the lesson in this day's verses, and I believe that I understand the lesson, but how do I put it into practice? When the Holy Spirit lives in me, then is the fruit an automatic outcome? A tree just stands there and produces fruit. Is that what I am supposed to do? I know the tree must have a good root system, but what are my roots sunk into? The tree needs sun and water. What are my sun and water? I know I must be rooted and grounded in *your love*, and that I am *watered by the Word of God*, and as Jesus is the *light of the world*. Therefore, producing fruit will be all of God and none of self, right? So, then, Lord God, produce fruit in and through me according to your timing and your will. In Jesus' name, Amen.

JUNE 6th

 One more reference we need to address before we move on to something else is Ephesians 5:15-21, which states: *"See then that ye walk circumspectly, not as fools, but as wise, redeeming the time, because the days are evil. Wherefore be ye not unwise, but understanding what the will of the Lord is. And be not drunk with wine, wherein is excess; but be filled with the Spirit; Speaking to one another in psalms and hymns and spiritual songs, singing and making melody in your heart to the Lord. Giving thanks always for all things unto God the Father in the name of our Lord Jesus Christ. Submitting ourselves one to another in the fear of God."*

Here we are told that we are to redeem the time, for the days are evil, and then it goes on to tell us how that is done. To redeem something means to buy it back. To buy something, you have to sacrifice something. We use money to do that today, but back then they used the barter system. You have to be willing to part with money in order to buy something.

But how do you redeem (buy back) time? And what do you use to sacrifice (give in exchange) for time? You give up your desire to complain, fret, rebel, or whatever is your way of not praising God. Instead, we are to sing songs, spiritual songs, and do it with one another. We are to be wise instead of unwise, make melody in our hearts (think on pleasant things and refuse to dwell on the negative), and give thanks always, no matter how much we want to complain, bellyache, or rebel. Remember, the Bible says we are also supposed to submit ourselves to one another. That shoe really pinches doesn't it? But that is how we buy back or redeem the time.

Let us also look Colossians 4:5, which reads, *"Walk* (that refers to our daily life) *in wisdom toward them that are without* (unbelievers who are watching you, the believer) *redeeming the time."* We either reflect Jesus in our lives, or we reflect our sinful nature, which is a reflection of Satan himself. In this verse, we see that redeeming the time is being mindful of our image, how others see us. You see, we have various images to watch over as Christians: the one family sees in our home when our guard is down, the one the people we work with see, and the one the people in our social lives see. There will be believers and unbelievers watching your reactions at all times, just as we watch other people's reactions to life's circumstances in their lives.

Does your life reflect your faith in a faithful God? When it does, then you have redeemed the time. We have been looking at how *time* is an important thing to God, and it ought to be important to us as well. To think that He has given us an opportunity to actually redeem time, and given us ways in which to do it!

PRAYER: Heavenly Father, I feel so blessed to know that I can actually redeem time. Thank you for giving me this insight into your heart of hearts. Help me be sensitive to my actions and reactions, because I want them to reflect the God I know in my life, so that others may know you also. In Jesus' name, Amen.

JUNE 7th

Have you ever wondered what faith is? Can you put it in a test tube and analyze it? I don't think so. Just exactly, what is faith? We have a tendency to have faith in what we see and what we understand. I believe trust could be another word for faith. However, faith goes just a bit beyond trust. Let's take a look at Hebrews 11:1-3, which reads: *"Now faith is the substance* (assurance) *of things hoped for, the evidence* (a conviction) *of things not seen. For by it the elders obtained a good report* (had witness borne to them). *Through faith we understand that the worlds were framed by the word of God, so that things which are seen were not made of things which do appear."*

Faith gives us an assurance of the future, that nothing that comes our way can shake our confidence and trust that the God of our faith will be there for us in any and every event of our lives. It *"is the substance* (assurance) *of things hoped for,"* and *"the evidence of things not seen."*

People, who have faith, real honest-to-goodness faith, seem to have about them an aura of such confidence that you actually feel safe and

213

secure around them. That is evidence of things not seen. You cannot actually see that confidence, that inner knowledge that everything is okay, because God is in charge and God is good. It cannot be held up for everyone to see, but you just know that you know that it is there. That, I believe is *"evidence of things not seen."*

So, again, what is faith? We will explore that in the next few days. I do want to leave you with one more thought for today, however. Romans 12:3 states, *"For I say, through the grace given unto me, to every man that is among you, not to think of himself more highly than he ought to think; but to think soberly, according as God hath dealt to every man a measure of faith."* We see here that every one of us who believes, has been given a measure of faith. You can be sure that the measure you have is big enough to carry you through any problem that may arise. We also see that it is a gift from God, and not something you have to go about and drum up for yourself. To accept Jesus as Lord and Savior, you had to have faith, and since you no doubt have faith (or you would not be reading this daily devotional), then you know you have been given a measure of faith.

Yet, the disciples asked Jesus to increase their faith, in Luke 17:5-6, which says, *"And the apostles said unto the Lord, 'Increase our faith.' And the Lord said, 'If ye had faith as a grain of mustard seed, ye might say unto this sycamine tree, "Be thou plucked up by the root, and be thou planted in the sea"; 'and it should obey you.' "* We will continue to search out the meaning of faith tomorrow.

PRAYER: I have often wondered just exactly what faith is. I am thankful, Father, that this subject has been opened for me. Help me to grasp the meaning of each passage, so that I can become enlightened about faith, according to your Word. Can faith be increased like the disciples requested? If so, how do I accomplish that? Open my eyes of understanding, so that I may lay hold of what it means to have spiritual faith. In Jesus' name, Amen.

JUNE 8th

There are many verses that speak of "little faith," and it is Jesus, Himself, who speaks about it. We will look at a few of the passages. Matthew 6:28-30 reads: *"And why take ye thought for raiment* (why are you anxious concerning this)? *Consider the lilies of the field, how they grow; they toil not, neither do they spin: And yet I say unto you, that even Solomon in all his glory was not arrayed like one of these. Wherefore, if God so clothe the grass of the field, which today is, and tomorrow is cast into the oven, shall He not much more clothe you, O ye of little faith?"*

Matthew 8:24-26 states: *"And, behold, there arose a great tempest in the sea, in so much that the ship was covered with the waves: but He was asleep. And His disciples came to Him, and awoke Him, saying, 'Lord, save us: we perish.' And He saith unto them, 'Why are ye fearful, O ye of little faith?' Then He arose, and rebuked the winds and the sea; and there was a great calm."*

And Matthew 14:29-31 says: *"And He said, 'Come.' And when Peter was come down out of the ship, he walked on the water, to go to Jesus. But when he saw the wind boisterous, he was afraid; and beginning to sink, he cried, saying, 'Lord, save me.' And immediately, Jesus stretched forth His hand, and caught him, and said unto him, 'O thou of little faith, wherefore didst thou doubt?' "*

There are things in life that cancel out other things, such as a cloud in the sky will cancel out the sun's warmth and light. When a cloud obstructs the sun, we do not doubt that the sun is still in the sky. We know and have faith that it is there. We do not doubt it's presence, we just do not see it.

Let us look at what Jesus said about the situation in a couple of these references. In regards to the storm and the waves, Jesus asked His disciples, *"Why were ye fearful?"* Do you see how fear had cancelled out their faith. Jesus was on the ship, and He would not allow a storm to swallow them up. They were His disciples, not the devil's.

215

Fear is a hard thing to corral. We talked about that kind of fear earlier this year, and we learned that we need to take a stand against fear when there is no fear around us, and we need to declare that we will not fear when sudden fear or terror surrounds us. The disciples needed to learn that lesson, and Jesus must have been thinking that the time was ripe for learning it.

In the other reference, Jesus asked Peter, *"Why did you doubt?"* Doubts about God are another way to canceled out faith. If you have doubts about God's love, or His keeping power over you, or His ability to keep and protect you, or even His willingness to protect you, then, for goodness sake, go to God with your doubts and ask Him to help you dispel them. God wants us to know all about Him, and how far He is willing to go on your behalf to take care of you. In fact, we expect too little from God, and that tells Him that we do not trust Him enough or that we have little faith.

Jesus knew that Peter's trouble was doubt, but I do not think Peter knew that for himself. He had doubts about Jesus' ability or willingness to give him the authority to walk on water. This had more to do with Jesus' power and authority than with His willingness to see Peter walk on water. How well do you know Jesus' authority and power? We will look at that tomorrow.

PRAYER: Does being anxious over our daily needs, like food or clothing, also cancel our faith? Oh, boy, do I need help from you if that is the case. Show me in your Word how to rely on you for everything, so that my faith will grow strong enough to withstand the storms of life. In Jesus' name, Amen.

JUNE 9th

In regard to Jesus' power and authority, let us look at Matthew 28:18-19, which reads, *"And Jesus came and spake unto them, saying, 'All power* (authority) *is given unto me in heaven and in*

earth." Let the magnitude of that verse soak into the very fibers of your body, because in the very next verse he says, *"Go ye therefore, and teach* (make disciples of) *all nations, baptizing them in the name of the Father, and of the Son, and of the Holy Spirit."*

When Jesus bid Peter to come and walk on the water, Peter was being upheld by the power and authority of the Word that created the universe. You cannot get much higher authority than that, can you? I believe that is authority you can trust.

That same authority is given to us, too, when we invite Jesus into our hearts to live there. Having doubts about that authority will cancel out our faith, making our faith look like "little faith". I must pose an important question right now. On what do you base your faith? Do you base it on other people's faith, or maybe your circumstances (with good circumstances equaling big faith, and bad circumstances equaling little faith)? Do you base your faith on your money, insurance, social status, job, or friends?

The only place your faith should rest is *on the Word of God.* That is why it is so important to know the Word of God. When your faith is based on God and His Word, then it will appear to be a strong, large faith. Tomorrow we will talk about where our faith comes from. Just as children ask their mothers, "Where did I come from?" we also need to know where our faith originated.

PRAYER: Heavenly Father, I really need this lesson on faith in my life. Thank you for leading me into this topic. Help me to grasp the truth about faith, and help me to apply it to my life. I can see how it will help me to live a more victorious Christian life, maybe even to enter in your rest. I give you all the praise for leading me in this direction. In Jesus' name, Amen.

JUNE 10ᵗʰ

 Hebrews 12:-1-2 states: *"Wherefore seeing we also are compassed about with so great a cloud of witnesses, let us lay*

aside every weight and the sin which doth so easily beset us and let us run with patience the race that is set before us. Looking unto Jesus the author and finisher of our faith; who for the joy that was set before him endured the cross, despising the shame, and is set down at the right hand of the throne of God."

In this passage, we see several things. The witnesses that compass about us are the list of faithful believers from the Old Testament recorded in Hebrews chapter 11. Then, we are admonished to lay aside every weight and sin that besets us.

Think of runners in a race. They strip themselves of everything that would hinder their running the race. Sin will hinder our race, and so do weights. What weights do Christians carry? I believe our weights are such things as worry, jealousy, anxiety, bitterness, and so on. We are to choose to lay them aside, deliberately choose to recognize them and cast them aside. Then we are fit to run the race. And notice that it is *the* race, it is one race, not many races.

We have one race in our Christian lives, and there is no rerun either. How are we to endure this race? We will finish the race by keeping our eyes on Jesus, who is the author and finisher of our faith. Ah, there is where our faith comes from. *Jesus is the author and finisher of our faith.* Some translations say He is the *"pioneer and perfecter"* of our faith. I believe that just as Jesus displayed God's love to the world, He also showed us what faith is. Therefore, He can be called the author of faith, or the pioneer of faith.

This, of course, leaves me with a question to which I do not know the answer. Did the people really *know* what God's love was like in the Old Testament, and did they *know* what faith was like? Since Jesus brought with Him the example of God's love and true faith, could those who lived before Jesus came to earth have really known love and faith?

We do know that our faith has an origin, which is Jesus. I am fairly sure that it all happened when Jesus came to earth to live and die and rise again, and I believe a couple verses in Galatians proves that. Galatians 3:23-25 reads: ***"But before faith came, we were kept*** (kept in ward) ***under the law, shut up unto the faith which should afterwards be revealed.***

218

Wherefore the law was our schoolmaster (tutor) *to bring us unto Christ, that we might be justified by faith. But after that faith is come, we are no longer under a schoolmaster* (tutor). *For we are all children of God by faith in Christ Jesus."*

I believe that these verses clearly teach us that it was different "before" and "after" Jesus came. So I see that faith is eternally connected to the work of Jesus our Savior.

PRAYER: Lord God, thank you for your Word which shows us the truth, and for revealing that truth to me in such a way that I can grasp it. Help me, Lord, to apply it to my life. In Jesus Name, Amen.

JUNE 11th

So, what do we know so far? We have all been given a measure of faith. A mustard seed measure has enough power and authority in it to remove a tree. (Another verse says it will move a mountain.) We have learned that things like anxiety, fear, and doubt, will make faith appear little, and we know that there is a "before" and an "after" in regard to the coming of faith.

We also know that Jesus is the author and finisher of our faith. But there is more to learn about faith. Can faith grow, and if so, how does that happen? And if it can grow, can it also die or diminish? We will see what Scripture has to say about that. In II Thessalonians 1:3, we read, *"We are bound to thank God always for you, brethren, as it is meet* (fitting) *because your faith groweth exceedingly, and the charity* (love) *of every one of you all toward each other abounded."* Here we see that faith can grow. In fact, it can grow exceedingly.

Next, we need to know how faith grows. II Thessalonians 2:13 states, *"But we are bound to give thanks always to God for you, brethren beloved of the Lord, because God hath from the beginning chosen you to salvation through sanctification of the Spirit and belief of the truth."* I believe our faith grows through the work of the Holy Spirit in us and our

219

desire to know the *truth*. The Bible has a lot to say about the *truth*. In John 14:6, Jesus says, *"I am the way, the truth, and the life: no man cometh unto the Father but by me."*

If we search for the *truth* (which is like a hidden diamond waiting to be discovered) in the Bible, I believe our faith will grow exceedingly. If you had a pet, you would feed it faithfully every day. Our faith needs feeding, too, and I believe we feed it by learning the truth.

PRAYER: Again, I thank you, Lord, for what I am learning about faith. I guess I never really gave faith much of a thought before. I am beginning to have a friendly feeling about my own faith, as if I did not know I had this thing called faith, and it has been with me all these many years. I feel like I want to say, "Hello" to my faith, like it is a friend I never knew I had. Help me to nourish that faith, to cherish it, and to give it the place in my heart that it deserves. In Jesus' name, Amen.

JUNE 12th

Romans 1:16-17 reads, *"For I am not ashamed of the gospel of Christ: for it is the power of God unto salvation to everyone that believeth; to the Jew first, and also to the Greek. For therein* (the gospel) *is the righteousness of God revealed from faith to faith: as it is written, 'The just shall live by faith.' "* In these verses, we see that God's idea of righteousness for us is found in the Gospel of Christ, and that truth is revealed little by little, *"from faith to faith.*

Think of faith as a foundation. A foundation is row after row of bricks, built up until there is a solid base upon which to put a structure. So it is with faith. Faith leads us into more faith, and more truth, and more faith, and more truth. I believe that truth is like the mortar that holds faith together to create a strong foundation for our salvation to rest upon. It is Jesus' love, faith, truth, sacrifice, His finished work on the cross, and His resurrection that defeated sin, death, and the power of the devil.

Do you see that it is all of God the Father, Son, and Holy Spirit, and none of *self* in salvation? All this was done for you, and all you need to do is to accept it by faith. That is a win-win situation. Do not let anything cloud out that truth so that it cancels out your faith in the One who did it all for you.

PRAYER: Heavenly Father, I confess that I had no idea that faith was so tangible. It has laid hold of me in a way I never dreamed possible. I need your help to allow my faith to grow in the measure you want it to grow. Reveal your Word to me so that I can build a strong foundation from faith to faith. In Jesus' name, Amen.

JUNE 13th

I Peter 1:5-7 states: *"Who are kept* (guarded) *by the power of God through faith unto salvation ready to be revealed in the last time. Wherein ye greatly rejoice, though now for a season, if need be, ye are in heaviness through* (have been put to grief in) *manifold temptations: That the trial of your faith, being much more precious than of gold that perishes, though it be tried with fire, might be found unto praise and honor and glory at the appearing of Jesus Christ."*

As much as we do not want to even think in terms of trials, hardships, or temptations, it is a fact of life, and God knows that. Therefore, we must address that side of our faith. In these verses, we see that our faith will be tried, and that is not a bad thing, unless that is the way we choose to look at it. To God, this is a good thing. It gives Him the opportunity to bring a great blessing into our lives when we withstand the trials that are testing our faith.

But, if we fold in the middle of the trial, if we look at our circumstances and let them overwhelm us, like Peter did when he began to walk on water, but looked at the waves and began to sink, then instead of us having a full-blown victory, we have to look to Jesus to help us *out of* rather than *through* the trial. Jesus helped Peter "out of," but we do see that Jesus

221

was there for Peter. He did not say, "Tough luck." and go on His way. Jesus has promised to never leave or forsake us.

Peter called out to Jesus, and He answered the call. We, too, can call out for that kind of help and expect it to be there for us. We have only looked at half of what is being said in this scripture for today. Our faith is compared to gold, and it is in fact more precious than gold in the eyes of God. It needs to be that precious in our eyes too, does it not? God loves it when you recognize that thing called *faith* in your life, and that you want it to grow, and to be of vital use in your life.

Do you take a vitamin pill faithfully every day? Well, you need to wake up your faith, too, every day. Say, "Hello, faith, what are we going to do today? I'm ready, faith, are you?" And then, see what *faith* and you can do that day. Then, at the end of the day, thank God for the gift of faith and all that was done. Tomorrow, we will talk about gold and faith and fire.

PRAYER: Lord Jesus, I am glad you are the author and finisher of my faith. When trials come, I can remember you are the finisher of my faith and know that the gift of faith is able to see me through the trial. I do not want to fold when faced with a trial. I want the sweet victory of going all the way through it, and coming out without even the smell of smoke on me as the three young Hebrew men experienced in the fiery furnace (Daniel 3:19-27). In Jesus' name, Amen.

JUNE 14th

I Peter 1:7 states, *"That the trial of your faith, being much more precious than of gold that perishes, though it be tried with fire, might be found unto praise and honor and glory at the appearing of Jesus Christ."* Remember, in order for gold to have any worth, it is refined, and that is done through a test by fire. A slab of gold is put into a very hot furnace, and as it becomes very hot, the impurities rise to the top. The refiner brings the slab out of the furnace and scrapes off the impurities. Then he looks at the gold, like he would look at a mirror, to see if he can

222

see his image in the gold. If not, the gold is put back into the furnace to go through the fire all over again.

When the refiner can see his image in the gold, then it is free from impurities and can reflect the refiner's image. So it is with us. Jesus wants to see His image in us. As we go through tests and trials, it is like the gold in the furnace. However, our faith is more precious than gold. Gold will perish, but faith will not. Instead, faith is for praise, honor, and glory when we stand before Christ to have our life examined and be given rewards. Do you begin to see how this all hangs together. A trial or test today may seem hard, but it is small when compared to those words of Jesus, Matthew 25:21 *"Well done thou good and faithful servant: You have been faithful over a few things, I will make you ruler over many things: enter thou into the joy of the Lord."*

PRAYER: Dear Lord Jesus, it is hard to grasp how much you have done for me, or that I am that important to you! First of all, you created me in your image. Then you died to save me from the penalty of sin, and you gave me your kind of faith to see me through life. Then you also gave me the Holy Spirit to give me the power to live a life pleasing to you. The only room left for failure is when *I choose* not to believe it, or to not put it all into *practice*. Forgive me, Lord, for the times I have forgotten all that you have done for me, and for disappointing you by my lack of interest or care. Cleanse me from sin and its hold on me. Help me to recognize the temptations and the tempter himself as he comes to stir up my circumstances, intending to trip me up and bring failure into my life. Thank you for the victory that is mine to claim.
In Jesus' name, Amen.

JUNE 15th

 II Thessalonians 3:1-3 reads, *"Finally, brethren, pray for us, that the word of the Lord may have free course* (run), *and be glorified, even as it is with you: And that we may be delivered*

from unreasonable and wicked men: for all men have not faith. But the Lord is faithful, who shall establish you, and keep you from evil (the evil one)." This may be a controversial portion of Scripture, but I believe we need to recognize that there are people out there that the devil can provoke into doing evil against those who are believers in Jesus Christ, and he will strive to work us woe.

Here it says *"they have not faith."* Have you ever been betrayed by someone with whom you never ever expected to have that kind of experience? How do you react to that? They did not exercise the kind of faith that we have been talking about these past days, but that does not give us an excuse to not use faith in our reaction. You may feel betrayed and hurt. You may contemplate revenge, or treating them in a very unkind way.

God calls us to forgive, to keep the peace in our heart, and not to talk to others about what was done to us, which only keeps the wound open and bleeding. What we need to recognize is that Satan was at work in that person to betray you, and then he turns around to work on you, to turn that betrayal into a high wave so you cannot walk on water, or into a big storm, so you become fearful. Whatever works, the devil will use it. Satan will tempt you first one way, and if that doesn't work, he will tempt you in another way, always keeping you looking at the circumstances. We are to "look to Jesus, the author and finisher of our faith," not at our circumstances. Go to a mature Christian for prayer help in such a situation. Pool your faith in God and agree together over the matter. Then see what happens to the devil's plans.

Let me remind you of Matthew 18:19, which reads, *"Again I say unto you, that if two of you shall agree on earth as touching anything that they shall ask, it shall be done for them of my Father which is in heaven."* Having prayer partners that you can depend on is a very desirable thing to bring forth victories, spiritual victories, into your life.

PRAYER: Heavenly Father, you have given me so many wonderful promises, and all for my benefit. Help me to exercise my faith to lay hold on these promises and glean the fruit of those promises, day by day, in my life. In Jesus' name, Amen.

JUNE 16th

There is a very short verse that says a lot. II Corinthians 5:7 reads, *"For we walk by faith, not by sight.* When you see the word "walk" it means "our daily life." In other words, if we live our daily lives by faith, and not by sight, we will be living it according to God's will.

How is that done? First of all, I believe we have to "unlearn" living by sight. We allow what we see, or hear, to rule our emotions and our reactions. If we see a mouse, we jump, scream, and head for the nearest chair to climb. That is a picture of walking by sight. When you walk by faith, you will realize the mouse is not going to attack you, that in fact it will want to run away from you as fast as it can. There is no need to jump, scream, or climb onto a chair. (Is this easier said than done? Yes, I can vouch for that! Mice have always brought an instant reaction, and not according to faith. I am improving however.)

How do you react to a piece of tragic news? Do you allow faith to kick in and start working? I can do that easier than I can cure my "mouseitis," but I have found that it is a process. First, I have had to learn how to depend on God the moment I get the bad news. My first question is, "Father, show me yourself *in* and *through* this." Then, as God leads my mind from one scripture to another, I am comforted with the knowledge that, even though my world is turned upside down, God is still in charge, and just as He has been faithful in the past, He will be faithful right now in the present.

That does not change my circumstances one bit, but it gives me a place to put my faith, and helps me not let the circumstances blow me away. I say this because my youngest son, at age 46, died in his sleep this past May 5th, apparently of a heart attack. My first question was, "Can my faith in the God with whom I have had a good relationship stand this test, this trial, or will I be tempted to allow a cloud of doubt in God to cancel my faith in God, or in the goodness of the God about whom the Bible has taught me?"

God is so faithful to cover you in a time like that, if only you will let Him, so I encourage you to learn how to walk (live your daily life) close to God, hand in hand in fact, having your eyes open to see the hand of God in the small, everyday details of your life. That will help you so much when a large trial comes your way. And, it is almost impossible to go through life without a large trial of some sort. After all, we live in a sin-ridden world, where diseases, catastrophes, accidents, etc., happen on a daily basis around us.

Give your life over to His control and you will not walk by sight anymore. You could plan and plan and plan, but if God has a different plan than yours, all your planning is in vain anyhow. Therefore, it is much easier on the nervous system to just put our day in God's hands first thing in the morning.

PRAYER: Lord God, whew, what a lesson this is! I can't help but think it is like the process of the person who learned to play the piano by ear, and then started to take lessons and learn it according to music notes instead of instinct. I have heard it was harder to unlearn what had been learned earlier than it was to learn to play by music notes. I am so used to living with one eye on the circumstances around me, and now I need to unlearn that way of living, and, first and foremost, depend on you completely. All I can say to that is, "HELP, HELP!" I know that you are willing to help me make a change. Be patient with me, Lord, as I make those adjustments in my life. In Jesus' name, Amen.

JUNE 17th

I John 5:4 reads, *"For what so ever is born of God over comes the world: And this is the victory that over comes the world, even our faith!"* I put an exclamation point after that verse because it is such a powerful verse. When we are born again, then we are born of God. That makes us a new creation. Things that were impossible for us before have become possible now.

226

A person's faith can overcome the world, that system dominated by Satan around us. People watch you to see how you react to things in the world, and they love to criticize the believer who tries to walk by faith. They think they can discredit God and have an excuse not to follow God in their lives, that is why they criticize those who do walk by faith.

When your faith shines forth like a beacon, it will overcome the world. God is counting on us to let Him shine forth through us, so the world can see the God we know. The God that helps us through the trial just might be able to help others through their hard times in life. Hard times come to both believers and unbelievers alike. We all live in the same sin-ridden, fallen world, and experience the same kinds of trials.

Death will visit every household sooner or later. It cannot be avoided. How will you react to that? Your faith will determine that. Your faith can overcome if you will be humble and let it. Go to God and ask for His help.

There is a beautiful verse to store up for yourself in this regard. Learn it by heart. Hebrews 4:16 states, *"Let us therefore come boldly unto the throne of grace, that we may obtain mercy, and find grace to help in time of need."* When you are able to know God so well that you can come boldly to His throne and expect that He will minister His grace in your time of need, then your faith is running on all eight cylinders, and no amount of high waves or stormy seas can detour that kind of faith. It will overcome the world! You can count on it.

PRAYER: Heavenly Father, I think I am ready to stand up and shout, "Hallelujah!" This is such good news, and I believe I can come into that realm of faith for my life. Thank you for opening my eyes to these truths. I am so grateful that I feel worthy to have what the Bible says I can have. I know I do not deserve it, but I do know that Jesus sacrificed His life, His blood, and His will to your will, to bring such a benefit to me as I am learning today. Therefore, I have been made worthy by His work on the cross, and I am so grateful! In Jesus' name, Amen.

JUNE 18th

Hebrews 11:6 reads, *"But without faith, it is impossible to please Him: for he that cometh to God must believe that He is, and that He is a rewarder of them that diligently seek Him."* I used to think that nothing was impossible with God, and that is true. However, people may think that they can do works to please God, and that is not true. It is impossible to please Him without first having faith. It was faith that first nudged us toward God, and as this verse says, in order to come to God at all, one must believe that He is.

Our faith is a gift to help us follow in Jesus' footsteps. Our faith is supposed to bring glory, honor, and praise to God, not to ourselves. In fact, I believe we were born for the purpose to bring honor, glory, and praise to God. Your whole existence on earth will have a much deeper meaning when you see that your purpose is to reflect God's love, mercy, and grace in the world. In order to do that it takes a good measure of faith. Then you will clearly see that *"without faith it is impossible to please God."*

He also wants us to *"diligently seek Him."* There is a verse in the Old Testament for this also. God's word verifies His word. It proves His word, just like mathematics proves mathematics. Deuteronomy 4:29 states, *"But if from thence thou shalt seek the Lord, thy God, thou shalt find Him, if thou seek Him with all thy heart and with all thy soul."* As you read the Bible, you are seeking God. As you give Him permission to lead your day, you are seeking Him. And when you tell others about His great love, mercy, and grace, you are seeking Him. You put Him right into the midst of your everyday life, and you seek ways to do that.

You must never push Him down other people's throats. That is unacceptable behavior. God is too gentle and gracious to be shoved around like that. You need to wait for open doors before you jump in and tell others what you know about God. Your responsibility is to say, "Here I am, Lord. Use me as you wish." Then wait on Him for open doors to do that.

That is what it means to walk by faith. There is a song that goes something like this: "If with all your heart you truly seek me, you shall ever surely find me, thus sayeth the Lord." I believe that we are never done

228

seeking the Lord. It is a lifetime endeavor. I also believe that when we die, we will enter heaven on the same spiritual level that we leave earth. Do you want to enter as a kindergartner, or do you want at least to enter on an elementary level? We can never exhaust the study of the Bible. I believe we will spend eternity finding out what it all contains.

PRAYER: Heavenly Father, I stand in awe of your majesty. Thank you, Father, for giving me the Bible to learn more and more about you. You come alive in the Bible, and I want to know you better so that I can be the proper reflection of your love toward others. Help me to seek you with all my heart. In Jesus' name, Amen.

JUNE 19th

Have you ever wondered what it would have been like to be one of Jesus' disciples? They were young men who had grown up in the Jewish traditions, and, I am sure, were aware that their nation would one day produce the Messiah. I believe they had been told that Messiah would be a "take charge" type of leader who would defeat all those nations who opposed Israel, and would also defeat all false gods, so that the God of Abraham, Isaac, and Jacob would be the God of the then-known world.

Then can you imagine what it would be like to come in contact with this man called Jesus of Nazareth? He certainly was a different sort of man. He did not live by the same rules the disciples had been taught to live by. Over the years, the law had been interpreted so minutely until it did not resemble the law that it was meant to be. Jesus did not follow the laws according to their interpretation, but He followed the law as it was meant to be.

The disciples could not deny what they saw Him do, like when Jesus fed the 5,000 with five loaves of bread and two fish, with twelve baskets left over besides! He raised three people from the dead, healed the

229

blind and the lame, and drove out demons. Surely, He must be someone sent by God. Could He be the Messiah?

He stilled the storm by taking authority over the weather, took authority over death and over demons, and He changed water into wine. It must have boggled their minds to follow and watch such a man. No one was able to outtalk Him. Neither the Pharisees, Sadducees, Elders, Scribes or Priests dared to ask him anymore questions because He would, with His own questions, put them into a corner from which there was no escape, because they could not answer His questions.

Picture yourself following such a man, and making a decision as to just exactly who He was. For a few days, we are going to look at one of his disciples, Peter, and see what we can learn about Jesus, Peter, and, finally, ourselves. Character study is so good for us, because we are all made from the same cloth. We are all born in sin and have a sin nature that Satan dominates, but we all have the gift of freedom of choice, and we all need to make up our minds as to what we will do with this Jesus.

John 1:35-42 reads: *"Again the next day after John stood, and two of his disciples: And looking upon Jesus as He walked, he saith, 'Behold the Lamb of God!' And the two disciples heard him speak, and they followed Jesus. Then Jesus turned, and saw them following, and saith unto them, 'What seek ye?' They saith unto him, 'Rabbi* (which is interpreted as Master), *where dwellest thou?' He saith unto them, 'Come and see.' They came and saw where He dwelt, and abode with Him that day: for it was about the tenth hour* (4:00 p.m.). *One of the two which heard John speak, and followed Him, was Andrew, Simon Peter's brother. He first findeth his own brother Simon, and saith unto him, 'We have found the Messiah* (which is interpreted as the Christ). *' And he brought him* (Peter) *to Jesus. And when Jesus beheld him, He said, 'Thou art Simon the son of Jonah: thou shalt be called Cephas '*(which is interpreted as a stone, Peter). *"*

We will talk about this encounter with Jesus at length tomorrow.

PRAYER: Dear Heavenly Father, I look forward with anticipation to learning about Peter and his journey with Jesus. I realize Jesus changes every life that comes in contact with Him. I can even see how my attitudes are changing as I read these devotions each day. I want Jesus to see His image in me a little more clearly each day. Give me the grace to allow that to happen. In Jesus' name, Amen.

JUNE 20th

In John 1:36, John said, *"Behold, the Lamb of God."* That statement should have been a wakeup call for every Jew who knew anything about the Bible. The Lamb of God was God's sacrificial Lamb, which would be slain for the sins of the world. God needed no Lamb for His sins, because He is sinless, so whose sins would the sacrifice cover other than the sins of the world?

Every Jew knew what a lamb was for. They had the Passover feast, which required a perfect, spotless, unblemished lamb. Knowing all this, is it any wonder that when Andrew found his brother Simon, he called Jesus, "Messiah"? The disciples called him "Rabbi," which means "master" in John 1:38, when they asked Him where He was staying. Yet Andrew knew more than that. He told his brother, Simon Peter, *"We have found the Messiah, which is interpreted, the Christ,"* in John 1:41.

In John 1:42, we see that when Peter met Jesus, Jesus changed his name, *"And he brought him to Jesus, And when Jesus beheld him, he said, 'Thou art Simon the son of Jona: thou shalt be called called Cephas, which is by interpretation, a stone (Peter)."* Cephas is Aramaic for stone.

A couple years later, Jesus renamed him Peter, which means "rock," after Peter had made a great confession to one of Jesus' questions. In Matthew 16:15-18, we see Jesus' question and Peter's response: *" 'But who do you say that I am?' And Simon Peter answered and said, 'Thou art the Christ, the Son of the living God.' And Jesus answered and said unto him, 'Blessed art thou Simon Barjona* (son of Jon), *for flesh and blood hath not revealed it unto thee, but my Father which is in heaven. And I say unto thee, that thou art Peter, and upon this rock* (the

231

confession that Jesus is the Christ, Messiah), *I will build my church; and the gates of hell shall not prevail against it.' "*

In the Bible, names have significant meaning and are important in the life of the believers. I think we have lost that art in our modern culture. Parents were very careful of what they named their children, because the name was like a prophecy for them. Many people in the Bible were named by God. Jesus is one of them.

PRAYER: Lord God, what does it mean to follow you? If you could or would change my name, what would it be? I want to be ready to go where you tell me to go and to do what you tell me to do, and be what you want me to be, and if that means having my name changed, then so be it. I am either a slave of yours or a slave of Satan's and I, for sure, do not want to be a slave of Satan's. In Jesus' name, Amen.

JUNE 21st

There are two more references I would like to look at in regard to Peter's calling. In Matthew 4:18-20, we read: *"And Jesus, walking by the sea of Galilee, saw two brethren, Simon called Peter, and Andrew his brother, casting a net into the sea, for they were fishers. And He saith unto them, 'Follow me, and I will make you fishers of men.' And they straightway left their nets, and followed Him."*

Notice that the disciples did not hesitate. They simply left their nets and followed Jesus. What do you think it meant for them to leave their nets? Can you imagine the president of a large company walking out and not looking back? I think that would be similar to these men leaving their nets.

Nets needed washing and constant care in order to be ready to do the job they were designed to do. And what about the disciples' boats? They must have left them too. They left the tools of their trade, just as an artist would his paints, brushes, and canvases.

It sounds so easy when we just read it, but get a grip on what they actually did to follow Jesus! Jesus has asked us to follow Him also, and what are we ready to lay down or give up to follow Him? Look at what Peter himself wrote about following Jesus in I Peter 2:21, *"For even hereunto were ye called: because Christ also suffered for us, leaving us an example, that ye should follow His steps."* Even as Jesus suffered, so, too, we will be asked to suffer for believing in Him and carrying His name. It comes with a price, but it is worth it, because it is through that name that we have salvation and victory over sin, and we get the better end of that deal. Peter, of all people, experienced that through his life as a believer, a disciple, and an apostle.

PRAYER: Heavenly Father, am I ready to pay the price of being a believer as Peter did? I pray that I am ready. I will need the power of your Holy Spirit to carry me through every tough time that comes my way. Help me to stand strong through every test and trial that comes into my life that your love and mercy and grace can at all times shine through. In Jesus' name, Amen.

JUNE 22nd

Mark 1:16-18 reads: *"Now as He walked by the sea of Galilee, He saw Simon and Andrew his brother casting a net into the sea: for they were fishers. And Jesus said unto them, come ye after me, and I will make you to become fishers of men. And straightway they forsook their nets, and followed Him."*

This is very similar to the reference in Matthew, but there are a couple of added insights. In both references, the men were at work casting their nets into the sea. They did not just throw the net and haul it back in right away. They left it there awhile to catch fish, and then hauled it in.

Now notice that in Mark it says that *"they forsook their nets."* Matthew said they *"left their nets."* I believe there is a difference between leaving something and forsaking it. To forsake throws an added dimension

233

to it. They had no intention of coming back to check the nets out, or even look back (like Lot's wife looked back, and consequently turned into a pillar of salt).

Jesus' addresses this in Luke 9:57-62, which reads: *"And it came to pass that, as they went in the way, a certain man said unto Him, 'Lord, I will follow thee wither so ever thou goest' And Jesus said unto him, 'Foxes have holes, and birds of the air have nests; but the Son of man hath not where to lay his head.' And He said unto another, 'Follow me.' But he saith ,'Lord, suffer me first to go and bury my father* (wait until my father dies).' *Jesus said unto him, 'Let the dead bury their dead: but go thou and preach the kingdom of God.' And another also said, 'Lord, I will follow thee: but let me first go bid them farewell, which are at home at my house.' And Jesus said unto him, 'No man, having put his hand to the plow, and looking back, is fit for the kingdom of God.' "*

These sound like harsh words, but it is the principle that counts here. If a person is halfhearted about choosing Jesus over the flesh and the world, then the flesh and the world will always win out. You are deciding to whom you want to be tied, connected, and fused. That is the one thing that determines your destination. The disciples left everything and they did it "straightway," "right away," "at once," as some of the various translations put it.

It is a decision we need to make also. Making no decision is itself also a decision, and it is a dangerous one to make. Doing nothing is actually denying there is a choice to be made. There is an old saying, "Do not put off for tomorrow what should be done today." That holds dangerously true in the case of deciding whether you will follow Jesus. I encourage you to seriously think about that choice. Surely God can be trusted with your life. It was He who created your life, and you in particular. It was God who saw the pitiful state of fallen mankind and provided a way back into fellowship with Him. It was God who knew we needed an added power to live a life pleasing to Him and sent us the Holy Spirit to empower us to live that life. Tell me, what else can He do for you? I believe that with a God like that it should not be at all hard to make a choice to follow Him.

PRAYER: Heavenly Father, it puts me in awe of you to realize all you have done for me. Yes, I want to follow you, and I do not want to look back. I think that is the hardest part of this. Help me to understand just what all "look back" means. I am going to ask you to reveal to me, day by day, the things that you consider as "looking back" as I follow you, so that I will understand when I am drifting off to the left or right. I will make the choice, and then depend on you to direct my steps. How does that sound to you, Lord? In Jesus' name, Amen.

JUNE 23rd

We are now going to look at some of Peter's experiences following Jesus. We will also take note of some of the emotions the disciples felt. In Luke 4:30-39, we read: *"But He, passing through the midst of them, went His way, And came down to Capernaum, a city of Galilee, and taught them on the sabbath days. And they were astonished at His doctrine* (teaching), *for His word was with power* (authority). *And in the synagogue there was a man, which had a spirit of an unclean devil, and cried out with a loud voice, saying, 'Let us alone; what have we to do with thee, thou Jesus of Nazareth? Art thou come to destroy us? I know thee who thou art; the Holy One of God.' And Jesus rebuked him, saying 'Hold thy peace, and come out of him.' And when the devil had thrown him in the midst, he came out of him, and hurt him not. And they were all amazed, and spake among themselves, saying, 'What a word is this! For with authority and power he commandeth the unclean spirits, and they come out.' And the fame of Him went out into every place of the country round about. And He arose out of the synagogue, and entered into Simon's house. And Simon's wife's mother was taken with a great fever; and they besought Him for her. And He stood over her, and rebuked the fever; and it left her: and immediately she arose and ministered unto them."*

235

In these few verses, Jesus displayed His power and authority over the demons and sickness (fever). In verse 32, they were astonished at His doctrine. In verse 36, they were amazed, for with authority and power He commanded the unclean spirits (notice that word is plural, there were many demons).

Jesus wasted no time in showing the disciples what would be expected of them. People do not follow anyone just for the exercise of it all, but to learn to do what that person does. The disciples found themselves exposed to a mighty power and authority. How do you suppose they felt about all this, besides astonished and amazed? Do you suppose they had second thoughts about their choice to follow Him? How do you feel about choosing to read this devotional book so far this year?

There are many sides to Jesus, not just a sweet baby in a manger, but a powerful, take-charge man of strength. He does not shrink from a confrontation of any kind. Have you noticed that? He is showing us how to live in a world in which Satan roams around like a roaring lion, seeking whom he may devour.

I Peter 5:8 reads, *"Be sober, be vigilant; because your adversary the devil, as a roaring lion, walketh about seeking whom he may devour."* Who better to have written this than Peter, whom we are studying. I'll just bet he knew first hand how the devil works, and he called him our adversary. How true that is.

PRAYER: Jesus of Nazareth, help me not to change my mind in following you. I want to become strong in my witness for you, and strong in my determination to take advantage of every chance to shine for you, and not miss one opportunity presented to me by your Spirit, to be salt of the earth or the light of the world. In Jesus' precious name, Amen.

JUNE 24th

 I want to remind you that Jesus said he would make Peter a fisher of men. Mark 5:35-43 states: *"While He yet spake, there came*

236

*from the ruler of the synagogue's house certain which said, 'Thy
daughter is dead: why troublest thou the Master any further?' As soon
as Jesus heard the word that was spoken, He saith unto the ruler of the
synagogue, 'Be not afraid, only believe.' And He suffered no man to
follow him, save Peter, and James, and John the brother of James. And
He cometh to the house of the ruler of the synagogue, and seeth the
tumult, and them that wept and wailed greatly. And when He was come
in, He saith unto them, 'Why make ye this ado, and weep? The damsel is
not dead, but sleepeth.' And they laughed Him to scorn. But when He
had put them all out, He taketh the father and the mother of the damsel,
and them that were with Him, and entereth in where the damsel was
lying. And He took the damsel by the hand, and said unto her, 'Talitha
cu-mi;' which is, being interpreted, 'Damsel, I say unto thee, arise.' And
straightway the damsel arose, and walked; for she was of the age of
twelve years, and they were astonished with a great astonishment. And
He charged them straightly that no man should know it; and commanded
that something should be given her to eat."*

This is the first time they had been witness to someone who was
dead and given back her life. There are a few things I want you to discover.
How many people did Jesus allow to be in the room when He brought the
girl back to life? There are three disciples, two parents, the dead girl, and
Jesus in that room. Does that number seven ring a bell for you? Do you
remember what that number stands for? Seven is a number that signifies
perfection, a complete entity, nothing more is necessary.

These things are not just happen stances. Jesus does everything
according to the *will* of the *Father*. What part did the disciples have in this
healing, restoration, service? All they did was watch the Master at work.
How did they feel? They were greatly amazed!

Now, as we read this scripture, how are we to feel? What are we to
learn? We will learn absolutely nothing if we do not believe it. So our first
decision is to believe that Jesus had the power to bring life back to the dead.
Then, since He gave us the power and authority, we are to believe we can
do what He did, raise the dead. Now that is where we have trouble, but

there are records of that very thing being done today, and it is done by faith in the Word of God.

PRAYER: Heavenly Father, how far can a person's faith be stretched? I see the disciples' faith in Jesus being stretched like a rubber band until one wonders if it will break. And apparently, my own faith will also get stretched like that if I am determined to follow Jesus. How strong or fragile is faith? Is it possible to loose the faith I have been given? I do not want that to happen to me, so help me hang onto my faith through all the tough times that life throws at me. Give me your Holy Spirit, and help me to turn it all over to Him for the help I need to live in this body so bent toward sinning, while I struggle to live according to the power of the Holy Spirit. That requires daily, even hourly, choices on my part, so assist me in that. In Jesus' name, Amen.

JUNE 25th

Mark 9:2-10 reads: *"And after six days, Jesus taketh with Him Peter, and James, and John, and leadeth them up into an high mountain apart by themselves: and He was transfigured before them. And His raiment became shining, exceeding white as snow, so as no fuller on earth can white them. And there appeared unto them Elias with Moses: and they were talking with Jesus. And Peter answered and said to Jesus, Master* (Rabbi), *it is good for us to be here: and let us make three tabernacles; one for thee, and one for Moses, and one for Elias. For he wist not what to say; for they were sore afraid. And there was a cloud that over shadowed them: and a voice came out of the cloud, saying, 'This is my beloved Son: hear Him.' And suddenly when they had looked round about, they saw no man any more, save Jesus only with themselves. And as they came down from the mountain He charged them that they should tell no man what things they had seen, till the Son of Man were risen from the dead. And they kept that saying with themselves, questioning one with another what the rising from the dead should mean?"*

It just keeps getting deeper and deeper. Think about such an experience! Jesus is seen in His glory, His clothes are so white there are no words to describe it! Then Moses and Elijah (also spelled Elias) appear! That proves that they are not dead, but alive! They converse with Jesus, so they are not only alive, but also able to have an intelligent conversation.

Right there, that ought to tell them, and us, something about heaven. Then a voice comes out of heaven declaring that Jesus' Father is well pleased with His Son! What a confirmation of who this man, Jesus, *is*! Then a cloud overshadows them and the whole scene is changed. They are standing with only Jesus. Was this a dream, a vision, or did they just imagine the whole thing? Who is the first to speak? Peter! It says he did not know what to say. Well, just maybe it would have been wise to have said nothing.

His suggestion of three tabernacles must have sounded rather dumb in hind sight, because later, to top it all off, they were told not to say a word about the whole experience until Jesus had risen from the dead. Everyone for miles around would have known about it if they went to work and built three tabernacles. They went, with their thoughts, from one extreme to the other. They went from building three tabernacles, to being forbidden to breathe a word of it.

When you are told to never say a word about something, have you ever noticed how tempted you are to spill the beans? That kind of command gives Satan a big challenge and he is up to the task. This is another instance where you have to make that decision now, before there is a challenge, so that when the challenge comes, you are up to the task of keeping the order. Then, to go on, what in the world did rising from the dead mean? Jesus had not even died yet, and I doubt they had even given it a thought that He, who had the power to raise people from the dead, would ever die. How their heads must have been spinning as they came down off that mountaintop experience.

Scripture says they discussed this among themselves, the three of them. They could not even tell the other disciples. Do you recall when I

239

told you earlier to not share the intimate and deep things of God that He had revealed to you with those who would not understand? This is a good example of that. Jesus had said, in effect, "Keep your mouths shut about this *until* …" There we see that perfect timing of God's again. There are no loose ends in God's Word. His timing is constant, His love is constant, His hate of sin is constant, and His faithfulness and goodness are constant also. He cannot plan evil or think evil. It is not in His nature. To follow Jesus will bring many surprises, and hard-to-understand experiences. Learn to accept them with joy and to appreciate them even if you do not understand them.

PRAYER: Dear Lord Jesus, I feel like I had better put on my seat belt, if I am going to follow you. Is this going to be a wild ride or what? Help me to learn how to keep my mouth shut when it needs to be kept shut. Help me not to talk out of turn as Peter did, and help me to understand the deep things of God. I see that God does not want to have us in the dark about spiritual things, because Jesus told them He would rise from the dead, and they didn't even know He was going to die yet. What is there in your Word that you have told me that I should know and have not discovered as yet? Help me see these things. In Jesus' name, Amen.

JUNE 26th

Matthew 10:1-10 states: *"And when He had called unto Him His twelve disciples, He gave them power* (authority) *against unclean spirits, to cast them out, and to heal all manner of sickness and all manner of disease. Now the names of the twelve apostles are these; The first, Simon, who is called Peter, and Andrew his brother; James the son of Zebedee, and John his brother; Philip, and Bartholomew; Thomas and Matthew the publican; James the son of Alphaeus, and Lebaeus, whose surname was Thaddaeus; Simon the Canaanite, and Judas Iscariot, who also betrayed Him. These twelve Jesus sent forth, and commanded them, saying, 'Go not into the way of the Gentiles, and into*

240

*any city of the Samaritans enter ye not: But go rather to the lost sheep of
the house of Israel. And as you go, preach saying, "The kingdom of
heaven is at hand." Heal the sick, cleanse the lepers, raise the dead, cast
out devils: freely ye have received, freely give. Provide neither gold, nor
silver, nor brass in your purses, Nor script* (wallet) *for your journey,
neither two coats, neither shoes, nor yet staves* (staff): *for the workman is
worthy of his meat* (food). *'"*

In this scripture, the disciples are called "apostles," and that is
because they were being sent out to minister. A disciple is a follower, and
an apostle is a "sent one."

What are we to learn from this experience? First of all, Jesus
called them to a specific task. You do not go unless you are called to go.
That is an important lesson to learn. Then Jesus gave them the authority
and power to do the job. It was their choice to use the authority and depend
on Him for the power. Then the job was presented to them. They began to
realize that the power they had been given was to take authority over such
things as unclean spirits, devils, sickness, and disease!

This was their *first* assignment, and it included all that. I can feel
my feet getting cold just reading about it! But also think about it from
Jesus' point of view. He had a tremendous task to do in just a few short
years, three and a half to be exact. He had to get a little crew of men ready
to take the message of salvation, with power, into a hostile world as soon as
Jesus had accomplished purchasing salvation, defeating the devil and all his
demons, and conquering death and diseases. The disciples would have to
be ready to face the opposing religious leaders who had sent Jesus to the
cross, and they would have to be willing to risk their lives and learn to live
on almost nothing, or depend on their provision coming from God Himself.

Think about it! The disciples had to be willing to give it their all.
This first excursion into the world with news that the kingdom of heaven is
at hand was not an easy message to bring. How would it be today if some
person came into town waving His Bible and shouting, "Listen up, the
kingdom of God is at hand, repent and be saved!" Would you be willing to
do that? What kind of a message has Jesus called you to preach, or teach,

or to share? God does not want us to keep that message to ourselves. There is more to be said about this scripture, but we will wait until tomorrow.

PRAYER: Dear Lord Jesus, I remember listening to someone sing a song about following you, and they kept saying, "Please don't send me to Africa." (It was a satire on how we want to serve God but only on a limited basis that would fit our agenda.) I believe that is the way I often think, Lord. However, I also realize that you do not ask me to do what you have not first worked a desire in me to want to do. Then, I know you will give me the power to also do it. Thank you, Lord, that I can trust you to put me where I will be a useful vessel in your kingdom work. I am not a disciple living in that day and age. I am living in this day and age, and I have neighbors, friends, relatives, and social acquaintances to whom I can witness when you open the right doors. I am also aware of the fact that it is you that gives the call to a particular service, so I do not have to make the move until you move first. Then you will give me the right to make a free choice. Help me see your hand in any call that comes my way so that I will know that it is you calling me and I can trust you to lead me. It is such a privilege to be used by you in this world that is so needy. Thank you for the insights I gain from these experiences the disciples had. In Jesus' name, Amen.

JUNE 27th

Let us look closely at Matthew 10:5-6, which explains that Jesus *"commanded them, saying, 'Go not into the way of the Gentiles, and into any city of the Samaritans enter ye not. But go rather to the lost sheep of the house of Israel.' "* Jesus is doing His Father's will at all times, and here we see how specific the Godhead is. They are told where *not* to go and where *to* go. He left no doubt about anything!

Now the hardest place to witness is among those who know you best, your own family, church members, and those with whom you work. It would have been really easy to go tell the Gentiles what *they* needed to do, but to tell the religious leaders what they did wrong in the eyes of God was another thing. Jesus had to be doing that all the time, and it got Him crucified.

Wouldn't you like to know where they went on this excursion of witnessing? What they said and how they said it? It might help us a lot right now to be an example to us, but we are all individuals and Jesus will use each of us on that basis, individually, because each of us has to learn how to depend on God entirely, no one else can teach us that. But God is faithful and He will provide what we need, even bring to our remembrance whatever we need to remember, especially scriptures we need to quote to someone.

Then we read Matthew 10:8-10, which says, *"...Freely you have received, freely give. Provide neither gold, nor silver, nor brass in your purses, nor script* (wallet) *for your journey, neither two coats, neither shoes, nor yet staves* (staff)." The Contemporary English Version (CEV) translates it as, *"You have received without paying, now give without being paid. Don't take along any gold, silver or copper coins, and don't carry a traveling bag or an extra shirt or sandals or a walking stick."*

In these verses we see the attitude they are to have. They were to depend upon God for everything. They were to travel light and give freely, just as freely as they had received. Have you ever tried to travel light? It is not an easy thing to do. We always want just one more thing in case of an emergency. In the natural, we depend on our own strength, however, it is necessary to plan ahead. In this time and place, Jesus is calling upon them to depend on Him and to take along only the bare necessities. Stories abound of people who have depended on God for every small thing in their lives as servants of God's. Most of us do not know what that is like. But, if we are ever called to do that, I believe we better decide to do it when we do not need that kind of help, because when it does come, and usually it is suddenly, it is much harder to put into practice what we know is the right way to react.

PRAYER: Lord God, how did the disciples pass their first test? I am wondering if I would pass the test. This is putting it all on the line and depending on you completely. It really makes me feel naked, stripped clean. I also know enough about your Word to know that you will not let anyone down, but will provide, even if it is at the last minute. But then again, you are never a minute early or a minute late. Help me, Lord, to learn quickly how to lean and depend on you for all things. In Jesus' name, Amen.

JUNE 28ᵗʰ

Matthew 10:10-15 Jesus says: *"For the workman is worthy of his meat* (food). *And into whatsoever city or town ye shall enter, inquire* (search out) *who in it is worthy; and there abide till ye go thence. And when ye come into an house, salute it. And if the house be worthy, let your peace come upon it: but if it be not worthy, let your peace return to you. And whosoever shall not receive you, nor hear your words, when ye depart out of that house or city, shake off the dust of your feet. Verily I say unto you, 'It shall be more tolerable for the land of Sodom and Gomorah in the day of judgment, than for that city.' "*

And the CEV translates it as: *"Workers deserve their food. So when you go to a town or a village, find someone worthy enough to have you as their guest and stay with them until you leave. When you go to a home, give it your blessing of peace. If the home is deserving, let your blessing remain with them. But if the home isn't deserving, take back your blessing of peace. If someone won't welcome you or listen to your message, leave their home or town. And shake the dust from your feet at them. I promise you that the day of judgment will be easier for the towns of Sodom and Gomorrah than for that town."*

These are some tough words to swallow. To God, there is a separation between what is right and what is wrong, between sin and righteousness. The line was drawn, and there was to be no compromise, none at all. The directions were very specific: to go into a town or village and size up the situation. If you should go to a house and find they are not

244

friendly to you or your message, take back the peace with which you had blessed that home.

You see, if they choose darkness rather than light, don't object, it is their choice. You can always pray for that household. That is *your* free choice, and God will honor your choice and will do everything He can short of going against their will, to reach that home with His Truth. They were to even shake the dust off from their feet as they leave as a sign against them. With God, there is no room for compromise when it comes to being for or against Him.

If you are the kind of person with the gift of mercy, this will be the hardest thing you would ever do. God is a merciful God, but He is also a God who obeys the laws, and there can be no fellowship between light and darkness. Water is either bitter or sweet. It cannot be both at the same time. Everywhere light is, darkness has to flee. When they choose darkness, then light is not welcome. But Jesus is talking here about the "lost sheep of the house of Israel." They are Jews who should know about the God of their fathers Abraham, Isaac, and Jacob.

And then, to add insult to injury, Jesus says that it will be more tolerable for Sodom and Gomorrah in the day of judgment than for this city. "Why?" you might ask. I venture to suggest that Sodom and Gomorrah did not have the Word of God to direct them like the Jews did, they did not know right from wrong, or sin from righteousness. Therefore, their judgment will be from that standpoint.

So, then, what does that say to us? Well, it tells us plainly that we are responsible for what we know about God's Word. With every privilege goes an equal responsibility. Do you want to know the Word of God, or would you feel better not knowing what God has to say to you? If you want to know the Word, then you need to realize you are also responsible to live according to that Word. The disciples as apostles are finding this out as well. They were willing to die for that Word after Jesus rose from the dead!

PRAYER: Heavenly Father, there is so much to learn about you and your idea of how to live and act as a follower of yours. I am glad you are patient with me, and will help me take this step, one day at a time. At least I am

245

not in Africa, but in my little old home of my own, and you have put me here and have fed me here, and given me friends and supporters here. I thank you that you are using me right where I am. Help me not to turn to the left or to the right unless that is what you want me to do. Then I can be content to be right where I am as I read these devotions. If you want me to move, then you will arrange it and all I will have to do is to follow your leading. Okay? In Jesus' name, Amen.

JUNE 29th

We are going to look at a few more experiences the disciples had with Jesus. Put yourself in the shoes of the disciples as they watch and learn from the Master. John 2:1-11 reads: *"And the third day there was a marriage in Cana of Galilee, and the mother of Jesus was there: And both Jesus was called and His disciples, to the marriage. And when they wanted wine, the mother of Jesus saith unto Him, "They have no wine.' Jesus saith unto her, 'Woman, what have I to do with thee? Mine hour is not yet come.' His mother saith unto the servants, 'Whatsoever He saith unto you, do it.' And there were set there six water pots of stone, after the manner of the purifying of the Jews, containing two or three firkins apiece* (about 20 to 30 gallons each)*. Jesus saith unto them, 'Fill the water pots with water.' And they filled them up to the brim. And He saith unto them, 'Draw out now, and bear unto the governor of the feast.' And they bare it. When the ruler of the feast had tasted the water that was made wine, and knew not whence it was (but the servants which drew the water knew), the governor of the feast called the bridegroom, And saith unto him, 'Every man at the beginning doth set forth good wine; and when men have well drunk, then that which is worst: but thou hast kept the good wine until now. This beginning of miracles did Jesus in Cana of Galilee, and manifested forth His glory; and His disciples believed on Him."*

This took place at the beginning of His ministry, and the disciples are just getting a glimpse into what this Jesus was able to do. A Jewish wedding was a time for a festival. They celebrated according to the riches of the groom. When we, the church body, become the wife of Jesus, there will be a very big celebration also.

See what Jesus said when He instituted the Last Supper, known to us as the Eucharist or Communion Service. Matthew 26:26-29 says: *"And as they were eating, Jesus took bread, and blessed it, and brake it, and gave it to the disciples, and said, 'Take, eat; this is my body.' And He took the cup, and gave thanks, and gave it to them, saying, 'Drink ye all of it; For this is my blood of the new testament, which is shed for many for the remission of sins. But I say unto you, I will not drink henceforth of this fruit of the vine, until that day, when I drink it new with you in my Father's kingdom.' "*

It is my belief that "that day" He is referring to here, is the wedding celebration of the Bride and Christ. And just as a bride and groom are to become One, so also will we, the church, and Christ will become *one*. Jesus will drink the wine with us at that wedding celebration in heaven. We will talk more about the wedding feast at Cana tomorrow.

PRAYER: Heavenly Father, I cherish the moments of communion celebration with you. It draws me so close to you, and I know in my heart that you have reached right down on my level to take me into your circle and declare to me that I am accepted. I pray for those who do not know you in that intimate way and ask you to leave no stone unturned to reach them with your love and your Word, and bring them into your circle as you have done for me. In Jesus' name, Amen.

JUNE 30th

You can reread yesterday's scripture (John 2:1-11), because today we are going to discuss some things that the disciples had to process in their minds. It could appear that Jesus' mother was intimately involved in this wedding, perhaps good friends or maybe even a relative. Another thing to note is that it was very embarrassing to run out of wine. The groom would not have gotten married if he could not have provided for the new bride, and this feast was his first example of what he could do for her.

Jesus' mother did not want the groom to be embarrassed, so she turned to Jesus. Did she know something that the others did not know, about Him? There is speculation about that. But we do know that she did not hesitate to bring the need to the attention of Jesus. His response is rather abrupt and pointed. First of all, He did not call her "mother," but instead called her "woman," and I have read various thoughts on that. Some have said it was not an unusual way to address her, while others claim that Jesus was reminding her that He was not just her son, but also the Son of God, and that had to come first. He did say, "Mine hour is not yet come," reminding her that He was not on her time schedule, but on God's time schedule.

We talked at length earlier on the importance of the right timing. Here is another example of that truth. However, if someone was hurting, Jesus would stop and minister to that need right away, and I think His mother knew that too. Of course, that is what happened. His mother told the servants to do whatever He asked. She had no idea what He would ask of them, but no matter how odd it was, they weren't supposed to question it, just do it.

What does that tell us? Jesus may ask you to do something way out of the ordinary, and if it is Him talking to you, you better do as these servants did. They filled the water pots to the brim, not half full, but full! This is a lesson for us, too. We have a tendency to only expect a small amount from God. God wants to bless abundantly, but He will only bless according to our faith. The servants had faith as they filled those water pots. How much wine did they need toward the end of the celebration? But they filled the pots to the brim! You and I are clay pots also, and Jesus wants to fill us to the brim too. Are we willing to allow Him to fill us with His Spirit to the brim? We will look at this more tomorrow.

PRAYER: Heavenly Father, do I want to be filled to the brim? That is a good question! Everything in me says, "Yes, yes," and then the old nature kicks in and says, "But what if He asks you to go to Africa?" and I go on that same old merry go round again. Instead I am going to bypass my old nature and say, "Yes" anyway and then give my "yes" answer over to you to work out in my day-to-day life. Give me the eyes to see your work in my life now, to be able to see that it is filled to the brim with your Spirit. In Jesus' name, Amen.

JULY 1st

Remember that in John 2:8, Jesus told the men to draw out the water and give it to the governor of the feast. Today, I want to talk about the faith of the servants who did as Jesus asked by giving the water to the governor.

The servants know that there is only water in the pots. Jesus asks them to draw it out and bring it to the governor (which is like the host) who had been asked to keep things moving so the wedding feast would go smoothly. The verse does not say whether they were afraid of being ridiculed for bringing water, but no one had explained to them that this water would turn to wine. They had to have had tremendous faith in Jesus' ability to do something about the situation.

The governor is not aware of what is going on at all. He must have been expecting pretty poor wine, since the best was usually served first and this would have really been the last. Think of his surprise when it was better than the first wine. Everybody's expectations are being turned upside down. All through Jesus' ministry, He turned people's expectations upside down, and He is still doing that today.

We need to recognize one more thing. John 2:11 says that *"...His disciples believed on Him."* What are some things we need to recap? Jesus was celebrating a wedding—just being a plain human being in the then-known world. He had His friends with Him, who would one day carry on His work here on earth. A problem arises, and His Mother turns to Him for help. Jesus has to be careful that He fulfills God's timing in all things. His

249

mother expects Him to fill the need, so He does, and the wedding goes on as though there had been no problem.

The disciples believe in Jesus. Could we speculate on the next day? The governor is told he had been drinking water, the groom had been told he had run out of wine, the servants know it had been water, but now it is wine, and so the story goes. How it must have spread throughout the country, and here you sit reading about it today. What did you learn about Jesus?

PRAYER: Heavenly Father, I thank you for including this account in your Holy Book, the Bible. It makes me realize how Jesus lived like me—living an ordinary life, meeting ordinary needs. I feel like I can bring any need to Him, or any want, and He will at least hear me. Then, too, I see how abundantly He is willing to bless me. I always have a problem with expecting abundance from you, Heavenly Father. I feel like I am being greedy, wanting more and more, and that I do not appreciate the abundance I have already been given by you. I think I will stick with, *"Seek ye first the Kingdom of God and all these things will be given unto you,"* (Matthew 6:33) and let you be in charge of the *things* in my life. In Jesus' name, Amen.

JULY 2nd

Today, we will look at one more of Peter's experiences before moving on to other phases of his life. Matthew 26:36-45 reads: *"Then cometh Jesus with them unto a place called Gethsemane, and saith unto the disciples, 'Sit ye here, while I go and pray yonder.' And He took with Him Peter, and the two sons of Zebedee* (James and John), *and began to be sorrowful and very heavy. Then saith He unto them, 'My soul is exceeding sorrowful, even unto death: tarry ye here, and watch with me.' And He went a little farther, and fell on His face, and prayed, saying, 'O my Father, if it be possible, let this cup pass from me: nevertheless not as I will, but as thou will.' And He cometh unto the disciples, and findeth them asleep, and saith unto Peter, 'What, could ye not watch with me one hour Watch and pray, that ye enter not into temptation: The spirit indeed is willing, but the flesh is weak.' He went away again the second time, and prayed, saying. 'O my Father, if this cup may not pass away from me, except I drink it, thy will be done.' And He came and found them asleep again: for their eyes were heavy. And He left them, and went away again, and prayed the third time, saying the same words. Then cometh He to His disciples, and saith unto them, 'Sleep on now, and take your rest: behold the hour is at hand, and the Son of man is betrayed into the hands of sinners.' "*

The disciples are not at all aware that this is Jesus' last night with them as the leader and friend. Jesus often went to this garden to pray. Also notice that Peter, James, and John are asked to go a "little farther," and then Jesus Himself went still farther on. That is a picture of how things work in the spiritual world. God is always at work, getting us to go on a little farther.

All Jesus asked of these three disciples was to wait and watch with Him. The others were to sit while He went to pray, but the three were told to wait and watch. What were they supposed to watch? I believe they were to watch Jesus' body language. He had told them that his soul was exceedingly sorrowful, even unto death. What time of the day was this? I am not sure, but it was after the meal and after Jesus had washed their feet after the meal, so the disciples were tired.

If you know anything about the enemy, you know Satan is able to make you so suddenly tired that no matter how hard you struggle to stay awake, it is almost impossible—especially if you are listening to a good speaker who is ministering to your spirit. I cannot help but believe the disciples' drowsiness was Satan's attempt to defeat Jesus' plan of salvation. Jesus was left without prayer support from anyone.

It is so important to have some prayer partners who are able to "watch" with you when you have a big need. In Matthew 18:19, Jesus says, *"Where two of you shall agree on earth as touching any thing that they shall ask, it shall be done for them of my Father which is in heaven."* Satan knew that Jesus was the "Lamb of God," and the Lamb would have to

251

die, and he wanted Jesus to be defeated. Three times Jesus checked in on them, and every time they were sleeping. What a disappointment that must have been to Jesus. I have often wondered how those disciples felt later, when they witnessed the crucifixion and the resurrection, in the light of their inability to watch with Him even one hour as He said. I am sure we disappoint Him in our life too, just as they did.

We need to be sensitive to Satan's traps to set us up for failures such as this. You see, I am a firm believer in the fact that we cover such situations today before they happen, not when they happen. If you wait until then, it is too late to get it all together. But today, while you are thinking about it, ask God to wake you up to what is happening around you so that you can be ready for the temptation when it comes. Then you will recognize what is happening, and you can be ready to obey the Spirit within you.

PRAYER: Heavenly Father, I know that you have said that the Holy Spirit lives within me—that my body is the temple of the Holy Spirit. Therefore, I ask you to help me to be sensitive to the willingness of the Holy Spirit to have me be prepared at all times to meet the crises that comes into my life. Help me to be aware of what is happening, so I will not act or react in a way that is not in keeping with the life of a believer. I have not seen any place where you give us the notion that we will fall under a burden, or become a "basket case," as they say, when something suddenly befalls us, or that we are to retreat. Therefore, I believe that I am to be victorious and not a failure, the head and not the tail—to be an "overcomer," not a loser. Help me as I reach for those goals in my life. In Jesus' name, Amen.

JULY 3rd

We have looked at several experiences that the disciples had as they followed Jesus for those three and a half years. Three times Peter, James, and John were given extra privileges—when Jesus raised the little girl from the dead, when He was transfigured on the mountain along with Moses and Elijah, and again when they were in the garden of Gethsemane. Peter was mentioned first each time.

I have often wondered how his brother, Andrew, felt about that. It was Andrew who brought Peter to Jesus and pointed out that He was the Messiah. I want to take you to the portion of Scripture where Peter made his great confession as to who Jesus is. Matthew 16:13-20 reads:

" 'Whom do men say that I the Son of man am?' And they said, 'Some say that thou art John the Baptist; some Elias; and others, Jeremiah, or one of the prophets.' He saith unto them, 'But whom say ye that I am?' And Simon Peter answered and said, 'Thou are the Christ, the Son of the living God.' And Jesus answered and said unto him, 'Blessed art thou, Simon Barjona (meaning "son of John")*: for flesh and blood hath not revealed it unto thee, but my Father which is in heaven. And I say also unto thee, that thou art Peter, and upon this rock I will build my church; and the gates of hell shall not prevail against it. And I will give unto thee the keys of the kingdom of heaven; and whatsoever thou shalt bind on earth shall be bound in heaven; and whatsoever thou shalt loose on earth shall be loosed in heaven.' Then charged He His disciples that they should tell no man that He was Jesus the Christ."*

Jesus asked a very direct question that required an honest answer. First, He asked who "men" said He was. After they described what was being said out there in the streets, Jesus asked them who they, the disciples, said He was. It is important what we say, too. So, who do *you* say Jesus is?

Peter was always quick to speak up, even when he should have kept his mouth shut. But this time it was all right to speak up. Although, I would have liked to know whether some of the other disciples were willing to say who they thought Jesus was, such as Andrew, who first said He was the Messiah.

Here, Jesus called Simon by the name Peter, which means "rock," and Jesus said that only God, His heavenly Father, could have revealed this truth to Peter. The same is true today. Neither you nor I are able to reveal what the Scripture is saying to anyone. It is the Holy Spirit's work to reveal these truths.

Then, Jesus said that upon this rock God would build His church. What rock is Jesus talking about? There are different opinions about this. Some verses in the Bible describe Jesus as a rock. Romans 9:33 says, *"As it is written (Isaiah 8:14), 'Behold I lay in Zion a stumbling stone and rock of offense; and whosoever believeth on Him shall not be ashamed."*

Jesus gave the keys to the kingdom of heaven to the disciples, and gave them authority to bind and to loose, both on earth and in heaven. I believe that all who have the Holy Spirit within them have the keys to the kingdom of heaven and is responsible for carrying that truth with them.

Jesus is also called the Rock in I Corinthians 10:4, which reads, *"And did all drink the same spiritual drink: for they drank of that spiritual Rock that followed them: and that Rock was Christ."* I believe the rock Jesus is talking about in Matthew is the *truth* that Peter had proclaimed in his confession as to who Jesus was. We who believe that truth are responsible for it. If we keep it a secret, then what have we done with it? We have withheld it and no one else will hear it from us. The Church will be built on that truth—that Jesus is the Christ, the Son of the living God. Think each word of that statement through, and let it penetrate your whole being.

God is a *Living God.* Jesus rose from the dead! And Jesus was the anointed Christ, Son of God, Son of man. No wonder He could be the mediator between God and man. What puzzles me is that Jesus told the disciples not to breathe a word of this to anyone. He must have wanted the people to find it out in their own timing, and I sometimes think that is our problem today, we want to push the truth at someone who is not at all ready in the eyes of God to receive the truth, and that can do more harm than good. I have always said, "It has to be the *right word*, to the *right person* at the *right time*, and only the Holy Spirit can determine when that is." So, depend on the Holy Spirit to tell you when it is the right time, and then ask Him to give you the right words and the right person.

PRAYER: Dear Lord Jesus, thank you for being that Rock in my life. Help me also to know what and when to bind things on earth and what and when to loose things in heaven. Also, thank you for these verses about

Peter and all the disciples. They help me to see that they are human like me, and make mistakes like I do. I see your patience with them, and know that you will be that patient with me too. In Jesus' name, Amen.

JULY 4th

Peter was also Satan's target, just like we are at times. Matthew 16:21-23 states: *"From that time forth began Jesus to shew unto His disciples, how that He must go unto Jerusalem, and suffer many things of the elders and chief priests and scribes, and be killed, and be raised again on the third day. Then Peter took Him, and began to rebuke Him, saying, 'Be it far from thee, Lord: this shall not be unto thee.' But He turned, and said unto Peter, 'Get thee behind me, Satan; thou art an offence unto me: for thou mindest not the things that be of God, but those that be of men.' "*

Here we see that Peter again spoke without first thinking it through. These men just did not get it, did they? But then, do we get it? They saw a man who had supernatural powers, and what in the world would such a man have to suffer and die for? They did not see the big picture. Do we?

Mankind, as it stood at that time, was estranged from God, and needed a way to be connected to Him again. Jesus was the One who was to bring the fellowship of God and mankind back into line again. That is what was meant by the term "Lamb of God."

Jesus came to be that perfect sacrifice, and He was trying to tell His disciples that it would happen soon. But they just were not getting the picture. Their idea of a Messiah and Christ was a man who would be all powerful and rule on this earth—putting all other rulers down and all other gods also. Well, that day will come, but only in God's right timing.

So, Peter spoke up again. Jesus made quick work of Satan's attempt to once again, invade Jesus' mind and break His will to do the Father's will. Can you imagine Peter being told off so harshly by Jesus? But Peter did not give up and go away in a big pout. Many would have done that, thinking, "Well, if He wants to be like that, I guess I will just go my own way then!"

PRAYER: Heavenly Father, it is so good for me to see the action and reactions between Jesus and His disciples. It helps me to understand how Satan steps into the scene so unexpectedly. Help me to recognize when such a time is happening, so that I can avoid being a tool in his hand. This devotion today also helps me to see how Jesus took authority over the situation and did not allow it to be stumbling block to Him. Help me to be quick to take authority over things in my life when Satan tries to trip me up and cause me to fail in my daily walk with you. In Jesus' name, Amen.

JULY 5th

 Luke 22:31-32 reads: *"And the Lord said, 'Simon, Simon* (notice that here he is *not* called Peter, the rock)*, behold, Satan hath <u>desired to have you</u>, that he may <u>sift you as wheat</u>: But <u>I have prayed for thee</u>, that <u>thy faith fail not</u>: and when thou art converted, strengthen thy brethren."* Imagine that! Jesus had been praying for Peter that his faith stay strong and not fail. Jesus knew Peter very well, and Jesus, being gentle, allowed Peter to open his mouth and put his foot into it again and again, and to give a word of advice along the way, in the hopes that Peter would begin to see in his own spirit what is wrong with him and what correction he needs. God will never invade our freedom of choice. He will allow us to make one mistake after the other *until we get it*—until we understand that we need to ask God for direction for everything we do.

But let us go on and see how Peter put his foot in his mouth again. We continue in Luke 22:33 states, *"And he said unto Him, 'Lord, I am ready to go with thee, both into prison, and to death.' And He said, 'I tell thee, Peter, the cock shall not crow this day, before that thou shalt thrice deny that thou knowest me.' "*

Peter would have been better off if he had said nothing. One thing to note about God's Word is that it does not gloss anything over. The Old

Testament is full of the "oopses" of mankind. God foretold of it all—the lies, fornication, idolatry and jealousy. Mankind's failures stand out in God's Word, and it is meant to teach us not to do as they did.

We are all like Peter in many ways. But, if we are smart, we will learn from Peter and avoid the same embarrassments that he had to endure because of his mouth. Peter's biggest problem was that he did not have his eyes on God and what was God's plan in Jesus' life. He had his eyes on his own plan for Jesus. For Peter, though, it gets worse. We will look

PRAYER: Lord Jesus, I am glad to read about Peter's experiences. They help me to see you as a patient, long-suffering God—One who is able to know how we feel inside. I am also glad to learn that you pray for our shortcomings as you did for Peter. I believe Satan would like to sift all of us as wheat, and I am so glad that I am on your prayer list. If Peter, who had walked with you, was on your list, then surely I, who am covered by your saving blood, am on your prayer list, too. That is comforting to me. I hope that I can be the witness to these truths that you would want me to be. Give me the strength to do that. In Jesus' precious name, Amen.

JULY 6th

We are going look at verses that describe the same event in Matthew, Mark, Luke, and John. Some may sound repetitious, but we will cover the subject better that way. Mathew 26:31-35 reads: *"Then saith Jesus unto them, 'All ye shall be offended because of me this night: for it is written, "I will smite the shepherd, and the sheep of the flock shall be scattered abroad." But after I am risen again, I will go before you into Galilee.' Peter answered and said unto Him, 'Though all men shall be offended because of thee, yet will I never be offended.' Jesus said unto him, 'Verily I say unto thee, that this night, before the cock crow, thou shalt deny me thrice.' Peter said unto Him, 'Verily I say unto thee, "Though I should die with thee, yet will I not deny thee."' Likewise also said all the disciples."*

257

All this was said right before they went to the garden of Gethsemane (where Jesus asked them to wait and watch with Him for an hour, but instead they went to sleep). Peter did not understand the power and trickery of the enemy, but he would soon get a lesson in it.

Peter was forever speaking up, and those words would become bitter in his stomach. He said he was willing to go to his death with Jesus. Was that really true? Peter said he would never be offended because of Jesus. Was that true? Did Jesus know the truth? He had always told his disciples the truth, so why did they doubt it at this late hour?

You can see how easy it is to get sucked into the devil's trap. We can deny Jesus that easily, too. Just don't challenge Satan to prove it like Peter did. It is no wonder Jesus had been praying for Peter. Peter had no idea how weak his human flesh was when it comes to, for instance, being threatened with crucifixion. As followers of Jesus, it would be understandable that they would be rounded up and crucified also. Peter had not reckoned on that. Then the weakness of his flesh was shown for all to see.

PRAYER: Lord Jesus, my desire is to not deny you, but I will need the strength given to me by the Holy Spirit to carry that out. I know my flesh is weak and cannot live up to the standard you expect from us. My desire is to live a life pleasing to you, and, again, I need your help to do that. I hand my life over to the guidance of the Holy Spirit to direct and guide me daily. In Jesus' precious name, Amen.

JULY 7th

Jesus had been arrested, taken away by the Temple Guards, and questioned by the High Priest. The disciples scattered as Jesus had said they would, but let's see what Peter did. Matthew 26:69-75 reads: *"Now Peter sat without in the palace: and a damsel came unto him, saying, 'Thou also wast with Jesus of Galilee.' But he denied before them all saying, 'I know not what thou sayest.' And when he had gone out into the porch, another maid saw him, and said unto them that were there, 'This fellow was also with Jesus of Nazareth.' And again he denied with an oath, 'I do not know the man.' And after a while came unto him they that stood by, and said to Peter, 'Surely thou also art one of them; for thy speech betrays thee.' Then began he to curse and to swear, saying, 'I know not the man.' And immediately the cock crew. And Peter remembered the word of Jesus, which said unto him, 'Before the cock crow, thou shalt deny me thrice.' And he went out and wept bitterly."*

We need to understand that when Jesus says such-and-such is going to happen, we ought to believe Him. He had told the disciples that He would have to suffer and die, and that He would rise on the third day. They were all in denial, right up to the bitter end. Not until He had risen did they begin to see the light, so to speak.

Are we just as hard-headed as them? What has God said to you in His Word that you have blown off like, "That will never happen," or, "One little sin won't send me to hell"? Remember, one lie leads to another. Peter told three, right in a row, even after Jesus told him point blank that Satan desired to sift him as wheat and that He had been praying for him.

He also told Peter that he would deny Him three times before the cock crowed. How much more straightforward could Jesus have been? Think about it. We are just as thick-headed as Peter was. Our old nature is working just as hard as Peter's to trip us up each day.

Learn a lesson from Peter. You do not have to go out and weep bitterly. You can pray now to be prepared to stand your spiritual ground when the time suddenly arises. And, believe me, it happens to all of us at one time or another. My word to you is, "Be prepared now for it!"

PRAYER: Heavenly Father, I do not want to have to go out and weep bitterly, so I ask you now, in the comfort of my surroundings, while there is peace all around me, to help me in that time when Satan strikes with malicious force to undermine my faith in you. Give me the Words from your Holy Book that will pop into my mind to help me be steadfast and stable, not compromising—to soothe my old nature that will be screaming

259

at me to compromise and question your goodness, mercy or wisdom, or even to deny your goodness, mercy and wisdom. In Jesus' name, Amen.

JULY 8th

The book of Luke gives us a small hint as to what Peter's problem was. See if you can find it. Luke 22:54-62 states: *"Then took they Him and led Him, and brought Him into the High Priest's house. And Peter followed afar off. And when they had kindled a fire in the midst of the court, and were set down together, Peter sat down among them. But a certain maid beheld him as he sat by the fire, and earnestly looked upon him, and said, 'This man was also with Him.' And he denied Him, saying, 'Woman I know Him not.' And after a little while another saw him, and said, 'Thou art also of them.' And Peter said, 'Man, I am not.' And about the space of one hour after another confidently affirmed, saying, 'Of a truth this fellow also was with him: for he is a Galilaean* (his speech was different from those around Jerusalem). *' And Peter said, 'Man, I know not what thou sayest.' And immediately, while he yet spake, the cock crew. And the Lord turned, and looked upon Peter. And Peter remembered the word of the Lord, how He had said unto him, 'Before the cock crow, thou shalt deny me thrice.' And Peter went out, and wept bitterly."*

Did you find the one thing Peter was doing that gave Satan a foothold on him? In verse 54, we see that Peter followed "afar off." Anytime we follow Jesus afar off, it tells the devil he has a right to test our faith. Did you ever think about that before?

Peter wanted to melt into the crowd, but he also wanted to know what was happening to Jesus. He just did not want to be identified with Jesus and the punishment He was about to receive. I say all this, because it is so important for us to know that what has happened to Jesus was *all* done for our benefit, so we will not have to suffer as He did. But when we choose to be identified with Jesus, the world and its systems will see us as the enemy, and will work to make us a laughing stock, or, on the other side of the pendulum, expect us to be more than perfect and try to find even one little fault in us to point a finger at us and exclaim, "I thought *you* were a Christian, but you did, said, thought, like that!"

We will be in trouble if we follow "afar off," and we will be in trouble if we follow close and even smell of Jesus. It is your choice. If you follow afar off, you will go out and weep bitterly. It is inescapable. If you follow close to Jesus, you will suffer having the world in conflict with who you are in Christ. But, you will not suffer separation from God. That is by far worse than not being accepted by the world around you. Never be ashamed of Jesus in your life, knowing the Word of God, or carrying His Word, the Bible, with you. You may be called a "Bible Banger," but is that so bad? Believe me, you will live through that, and God will exalt you for it. It just might encourage others to carry their Bibles, too.

PRAYER: Lord Jesus, I do not want to follow you afar off, and I do not want to weep bitterly, but I also do not want to stick out like a sore thumb in the world around me. How do I reach a balance? If I just hand myself over for you to lead, direct, guide, and use, then do the people around me also have your guiding hand to cause them to look at me with a positive attitude? Are you working in their lives at the same time as I am trying to live a life pleasing to you? I pray that I can just rest in your guidance and not even worry about making a mistake, or putting my foot in my mouth, like Peter did, and then having to be so sorry for what I said. Thank you for hearing my prayer. In Jesus' name, Amen.

JULY 9th

John 21:13-17 states: *"Jesus then cometh, and taketh bread, and giveth them, and fish likewise. This is now the third time that Jesus shewed Himself to His disciples, after that He was risen from the dead. So when they had dined, Jesus saith to Simon Peter, 'Simon, son of Jonas, lovest thou me more than these?' He saith unto Him, 'Yea, Lord; thou knowest that I love thee.' He saith unto him,*

'Feed my sheep.' He saith to him again the second time, 'Simon, son of Jonas, lovest thou me?' He saith unto Him, 'Yea, Lord; thou kowest that I love thee.' He saith unto him, 'Tend my sheep.' He saith unto him the third time, 'Simon, son of Jonas, lovest thou me?' Peter was grieved because He said unto him the third time, 'Lovest thou me?' And he said unto Him, 'Lord, thou knowest all things; thou knowest that I love thee.' Jesus saith unto him, 'Feed my sheep.'"

In these verses, we see that Jesus did not leave Peter in bitterness, but came and reached out to him right on the level of his need. The fact that Jesus asked him the same question three times could be to match his denial of Jesus three times. And Jesus reinstates Peter three times by calling on him to feed and tend His sheep—which may be referring to the "lost sheep of the house of Israel."

Peter knew that he was still considered a part of the group of disciples, turned apostles. He had not lost his place in the group of men who were left with the work of forming a church that would fill the earth with the story of salvation, redemption, justification, and sanctification.

PRAYER: Heavenly Father, it was so much like you to reach out to mankind when we failed you in a big way like Peter had done by denying knowing Jesus. It shows me that you will reach out to me too when I have made a big mistake. Thank you for the lesson I gain by looking at Peter's life. You said that you would never leave or forsake me, and you prove that is a part of your nature when you show me in your Word that you do not leave nor forsake others, such as Peter. I thank you for that assurance. Help me to follow you like the sheep follow their shepherd. In Jesus' name, Amen.

JULY 10th

Fifty days after Jesus rose from the dead, God sent the gift of the Holy Spirit to the believers, and they were imbued with power from on high. Then Peter preached a mighty sermon. This same

Peter (who had not seen the broader vision of what God was doing through Jesus for the human race) was able to preach a powerful sermon. But then, Jesus knew he had a mouth that could speak, didn't He?

Acts 2 opens with the outpouring of the Holy Spirit on the gathered believers, as we see in verses 2:1-4, which reads: *"And when the day of Pentecost was fully come, they were all with one accord in one place. And suddenly there came a sound from heaven as of a rushing mighty wind, and it filled all the house where they were sitting. And there appeared unto them cloven tongues like as of fire, and it sat upon each of them. And they were all filled with the Holy Ghost, and began to speak with other tongues, as the Spirit gave them utterance."*

Everyone there was amazed at such a happening. Jews from other parts of the world were there to keep the Feast of Pentecost, which every Jewish male was required to attend. They were able to hear the believers speak in their own language. People thought these believers were drunk with wine, but at that suggestion, Peter got up and told them this was the fulfillment of prophecy and that Jesus had promised the gift of the Holy Spirit.

Peter then launched into a great sermon to those gathered in Jerusalem. Some of what he said is found in Acts 2:21-24, which states: *"And it shall come to pass, that whosoever shall call on the name of the Lord shall be saved . Ye men of Israel, hear these words, Jesus of Nazareth, a man approved of God among you by miracles and wonders and signs, which God did by Him in the midst of you, as ye yourselves also know: Him being delivered by the determinate counsel and foreknowledge of God, ye have taken, and by wicked hands have crucified and slain; Whom God hath raised up, having loosed the pains of death: because it was not possible that He should be holden of it."*

A few weeks prior to this, Peter had denied even knowing who Jesus was, because he was afraid for his own life, but now he boldly stands up and talks to the people of Jerusalem with power and conviction. Jesus knew what Peter was really made of, and that he would be a powerful force for the Church that was to grow out of the ashes of the crucified and risen Lord Jesus Christ.

If you want to read the whole sermon, read all of Acts 2, but right now, let's look at verses 37-38, which read: *"Now when they heard this, they were pricked in their heart, and said unto Peter and to the rest of the Apostles, 'Men and brethren, what shall we do?' Then Peter said unto them, 'Repent, and be baptized every one of you in the name of Jesus Christ for the remission of sins, and ye shall receive the gift of the Holy Ghost.' "*

The people were convicted of their sins and did not know what to do. Think about it. Jesus came to pay the price for sin and the penalty of sin! That was His whole reason for coming, dying, and rising again—to settle the sin question between God and mankind. That was the truth that Peter's sermon had shown them. He also gave them the right answer to their question. It was so simple: Repent and be baptized and receive the Holy Ghost!

Acts 2:40-41 explain, *"And with many other words did he testify and exhort, saying, 'Save yourselves from this untoward* (crooked) *generation.' Then they that gladly received his word were baptized: and the same day there were added unto them, about three thousand souls!"* This was only Peter's first sermon, and 3,000 souls accepted Jesus as their Christ! Peter may have made many mistakes, but he also had a heart for God. Peter knew who Jesus was, and he willing to step up to the plate and give it his all. It was an "anointed sermon," we might say, and the results proved it.

PRAYER: Heavenly Father, there are times when I feel too weak to step up to the plate and give it my all. Is that when you minister strength for the weary to continue on anyway? I want to be the person who does not slack off, or backslide, but rather presses onward and upward in my daily walk with you. Give me the persistent strength and faith to do that. Help me to lay on you the burdens of the day first thing in the morning, so that I can have your help to carry me through to a triumphant victory at the end of the day. In Jesus' name, Amen.

JULY 11th

Acts 3:1-9 reads: *"Now Peter and John went up together into the temple at the hour of prayer, being the ninth hour* (3:00 p.m.). *And a certain man, lame from his mother's womb, was carried, whom they laid daily at the gate of the temple which is called Beautiful, to ask alms of them that entered into the temple: Who seeing Peter and John about to go into the temple asked an alms. And Peter, fastening his eyes upon him with John, said, 'Look on us,' and he gave heed unto them, expecting to receive something* (alms, or money) *of them. Then Peter said, 'Silver and gold have I none; but such as I have give I thee: In the name of Jesus Christ of Nazareth rise up and walk.' And he took him by the right hand, and lifted him up: and immediately his feet and ankle bones received strength. And he leaping up stood, and walked, and entered with them into the temple, walking, and leaping, and praising God. And all the people saw him walking and praising God."*

The frightened Peter of just a few weeks earlier has turned into a take-charge, powerful follower of Jesus Christ. He is ready to feed and tend His sheep, as Jesus commissioned him to do. The lame man has spent his life at this gate, put there by his parents no doubt, or some friends of theirs. To be there at the time of prayer was important. It was then that people were in a mood to do things God's way, and would be more apt to give money to him. It was his only means of support. And remember, God had told them to be generous to the poor and the needy in Deuteronomy 15:11, which states, *"For the poor shall never cease out of the land: therefore I command thee, saying, 'Thou shalt open thine hand wide unto thy brother, to thy poor, and to thy needy, in thy land.' "*

Also look at Proverbs 14:21, which says, *"He that despiseth his neighbor sinneth: but he that hath mercy on the poor, happy is he."* This day was to be a new day for that man who was born lame. Peter and John were passing that way to go to prayer, and even though he did not have money for alms, when Peter saw this man and his need, he stepped up to the plate once again to do what Jesus would do, meet the man on the level of his need, and bring to him a supernatural healing!

265

The man not only walked, but what else did he do? He praised God in the temple! I want to point out that the man was healed by the *name of Jesus*. Remember, Jesus said that if we prayed to the Father in His name, we would have what we ask for. In John 16:23, Jesus says, *"And in that day ye shall ask me nothing. Verily, verily, I say unto you, whatsoever ye shall ask the Father, in my name, He will give it you."* I don't think Peter gave a second thought to, "What if I do this and it doesn't work?" or "What will people think if this fails to work?" I believe Peter was so sure it would be done that he did not feel one bit of hesitation. He just knew that he knew this was what he was supposed to do, heal the man! I think we as Christians analyze too much, and debate within ourselves until we talk ourselves out of being the witness Jesus wants us to be. Peter gave the man a whole lot more than mere money. The man got back his life, a whole new life. And his response was to praise God, not silently, but with gusto, with his whole heart, leaping and praising God.

PRAYER: Heavenly Father, to follow Jesus brings us into unusual situations, as Peter's example shows us. Help me to be prepared for those times, so that I do not hesitate, but am ready to meet the challenge head on. It may seem scary to be sent to Africa, but it can be just as scary to live right where I am. Peter was on his way to church, which was an everyday activity in his familiar surroundings. I find myself almost afraid to think of what you might ask me to do. But I will, today, ask you to make me ready ahead of time so that when it happens, I will be ready to pray, give advice, or ask for your healing if that is what you want from me. But it will have to be all of you, Lord, because I am weak and afraid, afraid of not being able or ready. I look to you for the ability and strength to be and to do what you ask. In Jesus' name, Amen.

JULY 12th

 There is one thing we need to realize when we choose to follow Jesus, and that is that He will stretch our vision and our faith, stretch them almost to the breaking point. I want you to see how far Peter was stretched at one time. It caused him to throw out all his traditional teaching and to step out in a level of faith he did not even know he had.

In fact, his theology got turned on its head. We will look at parts of Acts 10 today, but I would suggest that you read the whole chapter. Acts 10:1-8 reads;, *"There was a certain man in Caesarea called Cornelius, a centurion of the band called the Italian band. A devout man, and one that feared God with all his house, which gave much alms to the people, and prayed to God always. He saw in a vision evidently* (openly, as it were) *about the ninth hour* (3:00p.m.) *of the day an angel of God coming in to him, and saying unto him, 'Cornelius.' And when he looked on him, he was afraid, and said, 'What is it, Lord?' And he said unto him, 'Thy prayers and thine alms are come up for a memorial before God. And now send men to Joppa, and call for one Simon, whose surname is Peter: He lodgeth with one Simon a tanner, whose house is by the sea side: he shall tell thee what thou oughtest to do.' And when the angel which spake unto Cornelius was departed, he called two of his household servants, and a devout soldier of them that waited on him continually: And when he had declared all these things unto them, he sent them to Joppa."*

Here was a gentile who believed in the God of the Jews, prayed regularly, and was generous in giving alms. In the Old Testament, the Jews were encouraged to have nothing to do with the gentiles. Remember how God kept them separated from the Egyptians during the days of Joseph? This was God's way of keeping them connected to Himself. It does not mean that God did not care about all other nations or people groups. God had to first of all get His nation established as a pure nation for Himself because it would be out of that nation that God would bring forth His Son to be the savior of the world. It was God's intention that all men should be saved, Jews and Gentiles alike. This was not the vision that the Jews had. After Jesus died, God began to reach out to all people and He is still doing that today. We will continue with this tomorrow.

267

PRAYER: Heavenly Father, so now you are going to ask a "dyed in the wool" Jew, Peter, to reach out to the Gentile world? I can see it coming! And this is how you will stretch my vision and faith as well, huh? Is this the way it is to follow you, Lord? I don't want to get cold feet, but how do I stick to it, hang in there, and keep on keeping on in the path that looks so steep? One day at a time, will that do it? You won't give me more to do and adjust to in one day than I can handle, right. I am putting my hand in yours and I won't let go, and I expect you to not let go either, and between the two of us, we will do it, okay, Lord? In Jesus' name, Amen.

JULY 13ᵗʰ

Today, we will look at a time when God gives Peter a great lesson about racism and about being moldable and flexible in His hands. Peter is hungry, and goes up to the rooftop to pray, as we read in Acts 10:10-16: *"And he became very hungry, and would have eaten: but while they made ready, he fell into a trance, And saw heaven opened, and a certain vessel descending unto him, as it had been a great sheet knit at the four corners, and let down to the earth: Wherein were all manner of four-footed beast of the earth, and wild beast, and creeping things, and fowls of the air. And there came a voice to him, 'Rise, Peter, kill and eat.' But Peter said, 'Not so, Lord: for I have never eaten anything that is common or unclean.' And the voice spake unto him again the second time, 'What God hath cleansed, that call not thou common.' This was done thrice: and the vessel was received up again into heaven."*

In the Old Testament, God made it very clear that His people could only eat certain kinds of animals, such as birds and fish. If you want to read about that, see Leviticus 11. Peter had kept a pure life in regard to not eating what was forbidden. So, when that sheet came down with forbidden meat to eat, Peter opposed the Lord, as he had done before. It is interesting to note that the sheet was brought down three times, or else the voice spoke three times and commanded him to eat. The fact that it happened three times did not escape Peter's notice, I am sure, since he denied Jesus three times and he was reinstated three times.

Take special note of the statement, *"What God hath cleansed, that call not thou common."* This was God's way of telling Peter (and us) not to prejudge anything or anyone. Peter was to follow God's leading. I cannot help but guess that Peter was totally puzzled as to what vision was all about. But the message will be so clear to him.

If he had not had this vision, he would not have been prepared at all for what was to come. Isn't this just like Jesus—to make us ready in every way to meet the challenge we are to face. I want to remind you of a verse we read before, Philippians 2:13, which states, *"For it is God which worketh IN you both to WILL and to DO of His good pleasure."* Can you see how God is working a change in Peter's heart and will here? Tomorrow we will see how he put the whole experience into focus and learned what God was trying to accomplish through him.

PRAYER: Heavenly Father, I realize that you gave Peter this vision in privacy. That is encouraging to me. Peter had time to ponder it and let it soak in, so to speak. That, too, is encouraging. You do not put us on public display as you give us these life-changing lessons. I pray that I will be able to hear and see your hand and voice in my life as Peter was doing here. Peter is indeed a stone, a rock in the faith. I know that is what you want from me, too, and I pray that I will not disappoint you. In Jesus' name, Amen.

JULY 14th

Acts 10:17-23 reads: *"Now while Peter doubted* (was much perplexed) *in himself what this vision which he had seen should mean, behold, the men which were sent from Cornelius had made inquiry for Simon's house, and stood before the gate, and called, and asked whether Simon, which was surnamed Peter, were lodged there. While Peter thought on the vision, the Spirit said unto him, 'Behold, three*

men seek thee. Arise therefore, and get thee down and go with them,
doubting nothing: for I have sent them.' Then Peter went down to the
men which were sent unto him from Cornelius; and said, 'Behold, I am
he whom ye seek: what is the cause wherefore ye are come?' And they
said, 'Cornelius the centurion, a just man, and one that feareth God, and
of good report among all the nation of the Jews, was warned from God by
an holy angel to send for thee into his house, and to hear words of thee.'
Then called he them in, and lodged them. And on the morrow Peter went
away with them, and certain brethren from Joppa accompanied him."

There are several points we need to zero in on, lessons from
Peter's experience. God was working on two fronts at the same time by
setting up a meeting in which many will hear the Word of God from a man
of God, which will result in glorifying God. It will be the *right words* for
the *right people* at the *right time*. Only God, the Trinity God, can perform
that kind of thing.

God gave Peter a vision that caused him great confusion as to what
the message meant. At the same time, a non-Jew was fervently praying to
the God of the Jews. God answered the Centurion's prayer by telling him
to get in touch with Peter. The Centurion was also told where to find Peter,
and God promised that Peter would tell him what he needed to do.

We see in verse 17 that Peter was still wrestling with doubt and
perplexity as to what that vision meant. At that moment, the Holy Spirit
spoke to him and told him that three men were looking for him. Have you
ever heard the Spirit speak to you? I am sure He has, but you did not know
how to listen to Him. He will put a thought into your head and you could
swear you heard a voice as well. And maybe you did, but you are not sure
and you wondered, "Where did that come from?" Well, guess what, it was
God speaking to you.

I also must warn you that Satan will try to mimic what God can do,
so you will need to discern whether the voice or idea is from God or Satan.
Remember, God is always good, never evil, but Satan is never good. The
devil may try to look and act good in order to deceive you, but his
intentions are always evil. I am sure Peter was struggling to determine
whether his vision was from God or from the enemy.

270

In verse 22, Peter is told about Cornelius, the man of faith, and how the angel told Cornelius to send for Peter to come *into* his house. If Peter had not had that vision, he would never have gone into Cornelius' house, because the Centurion was not a Jew.

Peter also lodged these three gentiles over night, which had been forbidden, just as the Jews had been forbidden to eat certain foods. Imagine that! Peter's faith is being stretched to the breaking point here, all because of a vision and God's command, "What God hath cleansed, that call thou not common." Peter is ready to see God's broader vision of salvation

I also want you to see the Trinity at work in this experience. Yesterday and today we saw God the Father and the Holy Spirit at work. But, so far, something has been missing. Peter is the one who can put the missing piece, Jesus, into that puzzle. Peter will be made ready to share the gospel of Jesus with Cornelius and his kinsmen and friends.

PRAYER: Heavenly Father, I am simply amazed at how you are at work among us and we are not even aware of what you are doing. I look at my life and begin to see more and more clearly how your hand has been there when I thought I was left alone. All I can do today is say a great big, *"Thank you Father, for being there for me even when I was not aware of it!"* In Jesus' name, Amen.

JULY 15th

Today we will look at Acts 10:24-33, which reads: *"And the morrow after, they entered into Caesarea. Cornelius waited for them, and had called together his kinsmen and near friends. And as Peter was coming in, Cornelius met him, and fell down at his feet, and worshipped him. But Peter took him up, saying, 'Stand up: I myself also am a man.' And as he talked with him, he went in, and found many that were come together. And he said unto them, 'Ye know how that it is an unlawful thing for a man that is a Jew to keep company, or come unto one of another nation; but God hath shewed me that I should not call any man common or unclean. Therefore came I unto you without hesitation,* *as soon as I was sent for: I ask therefore for what intent ye have sent for* *me?' And Cornelius said, 'Four days ago I was fasting until this hour;* *and at the ninth hour I prayed in my house* (Cornelius was keeping the ninth hour of prayer, Jewish custom, of which Peter would understand the significance right away)*, and, behold, a man stood before me in bright* *clothing, And said, "Cornelius, thy prayer is heard, and thine alms are* *had in remembrance in the sight of God. Send therefore to Joppa, and* *call hither Simon, whose surname is Peter, he is lodged in the house of* *one Simon a tanner by the sea side who, when he cometh shall speak unto* *thee." Immediately therefore I sent to thee; and thou hast well done that* *thou art come. Now therefore are we all here present before God, to hear* *all things that are commanded thee of God.' "*

Cornelius wasted no time in gathering his relatives and friends to hear what Peter had to tell them, speaking as a man of God. They are expectant. This is the way we are to go to church each Sunday. We are to expect to hear a word meant just for us. In order for that to happen, you need to be in prayer for the pastor to speak boldly the truth about the Word of God, and pray for yourself that you will have ears to hear the Word of God, and be able to receive it for yourself.

If you ever think, "I sure wish so-and-so was in church today. So-and-so sure did need this sermon," I want you to remember that you are the one hearing that message, and it is for you.

Cornelius had been in prayer, and this meeting is a result of that prayer. They are all expecting to hear a word for themselves. Not only that, but Peter also hears how this all came about. I am sure his head was in a whirl as he remembered his vision, and he realized, beyond a shadow of a doubt, that this was all of God and had nothing to do with anything Peter did to set it up.

Never forget, Jesus reinstated Peter three times, "Feed my sheep. Tend my sheep." Peter also tells Cornelius that it is unlawful for a Jew to enter the house of a person of another nation. To the Jews, there were only Jews and gentiles. In verse 28, Peter has a great big "but" in there. I have always said that "but" in the Bible turns you around, and Peter was turned

272

around by the vision God gave him. He says, *"But God hath showed me that I should not call any man common or unclean."* This was a revolutionary thought to a Jew! But, you see, Jesus died for the *whole* world, as is stated in John 3:16, *"For God so loved the world that He gave His only begotten Son, that whosoever believeth in Him shall not perish, but have everlasting life.."*

Now Peter wants to know what this meeting was for. What did Cornelius want? Cornelius told Peter just exactly what the angel told him, word for word. It is obvious that God wants Peter to teach them about Jesus, which is God's new dimension of salvation and fellowship with mankind. God gave Cornelius precise directions, with names, places and who he should speak to.

Imagine Peter's surprise when Cornelius knew his name and the name of the person with whom he was staying, and the name of the town in which to search for him. Get a picture here of the God's precision. I believe that when we totally depend on God, without any doubt or wavering, God will come through for us in a like manner. What will Peter preach or talk to them about? What will be his message? We will begin to look at that tomorrow.

PRAYER: Heavenly Father, I feel like I am learning so much about you, and your characteristics. My vision has expanded, and my faith is trying to catch up. If I had been in Peter's shoes, I wonder if I would have been able to go with the two men who came for me—to go into an unknown, uncharted area of service. I suppose this is recorded in your Word so that I will come to understand that I could experience this, too, as I follow you. Please help me to be prepared for such a time as that. I do not want a spirit of fear because you said you did not give us a spirit of fear, as I read in II Timothy 1:7, *"For God hath not given us the spirit of fear; but of power, and of love, and of a sound mind."* I lay claim to that verse, Lord, and I will depend on you to fulfill it. In the name of Jesus, Amen.

JULY 16th

Acts 10:34-43 reads: *"Then Peter opened his mouth, and said, 'Of a truth I perceive that God is no respecter of persons: But in every nation He that feareth Him, and worketh righteousness, is accepted with Him. The word which God sent unto the children of Israel, preaching* (good tidings of) *peace by Jesus Christ:* (He is Lord of all) *That word, I say, ye know, which was published throughout all Judea, and began from Galilee, after the baptism which John preached; How God anointed Jesus of Nazareth with the Holy Ghost, and with power: who went about doing good, and healing all that were oppressed of the Devil; for God was with Him. And we are witnesses of all things which He did both in the land of the Jews, and in Jerusalem; whom they slew and hanged on a tree. Him God raised up the third day, and shewed Him openly; Not to all people, but unto witnesses chosen before of God, even to us, who did eat and drink with Him after He rose from the dead. And He commanded us to preach unto the people, and to testify that it is He which was ordained of God to be the Judge of quick and dead. To Him give all the prophets' witness, that through His name whosoever believeth in Him shall receive remission of sins.' "*

This is a relatively short sermon, but it says so much. Peter states that God is no respecter of persons. God had included all mankind in His family after Jesus paid the price and penalty for all sin for all time. That meant that those sitting in that room were included in God's family. That must have just about blown them out of the water, as we say today.

Everyone who performs acts of righteousness and fears God is accepted by God. That is not a torment type of fear, but a reverential fear—a fear that brings honor to God and causes us to obey rather than disobey Him. Cornelius was a good example of that. Works of righteousness come out of that kind of fear. Someone with that fear will look for ways to bless God with good works, rather than appease God.

In his speech, Peter provides a little history of who Jesus is and what He is all about. He explains that Jesus came preaching good tidings of *peace* (with God I might add). Peter also assumes that they have heard about what happened to Jesus—that He was baptized by John, anointed with the Holy Ghost, and filled with power to go out and perform miracles and cast out demons. In fact, Peter was an eye witness to all of these events. Peter explains that they (the Jews) crucified Him, but that God raised Him up on the third day, and He was seen openly.

Although seeing Jesus did not happen in secret, not everyone saw Him. There was only a chosen, select group that witnessed the risen Christ. They even ate and drank with Him after He rose from the dead. For a moment, imagine sitting there and listening to Peter's sermon. Do you think they could believe it all? Was it too much for them?

Peter told them that those who had seen Him alive were commanded to go out and tell about this good news—to preach and to testify that Jesus will be the Judge of the living and the dead. Even the prophets left a witness that agrees with all Peter had told them.

Each one of us who reads these passages is also held responsible for this good news of salvation. And, like Peter, we need to be ready to tell it to anyone who wants to hear it. I take comfort in the fact that Peter was invited to share the news. I am not a pushy kind of person, and I do not want to push this sort of thing down anyone's throat. But, give me an opportunity to tell it to someone who wants to listen, and I am ready to roll—and you should be too. How did this affect these people when they heard it? We will look at that tomorrow.

PRAYER: Heavenly Father, how far are you going to stretch Peter's faith? He entered a gentile home filled with gentiles who were expecting to hear about the God of the Jews! Peter must have been struggling to keep in step with you, Lord. I feel the same way as I read this—thinking that the day will come when you begin to stretch my faith like that also. But then you seem to have been confident that Peter would be able to step up to the plate and get the job done. I will depend on you to give me the right words and the power to say and do what needs to be said and done. Thank you for holding my hand and for giving me the confidence that I need when I need it. In Jesus' name, Amen.

JULY 17th

Acts 10:44-48 explains: *"While Peter yet spake these words, the Holy Ghost fell on all them which heard the word. And they of the circumcision* (the Jews) *which believed were astonished, as many as came with Peter, because that on the Gentiles also was poured out the gift of the Holy Ghost. For they heard them speak with tongues, and magnify God. Then answered Peter, 'Can any man forbid water, that these should not be baptized, which have received the Holy Ghost as well as we?' And he commanded them to be baptized in the name of Jesus Christ. Then prayed they him to tarry certain days."*

They had a taste of the good news, and right then and there they wanted more and more. This should be the reaction of everyone who comes into that living relationship with Jesus Christ. Their appetite is whetted and they desire more of God, more of Jesus, and more teaching of His words of hope, comfort, assurance, righteousness, and, yes, even discipline, correction, and trials.

You grow the surest and quickest through trials. It is the experience of the trial that is hard, but once it is through, you enjoy a victory and rejoice with God over it. That is like a "high" not found anywhere else.

The trip Peter took, with some gentiles to attend a meeting with more gentiles in a gentile's home, is a fantastic example of what it is like to be called into the everyday life of a believer and follower of Jesus Christ. He was up to the task, Are you?

PRAYER: Lord Jesus, in your Word, you have said, *"I, if I am lifted up from the earth, I will draw all men unto me"* (John 12:32). I pray that I will lift you up at all times and be prepared to bring you into my conversation, into my everyday life, as naturally as I wave to my neighbor and say, "Hi." Peter was ready to leave for Cornelius' house right away, with no hesitation at all. That is the kind of response you are looking for, and I do not want to disappoint you, Lord. I lay my life before you to use for your glory. In Jesus' name, Amen.

JULY 18th

I believe we need to look at something else in yesterday's reading. Look again at Acts 10:44-45, which reads: *"While Peter yet spake these words, the Holy Ghost fell on all them which heard the word. And they of the circumcision which believed were astonished, as many as came with Peter, because that on the Gentiles also was poured out the gift of the Holy Ghost."*

You need to see, and be aware of the fact that this whole meeting had been planned by God and carried out by God. God used Cornelius and Peter, without them knowing it, to bring all this about. All Cornelius did was pray to God, and, as for Peter, he had a vision from God with the lesson that what God calls clean is no longer common. All Peter had to do was to obey, go, and preach.

If we are alert, we will see that is how God works in our lives too. He plans our lives, He sets up the situations, and He will provide the power to obey, go, and do what He wants us to. Then, we also need to see that the results are also from God. No one can take an ounce of credit for the outcome. In this instance, the whole congregation of listeners was gifted with the blessing of the Holy Ghost poured out upon them, just as it had been on the day of Pentecost.

This was God's way of showing Peter, and the believers with him, what that experience was all about. We also need to see that the wall of separation between Jew and gentile had been broken, so they could fellowship together in a way that had never been permitted before.

God was preparing the Jews for a new thing, but when we look at the situation today, many Jews still do not know that truth. As Christians, we need to pray that they will hear and believe the truth about Jesus Christ.

Did you notice how Peter and those with him felt? They were astonished! You see, they had seen the gentiles as outside of the covenant of Abraham, and therefore outside of a relationship with the God of creation. Not even in their wildest dreams would they have expected God to include the gentiles. And it was Peter, of all people, who had walked right into this situation.

277

The message was so clear that there was no way Peter could ignore it. Jesus knew Peter very well, and I believe that is why he got such a loud and clear vision with such a loud and clear message, and three times as well! Peter knew that he knew what God was telling him. He also knew that he had better believe it and not question it. He could say, "Been there, done that." But Peter was teachable.

I have seen people who are not teachable, and it is like hitting your head against a stone wall. It will not budge. Never be so hardheaded that you cannot learn some of God's precious truths.

Do you recall me explaining how God will use you either with your cooperation or without it? Can you see how that happened in this situation? Peter must have felt very reluctant as he went with a gentile to a gentile's house, because it is recorded here in Acts 10:28 that Peter said, *"Ye know how that it is an unlawful thing for a man that is a Jew to keep company, or come unto one of another nation."*

Peter's flesh must have just crawled as he put his foot into that gentile's house filled with gentiles. I don't think we can begin to imagine how he was feeling as he defied the law according to his upbringing. But he was willing to obey God in spite of it all, and obey the vision, and the voice from heaven.

PRAYER: Heavenly Father, again I thank you for using Peter to teach me this lesson on how you plan out our lives so thoroughly, and give people the wisdom and power to bring your plan together for the good of all. I can only imagine what the Cornelius' guests were learning. That is where I put myself in this scene—sitting there, listening to Peter tell such good news. And to think that it includes me, too. I, a gentile, am actually accepted by you, Father, in full communion! I accept the invitation with my whole heart. In Jesus' name, Amen.

JULY 19th

 For a few days, I want to share some truths from the first and second epistles (letters) written by Peter in the New Testament. Now, since we have learned truths from Peter's life, it is interesting to see those truths put into practice through his letters to believers in the early church. It is my prayer that these truths will bless you as you grow in grace and holiness.

Before we look at the first verses, I need to explain that the Jews, because of persecution, were scattered throughout that part of the world. If you are interested, you can look at a map, perhaps in your Bible, and find the provinces Peter speaks of listed there. Peter's letter is addressed to all those believers in that part of the world, but it is also a message for us today, since we are Christians, and it is written by a Christian to Christians. That is why we read and learn from these letters.

In I Peter 1:1-5, we read: *"Peter, an apostle of Jesus Christ, to the strangers scattered throughout* (believers who are sojourners of the dispersion in) *Pontus, Galatia, Cappadocia, Asia, and Bithynia, elect according to the foreknowledge of God the Father, through sanctification of the Spirit unto obedience and sprinkling of the blood of Jesus Christ: Grace unto you, and peace be multiplied. Blessed be the God and Father of our Lord Jesus Christ, which according to His abundant mercy hath begotten us again unto a living hope, by the resurrection of Jesus Christ from the dead. To an inheritance incorruptible, and undefiled, and that fadeth not away, reserved in heaven for you. Who are kept* (guarded) *by the power of God through faith unto salvation ready to be revealed in the last time."*

This needs a lot of explaining for you to understand its depth. As a believer, you are a part of the "elect," according to the foreknowledge of God the Father. To help you understand what that means, let us look at II Timothy 1:8-9, which states: *"Be not therefore ashamed of the testimony of our Lord, nor of me His prisoner: but be thou partaker of the afflictions of the gospel according to the power of God; Who hath saved us, and called us with an holy calling, not according to our works, but according to His own purpose and grace, which was given us in Christ Jesus BEFORE the world began."*

You see, you were called with a holy calling, not because of your works, but rather because God had a purpose in mind for you by His grace *in* Christ Jesus before there was a world! Now, if that doesn't stretch your faith, nothing will!

God knew you and had a purpose for you way back then, and in His timing you would be born and His purpose would be revealed from day to day in your life. With that, Paul could say, "Elect, according to the foreknowledge of God the Father ..." and speak of "sanctification of the Spirit."

It is the job of the Holy Spirit to help us to grow in our knowledge of God and want to serve Him to fulfill that purpose for which we were born. That process is called "sanctification." Notice that the reason for that sanctification is "unto obedience, since we are sprinkled with His blood," which means we are made pure and holy. We will talk more about this tomorrow. You need to dwell on what was said today.

PRAYER: Heavenly Father, to realize that you knew me before the world began does stretch my way of thinking. It means you must have had me in mind when you made the world and all that is in it. It is hard to grasp the depth of such a statement! Help me, Father, to want to fit into your purpose for me, to desire to please you, to be an obedient child of yours. Help me to see your hand in my life that I may know that I am fitting into your plan for me. In Jesus' name, Amen.

JULY 20th

Today we will continue with yesterday's reading. I Peter 1:2 reads, *"Grace and peace be multiplied."* Notice that it does *not* say "added," but multiplied! Just how much does God desire to bless you? More than you can imagine. But for that to happen, we need to be in obedience to Him.

Usually it is the little things in life that get in the way of our obedience—things like stretching the truth or diminishing the truth. No matter how you look at it, those things are lies. Ask God to show you what you do that displeases Him. Also, when we worry and fret over things in life, we show that we do not trust Him with our lives.

How do we stretch the truth? Well, how about when you say you *never* have a chance to take a break. When you say that, you give the devil legal rights to see to it you never do get a break and become overworked. You may feel overworked, but take charge of your life.

First, pray for some time for yourself. God knows you need it, and it is He who can provide it. And He will, if you ask. But also be careful of what you ask for. You do not want to break a leg in order to have some time for yourself, either.

Ask God to help you see things in your life that can be put on hold or eliminated to give you that self time you need, or plan a few minutes to just sit down with the children and have a floor picnic. You will feel better and so will they.

I remember a time when I needed to get out of the house. The walls were closing in on me. I took my four-year-old son out for a little picnic and went to a park in town overlooking a big river. We relaxed, looked for birds, watched boats on the river, and had a fun time. Then I was ready to go home, put the harness on, and go on with life. My son thought it was super fun, and said, "When can we do this again, Mom?"

PRAYER: Dear Lord, it is so encouraging to know that you desire to bless us abundantly, but to know it and to actually receive the blessings are two different things. Help me to lay hold of the blessings you are happy to bestow upon me, such as some time to just enjoy your creation, and a respite from the humdrum of everyday life. You know my heart through and through, I cannot hide anything from you. Thank you for loving me just the way I am. In Jesus' name, Amen.

JULY 21st

 I Peter 1:3 reads, *"Blessed be the God and Father of our Lord Jesus Christ which according to His abundant mercy hath*

begotten us again unto a living hope by the resurrection of Jesus Christ from the dead."

What is being said here? Peter is blessing God, the Father of Jesus. God, by His mercy, has given us a new birth (we are "begotten again"), all because Jesus rose from the dead.

Do you recall that we talked about that earlier in the year? Jesus got a brand new life, one that had never existed before, when He was raised from the dead. I believe it is that life that we get when we are born again. I call it resurrection life, and that life lives within us. It is that life that is the "power pack," if you will, that energizes us to do good works.

Notice that we have been born again "unto a living hope." Because of the resurrection of Jesus, we have a living hope, not a dead religion, and we serve a living Savior. Our salvation sort of comes in stages. We are saved for eternity the moment we accept Jesus as our Lord and Savior and invite Him into our hearts. That becomes a settled fact. There is also a *hope* stored up in heaven for us, and it will become a reality when we get there. That is our living hope.

When we see Jesus face to face, then our salvation will be complete. In the meantime, we live a life that reflects Him, serves Him, lifts Him up for all to see, and pleases Him. That is also a part of our salvation—our life on earth that is in harmony with God's will for us. All of that blesses God, our Father. It brings Him joy and satisfaction, which blesses Him.

Let's look at a couple more verses. Hebrews 13:16 states, *"But to do good and to communicate forget not: for with such sacrifices God is well pleased."* And II Corinthians 2:14-15 reads, *"Now thanks be unto God, which always causeth us to triumph in Christ, and maketh manifest the savour* (smell or aroma) *of His knowledge by us in every place. For we are unto God a sweet savour of Christ."* When we live for Jesus, we create a sweet smell that comes up to God and blesses Him.

PRAYER: Lord Jesus, I thank you for the gift of salvation that you purchased for me, and I ask you to help me live the life that reflects that gift of salvation. Let others see the joy in my life, and the peace also. Forgive me when I worry about "things," which give a false impression of who you are, and to what you are able to do in my life. I thank you for the truths I am learning that help me to see more clearly how I fit into that purpose you saw for me, before the world existed. In Jesus' precious name, Amen.

JULY 22nd

I Peter 1:4 reads, *"To an inheritance incorruptible, and undefiled, and that fadeth not away, reserved in heaven for you."* We have an inheritance waiting for us in heaven.

Notice the four things that are said about that inheritance. It is incorruptible and undefiled. This means it cannot rot or waste away, and its value will never diminish.

It does not fade away, either. And it is reserved. Have you ever been ushered into a nice eating place up to a fine table with a sign saying, "Reserved"? There is an inheritance with such a sign on it for you in heaven.

Let me remind you that the Peter that we studied about earlier is the same Peter who is writing this letter. God has shaped, corrected, molded, and fine-tuned him into a vessel of great value for the kingdom of heaven. He is that fisher of men that Jesus said he would be. God can do the same for you, if you will only let Him.

PRAYER: Heavenly Father, what can I say? It just keeps getting better and better. An inheritance reserved just for me? This life is only a small part of my existence. Eternity is a large part of my existence. I need to adjust my view of eternity and think about it on a level of reality *now*, rather than *later*. I know that my view of death has changed as I have studied your Word, and my view of heaven has also changed a whole lot, and I am grateful to you, Father, for this Word today about the inheritance in heaven awaiting me. Thank you, Father, for loving me that much. In Jesus' name, Amen.

JULY 23rd

I Peter 1:5 states, *"Who are kept* (guarded) *by the power of God through faith unto salvation ready to be revealed in the last day."* God is guarding us by His power, and it is by faith that we believe it. He will guard us right up to that day when we see Jesus face to face. It will be then that the whole story of our salvation will be revealed to us.

We go along in our lives and, many times, do not even give God a glance, but all the while He is watching over us and directing us, even though we are not aware of it. Ask God to give you the discernment of His hand in your life. You will be surprised at what you will begin to notice on a daily basis. You may experience telephone calls at just the right time or a stop light that either turned red or green at the right time. Do you think that is a coincidence? Not at all!

Peter knew that his vision of the sheet with unclean and clean animals at just the right time was not a coincidence, nor was arrival of the men who came to his place of lodging to look for him. Nothing that occurs in your life is a coincidence. We always need to see God as big enough to reach around each of us all the time, and small enough to live in our heart all of the time—to see the tear on our cheek, the hurt in our heart, and the wound in our soul.

He has promised to never leave us or forsake us. Can you hang onto that promise through thick and thin? God will help you do that if you ask Him for that help.

PRAYER: Yes, Lord, I do need your help to keep on keeping on. There are days when you seem so far away. Even though I know in my head that you are near, because you promised you would be, sometimes there is still that nagging doubt in my heart, as I look at the circumstances around me. So, yes, help me to fix my eyes on your Word of promise and not to look at the circumstances that threaten me. Satan is at work, I know. But I want to stand firm in your corner with you. Just as you prayed for Peter that his

JULY 24th

I Peter 3:15 reads: *"But sanctify the Lord God in your hearts* (sanctify in your hearts Christ as Lord) *and be ready always to give an answer to every man that asketh you a reason of the hope that is in you with meekness and fear."* Let me remind you of some things before we go on to explore this verse. Peter was not a naturally meek man. He struggled with jealousy, which we will address more later on, but he has learned to be meek. How did that happen? Peter became meek through the various experiences he had with Jesus, which we have already looked at.

I also want to point out that in this verse Peter is telling the people to sanctify Christ in their hearts. In order for them to do that, they have to know in their minds that Christ is worthy of sanctification. Once the mind knows a truth, it then moves into the heart, where it motivates us to a new way of acting. First, we develop a new way of thinking, and then a new way of acting.

To sanctify means to set aside as holy. How holy is Christ to you in your life? That will determine how much you sanctify Him in your heart. The idea of sanctifying Christ as Lord in our hearts is very interesting. It is one thing to have Jesus in our heart as Christ, the Anointed One, to save us from our sins, but it is quite another thing to have Him in our heart as Lord, the supreme boss.

We turn our whole life over, lock, stock and barrel, to the lordship of Jesus Christ. Satan will always fight that decision with all his strength and power. He knows that his defeat is sealed when we give our lives wholly to Jesus. Then, when we have done that, we should be *able* to *"Give an answer to every man who asketh you a reason of the hope that is in you."* If we cannot really tell anyone why we are not worried, or why we are full of joy, thanksgiving, praise, and peace, then something is radically wrong in our relationship with Jesus.

285

But, I want to point out that the most important part of this verse is, *"that asketh you."* That narrows down our audience considerably. Only those who have noticed a change and want to know what happened, or are inquiring about how we can face life with such a strong resolve, are those whose hearts have already been made ready to hear the answer.

Remember me telling you that witnessing must include the *right words* and the *right person* at the *right time*, and only the Holy Spirit can arrange that? When someone asks you about your faith in God, be ready to listen to the Holy Spirit for what to say, and then say it with *the right attitude*—with meekness and fear.

There will be a sense that you want to do it right, because this is a divine appointment—God has chosen you to fulfill a major role in His divine plan to reach this particular person.

It is interesting that this is from Peter, to whom Jesus had said in Matthew 16:23, *"Get thee behind me Satan: Thou art an offence* (stumbling block) *unto me: for thou mindest not the things that be of God, but those that be of man."* You see how Peter has learned from all his experiences? Are you learning from Peter's experiences, or do you have to experience such things in order to learn? The choice is yours.

PRAYER: Heavenly Father, I do not want to have to go through hard experiences of my own to understand and learn these lessons. Help me to know in my mind the truth of your Word, and then help me settle it in my heart that it is for me. Help me to be the witness that you have called me to be. I want to be able to give a good answer to every one *who asks* about the hope that is within me. In Jesus' mighty name, Amen.

JULY 25th

In I Peter 5:1-6, we read: *"The elders which are among you I exhort, who am also an elder, and a witness of the sufferings of Christ, and also a partaker of the glory that shall be revealed: Feed the flock of God which is among you, taking the oversight thereof, not by constraint, but willingly; not for filthy lucre* (money), *but of a ready mind; Neither as being lords over God's heritage, but being examples to the flock. And when the chief Shepherd shall appear* (notice that it says when, not if, Christ will return), *ye shall receive a crown of glory that fadeth not away. Likewise, ye younger, submit yourselves unto the elder. Yea all of you be subject one to another, and be clothed with humility for God resiseth the proud, and giveth grace to the humble. Humble therefore yourselves under the mighty hand of God, that He may exalt you in due season."*

I can see Peter all over in these verses. He is speaking from what he has learned. Experience is a wonderful teacher, even though it can be hard at times.

Peter is talking about feeding the flock. Where did that idea come from? I believe Peter learned that lesson when Jesus told him to "feed my sheep" and "tend my sheep." Peter came to find out that Jesus was, indeed, the Chief Shepherd.

Peter also drives home the fact that the older ones are to be authority figures over the younger ones, but they are all to be in subjection to one another. This is another lesson Peter learned as a disciple of Jesus.

He also learned humility, which he addresses here also. He knew first hand how dangerous pride was and how it would get in the way of true discipleship. Peter had also leaned that when he allowed God's mighty hand to humble him, God would also exalt him, but it would always be in "due season," again, in the right time.

God's timing is perfect and we need to learn that lesson. The sooner we learn that lesson, the better off we will be. God humbles us at just the right time, and God exalts us at just the right time, also.

PRAYER Heavenly Father, there is a sense of safety in knowing that you humble people at just the right time. I believe that it is pride that brings on the discipline of humbling. Help me, Lord, to see pride creeping up on me, so that I do not need to go through the discipline of being humbled, and help me learn to be in subjection to you also. I do not want to wait to be made humble for you to get my attention. I want my attention to be riveted on you in the first place. I thank you for the Holy Spirit who enlightens me in these spiritual truths to help me grow into the Christian you have in mind for me. In Jesus' name, Amen.

JULY 26th

When I think of learning humility in regard to Peter, the scene that comes to mind immediately is when Jesus asked Peter if the children had to pay tax (tribute) in Matthew 17:24-27, which reads: *"And when they were come to Capernaum, they that received tribute money* (the half shekel) *came to Peter, and said, 'Doth not your master* (teacher) *pay tribute?' He saith, 'Yes.' And when he was come into the house, Jesus prevented* (Jesus spoke first to John) *him, saying, 'What thinkest thou, Simon? Of whom do the kings of the earth take custom or tribute? Of their own children, or of strangers?' Peter saith unto him, 'Of strangers.' Jesus saith unto him, 'Then are the children free. Not withstanding, lest we should offend them,* (cause them to stumble), *go thou to the sea, and cast an hook, and take up the fish that first cometh up: and when thou hast opened his mouth, thou shalt find a piece of money* (shekel): *that take, and give unto them for me and thee.' "*

Peter had already told those who asked him whether his master pays tribute that, yes, He did. Then *Jesus* asked *Peter* who had to pay tribute or tax, strangers or the children of the country? You see, Jesus is the *Word* that created the whole world and all that is in it. Should He have to pay tax?

Then Jesus told Peter to go to the sea where he will find a shekel in the mouth of the first fish that he catches, with which to pay tribute for both himself and Jesus. When I first saw the implications here I bust right out laughing. Imagine Peter (the big fisherman who fished from a boat with nets that caught anywhere from 50 to 100 plus fish) being told to go and cast a line with a hook on the end of it into the sea for one fish at a time. The first fish was the one in whose mouth would be the money for the tax he had told the tax collectors that his master paid. The price was a half a shekel and the fish would have in its mouth a full shekel—enough for both Jesus and Peter.

What if some of his peers saw him there with a line in the sea, patiently waiting for that first bite on the hook so he could hurriedly bring it in and find the money and be on his way—no doubt abandoning the hook and line in the process. Do you think Peter might have learned humility from this? You bet!

However, here Peter is trying to pass on that lesson to all of us. Can we learn it by just reading it, or do we have to go through some embarrassing situation ourselves to learn it? Only you can answer for yourself, and I will have to answer for me. God promises to exalt us if we become humble, and that will be in due season—at the very right time, when our exaltation would bring about the best and most holy glory to God for His wondrous works in our lives. You see, it is never us who are to be exalted, but rather God exalts us so that we become a blessing to Him, and it is He who is really exalted.

Matthew 5:16 says, *"Let your light so shine before men that they may see your good works, and glorify your Father which is in heaven."* Again, it is God who is the one that is glorified, not the person. When God exalts you, it is not so you get the glory. It can bring you great joy and relieve you of strife, but its purpose is not to give you glory. Your joy and strife-free life will bring glory to God by the world seeing what God is able to do in your life.

God cannot do this for a proud person. That proud person would see to it he or she got the glory, and God would not even be recognized in that event. Peter had learned all these lessons the hard way. Then he has passed them on to us in his letters.

PRAYER: Heavenly Father, I am amazed at how your whole Bible hangs together. There are references to back up other references and it seems your message in one Book has the same theme in every other Book of the Bible. It becomes like a rock upon which I can stand and it will not be moved. I thank you for such a Word as this. I need your help to make the most of what I read in your Word. Help me to put it into practice, and to really believe, what it says. Help me to lay claim to that Word of truth for my own personal life. Again, I thank you for this Book called the Bible, and for the power of the Word in that Book. In Jesus' name, Amen.

JULY 27th

I Peter 4:16 reads, *"Yet if any man suffer as a Christian, let him not be ashamed; but let him glorify God on this behalf."* And I Peter 4:19 states, *"Wherefore let them that suffer according to the will of God commit the keeping of their souls to Him in well doing, as unto a faithful Creator."* Both of these verses talk about suffering from two different points of view.

What does it mean to suffer as a Christian? Christians knows who is in control of their lives—God is! And Christians are invited to give thanks for everything, no matter how bad it may look, knowing that God will exalt them in due season, and that God will restore double what the devil has stolen. No matter what, we win. No matter how awful it looks, God never says to retreat, nor does He encourage anyone to look back, but instead He tells us to keep our eyes on Him who is calling us forward.

Our sacrifice at that time is to offer up praise and thanksgiving, and to keep peace and joy in our hearts. We do not always feel like it, but we do it in spite of how we feel. That is our sacrifice. Our old nature has to die to its willful and selfish ways, and the new nature must step up to the plate and give a resounding, "Praise the Lord!" Nothing defeats the enemy, the devil, faster than that.

Then we see in verse 19 that we also suffer "according to the will of God." Remember that every situation has is two-sided—a temptation and a test. Satan tempts and God tests, and they both strike at our faith. If we will only look at every situation and ask God to show us the temptation and the test in each case, it would help us so much to "suffer according to the will of God."

I have mentioned that my son, Milton, died at age 46, just when his life was turning around for the good, and his life was on track for the first time in many years. Satan would like me to see Milton's death as a slap from God, to blame God for such an untimely death. Satan wanted me to grieve for what could have been, should have been, and would have been. God, on the other hand, wanted me to see Him as good, on time, in charge of Milton's own good, and a God to be praised.

There before me was the temptation and the test. Why should I choose the temptation that would only bring me heartache and depression? I chose to lay claim to the fact that God is good. He does not think or plan evil. He is also an "on time" God. He is never late or early. Therefore, He is to be praised for His goodness and for His timeliness. Yes, my heart was sad for the loss of the fellowship we could no longer have in this world, but one day we will begin our eternal fellowship that will last forever. Can you beat that? I don't think so.

So, I chose to suffer as a Christian and according to the will of God. It sure beats suffering as an unbeliever. Ponder on this truth for your own sake.

PRAYER: Heavenly Father, I feel like one of the disciples who asked you to increase their faith. I thank you for the faith you have given me, and the power to use that faith to the fullest. I decide right now to suffer as a Christian and according to the will of God, so that, when the time comes, when I need that kind of faith, it will be there at my disposal. In Jesus' name, Amen.

JULY 28th

II Peter 1:1-8 reads: *"Simon Peter, a servant and an apostle of Jesus Christ, to them that have obtained like precious faith with us through the righteousness of God and our Savior Jesus Christ: Grace and peace be multiplied unto you through the knowledge of God, and of Jesus our Lord. According as His divine power hath given unto us all things that pertain unto life and godliness, through the knowledge of Him that hath called us to glory and virtue: Whereby are*

291

given unto us exceeding great and precious promises: that by these ye might be partakers of the divine nature, having escaped the corruption that is in the world through lust. And beside this, giving all diligence, add to your faith virtue; and to virtue knowledge; and to knowledge temperance (self control)*; and to temperance patience; and to patience godliness; and to godliness brotherly kindness, and to brotherly kindness, charity* (love)*. For if these things be in you, and abound, they make you that ye shall neither be barren nor unfruitful in the knowledge of our Lord Jesus Christ."*

Peter is penning these words, by the direction of the Holy Spirit. But if he had not experienced these things himself, he may not have been the one God could use to write them down.

Grace and peace are multiplied to us as we store up knowledge of God and of His Son, Jesus our Lord. As you read and meditate on these devotions, it is my hope that you are storing up knowledge of God and of Jesus Christ. The Word says, *"My people perish for lack of knowledge"* (Hosea 4:6). Let that never be said of you. Learn how to read the Word of God, how to study it, and how to grow in grace and holiness.

You will enter heaven at the level you left earth. Who takes a trip without looking at the map and studying it to determine the best rout? We have a divine power at work in us to help us in this life here on earth (verse 3), and we are partakers of the divine nature of God (verse 4). We have escaped corruption that is in the world through lust. Our "want to" is changed when Jesus is given the reins, and therefore the corruption of the world does not hold us captive anymore.

In verse 5 we see that we are first diligent, and that adds virtue (morality, chastity, and merit) to our faith, which adds knowledge, then self control, then patience, brotherly kindness, and, finally love. You see, growth is a process. It does not happen all at once. It is a step-by-step process.

God works in progression. All you have to do is to look at the process of creation. It was a step-by-step work. Our spiritual growth is the same way, and so was Peter's.

Verse 8 explains that, since these qualities are in us as believers, we should display certain behaviors and attitudes. We should *"neither be barren nor unfruitful in the knowledge of our Lord Jesus Christ."* In other words, the way we live an witness should bear fruit of knowledge of Jesus Christ. God is interested in fruit. Why should we take up space on this planet and not bear fruit? This planet belongs to God, not to us. We are given a few years to enjoy life on this planet, and God is looking for fruit of the knowledge of Him, Jesus, and the Holy Spirit.

PRAYER: Heavenly Father, open my eyes to your vast knowledge. Help me to grasp your truths. Give me the grace to display your divine nature through me, and let me not be a disappointment to you. One day I want to hear those words from you, *"Well done, thou good and faithful servant. You have been faithful over a few things. I will make you ruler over many things. Enter thou into the joy of thy Lord."* In Jesus' name, Amen.

JULY 29th

II Peter 1:9-12 reads: *"But he that lacketh these things* (referring to the qualities listed in verses 5-7) *is blind, and cannot see afar off, and hath forgotten that he was purged from his old sins. Wherefore the rather, brethren, give diligence to make your calling and election sure: for if ye do these things, ye shall never fall* (stumble)*. For so an entrance shall be ministered unto you abundantly into the everlasting kingdom of our Lord and Savior Jesus Christ. Wherefore I will not be negligent to put you always in remembrance of these things, though ye know them, and be established in the present truth."*

In the CEV translation, these verses read: *"But if you don't grow, you are like someone who is nearsighted or blind, and you have forgotten that your past sins are forgiven. My friends, you must do all you can to show that God has really chosen and selected you. If you keep on doing this, you won't stumble and fall. Then our Lord and Savior Jesus Christ will give you a glorious welcome into His kingdom that will last forever.*

You are holding firmly to the truth that you were given. But I am still going to remind you of these things."

I hope that by now you have learned to count things that are listed! If so, how many things were added to faith? Those things that are added to faith helped your faith to grow. You can see that truth in the CEV translation where it says, *"if you keep growing in this way ..."* And Peter will continue to remind you of this fact. But if you do not grow in this way, you have forgotten that your past sins are forgiven and you are like one who is blind or near-sighted.

Peter had a lot to put behind him. I wonder how often he replayed in his mind that night when he denied knowing Jesus three times— especially after declaring that he would never do that, and was willing to die for Jesus. I am sure that you have all experienced those nagging thoughts that come back to you as you lay in bed at night trying to get to sleep—thoughts about things that you were sure you have been forgiven for, but Satan will remind you of them again and again.

Peter had to learn to put them behind him and *know* that Jesus had forgiven him and would not bring it up again. You see, you allow growth to stop when you harbor some doubt about your forgiveness. Satan is a pro at causing us to doubt God's goodness and security. Learn to recognize Satan's tactics and tell him to take it up with Jesus who is the new landlord in your life. He lives *in* you and you live *in* Him. You don't need to answer to Satan. You need only to answer to a forgiving Savior, so send Satan to the new landlord in your life. You will find he will soon leave you alone in that area.

Each one of us who has accepted Jesus as Lord and Savior has been chosen and selected. That is why Peter says to *"do all you can to show that God has really chosen and selected you."* Think of athletes who train for the Olympics. They practice and practice their art. They do not try to hide it at all. They see no need to apologize for practicing it. They glory in victory. They don't hide their face in embarrassment.

So, why do we as Christians hide our faith, which has grown by virtue, knowledge, self control, patience, godliness, brotherly kindness, and love? It is because Satan does not want us to show our faith to the world.

294

Others just might like it and want to know what we have that they don't and will ask us to give the answer for the hope that is within us.

There was a man who was walking down the street with a placard hanging over his shoulders. As you near him, you see that it reads, "I am a fool for Christ Jesus," and as he passed you by you turn and look at him from behind and there the placard reads, "Whose fool are you?" No more needs to be said.

PRAYER: Heavenly Father, there is something scary about stepping over the line to be a full-fledged follower of yours. I think it is that we see ourselves as utter fools for trusting in a God we cannot see—going into the next day depending on your grace, mercy and love, which is not tangible. I cannot put it in my hand and say, "Look at this." In fact, I cannot even explain what faith is to someone who asked me about it. On the other hand, I know by experience, it is the only way to happiness, stability, peace, and joy. Therefore, I will put the placard on myself and walk the street with the man who knows you as I know you. I will depend on you to grow me up in the faith, lead me in the way of everlasting life and receive me at that last day into your kingdom. All praise to you, Father, for your unconditional love for me. In Jesus' name, Amen.

JULY 30th

God saw in loud, impetuous, boisterous Peter a potential of humility, virtue, diligence, and patience. God also sees your potential. He put it there, after all! In each of us there is a divine potential that is just waiting for that perfect timing to come bursting out. Our desire to birth that potential will hasten that day, but if we are afraid to give ourselves over to the control of Jesus, we put a damper on that work in our lives.

Jesus took Peter, a rugged fisherman who was filled with self confidence, and molded him into a vessel that became a pillar in the early church. The same Lord seeks to mold you into a useful vessel, too. I believe there is one more verse we need to look at. I have used it earlier this year, but I do not mind repetition—the Bible is full of it. In II Peter 3:9, Peter says, *"The Lord is not slack concerning His promise, as some men count slackness; but is longsuffering to us-ward, not willing that any should perish, but that all should come to repentance."* I see this as a profound statement. It took me awhile before I saw the whole truth that was hidden in this verse.

Let me walk you through it. God will fulfill every promise He has made to us. God never gives up on us, but rather we are the ones who give up on Him. He is not that kind of God. In fact, if He were, He could not be God. Our universe would collapse. The verses to support that are found in (CEV) Colossians 1:15-17, which read: *"Christ is exactly like God, who cannot be seen. He is the first born Son, superior to all creation. Everything was created by Him, everything in heaven and on earth, everything seen and unseen, including all forces and powers, and all rulers and authorities. All things were created by God's Son and everything was made for Him. God's Son was before all else and by Him everything is held together."*

You see, by Him *everything* is held together. Now let's turn back to today's main reading. In II Peter 3:9, God is not slack concerning His promises, like man is, but God is longsuffering, He has patience more than we can imagine. We are the impatient ones, but not God.

I want you to notice with whom God is being patient. He is not looking to the disbeliever for patience. Instead, He is waiting for us believers to get busy. It is with us that He is being patient. He is longsuffering toward *us* that *none* should perish, but that *all* should *come to repentance*.

It is up to us to go out and tell the world about God's plan of salvation. Remember, Peter is sending this message out to us. Jesus told Peter to "feed my sheep," "feed my lambs," and "tend my sheep." That is what he is doing here in this epistle. We are to go out—to get the good news of the Gospel of Jesus Christ spread to the world around us. God is waiting on us patiently to get the job done.

Has our look at the life of Peter prompted you into action? Does it give you hope that God can use you too? Does it motivate you, inspire you, and help you to see an urgency to get a move on? Do you wonder whether time is running out, and just maybe God's patience is getting thin? I surely hope you are feeling such a reaction. All Jesus needs are willing hearts. We can see by Peter's letters that his heart was totally dedicated to His Lord. God grant that the same can be said of you and me.

PRAYER: Heavenly Father, I am glad that you know my potential, and I know you won't ask me to do what I am not able to do. Therefore, I willingly say, "Yes, I am prepared to do your will in the surroundings in which I find myself." Give me the right words, and the verses to back them up, so that I can be of help to others who are struggling to understand your Word and your ways in their lives. I desire to share your Word with others, but know you must prepare their heart first to hear what your Word says to them. I have confidence that you will go before me and get the ground work all done, since you have invited me to follow you. That means you were there before me, getting it all ready for what you have asked me to do or say. In Jesus' name, Amen.

JULY 31st

We have learned that there is a bitter enemy out there called the devil, with whom we do battle all the time. God has provided armor for us to use to withstand the devil's assaults. We are going to spend a few days looking at what that armor is and how to use it. It is all listed in Ephesians 6.

Since it is written in pieces, we will address it in pieces. First we will look at the reason for having armor, then what the battle is all about and why we need armor, and then what each piece of armor is.

Let us first turn to Ephesians 6:10-11, which reads, *"Finally, my brethren* (fellow believers), *be strong in the Lord, and in the power of His might. Put on the whole armor of God, that ye may be able to stand against the wiles of the devil. "* This journey of life is going to be a tough battle, God knows that better than we do. In fact many people who have accepted Jesus as Lord and Savior think that the battle is over, but it has only begun.

Now that you know Jesus and have accepted Him as Lord in your heart, you have a supernatural power to be an "overcomer." The devil knows that well, but he does not want you to ever know it, because you can use that power to defeat him. Notice that verse said, *"Be strong in the Lord and in the power of His might."* It will not be your strength that will win the battle, but rather His strength and His power.

Jesus just loves it when we allow Him to fight our battles for us. Our problem is that we do not always trust Him to do that. The way to improve our trust is to put on the armor that God provides for that battle. That is why it is so important for us to know what that armor is and what it can do for us. One of the words we will see again and again is "stand." There is no place in the Bible that I can remember ever hearing God telling someone to run away.

I do not think God ever calls for retreat tactics, so we need armor to protect us from Satan's assaults. We will look at this carefully for a few days. In the meantime, pray that you may understand what you read, so you can apply it to your life.

PRAYER: Heavenly Father, I never thought of being recruited into an army, but that is what it sounds like you are doing with me. Help me to want to be recruited. Take me slowly through this portion of my Christian walk and give me the courage to stick with it. Is this also a part of the abundant life you talked about earlier? If so, help me to see that too. I like the sound of abundant life so much better than putting on armor for a battle. I am thankful that I know you are the winner, which makes me a winner too. I will take courage in that fact. In Jesus' name, Amen.

AUGUST 1st

Ephesians 6:12 reads: *"For we wrestle not against flesh and blood, but against principalities, against powers, against the rulers* (world rulers) *of the darkness of this world, against spiritual hosts of wickedness in high* (heavenly) *places."*

This verse tells us who we are not to be doing battle with, and who we actually are fighting, or in battle with. It is very important that we get this truth settled right away. If we do not, we will be confused and not able to win a victory—we will always feel defeated, and Satan will have a circus with us. We do not battle with each other, but rather our battle is with the enemy, the devil.

In this verse, we are called flesh and blood. We are told that we fight with powers and principalities, rulers of this world, and hosts of wickedness in heavenly places. These are all different ranks of evil spirits, including Satan himself who is the head of all these evil powers. Satan's kingdom is highly organized, and he has an evil spirit or demon assigned to each one of us. Each must answer to those above them, and their job is to wear you down, tempt you to not obey God.

Satan wants to bring you to the place where you will deny God, if that is at all possible. He uses other people to do that. The interesting thing here is that he is always trying to use you, too, to be the thorn in someone else's side.

We all know people who are able to bring out the worst in us, and others who always seem to bring out the best in us. Say, for instance, you change jobs and you find that the new boss is a pain in the neck. You just cannot seem to please him, no matter what you do, and he is constantly finding fault with your work. Get a handle on what is going on. Satan is trying to get under your skin through this new boss. So what can you do? You can begin to pray for this man—ask God to bless him and his family, and to help you be a shining light to this man. Do not loose your cool, but stay positive and do your best. If that boss uses bad language and speaks harshly to his employees, you can ask God to push those words back down his throat and to make them bitter in his stomach. You can pray under your breath and God will hear you. In fact, you can just think those thoughts and God will read your mind. You cannot change your boss—no one can, except God. You cannot even change yourself. God is the only one who can change you.

You join hands with God when you pray such a prayer. God wants that boss to be a reflection of Him, and when you ask God to convict him of his harshness by having him taste his own bitter words, then God can do that in answer to your prayer, and over time the man will be so convicted of his bitter words he *will want* to change his ways.

If those words came out of his mouth, why can't I ask God to cause him to taste them? I feel I am in my perfect right to do that, and I have watched "change" take place in many people who use their mouth to cut people down. You can also let Satan know that you are aware of what he is up to in this whole situation, and you can declare to Satan that you will not run away or be defeated, but that you and God are always the winners.

PRAYER Heavenly Father, thank you so much for showing me that I have authority over situations in my life, and that I am not fighting against people, but against evil spirits that use people. That helps me to understand so much, such as why certain people get under my skin so often. I want to live a victorious life, and you have given me hope of doing that. In Jesus' name, Amen.

AUGUST 2nd

Referring back to yesterday's devotional, there will be times when God does want you to leave a job, but if God is in charge of my life, then the fact that I found work there in the first place would give me pause to think before trying to change the environment around me. We can do that since we know we are not fighting with flesh and blood, but with realms of satanic powers and principalities. They all shudder at the name of Jesus.

300

Claim the area around your workplace to be free of every evil spirit by commanding that they leave in the name of Jesus. Of course, you do not do that in a loud voice for all to hear, but rather you do this at home in your prayer time.

We have the right to take authority over Satan and all his hosts of wickedness, because of what Jesus said in Matthew 28:18-19, *"And Jesus came and spake unto them, saying, 'All power* (authority) *is given unto me in heaven and earth. Go ye therefore, and teach all nations, baptizing them in the name of the Father, and of the Son, and of the Holy Ghost:' "* You see, you have the power to change your environment—it is the power of prayer, how you react to your situation, and how you use the authority you have been empowered with.

You do not preach to the people around you unless they open the door by asking about your faith. When they ask, it is assumed that person wants to know about your faith, or the God you worship, otherwise they would not have asked. Satan would not prompt anyone to ask a question about a believer's faith. It is dangerous for him to prompt anyone to do that, to offer a believer the opportunity to share anything from the Bible.

When you are frustrated with your circumstances, look at your situation, analyze it and figure out what the source of the problem is. If it is a spiritual battle, then prepare to fight it on a spiritual level with prayer being your most powerful weapon. Pray in the name of Jesus!

Whatever you do, do not accept the ugly words that tear you down, unless you sense a nugget of truth about yourself in those words. If that is the case, go to God and ask Him to help you to change your behavior, or your response to correction. However, you do not need to *receive* unkind words. It is your choice.

Too many people receive the unkind words from others, and it serves to unnerve them and defeat them, and it undermines them becoming the people God created them to be. Keep in mind, a believer is to live an abundant life, not a defeated life. If you need to change, then do so willingly. Otherwise, do not allow this workplace, or boss, or other problem drain you of your own self respect. We do not wrestle with flesh

301

and blood. People are not the problem as a rule, but rather the evil spirits that seek to use people against us are the problem.

PRAYER: Heavenly Father, these are encouraging words, but will I be able to put them into practice when I need to? I am not used to using a prayer power rule in my life, and it feels like I am taking advantage of your power. Help me to get this settled in my mind so that I can feel comfortable praying with power. Show me in your word that I have the privilege and the right to live in this peaceful place of the abundant life you said I can have. In Jesus' name, Amen.

AUGUST 3rd

In Ephesians 6:13-14, we read: *"Wherefore take unto you the whole armor of God, that you may be able to withstand in the evil day, and having done all, to stand. Stand therefore, having your loins girded about with truth, and having on the breastplate of righteousness."*

There are five defensive pieces of armor listed in this chapter, and one offensive piece. Today we will discuss two of those pieces of armor, but first, we will look at the beginning of verse 13. We are admonished to take on (put on) the whole armor of God. We cannot afford to leave off one piece of that armor. The reason for the armor is to be able to *withstand* in the evil day, having done all, to *stand*.

We are never admonished to run from a fight with the devil. In every situation in life, the believer is to be a winner. Even when all evidence looks like a defeat, we are to stand, and stand, and stand. Notice that it says, *"having done all to stand."* We need to practice stubborn faith. God honors that kind of faith where we do not budge. Defeat is for Satan, not for flesh and blood believers.

So, what about the armor? The first piece of armor is having our loins girded with *truth*. What does it mean to have our loins girded? In those days people wore long flowing gowns, and if they wanted to walk

302

swiftly or run, they needed to gather those gowns up and secure them (with a belt or cord), so they would not be tangled up in the gowns.

If we are to really run this race called life, then we, too, need to be able to move quickly and not get tangled up in worldly things and stumble. The way to do that is to know the *truth* about the word of God. Jesus Himself said in John 14:6 that He is the way, the truth, and the life. Jesus *is* the truth, so to know Him is to know truth. How much do you want to know the truth? It is a protection against the devil's schemes. The more you know the truth, the more you can be an "overcomer" of Satan.

The other piece of armor is the *breastplate of righteousness*. A breastplate protects the heart and lungs, which are two vital organs we cannot live without. The key word here is "righteousness." There is no righteousness outside of Jesus Christ. He gained a righteous standing before God for all of us.

When you have Jesus in your heart, you also have His righteousness on you and in you—a right standing before God. That is an important piece of your armor and you need to know, really know in your heart of hearts, that you are righteous in the eyes of God. You are not a second-class citizen. You are a first-class citizen with all the privileges that righteousness brings with it. Know the truth about the privileges of your righteousness given you by the finished work of Jesus Christ. It will protect you from the wiles of the devil.

PRAYER: Heavenly Father, I thank you for the righteousness that your Son Jesus died to give me, and for the protection that it provides. I pray that I will remember whose I am, and who I am, when the devil arranges hardships and trials against me to weaken my faith. I ask your Holy Spirit to help me to remember the power of prayer and the power of your name, Jesus. That is a privilege I have to win the victory over every situation in my life. In Jesus' name, Amen.

AUGUST 4th

Ephesians 6:15 says that our feet are to be *"shod with the preparation of the gospel of peace."* We are to wear the preparation of the gospel of peace as shoes to take the gospel around the world. God's desire for peace is intense. Where God is, there is peace. The word "gospel" means "good news." God's plan of salvation is very good news, and everyone needs to hear it and to believe it.

Do you remember me telling you that there are three kinds of peace? First we have peace *with* God, which was established for us when Jesus died on the cross as payment for our sins. That made peace between sinful mankind and God. Jesus did it all and then gave it to us as a free gift, which we can accept if we just invite Jesus into our hearts.

Secondly, we have peace *from* God. God can now minister peace to us in the midst of any hardship, trial or circumstance. All we need to do is plug into that peace that has been made for us by accepting it as ours.

Thirdly, we have peace *of* God. This is God's kind of peace. His very own peace can also be ours. It belongs to us, since we belong to Jesus, and to God through Jesus. We are like children in God's family. Everything that belongs to that family also belongs to each child. Typically, in families, if the parents die, the children would inherit equally. Jesus is the Son of God, and we are sons and daughters, therefore, the peace of God is also ours.

It is that good news, or gospel, that our feet are to carry to the community around us. It also protects us, just as shoes protect our feet from the stones and stubble we would have to walk on. Satan would like to cause us to stumble, to stub our toes, or do anything to deter us from carrying the gospel to others.

Let me remind you that verse 11 said, *"Put on the whole armor of God."* We dare not leave one part of that armor off. Also remember that in Mathew 5:9, Jesus said, *"Blessed are the peacemakers: for they shall be called children of God."* And Isaiah 52:7 says, *"How beautiful upon the mountains are the feet of him that bringeth good tidings, that publisheth peace; that bringeth good tidings of good, that publisheth salvation; that saith unto Zion, 'Thy God reigneth!' "*

PRAYER: Dear Lord Jesus, I thank you for making peace between God and me, and I pray that I will be a peacemaker in my life. Thank you that I can experience that peace in my life, and know that it will be there for me whenever I have need of it. Also, help me to be a carrier of that peace, that my feet will be swift to carry it to whomsoever you ask me to go to and that my armor of shoes of peace will always be on my feet. In Jesus' name, Amen.

AUGUST 5th

In Ephesians 6:16, we read, *"Above all, taking the shield of Faith, wherewith ye shall be able to quench all the fiery darts of the wicked (evil one)."* A shield protects many parts of the body, and it is moveable. We will call on our faith to "be there" in many different situations. It has to be strong like a shield.

A shield is made from metal and can withstand fiery darts; it is not made of wood, which would not be strong enough to stop such an assault. How strong is your faith, and what makes one's faith strong? Faith is made stronger as it is tested and tried.

Although we do not like tests and trials, if we walk through them with an attitude of victory and with our faith firmly rooted in God's love, mercy, and grace, then our faith can take us through the toughest times and will grow stronger for it. Then our faith will be that strong shield, an important part of our armor.

Do you recall addressing our faith earlier in the year? Faith is a gift from God. He gives a measure of faith to every man, as it says in Romans 12:3, *"according as God hath dealt to every man a measure of faith."* We naturally live by faith all the time and think nothing of it. When you go to a restaurant and order your food, you expect it to be free from poison. That is faith. When you get into an airplane and expect the pilot to be alert and healthy, you fly by faith.

Think of your day-by-day activities. You live by faith every day of your life. Should it be any different in the spiritual realm? I don't think so! In order to have faith in God, you need to know God through His Word. You need to understand how He has been faithful throughout history to those who call upon His name. He is faithful to forgive. Therefore, He can ask us to be faithful to forgive.

Our faith will determine our faithfulness. It will protect us from quitting when the going gets tough, and quitting is what the devil wants us to do. He loves unfinished business, aborted plans, missing the mark, stalemates, and indecision. They are signs of a lack of faith. Not in one place in the life of Jesus do you see Him practice any of these things. He was always moving forward, toward Jerusalem and the cross. There was no turning back, no short cuts, no hesitation. He had faith in His Heavenly Father, and His faith never wavered.

We all reap the benefit of His faith. Yes, indeed, faith is a shield, a piece of armor to protect us on our journey in life.

PRAYER: Heavenly Father, I thank you for the faith you have given to me. I pray that I will store up your Word in my heart to draw on to support my faith when the tough times come crashing down on me. Also, help me to be faithful, so my faith can grow. I do not want to quit or take a shortcut in life. I want to be a part of your army, one who marches for your cause. Give me, I pray, the strength to persevere. In Jesus' precious name, Amen.

AUGUST 6th

Ephesians 6:17 instructs us to *"take the helmet of salvation."* A helmet protects a person's head, where the mind is located. Satan wants control of our minds, and if he gains control of it, then Jesus died for nothing—God gave His best for nothing!

What did that helmet cost God? God gave His Son to buy our salvation with His life! Philippians 2:5 says, *"Let this **mind** be in you which was also in Christ Jesus,"* and I Corinthians 2:16 states, *"For who* *hath known the __mind__ of the Lord, that he may instruct him?   But we have the __mind__ of Christ."*

According to those verses, whose mind do we have? Can we depend on that mind to help us our in times of need? You bet! But we have to apply it, since it is ours. Remember, Satan does not want us to know this truth, nor that we have the right to apply the mind of Christ when we need that kind of help. He can do nothing against us unless we give him the right to do it—and we give him that right when we doubt God's Word about what we have, or what we can do.

Look at Isaiah 26:3, which reads, *"Thou (meaning God) wilt keep him in perfect peace, whose __mind__ is stayed on thee, because he truesth in thee."* All we need to do is to keep our minds glued on God, and then we will have peace of mind and peace of heart. Focusing on God will show Him that you trust Him more than your circumstances.

It will take a stubborn faith to do that, but in the end it will pay big dividends. Another verse that is also important to know to make your helmet strong and impenetrable is Romans 12:2, which states: *"And be not conformed to this world: but be ye transformed by the renewing of your __mind__, that ye may prove what is that good, and acceptable, and perfect will of God."*

The mind is one area of our body that Satan seeks to control, but we are admonished not to allow our minds to be conformed to this world's systems, or values, but instead to allow our minds to be transformed by being renewed each day. That is done when we read and meditate on daily devotions or read the Bible. We can not only read, though, but also meditate on what it says to you and how it is supposed to change you from glory to glory.

What does your helmet look like? Is it a straw hat, a hard hat, or a real honest-to-goodness helmet that also covers the ears? We need to also be concerned about what we hear. Negative talk can settle in our hearts and produce negative actions, which is what Satan is only too happy to tempt you to do. The helmet of salvation, which is a positive message through and through, will help you recognize the negative suggestions that seep into your mind on a daily basis.

307

PRAYER: Heavenly Father, help me to make use of the armor you have provided for me. Help me to really understand each piece of my protective armor. Continue to teach me about that armor. I do not want Satan to coax me into leaving one piece lay idle, so help me to see and understand it when he is doing that very thing in my life. I want to live a life of victory *every day*, not just once in awhile. I realize that is the abundant life you talk about. In Jesus' name, Amen.

AUGUST 7th

 Ephesians 6:17 states, *"And take the helmet of salvation, and the sword of the Spirit, which is the Word of God."*
This verse is so full of truth we need to know and grasp that we need to spend a couple days on it.

Remember, the helmet is our salvation. What do you really know about your salvation? First of all, you need to know in your mind that you have salvation right now, not just a hope for a "someday" attainment way beyond the blue.

When we accept Jesus as Lord and Savior we became betrothed, or "engaged" so to speak, to Jesus. To flirt with the world is like an unfaithful spouse. Jesus *is* our salvation.

I Peter 1:18-19 explains: *"For as much as ye know that ye were not redeemed with corruptible things, as silver and gold, from your vain conversation* (meaning, way of life), *received by tradition from your fathers. But with the precious blood of Christ as of a lamb without blemish and without spot."*

Jesus did for us what no number of lambs could ever do—we are permanently redeemed from the curse of sin and death, from the world around us, from our own sinful nature. We are redeemed into a living hope and eternal life.

We have been given the power to live a life of victory over sin, death, and the power of the devil. All this is also included in that word "salvation." We must not forget the price of all this. No amount of silver or gold could ever have bought such a gift. It cost God His best, His own blood.

There was only one way God could bring that sacrificial blood into this world and do it "legally," and that was to send His own Son, in whom God's blood flowed. It was holy blood, and all this, too, is included in that word "salvation." Yes, indeed, we have as a part of our armor a helmet (protective covering for our mind) of salvation. Tell God that you consciously put on the helmet of salvation, and wear it proudly.

PRAYER: Thank you, Lord, for all the armor available to me to live that victorious life here on earth, where Satan rules and works to create chaos in the lives of believers. I also realize that he does not need to work so hard on those who have not believed in Jesus. Since they belong to him anyway, he can spend his energy on those who do believe in Jesus. It is sin that separates us from God, and the forgiveness of sin that brings us into union with Him. For that reason, Satan is continuously trying to cause me to sin. How clever of him to cause me to choose to sin, because he then thinks his hands are clean. I cannot blame him for it when I *chose* to do it. Thank you for your Word that helps me to know how Satan works, how he sets traps and snares to trip me up. May your Holy Spirit be at work day and night in my life to help me see those traps a mile away, not after they have entangled me. In Jesus' name, Amen.

AUGUST 8th

Ephesians 6:17 mentions *"the sword of the Spirit, which is the word of God."* I want to draw your attention to the fact that so far we have talked about defensive armor that protects us. Today, we change our stance and put on an offensive weapon, one that we can use to move forward, to attack, and to take over victoriously.

That weapon is the Word of God, the Bible. You would probably not think that such a thing would be a weapon, but when it comes to fighting Satan, it is the most powerful weapon in Heaven or on earth! I cannot stress strongly enough the importance of knowing the Word of God. I only hope that I will be given the right words to convey that message to you.

It is not only important for us to know the Word, but also to know how to use it. Remember, we do not wrestle with flesh and blood, so please do not use the Word as a sword against your fellow man, either believers or unbelievers. They are all flesh and blood. Great harm can be done if God's Word is used in such a way, as a whip over someone's head.

We can find some good advice in James 4:11, which reads, *"Speak not evil one of another, brethren. He that speaketh evil of his brethren, speaketh evil of the law, and judgeth the law: but if thou judge the law, thou art not a doer of the law, but a judge."* The "Message Bible" translates this verse as: *"Don't bad-mouth each other, friends. It's God's Word, His Message, His Royal Rule, that takes a beating in that kind of talk. You're supposed to be honoring the Message, not writing graffiti all over it. God is in charge of deciding human destiny. Who do you think you are to meddle in the destiny of others?"*

I have heard people quote the Bible in such a way as to condemn others right then and there, and push them into a change of lifestyle. Well, that is not what is meant by using the Word of God as a sword of the Spirit. Our battle is not with flesh and blood, but with the satanic forces at large in the world, even in the church. It is in that realm that we are to use the Word of God. Jesus, in His temptation for 40 days, has given us the example of such use of God's Word. We will address that topic soon.

PRAYER: Heavenly Father, in the name of Jesus, I ask you to help me use the Word of God, my sword, to fight the devil in all the right ways. Help me to only use the Word for people's good, to help them know and understand your love, mercy, and grace, never as a sword against them. Help me to depend on your Holy Spirit to guide me in this new walk with you. In Jesus' name, Amen.

AUGUST 9th

I want to talk a bit more about weapons as we see them in the Bible. Ecclesiastes 9:18 states, *"Wisdom is better than weapons of war: but one sinner destroyeth much good."* Our life is compared to a battle field, and God is telling us that our best weapon is "wisdom."

One might wonder how that could be. Remember, we found out that wisdom is the wise use of what we know and understand. We have just learned that the only weapon that will work against Satan is the *Word of God.* We cannot fight him with our faith.

Jesus' faith was tested when Satan tempted Him during his 40 days of fasting. Unless we know the Word of God, we are like soldiers going into battle with guns, but no bullets. If all you know is that Jesus loved you enough to die for your sins, then that alone will be like a million bullets for your gun. Think what it would mean to have ten such truths from the Bible committed to memory to quote back to Satan when he comes against you?

One person practicing sin is like a rotten apple in a barrel—it will destroy the whole barrel of good apples if left alone. As we just read in Ecclesiastes 9:18, *"but one sinner destroyeth much good."* Instead, practice wisdom from God and make wise use of His Word. The Word of God gives a believer a great deal of authority and power against the devil and all his hosts of helpers. Make wise use of that weapon in your faith journey.

PRAYER: Heavenly Father, I am so thankful for the sword of the Spirit, the Word of God, I can have at my disposal. Help me to practice using it when Satan confronts me, to tempt me to give up or lose faith. Help me remember to turn to your Word as Jesus did when He was tempted. I also ask the Holy Spirit to remind me of the Word that I have studied so it can help me in my hour of need. In Jesus' name, Amen.

AUGUST 10th

Isaiah 54:17 reads: *"'No weapon formed against thee shall prosper; and every tongue that shall rise against thee in judgment thou shalt condemn. This is the heritage of the servants of the Lord, and their righteousness is of me,' saith the Lord."*

When God says, "No weapon formed against thee shall prosper," we can see that it is not a weapon God has made. God is for us, not against us, so He would not form a weapon against us.

Satan is the one who forms weapons against us. He encourages other people to come against us to slander, abuse, steal, lie, cheat, and hate us. But, the good news is that we can claim this verse of scripture that states God will see to it that no weapon formed against us will prosper. You should quote it back to Satan. He knows God's Word. He quoted the Bible to Jesus when he tempted Jesus.

There is another part of this scripture we need to look at. It says that *" every tongue that shall rise against thee in judgment thou shalt condemn."* This sounds like a harsh thing to do, but I think God wants those people to come to know and understand the truth, and the only way that can happen is if they are convicted of their sin. Then, the next step is for them to ask for forgiveness and to receive forgiveness.

You can help the Holy Spirit's work by praying for that person as the Spirit leads you. Remember, Jesus said to pray for those who persecute you. You do not condemn the person, but rather you condemn the words of judgment that person has spoken. That is why I often say, "Lord, take those words, push them back down their throat and make them bitter in their stomach."

I believe that sometimes people need to "taste" their words and feel how bitter they are. As you reread the scripture for today, do you see how God has your victorious life in view at all times? Jesus called it "abundant life."

God gave us six pieces of armor to prepare us for the fight, and all we need to do is make sure we wear our protective armor. There is no question about the battle. There is one, and we are in it whether we know it or not. So, we better acknowledge it, know our enemy, and know our weapons, the One who created those weapons, and how to use them.

PRAYER: Heavenly Father, thank you for providing the weapons I can use against the enemy. Help me to know how to use my weapons and what they are. Give me the training I need to be a good soldier for your kingdom. One thing I do know is that you expect me to fight with love, show mercy, and minister grace, like you did. It is not a battle full of hate, except for Satan and his hosts of wickedness. I am to pray for and love even the people he uses against me. Give me the strength to do that. In Jesus' name, Amen.

AUGUST 11th

Satan forms weapons against us, but Jesus knows how that is done. Jesus also knows the Word of God is His weapon against Satan. So let's see how that played out while Jesus was fasting for 40 days. In Matthew 4:3-4, we read: *"And when the tempter* (Satan) *came to Him, he said, 'If thou be the Son of God, command that these stones be made bread.' But He* (Jesus) *answered and said, 'It is written, Man shall not live by bread alone, but by every word that proceedeth out of the mouth of God* (a quote from Deuteronomy 8:3). *And He humbled thee, and suffered thee to hunger, and fed thee with manna which thou knewest not, neither did thy fathers know; that He might make thee know that man doth not live by bread alone, but by every Word that proceedeth out of the mouth of the Lord doth man live.' "*

Jesus threw the Word of God right into Satan's face. He did it three times, one right after the other. We will look at those tomorrow. What I want you to see here is the fact that Jesus knows the Word, the Old Testament was all there was to the Bible of that day, and we need to know it that well, too, if we are going to use it as a weapon against Satan.

We also have the New Testament, which is all about Jesus and His victory over sin, death, and the power of the devil. Pay close attention to

313

how Jesus quoted the Word back to Satan. Satan even dares to quote the Word to Jesus, but in a half-truth sort of way.

If we do not know the Word, do you realize that you could sit under the teaching of a false prophet and never know it? You could be led astray by false teachings and not even know what has happened.

Get acquainted intimately with the Word of God in the Bible, so that you cannot be led into a false gospel. Matthew 7:15 warns us, *"Beware of false prophets, which come to you in sheep's clothing, but inwardly they are ravening wolves."* These were Jesus' words.

Paul also warned the church at Galatia. In Galatians 1:6-8, Paul says: *"I marvel that ye are so soon removed from him that called you into the grace of Christ unto another gospel: Which is not another* (another gospel); *but there be some that trouble you, and would pervert the gospel of Christ. But though we, or an angel from heaven, preach any other gospel unto you than that which we have preached unto you, let him be accursed."*

The amplified Bible says, *"let him be devoted to destruction, doomed to eternal punishment!"* Those are strong words, wouldn't you say? We are warned that there will be those who will try to lead believers astray, but Satan is behind it all. Know the true Word well enough to recognize a false teaching.

PRAYER: Heavenly Father, I pray that I will be careful how I use your Word in my conversations with those around me. Help me to be sensitive to the needs of others, so that I will not throw the Word of God around like a weapon, which it was not intended to be. Also help me to become comfortable in quoting the Word to the devil, who wants to use God's Word as a lie. Help me to fend off his lies about the God of my faith, and his attempts to make my God appear as a wimp who cannot help me in my time of need. You have promised to never leave me or forsake me, so help me to keep my eye on that promised Word and quote it to Satan when I need to. I also need your help in remembering what the Word of the Bible says, so it is available to me at a moment's notice to keep me from following a false gospel. In Jesus' name, Amen.

AUGUST 12th

I want to point out something I feel is necessary for all of us to understand. Satan will always tempt us at our weakest points. In the verses yesterday, we saw his attack on the weakness of the body. Jesus had been fasting for 40 days and was hungry, so Satan tempted Him to turn stones into bread. Jesus recognized Satan's tactic, and quoted straight from the Bible that food for the body is not as important as the Word of God—the Word of God is what brings eternal life to our souls.

Today, we will see how Satan tempted Jesus' soul, the seat of decisions. Matthew 4:5-7 reads: *"Then the devil taketh Him up into the holy City* (Jerusalem)*, and setteth Him on a pinnacle of the temple, And saith unto Him, 'If thou be the Son of God, cast thyself down: for it is written, "He shall give His angels charge concerning thee: and in their hands they shall bear thee up, lest at any time thou dash they foot against a stone." ' Jesus said unto him, 'It is written again, "Thou shalt not tempt the Lord thy God."*

If Jesus ever wondered whether He really was the Son of God, Satan was at work to create enough doubt in Jesus' mind. Satan wanted Jesus to test God to see if His Father would indeed protect Him if He threw Himself down from the height of the temple pinnacle.

Satan quoted Psalm 91:11-12, which said, *"For He shall give His angels charge over thee to keep thee in all thy ways. They shall bear thee up in their hands, lest thou dash they foot against a stone."* Imagine the boldness of Satan to get right into Jesus' face and quote Scripture back to Him! If he will do that to Jesus, don't you think he will do that to us too?

We need to know the Word of God so well that we can quote it to Satan and be ready to defend it by whatever Word of Scripture he will try to use against us. He will twist God's Word to his own gain, and we must be wiser than he is and know that God's Word was never intended to be used in that way.

In response to Satan's misuse of the Word, Jesus fired another scripture right back at him, referencing Deuteronomy 6:16, which says, *"Ye shall not tempt the Lord your God, as ye tempted Him in Massah."* Satan was trying to get Jesus to tempt God. If we think we can live recklessly and expect God to protect us, we are tempting God, and that is absolutely foolhardy.

Let's also look at James 1:13, which reads, *"Let no man say when he is tempted, 'I am tempted of God,' for God cannot be tempted with evil, neither tempteth He any man."* We can see plainly that God is not the tempter in our life, but rather Satan is the tempter. When we look at a situation, we need to remember that God is always good, and He does not plan or even think evil. Jesus remembered that when He was being tempted by the devil sitting high upon that pinnacle.

Can you begin to see how important it is for us to *know* and to be able to *use* the Word of God to bring victory into our lives at all times? Yes, indeed, the Word of God is our sword for a stance of victory over Satan all the time. He tempted Jesus in His seat of decision, the soul. It is in our soul that we make life-changing decisions.

This leads me to think of the people who "follow the crowd" because of peer pressure. It can lead them into a life of bondage to Satan, and, of course, that is exactly what he wants.

PRAYER: Heavenly Father, it just amazes me that there is a tempter out there with strategies to accomplish devious works that are way beyond my comprehension. And yet you expect me to outwit him! You have given me tools to overcome his wiles and schemes, and my job is to use those tools with confidence in the One who gave them to me. Help me, Lord, to think in that vein every time the devil comes at me with a temptation to doubt your goodness or your willingness to cover me with your grace. In Jesus' name, Amen.

AUGUST 13th

Luke 4:5-8 reads: *"And the devil, taking Him up into a high mountain, showed unto Him all the kingdoms of the world in a moment of time. And the devil said unto Him, 'All this*

*power will I give thee, and the glory of them: for that is delivered unto
me; and to whomsoever I will I give it. If thou therefore wilt worship me,
all shall be thine'. And Jesus answered and said unto him, 'Get thee
behind me, Satan: for it is written, "Thou shalt worship the Lord thy God,
and Him only shalt thou serve.' "*

There is so much to these verses, I only hope I can lead you
through them in such a way that you can grasp it all.

First of all, we see that Satan's goal in all of this is to make Jesus
actually worship him! Please get this truth firmly entrenched in your mind.
Satan has always wanted to be worshipped as God, and he will continue on
that foolhardy trek until he is cast into the lake of fire.

Satan wants you to worship him. Satan's whole tactic, from
beginning to end, is for you to put something before God in your life—
money, social status, somebody, *anything*, just so it is not God that is first.
If one thing does not work, he will try another.

This time, Satan was tempting Jesus' spirit, so we see the whole
gambit from beginning to end of his attempt to wear Jesus down. Jesus is
tired and hungry, so Satan tells Him to turn stones into bread. The devil
wanted Him to prove that He really is the Son of God, so he told Him to
throw Himself down from the pinnacle of the temple, essentially saying,
"God will protect you." Take a short cut to being King of kings and Lord
of lords on earth by falling down to worship me."

It is also plain to be seen that Satan is the god of this world's
systems. If he was not, how else could he claim that it was *his* to give to
Jesus? Satan will promise *you* the world, too, if you follow and worship
him.

This is a temptation of our spirit. First, Satan will tempt the body,
as he did to Jesus when He was hungry. Then he will tempt the soul, the
seat of desire. He may tempt you to prove to the world that you are a child
of God. And then he tempts the spirit, tempting you to worship him so you
can have worldly fame, money, prestige, and so on.

It is a dangerous route to take, and it is so sly and devilish that you
hardly notice you are heading down that path until suddenly your feet are
stuck in cement and there is no way to get out of the mess you are in. At

317

least, that is what Satan will tell you. He will try to convince you that you are hopelessly lost. Do not believe it! Remember, Jesus is in the "whosoever" business. Whosoever dares to believe that God loves him, that Jesus paid the price for his salvation, and that he can have eternal life and not perish, *is* a child of God!

Aren't you glad God the Father, Son, and Holy Spirit are in the "whosoever" business? There is no one on earth that is beyond hope. All anyone has to do is call on the name of the Lord and God will be there to deliver them from bondage and to minister peace to their souls. What a God we worship and serve!

To humble yourself under the mighty hand of God means to call out to Him in your time of testing, temptation, and need. He will be right there to help you. You can depend on this! Never fall for the lie that you are too far gone for God to rescue you!

I hope you saw how Jesus used the Word of God as a weapon against the tempter. That is what we need to learn to do, too. God says, "You are the head, not the tail. No weapon against you shall prosper. You are more than a conqueror." Believe it!

PRAYER: I am beginning to realize what a deceitful enemy we are up against. I also see how needy I am in the face of such an enemy. I come to you, Heavenly Father, to ask for all the help I can get to withstand such an enemy and not faint or falter, or become weary in my faith walk. I also need your help to use all my weapons daily so that I can make sure that victory is mine to claim. In Jesus' mighty name, Amen.

AUGUST 14th

Today, we will look at II Corinthians 10:4-5, which states: *"For the weapons of our warfare are not carnal* (of the flesh) *but mighty through God to the pulling down of strong*

holds; Casting down imaginations, and every high thing that exalteth itself against the knowledge of God, and bringing into captivity every thought to the obedience of Christ."

The Message Bible translates these verses as: *"The tools of our trade aren't for marketing or manipulation, but they are for demolishing that entire massively corrupt culture. We use our powerful God tools for smashing warped philosophies, tearing down barriers erected against the truth of God, fitting every loose thought and emotion and impulse into the structure of life shaped by Christ. Our tools are ready at hand for clearing the ground of every obstruction and building lives of obedience into maturity."*

The weapons God gives us to fight the spiritual battle we are in are *spiritual* weapons—the Word of God, prayer, worship, and praise of God (yes, even singing, which we will look at tomorrow). Satan wants to blind our eyes to the truth of God's power and love, but we have an arsenal of weapons to prevent and overcome that.

We can use these weapons not only in our own lives, but also in the lives of those we love and want to see take Jesus into their hearts. Only those who have stood fast and strong in this kind of prayer really know how powerful these weapons are. If one person will put his hand in God's, determined not to falter or faint, standing strong, add to that God Himself and you will have a majority that is second to none.

In fact, there will be four of you: God the Father, Son, and Holy Spirit, and you. With such a majority, nothing is impossible. Look at that today's verses again. Our weapons are mighty. They can pull down strongholds (that is, Satan's strongholds). If he has set up a stronghold in the life of a friend or relative of yours, your weapons of prayer and praise can actually pull down that stronghold.

It may take a few years, but if you do not give up, that stronghold will come down. Satan is no match for God, and when God and you team up, believe me, Satan is one defeated fallen angel.

PRAYER: Heavenly Father, I will need your help to know how to use those spiritual weapons you have given us. I have never done this kind of warfare before, so help me to learn how to be bold and take control over a small area, so that I can learn to step into the larger areas in my life. I am going to lay claim to the truth found in I Corinthians 10:13, which says: *"There has no temptation* (test) *taken you but such as is common to man* (that man can bear)*: but God is faithful, who will not suffer you to be tempted above that you are able; but with the temptation also make a way to escape, that to bear it* (that you may be able to bear it)*."*

Heavenly Father, I see in this Scripture that through everything God is faithful to His own Word. That is a real comfort to me. I also appreciate that you provide a way of escape when the going really gets tough. Thank you for those comforting words. In Jesus' mighty name, Amen.

AUGUST 15th

One more weapon I promised to share with you is the weapon of worship, such as singing praises to God. Before we look at the scripture for today in II Chronicles, you will need a little background. At this time, Israel was preparing to go into battle, and a lot of prayer had gone into their strategy for this battle.

We find a prophetic word from God in II Chronicles 20:15-17, which states: *"And he* (Jahaziel) *said, 'Hearken ye all Judah and ye inhabitants of Jerusalem, and thou king Jehoshaphat, Thus saith the Lord unto you., "Be thou not afraid nor dismayed by reason of this great multitude; for the battle is not yours but God's. Tomorrow go ye down against them, behold they come up by the cliff of Ziz: and ye shall find them at the end of the brook* (valley), *before the wilderness of Jeruel. Ye shall not need to fight in this battle; set yourselves, stand ye still, and see the salvation of the Lord with you. O Judah and Jerusalem: fear not, nor be dismayed; tomorrow go out against them: for the Lord will be with you.' "*

In verses 21-22, we read: *"And when he had consulted with the people, he appointed singers unto the Lord, and that should praise the beauty of holiness, as they went out before the army, and to say, 'Praise the Lord; for His mercy endureth forever.' And when they began to sing and to praise, the Lord set ambushments against the children of Ammon and Moab, and mount Seir, which were come against Judah; and they were smitten."*

Can you imagine fighting an enemy with a choir at the head of your army? When you are dismayed, afraid, or feeling hopeless, the best thing you can do for yourself is to begin singing praise songs or listening to praise music. It will drive away the enemy of your peace, joy, and hope. Instead, those things will be ministered to your soul. Singing is a strong weapon against the enemy, and we need to learn to make use of that weapon to the fullest.

I also want to point out that God chases fear and dismay away. According to God, there is no place in the lives of His children for those negative attitudes. First, you have to recognize that Satan is whispering words of fear and dismay into your ears, which should be protected with the helmet of salvation.

God is for His children, not against them, but to have a victory it is a two-sided thing. It is God and you against the enemy. Well, guess what? Jesus already won the battle on the cross over 2,000 years ago. Isn't it time that we lay claim to that victory and realize we do not need to fight in these battles anymore? Instead, all we need to do is lay claim to what has already been won for us!

That is a hard lesson to learn. It takes time to simply let the problem go and lay claim to the victory that has been won for us. It feels too much like magic, but it is reality. The enemy is real, the problem is real, and the fact that you are the target is real. You do not have the power to overcome it all, but God does, and He is standing ready to step in and solve the problem if you will call on Him to do that. Then it may be wise to just sing songs of praise to God to prove to Him that you have given the problem over to Him. He does not solve all problems in a day, or week, or even a year, but God knows best, and if we do not waver in our stance with our hand in His, we *will* experience the victory.

PRAYER: Dear Heavenly Father, how hard is it to put this teaching and lesson into practice? I can just see my feelings getting in the way of singing when I am hurt and in trouble. But I also realize that you know best and want me to see things through your eyes, so I will accept this lesson on using praise as a weapon against the enemy, and when I really need to practice it, I will depend on you to be there and help me to do it. In Jesus' name, Amen.

AUGUST 16th

 We need to talk about God's payroll program. Just as God is precise in all His dealings with people—with Satan, and with nations— so, too, is He precise in His dealings with paying wages. It is an extension of the law of sowing and reaping.

Nothing goes undetected by God. He sees it all. There will be no unsettled scores when all is said and done. Even our use of time will be noticed. Time is a gift from God, as are our talents and treasures. He will examine how we used those gifts.

The object of His examination will be to give us a reward, a payment if you will, for a job well done. The rewards are all ready to be handed out when that day arrives, and if you did not do anything with your gifts, the reward will go to others who have done their jobs well.

If we refuse to listen to God, He will speak to someone else to visit the sick, the lame, those in prison, and so on, and that person will receive the reward that was meant for us. We will lose out in the long run when we refuse to obey the Holy Spirit, who tries to encourage us to do that job in the first place.

Having said all that, look at Revelation 22:12, where the God says, *"And behold, I come quickly; and my reward is with me, to give every man according as his work shall be."* Also, in I Corinthians 3:8, we read, *"Now he that planteth and he that watereth are one: and every man shall receive his own reward according to his own labor."*

322

What we need to see most of all is that we cannot *work* for our salvation. It is a free gift bought for us by Jesus' life and death. Once we invited Jesus into our hearts, however, we then have an obligation to live a life that reflects Jesus within us. That will be seen in our actions, in the way we live our lives.

God wants to direct our lives to follow the plan He has in mind for us. As we do that to the best of our ability, He will reward our efforts. But, for now, be assured that a rewards day is coming. We will look at when that will be and what some of the rewards are. We are not to be taken by surprise, but rather we are to know understand these things as truths since they are recorded in God's Word so clearly.

PRAYER: Heavenly Father, just when I think there cannot be much more to learn, a whole new realm of truth emerges from the pages of the Bible. I never thought of you as having a payroll of any kind. It makes me so humble to even think that you would keep record of my efforts to serve you. I pray that I will be a faithful servant in your Kingdom here on earth. Fill me with your love and faith, so I may love as you loved and persevere to the end. Fill me with your grace and mercy, too, so that I may shower that grace on others and display mercy in a world so full of hate and confusion. In Jesus' name, Amen.

AUGUST 17th

Luke 14:13-14 reads: *"But when thou makest a feast, call the poor, the maimed, the lame, the blind: And thou shalt be blessed; for they cannot recompense thee: for thou shalt be recompensed at the resurrection of the just."*

God wants us to be as willing to give of ourselves as Jesus was, with no thought of being paid back by those we help. Here, the Bible is essentially saying, "Don't worry about getting reimbursed. That will be taken care of at the time of the resurrection of the just."

There will be two resurrection days: one for the just and one for the unjust. They are one thousand years apart, according to Revelation 20. I know we have looked at these verses before, but I believe it is necessary to quote them again at this time. Revelation 20:4-5 states: *"And I saw thrones, and they sat upon them, and judgment was given unto them: and I saw the souls of them that were beheaded for the witness of Jesus, and for the word of God, and which had not worshipped the beast, neither his image, neither had received his mark upon their foreheads, or in their hands; and they lived and reigned with Christ a thousands years. But the rest of the dead lived not again until the thousand years were finished. This is the first resurrection."*

Those who reign with Christ are the ones who will have received their rewards. One thousand years later, the people who refused to accept God's plan of salvation will be raised from the dead to hear what their punishment will be, as it is recorded in the Book of Life and "the Books."

Some scholars believe the Books contain the records of people's works, while others believe the Books are the 66 Books of the Bible. Personally, I think it would be more true to the Word of God that they are judged out of the 66 Books of the Bible.

The first resurrection is when Jesus will have rewards with Him to be given out according to how we, the believers, obeyed Him during our lives. Matthew 10:40-42 states: *"He that receiveth you, receiveth me, and he that receiveth me receiveth Him that sent me. He that receiveth a prophet in the name of a prophet shall receive a prophet's reward; and he that receiveth a righteous man in the name of a righteous man shall receive a righteous man's reward. And whosoever shall give to drink unto one of these little ones a cup of cold water only in the name of a disciple, verily I say unto you, he shall in no way lose his reward."*

There you have it. Rewards will be passed out for every fine detail of service given as a follower of Jesus. Some people will be shocked at the rewards due them, and others will expected much more when they do not receive what they thought they had coming. God will also take into consideration the motives of our hearts. The Pharisees served others with the intention of getting men's praise, and that did not sit well with Jesus.

324

Matthew 6:3-5 reads: *"But when thou doest alms, let not thy left hand know what thy right hand doeth: That thine alms may be in secret: and thy father which seeth in secret Himself shall reward thee openly. And when thou prayest, thou shalt not be as the hypocrites are: for they love to pray standing in the synagogues and in the corners of the streets, that they may be seen of men. Verily I say unto you, they have their reward."*

The reward of the people described here was to be seen by others. If what we do is for our own glory, if our intentions are to be seen by people, then God does not have to reward us according to His bookkeeping system. I prefer to be rewarded by God's system. How about you?

PRAYER: Heavenly Father, it seems as though we are in battle with our old nature, which wants to be noticed all the time. Does it ever quit doing that, or will I battle that all my life? I pray that your Holy Spirit will help me to overcome that urge to be seen by others. It is so worldly and so out of character with you. Will there be the same urge when I receive my rewards from you? Will I think, "Look at me and what I have done in the Kingdom of God on earth"? God forbid that such a thought will linger in my heart. I want all my motives to serve you, to be pure and righteous. All I can say is, "Help, help, help." In Jesus' name, Amen.

AUGUST 18th

It might be interesting to see how two different groups of people responded to Jesus when rewards were being determined. Today, we will look at Matthew 25:31-40, which describes when Jesus comes in power and glory, not when He comes as suddenly as a thief. You need to know the difference.

He will come as a thief when He silently, unexpectedly removes the church (Christians) from the earth. This is often called the rapture. When He comes in power and great glory, He will take authority over the whole world, put down the rule of the evil one, Satan, and rule with a rod of iron as was foretold in the Bible. Many Christians believe there will be a seven-year interval, called the "tribulation," between those two events, although some believe the tribulation will be shorter than that. It is a matter of how one interprets Scripture, and that is debatable.

In Matthew 25:31-40, we read: *"When the Son of man shall come in His glory, and all the holy angels with Him, then shall He sit upon the throne of His glory: And before Him shall be gathered all nations: and He shall separate them one from another, as a shepherd divideth his sheep from the goats: And He shall set the sheep on his right hand, but the goats on the left. Then shall the King say unto them on His right hand, 'Come, ye blessed of my father, inherit the kingdom prepared for you from the foundation of the world: For I was hungry, and ye gave me meat: I was thirsty, and ye gave me drink: I was a stranger, and ye took me in: Naked, and ye clothed me: I was sick, and ye visited me: I was in prison, and ye came unto me.' Then shall the righteous answer Him, saying, 'Lord, when saw we thee hungry, and fed thee? Or thirsty, and gave thee drink? When saw we thee a stranger, and took thee in? Or naked, and clothed thee? Or when saw we thee sick, or in prison, and came unto thee?' And the King shall answer and say unto them, 'Verily I say unto you, in as much as ye have done it unto one of the least of these my brethren, ye have done it unto me.' "*

Notice that Jesus is called "the Son of man" in the beginning (verse 31), and "the King," who has a kingdom, in the end (verse 34). Another interesting aspect of these verses is these people had been serving the Lord, day after day, and did not even realize it. They even had to ask Him to explain how they had actually done all this.

You see, that is the way it is when Jesus lives within people. They are living out His life through them, and it is as natural as breathing. Tomorrow, we will look at how the ones on His left, the "goats," addressed their service, or lack of it.

PRAYER: Heavenly Father, thank you for giving me opportunities to serve you here and there, and help me to recognize those opportunities so that I do not miss them. I do not want you to look at me and think, "I wasted my time on her." I can think of opportunities I have already missed, and should have been more aware of the immediate need before me. Forgive me, Lord, for my insensitivity. Maybe it was fear that held me back—fear of being taken advantage of, fear of not being able to finish what I started. There are people out there who, if you give then a dollar, stick around hoping it will become ten dollars, then fifty, and even a hundred. How do I deal with that, Lord? The Bible does say that they should find work so that they could become givers rather than takers. But that does not help me know how to deal with the situation when it arises right in front of me when I am being kind to help someone in need. Give me the wisdom to know which people you have placed before me that you want me to help. I will watch for your open doors. In Jesus' name, Amen.

AUGUST 19th

Matthew 25:41-46 reads: *"Then shall He say also unto them on the left hand, 'Depart from me, ye cursed into everlasting fire, prepared for the devil and his angels.* (These are harsh words, but God is a God of absolutes. Actions are either right or wrong. You are either for Him or against Him.) *For I was hungry, and ye gave me no meat: I was thirsty, and ye gave me no drink: I was a stranger, and ye took me not in: naked, and ye clothed me not: sick, and in prison, and ye visited me not.' Then shall they also answer Him, saying, 'Lord, when saw we thee hungry, or athirst, or a stranger, or naked, or sick, or in prison, and did not minister unto thee?' Then shall He answer them, saying, 'Verily I say unto you, in as much as ye did it not to one of the least of these, ye did it not to me.' And these shall go away into everlasting punishment: but the righteous into life eternal."*

Think of the question they are asking Jesus. They are essentially saying, "Jesus! We have given and given and given. Just name one time when we did not give." You see, I believe that they did not listen to the Holy Spirit and watch for open doors set before them. They may have given only when it would make them look good in front of other people.

I have always said that we need to have the right words for the right people at the right time, and only the Holy Spirit can determine when that precise time is right. There are times when we think someone needs a hand out, and just maybe God is trying to teach them a lesson on budgeting so they will not spend money they do not have. Or maybe God is trying to teach them to save for a rainy day, because they have the tendency to spend money as fast as they get it.

We need to do what God wants us to do, when He wants us to do it. Maybe a verse that has helped me will also help you to understand it all a little better. In Matthew 7:21, Jesus says, *"Not every one that saith unto me, 'Lord, Lord,' shall enter into the kingdom of heaven; but he that doeth the will of my Father which is in heaven."* There are those who do the will of the Father, and those who do not. I believe it is the difference between listening or *not* listening, to the Holy Spirit, following Him, depending on Him to guide you and lead you through this life. We will continue on this subject tomorrow.

PRAYER: Heavenly Father, I realize I seriously offend you when I neglect being of service, when I refuse to be a worker in your vineyard. I am also aware that your vineyard is right in my own backyard, so there is really no excuse. Forgive me, Lord, for the times I have been blind to the opportunities you have put before me. May your Holy Spirit prick my heart when I need to see with spiritual eyes what you want from me. Then give me the will and ability to do what you want me to do. In Jesus' name, Amen.

AUGUST 20th

Matthew 7:22-27reads: *"Many will say to me in that day* (the day we read about in Matthew 25:41-46 yesterday) *'Lord, Lord, have we not prophesied in thy name? And in thy name cast out devils? And in thy name done many wonderful works?' And then will I profess unto them, 'I never knew you: depart from me, ye that work*

iniquity.' Therefore whosoever heareth these sayings of mine and doeth them, I will liken him unto a wise man, which built his house upon a rock: And the rain descended, and the floods came, and the winds blew, and beat upon that house; and it fell not: for it was founded upon a rock. And every one that heareth these sayings of mine and doeth them not shall be likened unto a foolish man, which built his house upon the sand. And the rain descended, and the floods came, and the winds blew, and beat upon that house, and it fell: and great was the fall of it."

Those who listen to the Holy Spirit, study the Word of God, know God's will for them, and follows His will have a strong foundation for their faith. When the storms of life come along, their faith will carry them through, and they will not falter and faint, but will endure to the end.

People who try to fix things on their own essentially do not know God, and God does "not know them" because they do not ask Him for help, guidance, and support. They do not know how to totally depend on God. By not depending on God, they are telling Him that He is not worth their time or effort. How can God know them then?

It sounds harsh, but God is not to be mocked. We are not to turn to Him only when we are desperate. And if you have done that already, then you need to fall on your face before Him, confess that you have neglected Him, and ask to be forgiven. He will forgive you in a blink of an eye. Do not neglect Him again when things are going right, however, but keep your eye on Him through thick and thin.

In the verses for today, "doing" is the key. To hear the Word of God and then to ignore it will result in catastrophe, a great fall! We do not need to do more than ask the Holy Spirit to be our guide through our lives, and help us follow His direction. He was sent by the Father to be that helper, comforter, and guide into the truth, so that we will be the servants Jesus is calling us to be.

It is *all* of God and none of self. I felt that took me off the hook. I was not responsible for planning out my life, but instead I was responsible for following the leading of the Holy Spirit. Just leave it up to Him to show you what to say, what to do, and where to go. As you go over the verses for today, just follow the trail of those who listened to God and did what He told them, and then follow the trail of those who listened to Him but did not do what He told them, and I think you will see the reason God said, "I never knew you."

PRAYER: Heavenly Father, thank you for making it so clear to me. At first I began to wonder what kind of a God you are! But I also see you are duty-bound to respect my freedom of choice, and that great freedom can be used by the enemy to blind my eyes to my responsibility. I pray that the Holy Spirit will help me to see clearly the end results of my choices so I will walk closer to you day by day. Thank you for this Word, the Bible, in which I can explore your will, your desire for me, and your great plan for us all. I am ever so thankful for such a Word as this, which shows me the warnings you have already given to detour us from making similar mistakes in life. In Jesus' name, Amen.

AUGUST 21st

For a few days, we will explore the giving of crowns. There are five crowns spoken of in the Bible, and these are to be given for specific reasons. I believe there are those who will be able to earn all five of them. We will look at each one carefully.

I Thessalonians 2:17-20 states: *"But, we, brethren, being taken from you for a short time in presence, not in heart, endeavoured the more abundantly to see your face with great desire. Wherefore we would have come unto you, even I Paul, once and again; but Satan hindered us. For what is our hope, our joy, or crown of rejoicing* (glorying)? *Are not even ye in the presence of our Lord Jesus Christ at His coming? For ye are our glory and joy."*

Paul is writing this letter to a church at Thessonalica, a church that he had founded. He desired again and again to go back to them to see how they were doing. Remember, in that day and time, the church was being

330

persecuted by the Jews, and some believers were even killed. Paul's life had been threatened time and again.

Paul assures the church that his heart is with them, even if he is not there in body. Then he claims that their presence before Jesus when He comes again will be his crown of rejoicing. So, this crown is for those who are *soul winners*. They will receive a crown of rejoicing when they can see all those souls to whom they brought the good news of salvation, and who had heard it and accepted God's plan of salvation.

Some people have a burning desire to win souls for Christ. There are others who just love to help other believers learn how to live the life of faith. Each one has his or her own place in God's plan. You may say something to someone at one time that will make a big difference in that person's life and lead to a saving faith in Jesus.

It would be interesting to see God's chart of the life of just one individual, and see the scores of people God had chosen to use to influence that one individual during his or her lifetime. In fact, you may be amazed at how often God has used you to influence people during your lifetime. If you want to live a life that is full of surprises such as these, then ask God to use you and to give you the eyes to see, and ears to hear when He speaks to you, and a heart to accept His hand in your life.

You will find one surprise after another to prove that God does hear your prayers. When you look at people, do you see a soul that will live forever, either in heaven or in hell? Can you offer up a quick prayer for those people, that they will want to have Jesus in their hearts and want to live eternally with God? That will make you a soul winner. It all begins with prayer for souls to be saved by God's grace, which is Jesus' sacrifice, and the Holy Spirit who woos them to Jesus.

PRAYER: Heavenly Father, yes, I want to be a soul winner, but I always thought it was much harder then that. Help me to see those who need that kind of prayer, and give me a nudge so I will surely pray for them to come to the knowledge of the truth about Jesus and His love for them. If I am the one to speak to them, I will depend on you to give me the right words to say. I look forward to this adventure in my Christian life. You and I, Lord, ought to make a good team. I will pray, and you will answer, and together we will make headway. I rejoice at such a challenge as this. In Jesus' name, Amen.

AUGUST 22nd

In I Corinthians 9:25, we read, *"And every man that striveth for the mastery* (in the games), *is temperate in all things. Now they do it to obtain a corruptible crown; but we an incorruptible."* So, there is an incorruptible crown and it is the result of keeping yourself tempered, living a well balanced life.

The Bible has a lot to say about living that kind of life. Ephesians 5:18 states, *"And be not drunk with wine, wherein is excess* (riot)*; but be filled with the Spirit."* And I Peter 4:3 reads: *"For the time past of our life may suffice us to have wrought the will* (desire) *of the Gentiles, when we walked in lasciviousness, lusts, excess of wine, revellings, banquetings, and abominable idolatries."*

The CEV translates I Peter 4:3-4 as: *"You have already lived long enough like people who don't know God. You were immoral and followed your evil desires. You went around drinking and partying and carrying on. In fact, you even worshipped disgusting idols. Now your former friends wonder why you have stopped running around with them, and they curse you for it. But they will have to answer to God, who judges the living and the dead."*

In all these things we see an excess of behavior. God calls each of us to live a balanced life. There is an order to God's desire for our life. Matthew 6:33 says, *"But seek ye first the kingdom of God, and his righteousness; and all these things shall be added unto you."* God is to be first in our lives, then our spouses, then children, and then work. America seems to have it all turned around. Priorities are work, then family, and then God.

If we want to live balanced lives, we must put God first, and ask Him to help us put family and work in their proper order. Athletes who train know what has to be put first, and they put many hours into their training. It is a top priority and the crown or medal they receive is only a passing honor. Over time, that award loses its importance, but the crown we have the opportunity to win is eternal and it is kept in heaven for us.

PRAYER: Heavenly Father, this business of being a Christian touches every area of my life, right? Now you are talking about my leisure as well as my work, and I assume it means my money too. I hope, Lord, that changes can be made gradually in my life, so I am not overwhelmed. I also am aware that your Holy Spirit is there to help me make those changes. I have observed that those who choose to live a life pleasing to you seem to be much happier than those who live for themselves and the world. So, Lord, I choose to live that kind of life that pleases you, and I ask you to help me carry out my choice. In Jesus' name, Amen.

AUGUST 23rd

II Timothy 4:8 reads: *"Henceforth there is laid up for me a crown of righteousness, which the Lord, the righteous judge, shall give me at that day, and not to me only, but unto all them also that love His appearing."*

Here we see that the crown will go to those who look forward to the second coming of Christ, those who love His appearing. For many of us, it will be at our death, which will come before His second coming.

How much do you look forward to meeting Jesus face to face? It should be the highlight of our existence. Just imagine meeting the One who paid for your salvation and threw the door to heaven wide open for you and wrote a great big "welcome" sign over it.

If the thought scares you, then you need to get that issue settled between you and God right now. Ask God to forgive you your sins, and ask Jesus into your heart to live there. Then, you will be born again and in the family of God, and you will not need to be afraid of His coming to you, because He will come to you in love, mercy, and grace.

God has done everything necessary for you to live eternally with Him in Paradise. All you have to do is accept what He has done for you through Jesus. It is so simple, it is almost ridiculous. God has done it all for you. You can not buy it or work for it. All you need to do is believe and accept it. Is that so hard to do?

This crown is called a crown of righteousness, I believe, because Jesus *is* our righteousness. He became righteous for us, and then gave that wonderful condition to us, making us righteous before an Almighty God. Give yourself the freedom to look forward to His appearing.

PRAYER: Heavenly Father, it is amazing to me that God can take sinners and make us into saints through the work of His Son. As I contemplate that truth, I see a God of great mercy at work on my behalf. Without Jesus, I would be a miserable sinner with no hope of an eternity of bliss, peace, and joy. Instead, I am assured of an eternity with such beauty and wonder that it is hard to comprehend. My heart sings out a thank you to God the Father, Son, and Holy Spirit, and I worship the Trinity with all my heart. In Jesus' name, Amen.

AUGUST 24th

In I Peter 5:2-4, we read: *"Feed the flock of God which is among you, taking the oversight thereof, not by constraint, but willingly; not for filthy lucre, but of a ready mind. Neither as being lords over God's heritage* (lording it over the charge allotted to you)*, but being examples to the flock. And when the Chief Shepherd shall appear, ye shall receive a crown of glory that fadeth not away."*

The CEV translates these verses as: *"Just as shepherds watch over their sheep, you must watch over everyone God has placed in your care. Do it willingly in order to please God, and not simply because you think you must. Let it be something you want to do, instead of something you do merely to make money. Don't be bossy to those people who are in your care, but set an example for them. Then when Christ the Chief Shepherd returns, you will be given a crown that will never lose its glory."*

This crown of glory is given to those who are faithful in their ministry to others. Satan wants to make us weary in our efforts and lose heart. That can happen when we become tired and do not get enough rest. Satan will try to give us more jobs than we can handle and then make us feel guilty when we say no to one more job.

We need the Spirit of discernment to know whether a job that is presented to us is from God or from someone who is asking too much, for example, someone who has an idea but wants you to take the idea, work it up, and carry it out. If they had the idea, God wants them to bring it to pass, too.

Do not be fooled by such a trick of Satan. I have seen mothers who love to do the Lord's work, and they become overloaded and just cannot say no, and then their health fails and they have to give up all the jobs they enjoyed doing because they did not discern which ones were from the Lord.

Remember when we talked about those who called out, "Lord, Lord," and the Lord said, "I never knew you?" Not every job that comes our way is from God. The ones that are, though, we are to do with our whole heart and with joy. When it is directed by God, we will not get overtired and our health will not crumble. God wants faithful servants for His flock, and a crown of glory awaits those who are faithful.

PRAYER: Heavenly Father, thank you for the insight here on how to work in your kingdom and how to say no when I am overloaded. I want to be a faithful worker, carry out the obligations I am committed to, and work with a joyful heart. Help me to be that kind of worker in your kingdom's work. Forgive me for grumbling when I was tired and weary, and forgive me for not taking care to prevent myself from becoming tired and weary. I can plainly see that I did not exercise my freedom of choice in a wise way. Help me to recognize all these things in the future, so that I may be victorious in my faithfulness as a worker in your kingdom. In Jesus' name, Amen.

AUGUST 25th

Today, we will look at a few verses relating to the crown of life. First, turn to James 1:12, which reads, *"Blessed is the man that endureth temptation: for when he is tried* (has been approved), *he shall receive the crown of life, which the Lord hath promised to them that love Him."* Also, Revelation 2:10 states: *"Fear none of those things which thou shalt suffer: behold, the Devil shall cast some of you into prison, that ye may be tried; and ye shall have tribulation ten days: be thou faithful unto death, and I will give thee a crown of life."*

This crown is for those who have faced temptations and trials, but endured. Here is the struggle between God and Satan in the life of the believer. Satan wants us to give up halfway through a test, and he wants us to be so tempted to give up that we cannot endure. If we give in to the temptation, God will be disappointed that we did not trust Him to see us through, and Satan will beat us over the head with, "You are a miserable failure." Then, we will fail God again not letting Him help us through that part of the trial.

It takes a sort of stubborn faith to hang in there and declare to God, Satan, and those around you that you will put your faith in the God who created you and who is in charge of every circumstance in your life, and you won't back off or give up. When Jesus asked his disciples if they too would turn away from Him, some did and some did not. In John 6:66-69, we read: *"From that time many of His disciples went back, and walked no more with Him. Then said Jesus unto the twelve, 'Will ye also go away?' Then Simon Peter answered Him, 'Lord, to whom shall we go? Thou hast the words of eternal life. And we believe and are sure that thou art that Christ, the Son of the living God.' "*

Jesus was putting that squeeze to them that we often get when being tested mightily. What will our decision be—to give up and walk away or to persevere? Those who do not become disillusioned, discouraged, or disappointed, but who stubbornly believe that Jesus *is* in the midst of our troubles and that He *will* see us through them, are those who will earn the crown of life.

This is not the same as the "gift of eternal life." That gift is not something that can be earned. What we are talking about here is a crown that is named "Life," and that is given as a recompense for living a life faithful and obedient to the desire of God for your life.

First, God encourages you to repent and turn your life over to Him, and He offers you the choice to accept His plan of salvation, which is to accept Jesus Christ's death and resurrection on your behalf. All of that is called conversion, or being "born again."

Then another process is to take place, the process of "sanctification," which goes on for the rest of your natural life. Sanctification is your growth as a Christian, and the Holy Spirit is sent to help you grow in grace and holiness, through your daily choices. Those choices are what will either bring a recompense of the crowns we have been looking at or the loss of those rewards.

This whole process does *not* involve our *gift* of eternal life. We must keep those two things separated. I will address that later when I talk about our "state" and our "standing."

PRAYER: Heavenly Father, thank you for showing me the truth about the crowns and what they stand for. I realize that my job is to keep my thoughts focused on you and your will for my life, not on the crowns that will be given as rewards to the believers. Simply put, I shall "seek first the kingdom of heaven, and then all these things will be added unto me." But it is nice to know about the crowns, and for what they are rewarded. It helps me to understand your interest in every minute detail of my life and how I am to live to honor you. Guide me, Lord, to do just that. In Jesus' mighty name, Amen.

AUGUST 26th

Revelation 4:10 reads: *"The four and twenty elders fall down before Him that sat on the throne, and worship Him that liveth for ever and ever and cast their crowns before the throne saying, 'Thou art worthy O Lord, to receive glory and honor and power: for thou hast created all things, and for thy pleasure they are and were created.' "*

In this verse, it is plain to see that crowns are not to be worn by us, but are to bring glory to Jesus. The crowns will be cast at His feet because He is worthy to receive all glory, honor, and power.

There is a song in many hymn books entitled "Love Divine," and the final verse is:

Finish then Thy new creation;
Pure and spotless let us be;
Let us see Thy great salvation
Perfectly restored in Thee.
Changed from glory into glory,
Till in heaven we take our place,
Till we cast our crowns before Thee,
Lost in wonder, love, and praise.

Yes, indeed, we will cast our crowns at the feet of Jesus, for He deserves all the glory. The question is whether you will have a crown (or crowns) to cast before the Savior of the world. If you want to have them, you must choose now to live to earn a crown, or two, or even five, to cast at the feet of the One who died to take away our sins.

PRAYER: Heavenly Father, it sends goose bumps up my spine to think that I might have a crown, or even a few crowns, to cast at the feet of Jesus one day. Just to see that look of approval on His face would be worth it all. As I used to think of heaven, it seemed so big and so distant that I almost felt insignificant. I am beginning to see it more like a family reunion, where every individual there is an important person in the family of God. With that in mind, I realize that the people who are around me each day of

338

my life have a special place in the hearts of God and Jesus, and they need to be told the plan of salvation designed by God the Father, Son, and Holy Spirit. That becomes my purpose on earth. As I understand your Word and recompenses, I see that our lives on earth will determine the crowns given out to us one day. Please help me make wise use of that new knowledge and understanding. In Jesus' name, Amen.

AUGUST 27th

Look again at John 6:68, which reads, *"Then Simon Peter answered Him, 'Lord, to whom shall we go? Thou hast the words of eternal life.'"* Here, Peter asked a very important question, *"To whom shall we go?"* There is no other to whom we can go to get the help we need in order to stand up to Satan and his traps. The only One able to help us win the victory over Satan is Jesus. Peter answered his own question when he said, *"Thou hast the words of eternal life. And we believe and are sure that thou art that Christ, the son of the living God."* It was Peter who failed so dreadfully at the time of Jesus' arrest, yet, Peter was reinstated by Jesus Himself.

Never let the devil make you accept his words of accusation. Do not let him convince you that you are a miserable failure, or that you will never be fit for heaven, nor fit to serve God again. You need to learn to "tell Satan off," in no uncertain terms. "Satan, off with you. Go back to hell where you belong and leave me alone. God is my strength and my joy. You have no place in my life, so off with you!" Learn to do this as soon as possible. You may feel foolish talking to the thin air, so to speak, but believe me, Satan will hear you and know that you have made a stand not to listen to him, but to listen to God's Word instead.

PRAYER: Heavenly Father, it is plain to me that we are in warfare, a daily warfare, in fact. I feel like I have been fitted with boxing gloves and am in the ring ready for a fight. Thank you, Father, for being in the ring with me, and for giving me the tools (the spiritual weapons) for the fight and the help

I need to endure. It is my desire to live a life pleasing to you, so help me to endure to the end. In Jesus' name, Amen.

AUGUST 28th

For the next few days, we will look at the *standing* and *state* of a believer. To paint a clear picture, I will use a regular family as an example, and then reference some verses for further explanation.

First, let's imagine a family of a mother, father, six-year-old son, two daughters ages four and two, and baby boy who is only a few days old. This family is all excited about the new arrival, and is anxiously awaiting their first look him. The baby is given a first name, and his last name is the same as his three siblings.

If the parents met some tragic ending, this baby would inherit in equal measure as the other three siblings. His name is fixed and recorded as a member of this family. All of this is a picture of his *standing* in the family. He is equal in every way.

However, he cannot care for himself. He cannot do any chores, or actively provide any useful worth to the family's daily life. His capabilities, or lack thereof, is an example of his *state*. He needs a lot of attention, work, nourishment, and love. The six-year-old brother is able to do some of the chores in the family, but not a lot as yet, and the two sisters can do even less. Each one has a different *state* in the family life.

This is a picture of our lives as Christians in the family of God. When we were born again into the family of God, we inherited the name of "Christian." Our standing was complete. We became members in *full standing* in God's family.

But our *state* would have been as people in great need, with little ability as yet to be productive members of the family. But we would have potential to do great things in time. It is at this point that many Christians fail to realize that they have a responsibility to grow and be productive as a Christian.

340

Let us start to unravel this truth by looking at John 1:12, which states, *"But as many as received Him* (Jesus)*, to them gave He power* (the right) *to become the sons of God, even to them that believe on His* (Jesus') *name."* When Jesus lives in our hearts, we *are* the sons and daughters of God, through Jesus who is the Son of God. It is a spiritual birth.

Look also at Colossians and let the Word convince you of your standing in the family of God. Colossians 1:12-14 reads: *"Giving thanks unto the Father, which hath made us meet to be partakers of the inheritance of the saints in light: Who has delivered us from the power of darkness, and has translated us into the kingdom of His dear Son. In whom we have redemption through His blood, even the forgiveness of sins."*

Can it be much plainer that you are a member of the family of God through Jesus? You need to practice seeing yourself in that light.

Let us also turn to I Peter 1:3-5, which says: *"Blessed be the God and Father of our Lord Jesus Christ, which according to His abundant mercy has begotten us again unto a living hope by the resurrection of Jesus Christ from the dead, to an inheritance incorruptible, and undefiled, and that fadeth not away, reserved in heaven for you who are kept* (guarded) *by the power of God through faith unto salvation ready to be revealed in the last time."*

Lastly, let us look at II Peter 1:4, which reads: *"Whereby are given unto us exceeding great and precious promises that by these you might be partakers of the divine nature, having escaped the corruption that is in the world through lust."*

In the first reference, you can see that you are begotten, which means "born again by God" to a living hope kept safely for you. It is something God has done, not you. All you need to do is believe it. Tough job, huh? Not at all! You believe all the time. You believe the car will start when you drive somewhere, the restaurant will serve food that is not poisoned, and the lights will come on when you turn the switch. So, why not believe God's Word just as it comes to you? Then, in the second reference, you see that you were "made" a partaker of the divine nature of God. Again, this is not something you did, but that God did. You *are* a member of God's family in full standing.

PRAYER: Heavenly Father, these are some powerful references for me to ponder. Help me to receive them in all their truth. Give me the wisdom to put them into practice. It is plain that I will need your help to do this, since there is so much truth here for me to grasp. In Jesus' name, Amen.

AUGUST 29th

Today, we will look at your *state* as a member of God's family. In Matthew 13, the Word of God is described as a seed being sown. Matthew 13:3 says, *"And He spoke many things unto them in parables, saying, 'Behold, a sower went forth to sow.' "*

What do sowers sow? They sow seeds—usually grain seeds. In Jesus' parable, the seed had been scattered. Some fell by the way side, and birds came and ate it up. Some fell on stony ground and sprung up, but when the sun had risen, they were scorched and withered away because they had no roots. Some fell among thorns, and the thorns thrived and choked the seed out. But some fell on good soil and brought forth fruit— some 100 fold, some 60 fold, and some 30 fold.

One of the things you need to notice here is that everything from "stony ground" to "birds of the air" are out to get the seed before it can bear fruit. Jesus goes on to explain the parable in Matthew 13:18-19, which reads: *"Hear ye then the parable of the sower. When any one heareth the word of the kingdom, and understands it <u>not</u>, then cometh the wicked one* (the devil) *and catches away that which was sown in his heart. This is he which received seed by the way side."*

So, we see in these verses that the seed is the Word of the kingdom, the Word of God, the Bible, in fact. And we also see that it is sown into the hearts of believers. Satan does not want us to have the Word of God in our heart, because he knows that is death to him and his ability to defeat us.

What the believer did not have was *understanding*! Pray that you might have a spirit of understanding, so that the enemy cannot steal away the Word you do have in your heart. Keep an eye out to see how the enemy is at work to snatch away the seed that was sown in your heart. We will continue to explore this tomorrow.

PRAYER: Heavenly Father, thank you for helping me see myself as a child of God. I am in full standing as a member of your family, with Jesus as my brother, in addition to being my friend and Savior. I also want to learn everything that I can about the seed sown in my heart. I ask the Holy Spirit to reveal the truth to me in a simple way so I can grasp it and make wise use of what I know and understand. In Jesus' name, Amen.

AUGUST 30th

Today, we will look some more at Jesus' parable in Matthew 13:20-21, which reads: *"But he that received seed into stony places, the same is he that heareth the word, and at once receives it with joy; Yet has he not root in himself, but endures for awhile: for when tribulation or persecution ariseth <u>because of the word</u>, by and by he is offended (straight away he stumbleth)."*

The person described in these verses is one who has an accepting heart in the beginning, but when trials and persecutions come (notice that they come because of the Word), then he is "offended," or stumbles.

I would like to make two points in this reading for today. The first point deals with the truth of the Word sown in this person's heart. Here, the person heard the Word and received it joyfully. In other words, he had stored it up in his heart as a pillar of foundation for his faith.

As far as Satan is concerned, such a thing is very destructive to *his plans* for this person's life. That is why the battle kicks into high gear between the flesh and spirit (the old nature and the new) of a person with that kind of Word of truth in his heart. Satan launches an attack to *tempt* him to *decide* (that is, make a choice) that God's Word does not work for him. In these verses, that person chose to cast that Word of truth out as being worthless to him.

The second point I want to make is that when this person is tempted to abandon the Word, he is not at all aware of what is happening to him. When he fails this test, he is walking closer to Satan than to God. We have talked about the *difference* between a *test* and a *temptation*. Satan *tempts* you to choose to throw out God's Word, no matter how much you believe and know it is the truth. On the other hand, God is patiently waiting for *you* to see it as a *test of your faith*. He wants you to *know* that if you choose to stick with Him, He will see you through the test and give you the courage to rise to the challenge and claim victory over Satan.

Here is an example: You have received the Word of truth of I Thessalonians 5:18, which states, *"In everything give thanks for this is the will of God in Christ Jesus concerning you."* You begin to practice it and give thanks to God for everything. Then Satan launches his attacks. You lose your job, a family member dies, or you have a financial disaster. You do not feel like giving thanks, so you follow the *temptation* of the flesh and begin to fail the *test* part of what is happening. You neglect to be thankful.

God stands by patiently. He is waiting for you to call on Him to help you endure the test and to come out victorious in the end. The trouble that happened to the person in Jesus' parable is what is common to all humanity. We cannot escape it while we live in this world. How you deal with it in your everyday life will show you, the world around you, and God whose *will* you plan to follow, God's or Satan's.

If you choose to follow God's will, you will show that you have gone from a milk-drinking Christian to a meat-eating Christian. That kind of victory is very sweet to the taste because the truth of the Word is still firmly implanted in your heart at the end of the test/temptation.

PRAYER: Heavenly Father, thank you for putting these truths before me so simply that I can understand them. I am able to understand why so many people who have stepped out in faith by putting into practice what they have learned suddenly stopped doing anything for the Lord. They were overwhelmed by Satan's attacks and did not know that would happen. I thank you for this lesson, this "behind-the-scenes" peek into what goes on when seeds are planted in my heart. I look to you, Father, for the help I will need to withstand anything Satan throws in my direction. I do not want to lose any Word of truth that is sown in my heart. In Jesus' name, Amen.

AUGUST 31ˢᵗ

Matthew 13:22 states: *"He also that received seed among the thorns is he that heareth the word; and the care of this world, and the deceitfulness of riches, choke the word, and he becometh unfruitful."*

This verse describes a person who is not ready to be fully committed to a life of surrender to Jesus. He still looks for answers to his problems in the world, so much so that the cares of this world take up all of his time and effort and there is no room left for God. Bible reading is left undone, prayer time is neglected, and he thinks about his problems so much that the Word that was planted in his heart is not being depended upon. He is not using the Word to help him be victorious.

Notice that in every instance it is the sown Word that the devil is after, and he is after it so it will *not bear frui*t, or *"become unfruitful."* God is looking for fruit-bearing Christians. A child in a home will be given chores to do according to his or her age and ability. That is true with us as believers, too. This is a picture of our *state* in the family.

Our fruit-bearing will be a sign of our commitment and surrender to God, and it will also determine our state. As we grow, we need to become more and more familiar with how our Heavenly Father thinks and what He desires, just as we get to know what would please our earthly father and mother, who are the authority figures in our family. Our state is a constantly changing factor in our Christian walk, and God's goal for us is to grow up into the full stature of Christ.

PRAYER: Lord God, I had no idea how important it is to you that I bear fruit. I want to be a fruit-bearing Christian, and I want to do your will. I want to be a responsible part of the body of Christ, the Church. Help me, Lord, to put my trust in you and not in the world around me. Teach me where that fine line is between the two, so I can keep from stepping over the line by neglecting the Word that is planted in my heart. In Jesus' name, Amen.

SEPTEMBER 1st

Today, we will look at a few verses from Ephesians 4. In Ephesians 4:11-12, we read: *"And He gave some to be apostles; and some, prophets; and some, evangelists; and some, pastors and teachers; For the perfecting of the saints for the work of the ministry, for the edifying of the body of Christ."*

God has provided people to minister to the believers, who are called "saints" in this scripture. God provided prophets, evangelists, pastors, and teachers. They are given to us with a purpose: for the perfecting of the believers, for the work of the ministry (the planting of churches and feeding and tending the lambs), and for the edifying of the body of Christ. In short, this means to spiritually build up the believers who are the body of Christ.

Ephesians 4:13 continues:

"Till we ALL come in the unity of the faith, and of the knowledge of the Son of God, unto a perfect full-grown man, unto the measure of the stature of the fullness of Christ."

God's goal for every last one of us who believe in Jesus is for us to grow into a replica of Jesus. That sounds impossible, does it not? But the potential to grow that much is set before each one of us as a challenge to undertake, and it is reached day by day as we steadily grow closer to God. We draw nearer to that goal by stepping into His will for our lives a little more every day.

It is the "growth" that God is interested in. Anything that ceases to grow will begin to die, and Satan knows that better than any of us. Satan wants us to stop growing into a reflection of Jesus Christ—to get us to neglect God and His Word, to no longer fellowship with other believers or worship, and so on. In this verse, Paul calls on believers to become a group that is unified in faith and their knowledge of the Son of God.

Take a look at your life. In what state would you say you are? Are you the baby drinking milk, the toddler just learning to walk and balance, the teenager who wants to be independent and not listen to the authority of parents anymore, the young parents who are busy trying to make ends meet while raising a family and still have time to do something for themselves, the grandparents who now have more time and money to spend but are getting tired out and cannot accomplish what they used to, or are you like someone in a nursing home where time is running out and God has been neglected for so long that he does not know how to reconnect. Never forget, there is always God's call to come back and begin to grow again. See yourself becoming a full-grown spiritual person in Christ Jesus who loved you enough to die and rise again so that you can grow into a replica of Him.

When my mother was in a nursing home, she had a roommate who was over ninety, and she was the most positive, cheerful, person I had ever seen. She made quilts by hand, and found great pleasure in being useful. She believed in God, was a born-again Christian. She was full of the flavor of Christ Jesus, and I would say her state was truly that of a full-grown woman of God.

I told myself that when it would be my turn to reside in a nursing home, I would remember her attitude and decided to have a positive attitude also. That decision, just like that of your state, cannot be made after you are in that circumstance. It must be made ahead of time or it will not be there to support you in your time of need.

PRAYER: Heavenly Father, as I look at my state in the family of God, I think a better word, one that I can understand easier, is position. I want to reach the position you planned for me when you created me and put potential into me. I do not want a "high and mighty place" in the family of God, but I do want to be all that you planned for me to be. Help me to see, with spiritual eyes, what I am not doing that hinders my growth, what threatens the Word planted in my heart and keeps me from attaining your goal for me. I know that Satan is good at blinding my eyes to ways I can serve and worship you more and more. I come against his tactics, threats, and temptations and I proclaim victory in every area of my life. In Jesus' name, Amen.

SEPTEMBER 2nd

In I Corinthians 3:1-3, Paul says: *"And I, brethren, could not speak unto you as unto spiritual, but as unto carnal* ("carnal" being non-spiritual men of the flesh, those in whom the carnal nature dominates)*, even as unto babes in Christ. I have fed you with milk, and not with meat: for hitherto you were not able to bear it, neither yet now are ye able."*

Paul is explaining that he cannot talk to the people of this church as grown men who eat meat, but as babes who require milk. That tells us that their state in the family of God was that of a baby—fully a member of the family of God, but so immature they could not be talked to as a grown adults. Every church has members who are babes spiritually, and others who are mature and able to take in the Word at a depth that a babe could not understand.

Think of a pastor who is able to discern this variety in his congregation. He must be able to prepare a sermon that feeds both the lambs and the sheep in his fold. If you want to show yourself to be a mature, meat-eating Christian, begin praying for your pastor throughout the week, that he or she will be given the knowledge, understanding, and wisdom to preach a sermon that will feed the whole congregation.

It is our responsibility to invest into the worship service of our church, and we invest by praying for the pastor. You will get out of a worship service on Sunday exactly what you have invested in it during the week. That is being a fruit-bearing Christian. Your fruit is "doing" what you know you need to do to enhance your worship service.

Nothing is more powerful than prayer. And do not do it for one Sunday and then question on Monday why God did not answer your prayer. Ask God what else you need to do to invest in that worship service so that you will receive the blessing God has in store for you.

Do not criticize the music, but rather sing with all your heart. Singing is a powerful part of worshipping God. God created music to be used for His honor and glory. Satan has stolen much of the music of the world and has made it to glorify himself by drawing attention to sex, unfaithfulness, divorce, and so on. Determine right now that you will sing to the Lord next Sunday at worship in your church.

I have already talked about the principle involved with singing. However, I feel it is so important that I want to expand on what we learned before. God created music with seven notes—the perfect number. When King Jehoshaphat was faced with a large army coming at him to battle, he sought the Lord God to determine what to do.

Remember how Satan attacks the Word of God in our hearts? The Word from God was going to be attacked in Jehoshaphat's heart, and God told him to not be afraid nor dismayed. In other words, Jehoshaphat was to determine not to let fear or dismay defeat him before the battle even began. Are you looking at the circumstances of your life so much that you cannot see God in the midst of your battles?

349

In II Chronicles 20:15, we are told that *"...the battle is not yours but God's,"* and in verse 17 we read:

> *"Ye shall not need to fight in this battle; set yourselves, stand ye still, and see the salvation of the Lord with you, O Judah and Jerusalem: fear not, nor be dismayed; tomorrow go out against them: for the Lord will be with you."*

Jehoshaphat was encouraged and made battle plans. We see how the battle was won in II Chronicles 20:21-22, which states:

> *"And when he had consulted with the people, he <u>appointed singers unto the Lord, and that should praise the beauty of holiness</u>, as they went out <u>before the army</u>, and to say,' <u>Praise the Lord</u>; for His mercy endureth for ever.' And when they <u>began to sing and to praise</u>, the Lord set ambushments against the children of Ammon, Moab, and mount Seir, which were come against Judah; and they were smitten."*

In the hands of God, music is a tool used to defeat Satan and all his followers. It is also a tool in our hands to claim and receive victory over the enemy. Jehoshaphat's appointed singers praised God, and when we do that, God responds with favor on our behalf.

If you are down, put on good Christian music and let it minister to your emotions and spirit. This is a way for you to take the Words sown in your heart and put them into practice. This is spiritual growth, also called sanctification.

God will only spoon-feed you for so long, and then He expects you to feed yourself, get into His Word, and find out what it is saying to you. When you take a step like that in His direction, He is only too happy to give you more and more of His word to store up in your heart.

What did Jesus do the night before he was crucified? In Matthew 26:27-30 we see that:

"He took the cup, and gave thanks, and gave it to them, saying, 'Drink ye all of it: For this is my blood of the new testament, which is shed for many for the remission of sins. But I say unto you, I will not drink henceforth of this fruit of the vine, until that day when I drink it new with you in my Father's kingdom.' And when they had sung a hymn, they went out into the mount of Olives."

They *sung a hymn*! And what did Paul and Silas do when they were in prison? Acts 16:23-26 explains:

"And when they had laid many stripes (lashes) *upon them, they cast them into prison, charging the jailer to keep them safely: Who, having received such a charge, thrust them into the <u>inner prison</u>, and made their feet fast in the stocks. And at midnight Paul and Silas prayed, and<u> sang praises</u> unto God: and the prisoners heard them. And suddenly there was an earthquake, so that the foundations of the prison were shaken, and immediately all the doors were opened, and every one's bands were loosed."*

God's hands are moved by praying and singing believers. God is not bound by prisons, time, or mankind's rules. All in that prison were set free. Who was in control then?

Do not mess around with God. Instead, join hands with Him and His power and do things His way, then you win, too.

PRAYER: Heavenly Father, thank you for showing me how important music is in the life of a believer. I realize that music has a great influence on my emotions. When I am down, some kinds of music will only bring me down more, but when I listen to hymns of assurance, I am lifted up. I am glad that I can expect victory over the enemy through music, and I am thankful for knowing about this tool for both praise and for assurance— praise toward you and assurance within my heart. In Jesus' name, Amen.

SEPTEMBER 3rd

Today, we will look at the last type of soil the seeds fell into in Jesus' example. Matthew 13:23 reads:

"But he that received seed into the good ground is he that heareth the Word, and understandeth it; which also beareth fruit, and bringeth forth, some 100 fold, some 60, and some 30."

The heart with "good ground" is one where the Word is not only heard, but also understood, and goes on to bear fruit for the kingdom of God. I believe that the better we understand the Word, the more our "fruit increase" will be.

I told you earlier that it is important to pray for knowledge, understanding, and wisdom. In today's scripture, we see that underscored again. Knowledge (which is the Word sown in your heart) will not bring the intended benefits if there is no understanding of that Word. For example, you may try until you are blue in the face to tell a child that something is hot, but not until the child actually touches the object and feels the heat does he fully understand the potential for harm in that word "hot."

If you saw a person who has learned to ride a bike (and thinks him- or herself fully capable of riding it anywhere) coming faster and faster down a steep hill where there is a curve to maneuver at the bottom, you understand that there is no way that person is going to make that curve and stay on the bike in one piece. How did you come to understand that? You may know it through years of experience, by observation, or by the fall you took yourself once.

Well, God will give us a spirit of understanding if we ask Him, and we can avoid those experiences that cause us so much harm. Think of how your parents tried to teach you what not to do, and what to do, to make your life easier. If you listened to and obeyed them, you probably did well. But, if you did not, you had to suffer the hard knocks yourself.

352

God is our Heavenly Father, who has recorded His Word, the Bible, and it is full of examples of advice and directions, with "thou shalts" and "thou shalt nots," for us to have all the understanding we would ever need to live a life of victory. Let us decide to make use of them all, and thereby have the seed fall into good ground.

PRAYER: Heavenly Father, I want my heart to be one that is full of good ground. I also want the Spirit of knowledge, understanding, and wisdom to help me live a life of victory. I pray that you give me all of these, and I pray that your Holy Spirit will also help me to make the best use of those seeds, the Word of God, that has been sown in my heart. In Jesus' name, Amen.

SEPTEMBER 4th

There are so many truths hidden in the Word of God, and I believe we need to look at another truth about the will of God. It is hard to understand the full character of God if we only have half a picture of Him. For example, when you see that God created man to occupy earth and to be the "giver" to the earth, and then you see that God sent a flood to completely destroy what was on the earth with the exception of Noah, his three sons and their wives, you may wonder how that all figures into God's will.

Something about that was explained to me some years ago, and it was such a help for me to understand the *wills* of God. I was told that there are four *wills* of God: His directive will, permissive will, determinate will, and terminate will.

God's *directive will* was to create the heavens and the earth and everything in them. It was also His *directive will* to create mankind in His own image, and to give mankind the freedom of choice. We were not created to be

353

robots—to be programmed to love God and obey Him. Instead, we are given the freedom of choice.

Adam and Eve chose to disobey God when they ate the forbidden fruit. When Eve stretched out her hand to take the fruit, God did not slap her hand and ask her what she thought she was doing. It was God's *permissive will* that allowed her to take the forbidden fruit. God knew the sad consequences of such an action, and yet, He let her do it. It would cost God dearly for Eve to disobey Him that way. It cost His Son even more dearly, because He had to die to reconcile mankind to Himself. Yet, God did not stop Eve.

God will not interfere with *your* choices either. That is His *permissive will*. Be careful about taking advantage of His permissive will. He will let us sow bad seed, and then He will go through the resulting trials with us. God did not forsake Adam and Eve, but they did have to suffer the consequences of their choice. We will also suffer the consequences of our bad choices.

There are many examples of God's directive will in the Bible. To have a nation of His own on earth was God's directive will, and that nation is Israel. They made many bad decisions with their freedom of choice throughout their history, which brought untold suffering to their people.

Again, it was God's *permissive will* to allow them to make those bad choices. Now, I can just imagine some of you thinking, "Well, why did so-and-so survive when so-and-so was killed in a storm?" There can be a number of reasons. Maybe the one that survived had a faithful family member praying for his safety or for his salvation to be secured. Or, maybe the survivor had prayed for himself at that time. Or, just maybe, the person who died had completed his work on earth already, and it was time to go and be with the Lord.

The one thing that we must not do is question God's goodness and mercy. God is always good. He never plans or thinks evil. And He is the One who is sovereign. His will is always the best.

When you experience tragedies, learn to hand the situation over to God and ask Him to comfort you and uphold you through it all. One thing you can be sure of is that the one that went to be with the Lord is the one who is the blessed one. Is not our life with God in heaven our goal in life anyway? Or maybe the one who survived was the one who did not know the Lord, and was given more time to accept Jesus as Savior.

Although most people think life on this earth is the only important thing, God's eye is on eternity. That is the important factor in our lives.

PRAYER: Heavenly Father, grant that I will not have a spirit of confusion, but a spirit of truth. You have promised in your Word that the truth will set me free, and I lay hold of that promise today. In Jesus' name, Amen.

SEPTEMBER 5th

Today, we will continue to look at God's *directive will*, which is God's first choice to accomplish a certain thing. Genesis 1:1 reads, *"In the beginning, God created the heavens and the earth."* The creation of mankind was His directive will.

Genesis 1:26 reads:
"And God said, 'Let us make man in our image, after our likeness: and let them have dominion over the fish of the sea, an over the fowl of the air, and over the cattle, and over all the earth, and over every creeping thing that creepeth upon the earth.'"

355

It was also God's directive will to give mankind dominion over the earth. It was God's directive will to put His name in Jerusalem as a permanent dwelling place. Deuteronomy 12:10-11 states:

"But when you go over Jordan, and dwell in the land which the Lord your God giveth you to inherit, and when He giveth you rest from all your enemies round about, so that you dwell in safety; Then there shall be a place which the Lord your God shall choose to cause His name to dwell there; thither shall ye bring all that I command you; your burnt offerings, and your sacrifices, your tithes, and the heave offering of your hand, and all your choice vows which you vow unto the Lord."

This was to take place in the future, when they had settled in the promised land after leaving Egypt. God chose to have a house for Himself where His Name may dwell in Jerusalem.

II Chronicles 6:5-6 explains:

"Since the day that I brought forth my people out of the land of Egypt, I chose no city among all the tribes of Israel to build an house in, that my name might be there; neither chose I any man to be a ruler over my people Israel: But I have chosen Jerusalem, that my name might be there; and have chosen David to be over my people Israel."

God had made His directive will known to the people, and that "will" still stands today. As we view the problems Jerusalem is having, one might wonder how it will all play out, since God's Will has not changed. One day, there will be a new temple in Jerusalem. Israel will be God's nation among nations, and Jesus, a descendent of King David, will rule over the whole world. It is God's directive will. Tell me, who can stand in the way of such a will?

There is a day in the future when Jesus will return to take His bride, the Church, to Himself for the marriage. Revelation 19:7 states, *"Let us be glad and rejoice, and give honor to Him: for the marriage of the Lamb* (Jesus) *is come, and His wife hath made herself ready."* And Revelation 19:9 reads:

> *"And He said unto me, 'Write, "Blessed are they which are called unto the marriage supper of the Lamb."' And He said unto me, 'These are the true sayings of God.'"*

These are just a few examples of God's directive will. Since He said it, it shall be done. Jesus' death on the cross was also God's directive will. Your salvation is too, but you must understand that your freedom of choice to rebel at God's directive will has the power to over-ride God's good will for you.

Jesus has already paid the price and penalty for your sins. That is how determined He was to have you saved and to spend eternity with Him. But we have the freedom of choice, a gift from God, and He does not take it back when we disobey Him. That freedom was given to us once and for all. Choose wisely. Your eternal life depends on it.

There is some unusual text in Matthew 22:14, which reads, *"For many are called, but few are chosen."* I pondered that verse for a long time until I finally felt that God showed me what it meant, and it involved His *directive will* and His *permissive will*. It is God's directive will that everyone is saved, and the truth of the gospel of salvation goes out over the air waves by both T.V. and radio. It also goes out in thousands of churches across our country calling to you. Few people in America can say they never heard the call.

People are hearing the call, but if they do not choose to follow that call and give their lives to Jesus, then how can God choose them? He must honor their freedom of choice, and He will permit them to make that disastrous choice.

357

But, on the other hand, when they choose to accept that call and give their hearts to Jesus Christ by inviting Him in, then God will choose them. The reason "few are chosen" is because the sinful nature of many people chooses to not have Christ Jesus as their Savior. Do not let your eternal life be in jeopardy by neglecting to make Jesus your Lord and Savior.

PRAYER: Heavenly Father, the explanation of these wills of God helps me to understand so much better what is going on. Thank you, Father, for helping me to see and understand your work in my life. The more I get to know you better, the more I grasp your great love for me, and just how far you have gone to assure me of salvation. Father, I have nothing but praise and adoration to offer you, and a willing heart to serve you. Help me to be that faithful servant you desire me to be, that light and salt of the earth you have said that I am. In Jesus' name, Amen.

SEPTEMBER 6th

Let's look at a few more examples of God's permissive will. I believe God's permissive will usually come into play when His children *choose* to rebel against His directive will.

God told Adam that they were not to eat of the fruit of the tree in the midst of the garden of Eden, and that if they did, they would surely die, as we see in Genesis 2:15-17:

> *"And the Lord God took the man, and put him into the garden of Eden to dress it and to keep it. And the Lord God commanded the man, saying, 'Of every tree of the garden thou mayest freely eat: But of the tree of the knowledge of good and evil, thou shalt not eat of it: for in the day that thou eatest thereof, thou shalt surely die.'"*

God warned them of the consequences of disobedience, and He gave them His directive will for their lives. Then, along came Satan in the form of a serpent who talked to Eve. Genesis 3:1-3 explains:

> *"Now the serpent was more subtle than any beast of the field which the Lord God had made. And he said unto the woman, 'Yea, hath God said, "Ye shall not eat of every tree of the garden?"' And the woman said unto the serpent, 'We may eat of the fruit of the trees of the garden: But of the fruit of the tree which is in the midst of the garden, God hath said, "Ye shall not eat of it, neither shall ye touch it, lest ye die."'"*

The serpent placed doubt in Eve's mind—doubt that God was a generous God. He made her wonder why a loving God would withhold any good thing from her. Notice the boldfaced lie that Satan fed Eve in his response in Genesis 3:4-5:

> *"And the serpent said unto the woman, 'Ye shall not surely die: For God doth know that in the day ye eat thereof, then your eyes shall be opened, and ye shall be as gods* (God) *knowing good and evil.'"*

In other words, Satan is telling Eve that God is withholding something wonderful from her, and she surely wouldn't die from taking the fruit.

It is interesting that, in the beginning, when all was life, God warned mankind of death, and Satan *voided God's warning of death*. Today, when all is death, Satan tries to *void God's promise of eternal life*.

Genesis 3:6-7 states:

> *"And when the woman saw that the tree was good for food, and that it was pleasant to the eyes, and a tree to be desired to make one wise, she took of the fruit thereof, and did eat, and gave also unto her husband with her; and he did eat. And the eyes of them both were opened, and they knew that they were naked; and they sewed fig leaves together, and made themselves aprons."*

Right here, we see God's permissive will. He allowed Eve to eat of the fruit and give some to her husband. As a result of that choice, death entered into the world.

We need to see the progression of events that wore down Eve's resistance. In Genesis 3:3, we see that Eve modified God's command when she said, *"God hath said, 'Ye shall not eat if it, neither shall ye touch it.'"* God had not told Adam that he could not touch the fruit, so why did Adam add that word of warning to Eve? When we add to God's Word, we are getting ourselves into trouble, but, again, that is God's permissive will.

Remember when we saw how Jesus was tempted in the body, soul, and spirit? Well, we can see the same pattern with Eve. Genesis 6:6 reads, *"She saw that the tree was good for food* (temptation of the body) *and that it was pleasant to the eyes* (temptation of the soul, the seat of desire)*."*

Our eyes will see what our souls desire. How long had Eve looked at that tree and wondered just how delicious its fruit was? Maybe she even touched it and discovered that nothing happened, so she wondered if she could also eat the fruit.

Then, we also see the temptation of her spirit in verse 6, when it states that the tree was *" to be desired to make one wise."* Take a look back to what the serpent told her in verse 5, *"For God doth know that in the day ye eat thereof, then your eyes shall be opened, and ye shall be as gods* (God) *knowing good and evil."*

Remember when Jesus was tempted in the body, soul, and spirit? Satan told Jesus to turn stones into bread for His hungry body, throw Himself down, because angels will not let Him be hurt to prove to the world He was the Son of God, and bow down and worship Satan to receive authority and power over the world. Eve was tempted the same way. Satan told her that

360

she would <u>be like God</u>, knowing good and evil. And she fell for the whole package.

God did not stop her, either. There is much speculation as to why God allowed Eve to drag the whole world into such a sink hole of sin and death, but I will not go into that here. But I want you to realize how dangerous it is to rebel at God's directive will and push Him into His permissive will.

PRAYER: Heavenly Father, thank you for teaching me the difference between your directive will and permissive will. It helps me sort though things that I have wondered about for so long. Help me to stick to your directive will, rather than rebel and allow my own will to overrule yours. I am thankful that you are a forgiving God, and that there is always the hope of restoration with you when I make poor choices. However, I do not want to take advantage of that forgiving spirit and patience that you have toward us sinners, so help me to see Satan's snares and trickery, so I can resist his temptations. In Jesus' name, Amen.

SEPTEMBER 7th

Today, we will address God's *determinate will*. There are things that God has said *would happen*, and there is no changing His mind over those things. He is *determined* that those events shall occur.

Daniel, who had been taken among the captives into Babylon, never turned away from God. Daniel was also aware that his nation, Israel, had been handpicked by God to be the light in the world, to show the nations that there is one true God, the Creator of heaven and earth. Other nations had many gods, all of which were false.

Daniel also knew, by the prophecy of Jeremiah, that they would be captives in Babylon for 70 years. That time was coming to an end, and Daniel prayed earnestly for God to show him what would happen to Israel. Then in Daniel 9:24, we read:

"Seventy weeks are <u>determined</u> upon thy people and upon thy holy city (Jerusalem, remember, is where God chose to put His name) *to finish the transgression, and to make an end of sins, and to make reconciliation for iniquity, and to bring in everlasting righteousness, and to seal up the vision and prophecy, and to anoint the most Holy."*

There is a determined time line for the nation of Israel. Jesus would come to do away with sin, and would usher in a reconciliation for iniquity and everlasting righteousness, but this prophecy and vision would be sealed up until later, when the most Holy is anointed. This is a date that was determined, and it will not be changed.

PRAYER: Heavenly Father, as I study your Word, I see more and more how much you are in control of everything. That is a comfort to me, and I thank you for giving me this knowledge. Your Word tells me that I should know the truth, and the truth shall set me free, and that is so true. Help me make the right choices with the truth you have been giving me. In Jesus' name, Amen.

SEPTEMBER 8th

Let's look at a few more examples of God's determinate will. I Corinthians 15:51-54 reads:

"Behold, I show you a mystery; We shall not all sleep (die), *but we shall all be changed. In a moment, in the twinkling of an eye, at the last trump: for the trumpet shall sound, and the dead shall be raised incorruptible, and we shall be changed. For this corruptible must put on incorruption, and this mortal must put on immortality. So when this corruptible shall have put on incorruption, and this mortal shall have put on immortality, then shall come to pass the saying that is written, 'Death is swallowed up in victory.'"*

When Jesus comes as a thief in the night to take us with Him to heaven, there will be those who are alive on the earth, and they will be changed from mortal to immortal—from a body that corrupts to a body that will not corrupt any more. Then, "death will be swallowed up in victory."

One more reference we should look at in regard to this event is I Thessalonians 4:14-18, which reads:

"For if we believe that Jesus died and rose again, even so them also which sleep (have died) *in Jesus will God bring with Him. For this we say unto you by the Word of the Lord, that we which are alive and remain unto the coming of the Lord shall not precede them which are asleep* (have died). *For the Lord Himself shall descend from heaven with a shout, with the voice of the archangel, and with the trump of God, and the dead in Christ shall rise first. Then we which are live and remain shall be caught up together with them in the clouds, to meet the Lord in the air: and so shall we ever be with the Lord. Wherefore comfort one another with these words."*

Notice that it says, *"even so them also which sleep in Jesus will God bring with Him."* When we die, our souls go to be with Jesus and our body is buried. So, when Jesus comes for His Church, the graves will open and our bodies will be resurrected, and Jesus will bring our souls with him to be united to our glorified bodies—the immortal and incorruptible bodies.

This is also described in Matthew 24:37-42, which reads:

"But as the days of Noah were, so shall also the coming of the Son of man be. For as in the days that were before the flood, they were eating and drinking, marrying and giving in marriage, until the day that Noah entered into the ark, and knew not until the flood came, and took them all away; so shall also the coming of the Son of man be. Then shall two be in the field; the one shall be taken, and the other left. Two women shall be grinding at the

mill; the one shall be taken, and the other left. Watch, therefore:
for ye know not what hour your Lord doth come."

PRAYER: Heavenly Father, I can see that there is a date set in time that only you know about, and I also see that I am to trust in you for all things. So, I guess that means that my obligation is to be ready for that day and hour at all times, and not to worry or have a concern about when it will happen. I am grateful that I can depend on the Word, which teaches me that you will never leave me nor forsake me, but that I am in the safety of your hands. I thank you for that assurance. Help me to stay steadfast in my faith, never wavering. In Jesus' name, Amen.

SEPTEMBER 9th

Today, we will look at God's *terminate will*, which means things have gone far enough, and He will not permit them to continue further. Terminate means to end or finish.

I believe the first example in the Bible of God's terminate will is seen in Genesis 6 and 7. Genesis 6:3 reads, *"And the Lord said, 'My spirit shall not always strive with man, for that he also is flesh: yet his days shall be an hundred and twenty years.'"* And Genesis 6:7-8 reads:
> *"And the Lord said, I will destroy man whom I have created from the face of the earth; both man, and beast, and the creeping thing, and the fowls of the air; for it repenteth me that I have made them. But Noah found grace in the eyes of the Lord."*

Also look at Genesis 7:1, which states, *"And the Lord said unto Noah, 'Come thou and all thy house into the ark; for thee have I seen righteous before me in this generation.'"* Things had gotten so bad on the earth that God was ready to put His terminate will into practice. Sin was everywhere, to the point that God was sorry He had even created man.

364

However, Noah had held the line and was righteous before God, even in the midst of all that sin. God instructed him to build an ark to preserve himself and his family. Noah had to make a choice. Should he build the ark on dry ground when, as yet, there had been no rain upon the earth? Should he believe God when He told him that there would be a flood, and that it would not come for 120 years?

Imagine keeping that thought alive for that long, with a terribly sinful world all around you. God was not fooling. The flood did come, and everything was destroyed except for Noah, his wife, and his three sons and their wives.

I would like to suggest that you read Genesis 6:11-13 to get a glimpse of how corrupt the earth had become in Noah's day. You may wonder at God's patience with things in our day! Will His terminate will be needed again soon? Does the Bible have anything to say about that?

PRAYER: Heavenly Father, if I did not know your abundant love for me, and your mercy and grace, I could become anxious as I look at our world today. But just as you saw the righteousness of Noah (and I realize that the Bible doesn't even say his sons were righteous—all they had to do was to believe their earthly father and get into the ark to be saved from sure death), I can be sure that you see my righteousness in Christ Jesus. This assures me that I will always be in a safe place according to your grace. Thank you for that assurance. In Jesus' name, Amen.

SEPTEMBER 10th

Today, we will look at another example of God's directive will, as it set's the stage for tomorrow's example of His terminate will. The scene takes place in Egypt, when God is about to remove His nation, Israel, from the bondage of slavery there. God called Moses to bring the people out of Egypt, as we see in Exodus 3:9-10:

"Now therefore, behold, the cry of the children of Israel is come unto me: and I have also seen the oppression wherewith the Egyptians oppress them. Come now therefore, and I will send thee unto Pharaoh, that thou mayest bring forth my people the children of Israel out of Egypt."

Moses argued with God, telling God that he was not fit for such a big task, but one cannot argue with God. God will win every time, unless you rebel to the point of no longer being a follower of God. And who wants to rebel that far? Not me!

The verses above are an example of God's directive will. Moses was God's first choice to do this job. Guess what? God has a directive will for you too. You are a first choice for something. Ask God to help you see what He has chosen for you to do.

God also gave Moses a "job description" in Exodus 3:7-8, which reads:
"And the Lord said, 'I have surely seen the affliction of my people which are in Egypt, and have heard their cry by reason of their taskmasters; for I know their sorrows. And I am come down to deliver them out of the hand of the Egyptians, and to bring them up out of that land unto a good land and a large, unto a land flowing with milk and honey; unto the place of the Canaanites, and the Hittites, and the Amorites, and the Perizzites, and the Hivites, and the Jebusites.'"

Moses was to bring them <u>out</u> of Egypt and <u>to</u> a good land flowing with milk and honey. However, it was occupied by these other six nations. All of this is a picture of God's directive will, His first choice. No matter how much man will choose to rebel at God's first choice, that directive will of His will be done, either with your cooperation or without your cooperation. If you refuse to do your part in His will, God will find someone else to take your place and do it His way.

PRAYER: Heavenly Father, open my eyes to see your directive will in my life. And when I do see it, help me not to rebel or try to get out of it. Help me to understand that you would not ask more of me than I am able to do, and that you are able to equip me for the task at hand. Help me to be a faithful and obedient servant. In Jesus' name, Amen.

SEPTEMBER 11ᵗʰ

Moses obeyed God to the letter. Following God's instructions, he brought ten plagues upon the Egyptians, because Pharaoh would not allow the Israelites go out into the wilderness to worship Him.

Each time Pharaoh asked Moses to lift the plague, the plague was lifted. But Pharaoh hardened his heart over and over again. God knew that would happen, as you can see in Exodus 7:4-5, where God says:

> *"And I will harden Pharaoh's heart, and multiply my signs and my wonders in the land of Egypt. But Pharaoh shall not hearken unto you, that I may lay my hand upon Egypt, and bring forth mine armies, and my people, the children of Israel, out of the land of Egypt by great judgments. And the Egyptians shall know that I am the Lord, when I stretch forth mine hand upon Egypt, and bring out the children of Israel from among them."*

What we need to see here is that when Pharaoh kept hardening his heart, he was giving God the right to harden his heart. Now, Pharaoh would not be able to obey God and let the people go in peace. With that, God had His legal right to destroy Egypt's power. And what was Egypt's power? It was all the false gods they worshipped.

God's terminate will was going to be twofold here. He would terminate the slavery of His children in Egypt, and He would judge all the gods of Egypt. Exodus 7:22 says, *"And the magicians of Egypt did so with their*

367

enchantments: and Pharaoh's <u>heart was hardened</u>, neither did he hearken unto them, <u>as the Lord had said.</u>"

There is a reason behind all this. In Exodus 9:13-14, God instructs Moses to tell Pharaoh:

"Thus saith the Lord God of the Hebrews, 'Let my people go, that they may serve me. For I will at this time send ALL my plagues upon thine heart, and upon thy servants, and upon thy people; that thou mayest <u>know that there is none like me in all the earth.</u>'"

God wanted Pharaoh to come to know Him, and not to worship all those false gods, but Pharaoh would not bend. We see the same thing happening in the world today. All of Egypt suffered because of a leader who would not listen to God or see the truth.

One more verse we need to read while addressing God's terminate will is Exodus 12:12, which reads:

"For I will pass through the land of Egypt this night, and will smite all the firstborn (including Pharaoh's firstborn son, who was destined to sit on the throne and be worshipped as a god)*, both man and beast; and against ALL the gods of Egypt I will execute judgment: I AM the Lord."*

God terminated the *power* of the false gods over the land of Egypt. This is a picture of Jesus, who terminated the power of Satan over the world, especially in the lives of Christians. Satan can only be as powerful as you permit him to be in your life. We need to know and understand this truth, not only in our heads, but also in our hearts.

Jesus has broken the power of the devil over sin and death. You can dethrone Satan and ask Jesus to sit on the throne of your heart.

PRAYER: Heavenly Father, I give you all the praise and glory for your wonderful plan of salvation, justification, and sanctification. I am so thankful to be a part of that plan that my heart flows with gratitude. Keep me daily in your Word, that I might be fed the spiritual food I need to stay close to you. Give me those to whom I can share what I know about you. In Jesus' precious name, Amen.

SEPTEMBER 12th

There are a couple more examples we need to look at regarding God's terminate will. We need to grow in our trust of God and know that He has only good in His heart toward us, never evil.

Satan does not want us to trust in God, but wants us to see God as untrustworthy instead. Anyone who is overwhelmed with problems that look impossible to solve can easily adopt that viewpoint. We need to realize that God cannot wink at sin. It is an ugly thing that has invaded His universe, and it needs to be judged and removed.

The trouble is that every man, woman, and child is born a sinner. God wanted those who are willing to accept His plan of salvation to have a way to be saved to spend eternity with Him, and not be judged with sinners or judged like sinners. But, make no mistake, one day sin and all that is sinful will be removed from this universe—all evil will be gone, including the devil himself.

So, as we look at that terminate will of God, never forget that you, who are in Christ Jesus, will not be involved in that terminate will of God's. I want to make that clear. One day Jesus will come for His bride, the Church, and then the Church's influence on this earth will be terminated.

I Thessalonians 4:14-18 states:

369

"For if we believe that Jesus died and rose again, even so them also which sleep (have died) *in Jesus will God bring with Him. For this we say unto you by the word of the Lord, that we which are alive and remain unto the coming of the Lord shall not precede them which are asleep* (dead)*. For the Lord Himself shall descend from heaven with a shout, with the voice of the archangel, and with the trump of God: and the dead in Christ shall rise first: Then we which are alive and remain shall be caught up together with them in the clouds, to meet the Lord in the air: and so shall we ever be with the Lord. Wherefore comfort one another with these words."*

Since Jesus died and rose again, He has the legal rights to every soul who puts his or her trust in Him, and when that beliver dies (is "asleep" in Christ) his or her soul is safely with Jesus. Then, when He returns for us and there is the resurrection of the body, Jesus will be bringing our souls with Him and they will be reunited with our glorified resurrected body. And then, those who are alive when that event takes place will have their bodies changed in the twinkling of the eye.

We will look more at that tomorrow. According to today's reference, each step in this resurrection is precisely spelled out. Reread the scripture and watch the procedure. The ones who have died a believer in Jesus will be raised first, then those who are alive will be changed. (I call that being made fit for space travel. Flesh and blood bodies cannot travel in space so those bodies will be changed in a twinkling of an eye). And then all will meet Jesus in the cloud in the air and go to a place prepared for us all.

The Bible is so precise, it is just amazing. I want to quote a verse in Acts in regard to "the cloud." Acts 1:9-11 reads:
"And when He had spoken these things, while they beheld, He was taken up; and a cloud received Him out of their sight. And while they looked steadfastly toward heaven as He went up, behold, two men stood by them in white apparel; Which also

said, 'Ye men of Galilee, why stand ye gazing up into heaven?
This same Jesus, which is taken up from you into heaven, shall
so come in like manner as ye have seen Him go into heaven.'"

How had they seen Him go? Was it not by way of a cloud? So, that is the
way He will return for us also. It is the *determined will* of God. And our
exit from this earth is God's *terminate will* for this earth. There will be no
more Christian influence on earth.

If the people of the world want freedom *from* the restraints of "religion,"
they shall have what they think they want, only to find out that when Satan
has nothing to restrain him, this world will not be a fit place to live. God's
terminate will is not designed for the Christians. God wants everyone to
come to the knowledge of the truth and to accept Jesus as the substitute for
sin and escape the wrath of God. That decision is made now, not later.

PRAYER: Heavenly Father, I see so much hope in your Word, and yet I
have a heavy heart for those who do not know your truth about the
availability (through Jesus' life, death, and resurrection) of salvation from
sin, death, and the power of the devil. I name many in my heart before you
and ask that you leave no stone unturned to meet them on the level of their
need. If I am the one who is supposed to speak to any of them, then you
prepare their hearts to hear what you would have me tell them. I put myself
at your disposal to accomplish what is needful. In Jesus' name, Amen.

SEPTEMBER 13th

We have one more verse to look at in connection with yesterday's
devotion. In I Corinthians 15:47-58, we read:
"The first man (Adam) *is of the earth, earthy: the second*
man (Jesus) *is the Lord from heaven. As is the earthy, such are*
they also that are earthy: and as is the heavenly, such are they
also that are heavenly. And as we have born the image of the

earthy, we shall also bear the image of the heavenly. Now this I say, brethren, that flesh and blood cannot inherit the kingdom of God; neither doth corruption inherit incorruption. Behold I show you a mystery; We shall not all sleep (die), *but we shall all be changed, In a moment, in the twinkling of an eye, at the last trump: for the trumpet shall sound, and the dead shall be raised incorruptible, and we shall be changed. For this corruptible must put on incorruption, and this mortal must put on immortality. So when this corruptible shall have put on incorruption, and this mortal shall have put on immortality, then shall be brought to pass the saying that is written, 'Death is swallowed up in victory. O Death, where is thy sting? O grave* (death), *where is thy victory?' The sting of death is sin; and the strength* (power) *of sin is the law. But thanks be to God, which giveth us the victory through our Lord Jesus Christ. Therefore, my beloved brethren be ye stedfast, unmoveable, always abounding in the work of the Lord, for as much as ye know that your labor is not in vain in the Lord."*

We need to follow this scripture through. Jesus is called the "second Adam." The first Adam sold the whole world into sin, and the world is still under that curse. God sent His own Son as a second Adam to buy back what was taken away by the enemy, namely Satan. The first Adam was of the earth, but Jesus, the second Adam, was from the heavenly realm. Everyone on earth can change his or her status by accepting God's heavenly intervention, and by that choice will become heavenly bound, not earthly bound.

Flesh and blood as it is today (sin-sick and disease-ridden) cannot inherit things of the heavenly realm. That is why I say we need to be fitted for space travel. When astronauts go up into outer space, they have to take with them the earthly environment. Therefore, there is a mystery—those who are alive when this momentous event comes, will be changed in "the twinkling of an eye," which is really fast. There will be a voice of an archangel, a

372

trumpet sound, and a shout out of heaven, and a cloud that will receive us all together with Jesus to make a trip to heaven. No space suit will be needed. God has it all arranged.

Behind it all is God's determinate will for the believers, and the terminate will for the earth. This world will lose its Christian witness that restrains Satanic activity.

PRAYER: Heavenly Father, we keep going deeper and deeper into this subject, but I do see that your favor is always with the believers. You have done everything possible for us to be safe from the enemy, and to enjoy eternal life with you. That message needs to be shouted from the rooftops, but how hard it is to tell the people of the world about you. Their interests are not bent in that direction. But I will lay the names of those I love before you and intercede on their behalf, believing that you hear my prayer for them and will act upon it. In Jesus' name, Amen.

SEPTEMBER 14th

Today, as we will continue we will look at Revelation 12:7-12, which reads:

"And there was war in heaven: Michael and his angels fought against the dragon; and the dragon fought and his angels, And prevailed not; <u>neither was their place found any more in heaven</u>. And the great dragon was cast out, that old serpent, called the Devil and Satan, which deceiveth the whole world: he was <u>cast out into the earth</u>, and his angels were cast out with him. And I heard a loud voice saying in heaven, 'Now is come salvation, and strength, and the kingdom of our God, and the power (authority) *of His Christ: for the accuser of our brethren is cast down, which accused them before our God day and night. And they overcome him by the blood of the Lamb, and by the word of their testimony; and they loved not their lives unto*

the death. Therefore rejoice ye heavens, and ye that dwell in them. Woe to the inhabiters of the earth and of the sea! For the devil is come down unto you, having great wrath, because he knoweth that he hath but a short time.'"

Yesterday, we saw the necessity to be changed bodily for us to go with Jesus to paradise when He comes for the Church. That is a date determined by God. That event will also usher in a whole new condition on earth, and our reference for today describes that event.

There will be a spiritual war in heaven, and the archangel Michael, with his angelic hosts, will fight with the dragon and his spiritual hosts. Please understand that the dragon is Lucifer, who rebelled against God whom Jesus saw him fall like lightening to the earth. His fall, however, was not a total fall.

Lucifer still has some rule and freedom in the heavenly realm today, but the day will come when he will not be allowed that freedom anymore. Our scripture describes that event. It says there will be found *no* place for Satan anymore in heaven. Only on earth will he be able to function.

Remember when I said that earth will not be a fit place to live when that happens? The influence of the church will be removed, and it is for a specifically designed period of time. Some say it will be for 7 years, some say half that time. That is a controversial prophetic period of time, but there is no doubt that the event will happen. It is God's terminate will.

The Church's influence on earth will be terminated. All sin and wickedness will be allowed to reign. There will be no argument about the 10 commandments being in any law office or court room, because they will not be allowed anywhere.

The way I see it, it will be similar to the time of Pharaoh. Pharaoh would not listen to Moses, and plague after plague came upon the people of Egypt.

It was not until the plague of the death of all firstborns (both of animals and mankind) finally fell upon them that Pharaoh said they could leave Egypt.

Today the world is clamoring for more and more legal freedom to thumb its nose at God. People want to take God out of the Pledge of Allegiance and keep prayer out of the schools, claiming it to be illegal. Some want to take away any mention of Christmas or Easter, and I could go on and on. One day, God will say, "If that is what you really want, then that is what you shall have." And God will give the world a life full of Satan, with no respite at all.

Look again at the reference for today. Revelation 12:10 says:
"And I heard a loud voice saying in heaven, 'Now is come salvation, and strength, and the kingdom of our God, and the power (authority) *of His Christ: for the accuser of our brethren* (none other than Satan himself) *is cast down, which accused them before God day and night.'"*

Satan will no longer be able or allowed to come up before God and point a finger at you or me and accuse us before God. It will be a day of great rejoicing for the believers, but for those who had refused to believe what this Book, the Bible, had been saying to them, it will be a day of great sadness. We need to have our eyes wide open, know the truth, believe the truth, and then act upon that truth.

PARYER: Heavenly Father, thank you for making this so plain to me. I pray that I will be willing to inform anyone who should ask me about your plan for the future and that you want everyone to be in the safety of your place for them in paradise. Give me the right words to say to the right person at the right time. My desire is in sync with your desire, and together we can accomplish great things. In Jesus' name, Amen.

375

SEPTEMBER 15th

There is a day in the future when everything evil will be put out of the way. That day is also a part of God's terminate will. Let us look at a few references in regard to that. Revelations 19:20 reads:

"And the beast was taken, and with him the false prophet that wrought miracles before him, with which he deceived them that had received the mark of the beast, and them that worshipped his image. These both were cast alive into a lake of fire burning with brimstone."

The beast and false prophet are two personages who reign with Satan during the time when all evil rules over the earth. They will be the first two who are thrown in the lake of fire, and the Bible says they will be thrown in alive. Their time of freedom to defy God Almighty will come to an end, be terminated.

Now we will look at Revelations 20:10, which states:

"And the Devil that deceived them was cast into the lake of fire and brimstone, where the beast and the false prophet are, and shall be tormented day and night for ever and ever."

Finally, the devil himself will be thrown into that lake of fire, where he will remain forever. Step by step, all the evil that had invaded God's universe will be eliminated, terminated.

Let us also look at Revelation 20:12-14, which reads:

"And I saw the dead, small and great, stand before God (before the throne)*; and the books were opened: and another book was opened, which is the Book of Life: and the dead were judged out of those things written in the books according to their works* (their lifestyle will be examined)*, And death and hell* (Hades) *were cast into the lake of fire. This is the second death."*

Eventually, even death and Hades (the place where the wicked dead go now when they die) will be eliminated from the universe. God will one day have His universe back the way He had intended it to be in the first place.

Have you ever heard someone say, "If God is a loving God, why would He send anyone to Hell?" That person is putting all the blame on God for the evils in the world. It is the other way around, though. All the evils in the world come from Satan, who is able to use mankind to do his will on earth. God has done everything He could possibly do to create a way for sinful man to have fellowship with an Almighty God and to live eternally with Him in heaven.

Satan deceives people into believing that God is not fair, that He does not love mankind, and that he has taken everyone's fun away and made life miserable. So, people blame God for the troubles in the world.

It is a sad thing when people fall for that view of life and death. If you want to know that there is a better way, just ask Jesus (God's answer to the sin problem) to come into your heart and to make it His home. Your life will be changed forever, and for the better I might add.

PRAYER: Heavenly Father, I do want to live eternally with you, and I do want you to live in my heart. I ask you to forgive me all my sins, and help me to live a new life in you, one that is pleasing to you. Give me the strength to follow through on this desire. Lead me, step by step, in this new life, so that I can keep up with you. I see that at times you take a giant step, and wonder whether I am ready to take that giant step with you. That is when I will really need your help. In Jesus' name, Amen.

SEPTEMBER 16th

There is one more giant step in God's overall plan that we need to look at, the new heaven and new earth that will one day be. II Peter

3:10-13 reads:

> *"But the day of the Lord will come as a thief in the night; in which the heavens shall pass away with a great noise, and the elements shall melt with fervent heart, the earth also and the works that are therein shall be burned up. Seeing then that all these things shall be dissolved, what manner of persons ought ye to be in all holy conversation and godliness, Looking for and earnestly desiring unto the coming of the day of God wherein the heavens being on fire shall be dissolved, and the elements shall melt with fervent heat? Nevertheless we, according to His promise, look for new heavens and a new earth, wherein dwelleth righteousness."*

I want to remind you that this is written by that same Peter who denied even knowing Jesus the Christ, but that was before the Holy Spirit was poured out on the apostles at Pentecost. Peter, at this time, had been endowed with power from on high, and He was writing with the power of the Holy Spirit.

So, what did Peter say here? He explains that there will be a time when this earth will be burned up, and also the heavens as we know them. Just how that will happen we do not know, but since it was said here in God's Word, we know it will happen.

Then Peter asked a very good question. Since we know this world will be burned up and everything will be new, what kind of persons should we be? He stated, *"Seeing then that all these __things__ shall be dissolved, what manner of persons ought ye to be in ALL holy conversation* (meaning our daily life), *and godliness?"* How much importance should we put on the *things* of this world? One day it will all be gone. There will be a new heaven and earth where only righteousness will rule.

We need to have our priorities in order, and that is to, *"Seek ye first the kingdom of God and His righteousness, and all these__things__ shall be added unto you"* (Matthew 6:33). If we seek God first and foremost, then

378

God will see to it that all the *things* of this world will be added to us. The question is whether things control you or you control things.

PRAYER: Heavenly Father, help me to be able to grasp all the truths that are in your Word, and to put them into practice in my life. When I see the overall picture of your universe and how you want it back into the good working order you had in mind for it when you created it, I almost feel insignificant in my small part here. I think of the generations of people who have come and gone over the eons of time, and wonder "Who am I that I should make a difference?" And yet, that is the very message that I believe you are trying to convey to me. Help me to grasp that truth and to make good use of it so that I will be a perfect fit for your plan. In Jesus' name, Amen.

SEPTEMBER 17th

We find the warning and promise of the earth and heavens passing away and the new heaven and earth arriving not only in II Peter, but also in Revelation. Let us look at it in Revelation 21:1-5, which states:
"And I saw a new heaven and a new earth: for the first heaven and the first earth were passed away; and there was no more sea. And I, John, saw the holy city, new Jerusalem (There will be not only a new heaven and earth, but also a new Jerusalem. Keep in mind, Jerusalem is the place where God chose to put His name), *coming down out of heaven, prepared as a bride adorned for her husband. And I heard a great voice out of heaven* (the throne) *saying, 'Behold, the tabernacle of God is with men, and He will dwell with them, and they shall be His people, and God Himself shall be with them, and be their God. And God shall wipe away all tears from their eyes; and there shall be no more death, neither sorrow, nor crying, neither shall there be any more pain, for the former things are passed away.' And He that sat upon the*

throne said, 'Behold I make all things new.' And He said unto
me, 'Write: for these words are true and faithful.'"

Notice what shall be no more: death, sorrow, crying, and pain! Did you
realize that all these things were the result of sin in the world? Where God
dwells these things cannot exist. God will dwell with those who have
chosen to live for Him, therefore all these things that are the result of sin
will not be able to exist there. What a place God has in mind for us for
eternity! I am all for following a God that can promise me this kind of
eternal life. How about you?

PRAYER: Heavenly Father, I am reminded of Isaiah 55:9, which says,
"For as the heavens are higher than the earth, so are my ways higher
than your ways, and my thoughts than your thoughts." Your ways and
your thoughts are so much mightier and grand than mine. When I try to
comprehend your thoughts and ways, I find that our level of communication
at times comes to a sharp bend in the road and I am going back and trying
to figure out where I landed on a detour. But, the one thing I do know is that
you want me to know all the truth, and to be able to comprehend it and to
put it into practice. Therefore, I realize I can depend on the work of the
Holy Spirit in my life to unravel any part I am not able to comprehend, and
to come into a place where I can be confident that I can "copycat" you.
Lord, there is so much to be said about those two words, "as" and "so."

In John 20:18, you said, *"As thou* (Father) *hast sent me* (Jesus) *into the*
world, even so have I sent them (you and me) *into the world."* Jesus was
sent into a dying world that needed a Savior, and He obeyed and did the
work of redemption. In a like manner, Jesus has sent me into a sin-sick
world to tell of that completed work of redemption. And just as earth is far
below heaven, so my ways and thoughts are also far below yours, but I can
depend on your ways and thoughts to bring me up higher to complete the
work. And for that, I want to thank you so much, it will be *all* of you and
none of self. Your higher thoughts and ways are the power to bring me up
higher also. In Jesus' name, Amen.

(Prayer is not just requesting, "Give me, give me," but it is also meditating on God's character and talking to God about that. Your spiritual growth is of great importance to God. He loves it when you "reason" with Him. That, too, is prayer.) I pray in Jesus Name, Amen.

SEPTEMBER 18th

Some years ago, I began to make a list of all the places where "as" and "so" were found in the Bible. I have such a long list now that I have lost count, but I would like to share just a few of them with you to give you an idea of how much they teach us about God.

Joshua 1:5 reads, *"There shall not any man be able to stand before thee all the days of thy life: as I was with Moses, so I will be with thee: I will not fail thee, nor forsake thee."* Here God is encouraging Joshua to lead the people into the promise land after Moses had died. God's promise in this verse is a huge one! No man on earth will be *able* to withstand Joshua as he leads the people into the land that was promised to the children of Israel way back in the days of Abraham, when God told Abraham that He would give him a land, a people, and a blessing.

Then God also promised Joshua that just *as* He was with Moses, *so* also He would be with him. Therefore, because of that as-so comparison, Joshua could be ever so confident that this would be a successful journey into the promise land.

Another as-so comparison can be found in Psalm 103:12, which states, *"As far as the east is from the west, so far hath He removed our transgressions from us."* When God takes away our sins, he takes it so far away that it cannot be found again—as far as the east is from the west. It cannot be taken away any farther than that, can it?

381

Now, if you have repented and confessed your sins, and asked God to forgive you, and you know in your heart of hearts that God has taken it away to a place where you cannot find it, then why would you allow Satan to bring it up before you again and again to torment you? Satan will try to convince you that it just might not be taken out of the way or forgiven. Why else would you remember it as though it happened yesterday?

Well, this is that test and temptation deal all over again. God will use this to test whether you will depend on His Word that the sin once confessed is put as far away as the east is from the west away. Will you believe, or will you be tempted to doubt the Word of God? If you believe that the sin is taken away for good, then you will tell Satan to get behind you and to stop tormenting you with those doubts. Tell Satan to take it up with Jesus, whose blood has already cleansed you and set you free from the curse and penalty of sin.

We are to believe God, the tester, and take authority over Satan, the tempter. We need to learn to distinguish between the two and exercise our legal rights. Everything that needs to be done to ensure our victory in this life has been done, and God is just waiting for us to take our position. On whose side are you willing to stand? Those two little words, "as" and "so," ask us that over and over again.

PRAYER: Dear Lord God, here I sit with so much information that I hardly know how to handle it all. Give me the grace to believe it is alright for me to take such authority over Satan and not be an offense to you. I think my problem is being able to rely on your finished work on the cross, to the extent that I now have authority in my hand to confront Satan. I need to be confident in that finished work that was done on my behalf. Help me, Lord, to put all this into practice. In Jesus' name, Amen.

SEPTEMBER 19th

There is a group of scriptures in Romans 5 that I believe we need to examine carefully in regard to those two words, "as" and "so." I hope it will open up a whole new realm of truth for you.

Romans 5:12 reads, *"Wherefore, as by one man sin entered into the world, and death by sin: and so death passed upon all men, for that all have sinned."* Here we see clearly what the dilemma is and how it happened; one man sinned, death entered the world, sin passed to all men, and, therefore, death passed to all men. "As" through one man sin entered the human race, "so" death also entered and has passed onto all mankind.

Then, in Romans 5:13-15, we read:
> *"For until the law, sin was in the world: but sin is not imputed when there is no law. Nevertheless death reigned from Adam to Moses* (through whom the law came into the world), *even over them that had not sinned after the similitude of Adam's transgression, who is the figure of Him that was to come. But not as the offense, so also is the free gift. For if through the offense of one many be dead, much more the grace of God, and the gift by grace, which is by one man, Jesus Christ, hath abounded unto many."*

So, before the law was given (at the time of Moses), sin could not be measured or imputed (registered to one's account, so to speak), but death, which was the result of sin, was at work in the human race anyway. The rest of mankind did not sin in the same way Adam had, who had had a direct command from God that he disobeyed. But death still reigned, nevertheless. Adam, was a picture of the One to come, Jesus, who would set in motion a new pattern to make things right again.

The CEV translates Romans 5:13-15 as:

383

"Sin was in the world before the Law came. But no record of sin was kept, because there was no Law. Yet death still had power over all who lived from the time of Adam to the time of Moses. This happened, though not everyone disobeyed a direct command from God, as Adam did. In some ways, Adam is like Christ who came later. But the gift that God was kind enough to give was very different from Adam's sin. That one sin brought death to many others. Yet in an even greater way, Jesus Christ alone brought God's gift of kindness to many people."

I have mentioned before that God plays by the rules. He is a legal God, with a universe run on a legal system, and has rules to which He will hold Himself responsible. This can work both ways: for His advantage and also for His disadvantage. When we obey Him, it will all work to His advantage and ours, but when we disobey Him, it will work for both His and our disadvantage.

Remember, God cannot wink at sin. When we sin, there is a consequence to suffer. He will help us through the resulting consequence. He will not forsake us, but we must still go through the result. However, if sin can enter the universe through *one* man, why cannot *grace* enter by *one* man, namely Jesus? We will look at that "as" and "so" comparison tomorrow.

PRAYER: Heavenly Father, it is so comforting to realize that you have been able and willing to have a plan in which we sinners can come into your presence and be cleansed and accepted by you. It is also comforting to know that you love us so much that you were willing to sacrifice your Son, Jesus Christ, so that we could come into your presence as white as snow. I pray that all people may come to know and understand this marvelous plan of salvation of yours. I want to be a part of your work force to bring that message to those who want and need to know it. In Jesus' name, Amen.

SEPTEMBER 20th

Today we will continue with Romans 5:16-18, which reads:
"And not <u>as</u> it was by one that sinned, <u>so</u> is the gift: for the judgment was by one to condemnation, but the free gift is of many offenses unto justification. For if by one man's offense death reigned by one; much more they which receive abundance of grace and of the gift of righteousness shall reign in life by one, Jesus Christ. Therefore <u>as</u> by the offense of one (through one trespass) *judgment came upon all men to condemnation; even <u>so</u> by the righteousness of one* (through one act of righteousness) *the free gift came upon all men unto justification of life."*

And the CEV translates these verses as:
"There is a lot of difference between Adam's sin and God's gift. That one sin led to punishment. But God's gift made it possible for us to be acceptable to him, even though we have sinned many times. Death ruled like a king because Adam had sinned. But that cannot compare with what Jesus Christ has done. God has been so kind to us, and he has accepted us because of Jesus. And so we will live and rule like kings. Everyone was going to be punished because Adam sinned. But because of the good thing that Christ has done, God accepts us and gives us the gift of life."

You do not see the play on the words "as" and "so" in the CEV translation, but I think it helps to see the comparison somewhat better. However, I see the legal aspect in the King James translation. If Satan can bring sin and death to the whole human race, then why cannot God bring righteousness to the human race by the righteous act of One?

You see, Satan is watching God's legal actions like an eagle, trying to find a loophole through which he can escape the Lake of Fire judgment. That is why Satan tries so hard to get us to disobey God, so that he can have a legal right to occupy our hearts and drag us further into disobedience. God has made it legally acceptable for us to come into His presence, fully forgiven, and cleansed from all unrighteousness. He has given us the power of the Holy Spirit to live a life of victory over sin, death, and the power of the devil. Isn't that the best news yet? And it is all a free gift!

PRAYER: Heavenly Father, thank you for giving me the power to overcome, to live a life of victory over sin and the world around me. Help me to see Satan's snares and traps in which he is always trying to catch me. Give me the Spirit of Wisdom to make wise use of what I know and understand, so that I can be a reflection of your wisdom. I also want to be a reflection of your grace, mercy, and love. Fill me with your Spirit, Lord. In Jesus' name, Amen.

SEPTEMBER 21st

Today, we will look at Romans 5:19-21, which reads:
"For as by one man's disobedience many were made sinners, so by the obedience of one shall many be made righteous. Moreover the law entered, that the offense might abound. But where sin abounded, grace did much more abound: That as sin hath reigned unto death, even so might grace reign through righteousness unto eternal life by Jesus Christ our Lord."

The CEV translation reads:
"Adam disobeyed God and caused many others to be sinners. But Jesus obeyed Him and will make many people acceptable to God. The Law came, so that the full power of sin could be seen. Yet where sin was powerful, God's kindness was even more powerful. Sin ruled by means of death. But God's kindness now rules, and God has accepted us because of Jesus Christ our Lord. This means that we will have eternal life."

In the CEV translation, the word "ruled" emphasizes the legal implications found in "as" and "so." Sin ruled by means of death, but now God's kindness rules. Do you see the legal tone here? Jesus loves, but Satan hates. Jesus is kind, patient, and trustworthy. Satan is dirty, hateful, impatient, and not to be trusted, ever.

Light will always rule over darkness. Wherever there is light, darkness has to flee. Just *as* light will dispel darkness, *so* also will love overcome hate.

Proverbs 16:7 comes to mind, states, *"When a man's ways please the Lord, He maketh even his enemies to be at peace with him."* Do you see how love will overcome hate? God's kindness, spread abroad in your heart, will even drive out the hate in other people's hearts toward you. Just *as* gravity is a Law, and we obey it constantly, *so* also is there a royal law called *love*. When that law is obeyed, it conquers enemies, as we see in James 2:8, which reads, *"If ye fulfill the royal law according to the Scripture, 'Thou shalt love thy neighbor as thyself,' ye do well".*

PRAYER: Heavenly Father, I believe I am coming closer to your pattern of an overcoming Christian. It is not a bunch of magic. It is a well-ordered plan, all spelled out, step by step, in Scripture. It is not hard to follow or understand. You have given me everything I need to claim it as my own and the power to follow it. I pray that I will be diligent to read your Word daily and keep in touch with you through that Word, so that I will not drift away like a leaf in a river, drawn away by the current's flow. Help me to keep my focus on you, my priorities in order, and my thoughts and imaginations under your control. Help me, too, to give my time to you to control. In Jesus' name, Amen.

SEPTEMBER 22nd

Today, I want to comment some more on the reference from yesterday, so read it again to refresh your memory.

Where there is no law, no one can be found guilty of breaking the law. If you see no sign that tells you what the speed limit is, you can hardly be charged with speeding, now can you? In Romans 5:19-21, God is debating on this level.

Although no one could be charged with sinning before the law, the result of sin, which is death, still ruled. So then, death became a law of sin, even when sins were not written down. But, God did introduce the law into the human race and *then* sin abounded.

The Ten Commandments spelled out what God wanted and did not want, just like a sign posting the speed limit along the highway. Since the law came, sin could be recorded, but because God is a God of love, His grace abounded much more after the law was introduced. It was through grace that God sent His Son to be the sacrifice (pay the penalty) for sin, so that righteousness could rule.

You can almost see this whole section of Romans being presented as a court case to prove a legal point. God is right and He *is* righteousness. There is no evil intent in the heart of God at all. This world will be judged in righteousness. You and I can not claim any righteousness in ourselves, because our righteousness is in Christ Jesus. When we are in Him, covered by His blood, then we are seen through God's eyes as righteous. God sees Jesus' red blood *before* he sees our red sins, and, as you will remember from earlier in the year, the color red will wipe out the color red and make it white.

I hope this exploration on the "as" and "so" references in the Word of God has been a blessing to you, as it was to me when I first saw the truth of it. There are many more such references in the Bible. Be sure to stop and ponder them when you come across them. Ask God to reveal the truth of the verses to you and He will be happy to do that.

PRAYER: Heavenly Father, my cup runneth over! I thank you for being so generous in your love, mercy, and grace. I also thank you for your patience, long-suffering, and kindness. I know I don't deserve any of this, but you have given it to me just because you have showered your love on me. It is wonderful to know that you have chosen each one of us as your own, given us your name, and appointed us a position in your kingdom's work. I pray that I may daily walk to your drum beat, keep in tune with your hymn for the day, and have a song in my heart all day long. In Jesus' name, Amen.

SEPTEMBER 23rd

I would like to expand on the phrase "much more" we saw in yesterday's scripture. Paul used that phrase in much of his Epistles. I believe it would be wise for us to examine a few of them.

Look at Romans 5:8-10, which reads:
> *"But God commandeth His love toward us, in that, while we were yet sinners, Christ died for us. Much more then, being now justified by His blood, we shall be saved from wrath through Him. For If, when we were enemies, we were reconciled to God by the death of His Son, much more, being reconciled, we shall be saved by His life."*

Paul is trying to make the point that now, since Jesus came and did the work God had assigned for Him to do, we have *much more* of everything spiritual. Look at the first part of the scripture for today, *"God commanded His love."*
Think about that. God told His love to obey Him *"while we were yet sinners."*

God did not ask us to clean ourselves up first and wait for that before He would give a sacrifice for our sin. No, indeed. Instead, God rescued us from the grip of sin through His Son Jesus Christ *"while we were yet sinners, Christ died for us."*

That is the big picture of God's grace. Then Paul slips in that *much more* phrase! Could there be much more than what has already been said? But just look at what is being said, *"Much more then, being now justified by His blood, we shall be saved from wrath through Him."* Through Jesus' death, we were justified before God. But, since it was through Jesus' shed blood that we were justified, we are also saved from the wrath of God over sin. God has a constant wrath for sin, and since He has done everything possible to rescue us from Satan's hold, He cannot do anymore than He has already done for us. All we have to do is to accept His free gift of salvation, which is through Jesus (His sacrificial Son, the Lamb of God). To refuse that gift is to call the wrath of God down on ourselves.

No wonder Paul can say, *"Much more then, being <u>now</u> justified by His blood, we shall be saved from wrath through Him."* You can see by the "shall be" that this is a future event. There will be a day when God's wrath over sin will be poured out over disobedient mankind. No one wants to think about that, but it is a fixed day in the future.

Concerning the wrath of God, let's look at I Thessalonians 5: 9-10, which states:

> *"For God hath <u>not</u> appointed us* (meaning those of us reading this scripture, believe in Jesus and have accepted Him into our hearts) *to wrath, but to obtain salvation by our Lord Jesus Christ. Who died for us, that, whether we be living or dead, we should live together with Him."*

We will not be subject to that wrath, simply because the blood of Jesus has saved us from that judgment.

PRAYER: Heavenly Father, how grateful I am that I live in the "much more" era and am saved from the wrath of God toward sin. Thank you,

Father, for having such a foolproof plan. And thank you, Jesus, who obeyed the Father and did the necessary work to secure my salvation. And thank you, Holy Spirit, for ministering that whole truth to my mind and spirit. I am blessed, and blessed again, by such good news. In Jesus' name, Amen.

SEPTEMBER 24th

Today we will look at the last half of the verses we quoted yesterday. Romans 5:10 states, *"For if, when we were enemies, we were reconciled to God by the death of His Son, MUCH MORE, being reconciled, we shall be saved by His life."* Jesus did not only die for us, He also was raised for us. This also brought about a benefit to the body of believers, the Church. That is what this "much more' is referring to here.

"While we were yet sinners" and *"when we were enemies"* are addressing the same time. They refer to the period before Christ entered our lives. After Christ has entered our lives, we were *justified* and *reconciled* to God. To be justified suggested that God's justice system was satisfied. To be reconciled suggests we enter into agreement with God, as if a broken relationship has been mended.

God did it all. He planned and carried out the justice through the blood of Christ, and God raised Jesus from the dead to give us a new life like Jesus', and the broken relationship between God and mankind was then mended. For example, imagine you have committed a crime are in court, to settle the situation with a judge. What chance do you have? But someone steps in and pays the whole penalty for your wrongdoing. The judge is then justified in not giving you a penalty to pay.

But, let's say the judge is still not very friendly with you, and this is a sore on your heart. You are a great friend with his son, so the son steps in and pleads your case to the judge, and the relationship is also restored between you two. This may not be the best example, but should give you an idea of what reconciliation means.

Webster's dictionary defines reconciliation as to "return to harmony, make compatible, settle amicably, make acquiescent." I believe the statement, *"We shall be saved by His life,"* refers to our daily life here on earth. Our life in Christ is a brand new life with God, other people, and within ourselves. This new life is the result of the resurrected life of Jesus Christ. He gave us His new life so we can live a victorious life here on earth.

The greatest reconciliation in the world is the one made between God and mankind, and again, God made that all possible! Every other reconciliation is also possible because of the one made between God and mankind. The resurrected Jesus Christ is the one who lives within you, and that is what makes reconciliation possible at all.

PRAYER: Heavenly Father, I do not cease to be amazed at all you have done and keep on doing to make it possible for us to live a life of victory. I thank you from the bottom of my heart for all you have done for me. Help me to appropriate these blessings in my life, and to share what I know with those around me. In Jesus' name, Amen.

SEPTEMBER 25th

Romans 5:14-15 reads:
"Nevertheless death reigned from Adam to Moses, even over them that had not sinned after the similitude of Adam's transgression, who is the figure of Him that was to come. But not as the offense, so also is the free gift. For if through the offense of one many be dead, MUCH MORE the grace of God, and the gift by grace, which is by one man, Jesus Christ, hath abounded unto many."

392

The as-so comparison is overshadowed by the comparison of "much more." The grace that was brought to mankind is *much more* powerful than the offense that sin brought on mankind. I believe these verses are saying that grace is much more powerful, influential, and carries greater strength than the death that sin brought into the world.

Think about how grace lays hold of our lives the moment we have turned our lives over to Jesus. In fact, it was at work on our behalf even before we turn our attention toward God. But, with Christ in our hearts, it works in and through us every day and night.

Fear of death will cripple our lives, but we die only once, grace will attend us at the time of death. I have had to face death three times in my life, and I was amazed at how "at peace" I was. There was no fear. You *know* that it is a supernatural, God-given peace reserved for such a time as that in your life. That is God's grace at work in the life of the believer, and it is much more powerful than death.

PRAYER: Heavenly Father, I am so grateful for your abundant grace shed upon us so generously. I know you want us to reflect that grace in our lives, so others can see you through those of us who believe in you. How can you attempt to display that grace through you sinful children? We fall so short of what your grace is all about. Yet, you want us to join hands with you in your effort to get this good news out to every ear that will listen, and that can only be done by your grace. Thank you, Father, for even considering it worthwhile to use someone like me to be the carrier of your grace to the world. Let me not disappoint you. In Jesus' precious name, Amen.

SEPTEMBER 26th

There are some interesting things we need to look at in Hebrews. We begin in chapter 8:6, which says: *"But now hath He obtained a more excellent ministry, by how much also He is the mediator*

393

of a __better__ covenant, which was established upon __better__ promises." The old covenant is the Old Testament, which pointed, like an arrow, to Jesus as the promised Messiah. The "better covenant" is the New Testament, which tells in the Gospels all about the Messiah and the covenant that now exists because of Him. The promises that go with that new covenant are also better than the promises in the old covenant.

The Epistles in the New Testament help us to understand what this new covenant is all about, how it has affected our lives, and what it can do for us if we will only obey it. Jesus turned the Jewish world upside down. Many misunderstood God's love for His creation and what He was willing to do to restore His creation to its original design.

God wants us to be a part of the solution, instead of being a part of the problem. This had escaped the minds of the people of God in the Old Testament. The writer of Hebrews wants his readers to see that after Jesus came, things were so much better.

We, too, should move steadily toward a better life in Christ. God is a God of progression. A pool that has no inlet or outlet will have stagnant water in it. When God's Word is taken into our hearts, it is to move through us—not be bottled up. That would be like Christ's parable about the man who buried his treasure so that he can present it back to the investor when he comes for an accounting. It had gained no interest (had been stagnant), and that man was punished rather than blessed. His portion was taken away from him and given to another. Do not let that happen to you. Be willing to share with others what God has taught you. Then you will become a part of the solution rather than a part of the problem.

I must remind you that there are steps in this process. First, you need to tell God that you are willing to share. Then, when God presents an open door (for example, someone asks you why you have such a hope in you, or why Jesus is so precious to you), you can share your faith with them and know that it is a divine appointment set up by God. If that person does not seem to accept what you are saying, don't be upset. You planted seeds, and it takes time for seeds to germinate. Some day, perhaps years later, that same person may tell you that what you said made all the difference in the world. I have had that happen many times.

PRAYER: Heavenly Father, I do want to be a part of the solution rather than a part of the problem, so help me to hear you loud and clear. Then I will know it is you who is nudging me to share what I know with others. I am also very thankful for the new and better covenant that we have the privilege to live under, which also carries better promises, such as eternal life and fellowship with God the Father, Son, and Holy Spirit. In Jesus' name, Amen.

SEPTEMBER 27th

Today we will explore the idea of a *better hope*. Hebrew 7:19 reads, *"For the law made nothing perfect, but the bringing in of a better hope did; by the which we draw nigh unto God."* The law was the first covenant. God gave it to Moses, who then gave it to the people.

What did the law accomplish? Before we look at that, let's think about what the law did not accomplish. It could not take away sin, but only expose sin. God provided a way to cover each particular sin in the form of a sacrifice. People would bring the blood of certain prescribed animals to cover that singular sin. But, shortly after presenting that sacrifice, they would have already broken another part of the law. So, you see, they were constantly condemned.

Jesus, on the other hand, carried our sins away by His holy blood. His sacrifice was once and for all—for all who accept Jesus as their Lord and Savior. He was God's sacrifice for you, because God knew there was no other way to make you completely free from the curse of sin, which is death. God's Sacrifice made you perfect in God's eyes. If you are *in* Christ, and Christ is *in* you, then you are constantly covered by Christ's blood, and God sees you as perfect.

Now, let's turn back to the word "hope" in this verse. When we say that we hope, it usually means we wish for something, such as "I hope the sun shines tomorrow." That is not what the word "hope" means in the Bible. In the Bible, hope is a *sure thing*, and it is laid up in heaven for us where it is safe.

Jesus is our sure hope. And that is a *better hope*. Because of that hope, we can draw close to God. The way is paved for us to go directly to God with our dreams, concerns, and disappointments—our everything. Pray that the blinders will be taken off the eyes of the people of Israel that they may see this truth and know Jesus as their personal Savior.

Let me remind you of Romans 11:25, which reads:
> *"For I would not, brethren, that ye should be ignorant of this mystery, lest ye should be wise in your own conceits; that blindness* (a hardening) *in part is happened to* (Hath befallen) *Israel, until the fullness of the Gentiles be come in."*

We are to pray that blinders be taken off the eyes of the people of Israel so they can see (understand) the truth that Jesus is the Messiah they are looking for. I also want you to notice one important word in this verse, "until," which indicates a time limit. We are living in the time when God is gathering a bride for His Son, and she is being gathered out of the gentile nations. When that time in finished, the blinders will be taken off the eyes of the people of Israel. However, there are many Jews today who are beginning to see the truth, and have accepted Jesus as their Savior. That trend is growing and that makes me believe that the day is drawing close when the time of the gentiles will be complete.

PRAYER: Heavenly Father, I am so grateful to Jesus who has brought in a better hope, so we can now draw close to you and have fellowship with you. It is my prayer that none of us who go by the name Christian will neglect such a privilege to fellowship with you. I realize, too, that Satan does not want us to come close to you, and that he will put barriers in the way to take up our time so that we neglect our time of prayer. Help us to make it a priority each day. In Jesus' precious name, Amen.

SEPTEMBER 28th

Hebrew 10:34 states:
"For ye had compassion of me in my bonds (he was in jail),
and took joyfully the spoiling of your goods (possessions),
*knowing in yourselves that ye have in heaven a <u>better</u> and an
enduring substance* (a better possession and an abiding one)."

The possessions we have here on earth cannot hold a candle to the possessions that await us in heaven. Remember what Jesus said about our treasures? Matthew 6:19-20 reads:
*"Lay not up for yourselves treasures upon earth, where moth and
rust doth corrupt, and where thieves break through and steal:
But lay up for yourselves treasures in heaven where neither moth
nor rust doth corrupt, and where thieves do not break through
nor steal."*

The only safe place for our treasures is in heaven. Also see Matthew 6:21, which says, *"For where your treasure is, there will be your heart also."*

We also find a warning to those who store up goods for themselves and plan to lay back and take it easy. Luke 12:20-21 reads:
*"But God said unto him, 'Thou fool, this night thy soul shall be
required of thee: then whose shall those things be, which thou*

397

hast provided?' So is he that layeth up treasures for himself, and is not rich toward God."

There is nothing wrong in becoming rich. That is a blessing from God. But if those riches were gained by leaving God out of the equation, or if, after you have become rich, you forget about the God who blessed you, then you are in big trouble.

Notice that the scripture above address those who are *"not rich toward God."* You see, Satan is only too glad to make us lose sight of God in our lives, and riches are often a tool in Satan's hands to do that very thing. Keep a close watch on that tactic in your life.

PRAYER: Dear Heavenly Father, every time I hear a lesson on this very thing, I have more insight into just what is going on. I can see so easily how riches can come between me and you. The more one possesses, the more there is to tend to and take up one's time, which should also belong to God. The more money one has available, the more one can travel and neglect going to church or even supporting the church, and the less you are able to be an active member of a church which will put us on the shelf as a growing Christian. Thank you, Lord, for this lesson, and help me to be sensitive to what riches can do in my life. I may not feel that I am rich right now, but there are others in this world who have far less than I do and would call me rich in their eyes. So, those things that can happen when one is rich can also happen to me right now. I put my trust in you to help me never fall into those traps of Satan. In Jesus' name, Amen.

SEPTEMBER 29th

Hebrews 1:4-6 reads:
"Being made so much <u>better</u> than the angels, as He hath by inheritance obtained a more excellent name than they. For unto which of the angels said He (God) *at any time, 'Thou art*

my Son, this day have I begotten thee'? And again, 'I will be to Him a Father, and He shall be to me a Son'? And again, when He bringeth the first begotten into the world, He saith, 'And let all the angels of God worship Him.'"

And Hebrews 1:13 asks, *"But to which of the angels said He at any time, 'Sit on my right hand, until I make thine enemies thy footstool'?"*

In order to see this in all its beauty, you also need to look at Hebrews 2:7-9, which states:

"Thou madest Him a little lower than the angels; thou crownedst Him with glory and honor, and didst set Him (Jesus) *over the works of thy* (God's) *hands: Thou hast put all things in subjection under His* (Jesus') *feet. For in that He* (God) *put all in subjection under Him* (Jesus), *He left nothing that is not put under Him. But now we see not yet all things put under Him. But we see Jesus, who was made a little lower than the angels for the suffering of death, crowned with glory and honor; that He by the grace of God should taste death for every man."*

Angels are a higher creation than mankind. Just as other animals are a lower creation than mankind, so also is mankind lower than the angels. God did not send an angel to earth to be a savior for mankind. He sent a Man to be the perfect mediator between God and mankind. Mankind was the crowning glory of God's creation, and mankind was put in charge of the rest of creation on earth.

Not only that, but none of the angels can claim God as their Father like Jesus can, or like we can because of Jesus. Jesus taught us to pray, *"Our Father* who art in heaven ..." We were immediately included in that privilege to call God our Father, according to Jesus. Is it any wonder that the writer of Hebrews could say that Jesus was *"made so much **better** than the angels, as He hath by inheritance obtained a more excellent name*

399

than they"? He inherited His Father's name, and could be called the Son of God.

To get a glimpse of what we are because of who Jesus is, look at John 1:12, which reads, *"But as many as received Him to them* (that's us) *gave He* (God) *power* (the right) *to become the sons of God, even to them that* *believe on His* (Jesus') *name."* There is a "trickle down" effect. When we are in Christ, all that *Jesus is* becomes *who we are* as well. No wonder Jesus is so much better than the angels.

I know we have addressed some of this before, but I am compelled to emphasize here that Jesus, despite being created lower than the angels, defeated one of the chief archangels, Satan himself. Can you imagine the blow that had to be to Satan? And because of that, Jesus also gave us the power to take authority over Satan and his kingdom. What a blow to the whole Satanic system. Is it any wonder Satan is so furious with the Christian community, especially those who have bothered to learn who they really are in Christ, "more than conquerors"?

I Corinthians 6:3 reads, *"Know ye not that we* (Christians) *shall judge angels? How much more things that pertain to this life."* Here you have another "much more" phrase. But which angels will we judge? I believe it will be the fallen angels who rebelled against God, and Satan is the chief one. Is it any wonder he wants you to go with him to hell, so you won't be among those who will judge him one day? All this we learn because we saw in Hebrews 1:4 that Jesus was made <u>better</u> than the angels!

PRAYER: Heavenly Father, it just amazes me how intricately this Bible is put together, and how truths are so evident, and yet so hidden, from the casual reader. I am so thankful, too, that you have seen fit to open my eyes to see your truths all over the pages of this wonderful Book. Help me to be an "overcomer" in my everyday life. It must give you great joy to see your people take what they know and put it into practice and see them come out victorious. I am grateful to the Holy Spirit for helping me see the truths of your Word. I want to keep my hand in yours every day of my life. It is the safest place I know. In Jesus' name, Amen.

SEPTEMBER 30th

Hebrews 11:40 states, *"God having provided some better thing for us, that they without us should not be made perfect."* In the CEV translation, Hebrews 11:39-40 reads:

"All of them pleased God because of their faith! But still they died without being given what had been promised. This was because God had something better in store for us. And He did not want them to reach the goal of their faith without us."

All of chapter 11, up to verse 40, is about the people in the Old Testament who had stood strong in their faith through thick and thin, from Abel to Noah, Abraham, Joseph, and Moses—all the way to the New Testament. In verse 40, where the writer is speaking of two groups of people, "us" refers to the believers since the beginning of the New Testament. And "they" refers to those who had lived before Christ (the promise) came, and had lived by faith in the coming of that promise and in the God of the promise.

What we are to look at is that *"God had provided some better thing for us."* Jesus is that better thing. The people who had lived by faith in the Old Testament did not have what we have. They had only the promise in God's Word, yet they stood strong in their faith. Think of the faith of Noah. He built an Ark on dry ground, believing what God told him, that one day, 120 years from then, He would send a flood to destroy the whole creation on the earth, all life. How long would your faith last on such a project? Oh, yes, God had sent a better thing. In fact, it was His best thing.

PRAYER: Heavenly Father, you sent your best to earth, to complete a task no one else could. And what do we do with that gift? I remember back when I did not think I was good enough to receive such a gift, or that you wanted me to have that gift. Forgive me, Lord, for having such a warped view of who you are and who I am, or who I could be. Thank you, Father, for bringing your word to me in such an understandable way that even I could grasp the truth, and yearn to own it as my own. Even that desire was created in my heart by you, for which I am also grateful. Help me spread this good news to others, just as others gave it to me when I needed it. In Jesus' name, Amen.

OCTOBER 1ˢᵗ

In Hebrews 12:24, we read, *"And to Jesus the mediator of the new covenant, and to the blood of sprinkling, that speaketh better things than that of Abel."* The CEV version translates this verse as, *"And Jesus is here! He is the one who makes God's new agreement with us, and His sprinkled blood says much better things than the blood of Abel."*

In the Old Testament, blood was sprinkled on various pieces of furniture in the Tabernacle and on the garments of the High Priests. I believe the sprinkled blood spoken of in this verse is referring to that practice which was given to them by God when He gave Moses the directions for building the Tabernacle in the first place.

When we look at the blood that Jesus shed, it was scattered from Jerusalem to Golgotha (Calvary). Let me walk you through the way His blood was shed. They beat His back with 39 whip lashings and then put a crown of thorns on His head. Then they put a spike through both of His feet and both hands. Finally, they put a spear into His side. That makes seven places on His body from which His blood flowed and sprinkled on the ground. His was holy blood, and it has cried out to God ever since.

Look at Genesis 4:3-11. In Genesis 4, we see that after Adam and Eve sinned against God by eating the forbidden fruit, they had two sons, Cain and Abel. Cain is the first to bring an offering to the Lord. Genesis 4:3-11 reads:

"In the process of time it came to pass that Cain brought of the fruit of the ground an offering unto the Lord. And Abel, he also brought of the firstlings of his flock and of the fat thereof. And the Lord had respect unto Abel and to his offering. But unto Cain, and to his offering he had not respect. And Cain was very wroth, and his countenance fell. And the Lord said unto Cain. 'Why art thou wroth (angry)*? And why is thy countenance fallen? If thou doest well, shalt thou not be accepted? And if thou does not well, sin lieth at the door. And unto thee shall be his desire, and thou shalt rule over him.' And Cain talked with Abel his brother: and it came to pass, when they were in the field, that Cain rose up against Abel his brother, and slew* (killed) *him. And the Lord said unto Cain, 'Where is Abel thy brother?' And he said, 'I know not: Am I my brother's keeper?' And He said, 'What hast thou done? The voice of thy brother's blood crieth unto me from the ground. And now art thou cursed from the earth, which hath opened her mouth to receive thy brother's blood from thy hand.' "*

Please notice the questions that God asked Cain. Why would God ask those questions, since He already knew the answers to them? Also, notice the question Cain asked God! The thing we need to see here, as it refers to the reference in Hebrews, is the fact that Abel's blood cries out to God from the ground. I believe that Jesus' blood speaks to God from the ground also, but it speaks of redemption, rather than revenge.

Cain had sinned a great sin, and brought about the first death in the Bible, which was a result of the sin of his parents. They found out that, sure as anything, there is such a thing as *death*. Who do you supposed purposed in Cain's heart to kill Abel? Satan, of course, and he has been up to *no good* ever since.

Jesus' blood does speak of better things than that of Abel's. His blood speaks of redemption to the "who-so-evers" of the world. Is Jesus' blood a better thing to you? Have you applied it to your life? All you need to do is ask God to forgive you all your sins, and decide to live a new life that will reflect God's love, mercy, and grace. Then ask Jesus to come and live in your heart. You will never be sorry you did that. God is able to give you a brand new life with a taste of victory and freedom you can only imagine. You will find that out for real if you ask Jesus to come into your heart.

PRAYER: Heavenly Father, can you really make a new creation out of a person like me? It just seems too easy. I realize there is no other way to have peace on this earth, or to avoid being a defeated, tired-out warrior day after day. I will choose to do it your way and say, "Come into my heart, Lord Jesus. Come in today. Come in to stay. Come into my heart, Lord Jesus." Amen.

OCTOBER 2nd

Today, we will look at why Cain's offering was rejected. Hebrews 11:4 reads: *"By faith, Abel offered unto God a more excellent sacrifice than Cain by which he obtained witness that he was righteous, God testifying of his gifts: and by it, he being dead yet speaketh."*

The CEV version translates this verse as: *"Because Abel had faith, he offered God a better sacrifice than Cain did. God was pleased with him and his gift, and even though Abel is now dead, his faith still speaks for him."*

What was wrong with Cain's offering? For one thing, since the ground had been cursed after the fall of man, it was like an insult for Cain to bring Him an offering from the ground. I also believe that since God had to kill an animal to get skins to cover Adam and Eve's sin and nakedness, it should have been an indication for them of what kind of sacrifice God needed in order to be acceptable. Cain brought an offering, Able brought a sacrifice.

Why would Abel know that and not Cain? Satan was at work in every way possible to wipe out God's small family, or to make it so sin-sick that it would be worthless to God. (That finally did happen, and God sent a flood to cleanse the earth with only Noah and his family, a total of eight people, being saved. You can read about that in Genesis 6-8.)

Cain, to me, is a picture of those who want to live a life pleasing to *themselves*, and when they have to reap what they have sown they don't like it. They will blame God for the trouble they are in and not see that they had something to do with it. Isn't that the way Cain acted? Learn a lesson from Cain.

PRAYER: Heavenly Father, I look at Cain and wonder if I would have had the wisdom to have brought the right sacrifice. I think that just maybe the key to the knowledge here is in that word *sacrifice*. I see it was called an offering in Genesis. It is called a sacrifice in Hebrews. Just maybe it was a matter of the heart's attitude. Was it an offering to Cain and a sacrifice to Abel? There really is no sacrifice to bringing produce from the ground as there is to bringing a lamb or other animal that had to give up its life, blood, and maybe even its coat, as was the case of the animal whose skin was made a covering for the sinful nakedness of Adam and Eve. Lord God, it is good for me to search your Word for an insight into your way of working in the life of us human beings. Thank you for showing me the truth of today's scripture. In Jesus' name, Amen.

OCTOBER 3rd

As long as we are in Hebrews, it might be interesting to look at a few other verses from that book. The list of names of the faithful in Hebrews 11 is an awesome lot. But there is an interesting thing about that list. There are three people who were listed but who are not in that elite group. The first one is Cain, who we already addressed. Today we will look at Esau's story.

Hebrews 11:20 reads, *"By faith, Isaac blessed Jacob and Esau concerning things to come."* We will need some background on this in order to understand what is happening. The "blessing" that God promised

405

to Abraham was passed on to Isaac, his son. Then Isaac and his wife Rebekah had twins.

Let's look at what God had to say about the blessing when Rebekah was pregnant with the twins. Genesis 25:22-23 states: *"And the children struggled together within her; and she said, 'If it be so, why am I thus?' And she went to enquire of the Lord. And the Lord said unto her, 'Two nations are in thy womb, and two manner of people shall be separated from thy bowels; and the one people shall be stronger than the other people; and the elder shall serve the younger.' "*

It was not common for the older to serve the younger, but in this case God had declared it to be so. Now look at Genesis 11:24-28, which reads:

"And when her days to be delivered were fulfilled, behold there were twins in her womb. And the first came out red all over, like an hairy garment; and they called his name Esau . And after that came his brother out, and his hand took hold on Esau's heel; and his name was called Jacob: and Isaac was 60 years old when she bare them. And the boys grew: and Esau was a cunning hunter, a man of the field; and Jacob was a plain man, dwelling in tents. And Isaac loved Esau, because he did eat of his venison; but Rebekah loved Jacob."

So, here we see that Esau was the first born, the elder one, and it was determined by God that he would serve his brother Jacob. The name "Jacob" means, "cheat, supplanter, swindler." God had told Rebekah that the older shall serve the younger, but God had not told Isaac. Keep that in mind. I believe that Rebekah had shared that knowledge with Jacob, however.

The boys grew up, each being the favorite of one parent, which is not a good situation. On top of that, Esau did not cherish the blessing that goes with being the eldest son, and Jacob wanted it. So, when an opportunity came for Jacob to persuade Esau to give him the blessing, Jacob took full advantage of that situation. Genesis 25:29-34 explains: *"And Jacob sod* (was boiling) *pottage* (stew)*: and Esau came from the field, and he was faint: And Esau said to Jacob, 'Feed me, I pray thee, with that same red stew; for I am faint;' therefore was his name called*

Edom (meaning red). And Jacob said, 'Sell me this day thy birthright.'
And Esau said, 'Behold, I am at the point to die: and what profit shall
this birthright do to me?' And Jacob said, 'Swear to me this day,' and he
sware unto him: and he sold his birthright unto Jacob. Then Jacob gave
Esau bread and stew of lentiles; and he did eat and drink, and rose up,
and went his way: thus Esau despised his birthright."

Later, when Isaac was an old man and sick in bed, he wanted to
give Esau "the blessing" that was customary for the men of that day to pass
onto their firstborn. Rebekah heard Isaac tell Esau to bring him venison,
which he loved, and that he would then give him the blessing. Rebekah and
Jacob schemed to have Jacob stand in for Esau, and since Isaac could no
long see well enough to know that it was not Esau, Rebekah felt they could
pull it off. That is how Jacob stole the blessing from Esau. You can read
about it in Genesis 27.

Rebekah did not want Jacob to be married into the wrong family as
Esau had done, so, in Genesis 28, Isaac also gives Jacob a blessing to go off
to where Rebekah was from to find a wife. When Esau found out that his
father had given the real blessing to Jacob, he also asked for just a little
blessing. Those two blessings are referred to in the Hebrews 11:20 at the
beginning of today's devotion. Read it again, and then we will look at
those blessings some more tomorrow.

PRAYER: Heavenly Father, we can come to you for a blessing, can we
not? You desire to bless us abundantly. Open my eyes to see the blessings
you shower upon me every day. You have said that we are the head and not
the tail, that we are more than conquerors, that we are not under the curse of
death, and that we have inherited eternal life. If those things are not
blessings, then I don't know what I should call them. You have also said
that our body is the temple of the Holy Spirit, and that we have the divine
nature of Christ Jesus. I need to stop and bask in the blessings that I have
been given, and turn around and thank you and send my humble gratitude
back to you as a blessing. Help me to also be a blessing to others around
me. Help me to see the opportunities that you place before me to do that. In
Jesus' name, Amen.

OCTOBER 4th

Today, we will finish addressing Isaac's blessing for Esau and Jacob. Jacob had tricked Isaac into thinking he was Esau. And no sooner had Jacob left his father after Isaac pronounced the blessing than Esau came to receive his blessing.

Then the whole scheme becomes evident then Esau cried bitterly for losing the blessing. Esau pleaded with his father for just some blessing in Genesis 27:38, which reads, *"And Esau said unto his father, 'Hast thou but one blessing, my Father? Bless me, even me also, O my father.' And Esau liften up his voice and wept."* So, Isaac gave a blessing to Esau. We learn of this blessing, and the hatred between Jacob and Esau in Genesis 27:39-41, which states: *"And Isaac his Father answered and said unto him, 'Behold thy dwelling shall be the fatness of the earth, and of the dew of heaven from above; And by the sword shalt thou live, and shalt serve thy brother; and it shall come to pass when thou shalt have the dominion* (will break lose)*, that thou shalt break his yoke from off thy neck.' And Esau hated Jacob because of the blessing wherewith his father blessed him: and Esau said in his heart, 'The days of mourning for my father are at hand; then will I slay my brother Jacob.' "*

Remember the blessing Isaac gave to Jacob, thinking it was Esau, is in Genesis 27:27-29: *"And he* (Jacob) *came near, and kissed him: and he* (Isaac) *smelled the smell of his raiment and blessed him, and said, 'See, the smell of my son is as the smell of the field which the Lord hath blessed: Therefore God give thee of the dew of heaven, and the fatness of the earth, and plenty of corn and wine: Let people serve thee, and nations bow down to thee: be lord over thy brethren, and let thy mother's sons bow down to thee; Cursed be every one that curseth thee, and blessed be he that blesseth thee.' "*

The part about the cursing and blessing is exactly what God had promised to Abraham, and you see that this blessing is passed on down to Jacob. This is that same Jacob that had twelve sons who made up the 12 tribes of Israel. I want to point out to you that Esau is the father of the Arab people and Jacob is the father of the twelve tribes of Israel.

Today we see those ancient hatreds still boiling in the Middle East. Satan has tried to destroy Israel many times, and he has tried to interfere with the coming of the Savior out of the Israeli lineage, but God's *directive will,* will be done, and no man can stop it. Notice also that they both were blessed with the "fat of the land." Many people believe that means the rich oil fields of that region. As yet Israel has not found any oil in the land they have, but I have read that people who study prophecy think that they will yet find oil on their land.

PRAYER: Heavenly Father, the Bible really tells it like it is. Such trickery that went on, and they tried to use their own schemes to get your will done! I wonder how often I have tried to do that also. Satan knows just how to use people for his own gain, and are we to be a match for him? I see just how much I need the help of the Holy Spirit to live a holy and virtuous life. Guide me daily so that I do not bring shame to your name. In Jesus' name, Amen.

OCTOBER 5th

Esau's name, like Cain's, was listed in that "faith" section of Hebrews 11. There is one more person in that chapter that stands out, and that is Pharaoh. Hebrews 11:24-25 reads: *"By faith, Moses, when he was come to years, refused to be called the son of Pharaoh's daughter: choosing rather to suffer affliction with the people of God, than to enjoy the pleasures of sin for a season."*

Pharaoh was against the people of God and would not let His people go a three days' journey into the wilderness to worship Him. Pharaoh wanted nothing to do with their God. He had his own gods. Yet the God of heaven and earth brought down defeat to all the gods of Egypt, and that battle is still going on today in the world.

Many years ago, I followed a study on these three people in Hebrews. Each one represents an element of evil in the world today. Cain represents the devil himself, who is out to kill and destroy anyone who

409

would put God first in his or her life. Esau represents our old nature, which only looks for instant gratification, and does not pay attention to the things of the eternal realm. Only after the eternal blessing was lost did he mourn for what could have and should have been.

And Pharaoh represents the world with all its evil around us, just waiting to slow us down, ensnare us, and keep us in bondage—just as the people of God were in Egypt for those many years. The world will try to lure us into its systems, just as the people of God would yearn for the "good life" back in Egypt when some hardship hit them in the wilderness. They would forget they had been in bondage there. They would yearn for the good food in Egypt, and complain to Moses that their suffering was all his fault. If these three people in Hebrews are to teach us such a lesson, then learn it and apply it to your life so you don't have to go through some tough time in order to learn it.

PRAYAER: Heavenly Father, I am so thankful that you do not cover up the sins of the people you have chosen to use to bring about your directive will over the ages. It helps me to see how you continue to work on our behalf in spite of ourselves—our shortcomings, our failures, and our sins. I am also amazed at your patience and how far it will stretch to help us get back on track. I think that, as I was growing up, I must have heard nothing but law preached to me, and there is no hope in that message. I am so grateful that there is another part of that message and that is your grace! Thank you for your grace. It has given me hope beyond measure, and assurance of the truth of your Word and of eternal life. I feel I am so blessed. Thank you, Father, for the gift of life eternal. In Jesus' name, Amen.

OCTOBER 6th

There is one more name that sticks out like a sore thumb in Hebrews 11, but for a different reason. Hebrews 11:31 reads, ***"By faith the harlot Rahab perished not with them that believed not*** (were

410

disobedient), *when she had received the spies with peace."* Rahab was not a Jew, but she hid the spies Joshua had sent to scope out Jericho before attacking it. Because she did the Jews that favor, she and her whole household were saved when Joshua and his people attacked Jericho, and she gained a place in this great chapter of faith in Hebrews.

We have been looking at Hebrews 11, which tells about all the great people of faith in the Old Testament. They conquered their situations by faith and persevered. Now we will step into Hebrews chapter 12, were we are going to shift gears a bit. Hebrew 12:1-2 states: *"Wherefore seeing we also are compassed about with so great a cloud of witnesses, let us lay aside every weight and the sin that does so easily beset us, and let us run with patience the race that is set before us. Looking unto Jesus the author and finisher* (perfecter) *of our faith; who for the joy that was set before Him endured the cross, despising the shame, and is set down at the right hand of the throne of God."*

Here we are told how to respond to what we read in chapter 11. That word, "wherefore," points back to the whole of chapter 11. So, because all those who have gone on before us are like a cloud of witnesses (cheering us on perhaps), *"let us lay aside every weight and sin that doth so easily beset us."*

We know that sin is what we are to lay aside (again, it is all a choice we make), but what is a weight? We are to lay aside the weights in our life. I like to paint a picture of runners prepared to run a race. They are all at the line waiting in position for the shot to go off. Imagine that when it does one racer picks up a backpack, which becomes nothing more than excess baggage. He will not win the race with excess baggage. So it is with the race in our Christian lives also.

And why is it called a race? We have all been given a prescribed amount of time on this earth. Remember when we talked about time? There is a time to be born and a time to die. That amount of time is our race. We are to accomplish as much as possible for the Kingdom of God in that time period. That is why it is called a race. That shows me that God knows what our life ought to be. It was planned before time was.

411

Tomorrow we will talk about what excess baggage we often pick up on our walk (our race) of life.

PRAYER: Heavenly Father, I had no idea that I had picked up excess baggage to weigh me down in my walk with you. I am glad you are going to address this subject so I can be aware of what I need to lay aside. Give me the inner revelation of how to lay it aside, or what I need to do to set it aside. In Jesus' name, Amen.

OCTOBER 7th

Today we will look at I John 1:8-9, which reads: *"If we say we have no sin, we deceive ourselves, and the truth is not in us. If we confess our sins, He is faithful and just to forgive us our sins, and to cleanse us from all unrighteousness."*

How many people can read that and know that it is true, but are still unable to accept it for themselves? They have a grain of doubt that God will forgive them, to say nothing of being cleansed from all unrighteousness. So, the question is, can you lay full claim to the truth that is stated in those verses?

When we lay claim to that truth and believe without a shadow of a doubt that God heard your confession and is more than willing to forgive you, and cleanse you from *all* unrighteousness, then you have not picked up excess baggage of *doubt.*

Doubt about God's Word will always put an extra burden on your heart and water down your faith. Doubt is what got Eve into trouble, and we all live with the death that was brought into the world through her sin. Doubt is one of the big snares of the devil, so watch that excess baggage to ensure it will not be a part of your faith walk.

Being tempted with doubt is not the sin or weight itself, but succumbing to it is a weight, which can turn into a sin over time. Doubting God's Word caused Eve to eat the forbidden fruit, and she sinned the sin of disobedience. Personally, I believe that doubt will lead one into the sin of "unbelief." That is a dangerous sin to fall into, it hardens one's heart to the gospel message, and that leads to spiritual death. So, when you doubt anything about the Word of God, let that doubt drive you *into* God's Word to find the truth that will set you free from that excess baggage. Doubt will either lead you into unbelief or into the truth. You choose!

PRAYER: Heavenly Father, doubt is such a sneaky thought in the mind, and it can take over without my even noticing it. Help me to see the doubts that creep into my thinking in regard to trusting your Word, and trusting you, Lord. In Jesus' name. Amen

OCTOBER 8th

Mathew 11:28-30 reads: *"Come unto me, all ye that labor and are heavy laden, and I will give you rest. Take my yoke upon you, and learn of me; for I am meek and lowly in heart: and ye shall find rest unto your souls. For my yoke is easy, and my burned is light."*

How often do we carry burdens that are totally unnecessary? Jesus wants us to come to Him with our burdens in life, and to share them with Him and leave them there with Him. He knows the answers and will show us what those answers are in His own perfect timing.

Burdens we carry might include worry over what tomorrow will bring, worry about losing our job or whether accidents will happen, and on and on. Another burden is anxiety over our children, the choices they make, and the trouble that they can get into. Worry will wear you down physically, mentally, and spiritually. These things make up the excess baggage that slows down your race of life.

God wants us to enter into His rest, but in order to do that you need to do what the Lord suggests you do today, *"Take my yoke upon you, and learn of me; for I am meek and lowly in heart: and ye shall find rest unto your souls."* A yoke would connect two animals together who could then pull a much bigger load. Being yoked together with Jesus will give

413

you the help you need to put your burdens on Him and be at rest like He is. You cannot solve the problems by yourself anyway, and the sooner you learn that lesson the sooner you will leave your burdens with Jesus and walk in step with Him like the two animals that are yoked together. Worry and anxiety are weights that slow us down and steal our rest, peace of mind, and joy.

PRAYER: Heavenly Father, I feel lighter already. But to *know* a truth and to *practice* it are two different things. Help me give my burden of worry and anxiety over to you and then to leave it there. When I pick it up again, and begin to whirl it around in my mind, remind me that you have it and are working on it for my good. In Jesus' name, Amen.

OCTOBER 9th

 We saw in Matthew that Jesus wants us to have rest. What keeps us from having rest? In Hebrews 3:10-12, we read: *"Wherefore I was grieved with that generation, and said, 'They do always err in their heart; and they have not known my ways. So I sware in my wrath, They shall not enter into my rest. Take heed, brethren, lest there be in any of you an evil heart of unbelief, in the parting from the living God.' "*
Unbelief is the reason they could not enter into God's rest. Unbelief usually begins with doubt, and, when followed, leads to *"parting from the living God,"* and that will definitely lead to disaster. So beware of unbelief. It could be another weight, but again, when acted upon will lead to something else which inflicts God's wrath.

Are you beginning to see the trouble a weight can become in the life of a Christian? Before we look at our next reference in Mark, I want you to have some background. While Jesus and three disciples had been up in the mountain, a father had brought his demon-possessed son to the rest of the disciples at the foot of the mountain, to deliver him from demon possession. The disciples were not able to do it, so when Jesus came down,

He took over and delivered the boy. Mark 9:19-24 states: *"He* (Jesus) *answereth him* (the boy's father) *and saith, 'Oh faithless generation, how long shall I be with you? How long shall I suffer you? Bring him unto me.' And they brought him unto Him : and when he saw Him, straightway the spirit tare him; and he fell on the ground, and wallowed foaming. And He asked the father, 'How long is it ago since this came upon him?' And he said, 'Of a child. And oft times it hath cast him into the fire, and into the waters, to destroy him: but if thou canst do any thing, have compassion of us, and help us.' Jesus said unto him, 'If thou canst believe, all things are possible to him that believeth.' And straightway the father of the child cried out, and said with tear, 'Lord, I believe; help thou mine unbelief.' "*

This man was able to identify his own limitation of belief and cried out for help for his unbelief. Learn this lesson. Identify your own unbelief and ask God to help you overcome the weight of unbelief. Unbelief is like a lack of trust, a lack of assurance that God is capable, or that He is even willing, to give you the help you need. Unbelief can cripple us in our faith walk. This is something we need to be ready to fight off during our spiritual walk with God most of our lives. As you gain victory over it once, it will be easier to do again and again.

PRAYER: Heavenly Father, I want to make sure that I do not practice unbelief, so I will need your help to point it out to me, day by day. You have promised me the power of the Holy Spirit in my life so that I will lead a life pleasing to you. Unbelief is not pleasing to you, so I will depend on the Holy Spirit to direct my steps. Thank you for that promise. In Jesus' name, Amen.

OCTOBER 10th

There is another weight, or piece of excess baggage, that we need to identify. In Exodus 3:10-11, we see part of a conversation between God and Moses: *" 'Come now therefore, and I will*

415

*send thee unto Pharaoh, that thou mayest bring forth my people the
children of Israel out of Egypt.' And Moses said unto God, 'Who am I,
that I should go unto Pharaoh, and that I should bring forth the children
of Israel out of Egypt?' "*

Can you identify Moses' problem? God is having a very difficult
time persuading Moses that he is the man for the job. Exodus 3:13
continues: *"And Moses said unto God, 'Behold, when I come unto the
children of Israel, and shall say unto them, "The God of your fathers
hath sent me unto you;" and they shall say to me, "What is His name?"
What shall I say unto them?' "*

And the debate continues between God and Moses in Exodus 4:10,
where we read: *"And Moses said unto the Lord, 'O my Lord, I am not
eloquent* (a man of words)*, neither heretofore, nor since thou hast spoken
unto thy servant: but I am slow of speech, and of a slow tongue.' "*

God assured Moses that He would have his brother Aaron do the
talking for him, so God would not let Moses off the hook. But Moses tried
to squirm out of the job God was calling him to do once more, in Exodus
4:13, which explains, *"And he said, 'O my Lord, send, I pray thee, by the
hand of him whom thou wilt send.' "*

God became angry and told Moses that He was in charge of the
mouth, his brother Aaron was on his way (and he would do the speaking for
him), and that Moses *was* the man for the job. There was nothing for
Moses to gain from trying to get out of it. So, as you look back at the
excuses Moses used, what would you say was his problem? I would say it
was low self-esteem. Just look at what he said, *"Who am I that I should
go unto Pharaoh, and that I should bring forth the children of Israel out
of Egypt."* His low self-esteem is very evident, I believe.

Moses even indicated that he does not even know God's name, and
he would not be able to answer his people when they would ask him that
simple question. He saw himself as a failure before he had ever made one
step of faith.

Low self-esteem can slow us down in our lives too. It becomes
another piece of excess baggage. Can you think of other things that are
weights you need to lay aside? Fear, I believe, is a terrible piece of excess

baggage. Nothing cripples us more than fear—fear of failure, fear of criticism, fear of death, and even fear of success. You may be able to name other fears. The children of Israel saw the giants in the Promised Land, and I believe it was fear that kept them from going in to take the land when God had led them right up to its border. That resulted in going back into the wilderness for 40 years.

PRAYER: Heavenly Father, I know that you are willing to forgive sins that have been confessed, but when it comes to weights that we are to lay aside, there is a phrase in that verse that says so much. These are weights *"that so easily beset us."* With so many things that can become weights, how do we keep a watch over them in our lives? I do not want to lay hold of weights to burden me down during my walk with you, Father, so I come to you for the help I will need to recognize each weight that my flesh desires to carry. In Jesus' name, Amen.

OCTOBER 11th

The first big defeat the army of Israel suffered as Joshua led them into the Promised Land was the result of lust, also called covetousness. One whole battle was defeated as a result of that sin. Although to actually covet is not the sin, acting upon that desire is.

Let's look at an example in Joshua 7:21 *"When I saw among the spoils a goodly Babylonian garment (mantle), and two hundred shekels of silver and a wedge of gold of fifty shekels weight, then I coveted them, and took them; and, behold they are hid in the earth in the midst of my tent, and the silver under it."*

If you read the whole story surrounding this, you will see the steps in the process of this sin. God had told His people what they should or should not do when they went into Jericho, and I am sure that would be true of any other city in that land. In Joshua 6:17-19, God told them: *"And the city shall be accursed, (devoted) even it, and all that are therein, to the Lord: only Rahab the harlot* (who had hidden the spies of Israel when they

417

scoped out the city) *shall live, she and all that are with her in the house, because she hid the messengers that we sent. And ye, in any wise keep yourselves from the accursed thing, lest ye make yourselves accursed, when ye take of the accursed thing. And make the camp of Israel a curse, and trouble it. But all the silver, and gold, and vessels of brass and iron, are consecrated unto the Lord: they shall come into the treasury of the Lord.*"

So, when they went to capture the small city of Ai and were defeated, it was because Achan (who confessed in the first verse for today) had coveted and taken the garment, silver, and gold. The garment made Israel accursed, and the silver and gold belonged to God to be put into the treasury.

You need to see the steps in the covetousness of Achan. First he *saw* the items, and then he *coveted* (experienced temptation of the old nature, temptation of the body). He *desired* to make himself *beautiful* or *powerful* (experienced temptation of the soul), and then he *took* the items (gave in to temptation on the spirit) and the act was complete. He also hid what he had done, which was as much as thinking he could hide this from God or that he would not be accountable to God.

As a result of all this, God ordered that he and his family be stoned, and then everything Achan owned was burned. You can read about that in Joshua 7:22-26.

Like I said, a weight (such as covetousness) can lead to destruction. There are many examples of this same process (seeing, coveting, taking, and the resulting destruction) in the Bible. Our job is to learn from these examples and avoid doing the same things. You will need to keep a close watch on your heart to avoid these weights in your life.

PRAYER: Heavenly Father, I pray that these eyes of mine will not look upon those things that will bring my whole body into sin and destruction. I look to you, Lord God, to help me in my time of need, so that covetousness does not overtake me so easily. I ask you for this now, while I am not being tempted, so that when I am tempted, you can step in and prevent me from falling for that weakness of my old nature. Thank you, Father, for being there when I need you. In Jesus' name, Amen.

OCTOBER 12th

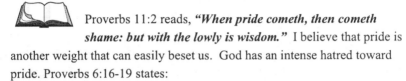 Proverbs 11:2 reads, *"When pride cometh, then cometh shame: but with the lowly is wisdom."* I believe that pride is another weight that can easily beset us. God has an intense hatred toward pride. Proverbs 6:16-19 states:

"These six things doth the Lord hate: yea, seven are an abomination unto Him. A proud look, a lying tongue, and hands that shed innocent blood. An heart that deviseth wicked imaginations, feet that be swift in running to mischief, A false witness that speaketh lies, and he that soweth discord among brethren."

God hates pride. God knows what damage can be done by pride. Proverbs 29:23 explains, *"A man's pride shall bring him low: but honor shall uphold the humble in spirit."* Also see Proverbs 16:18, which reads, *"Pride goeth before destruction, and an haughty spirit before a fall."* Haughty means arrogant, which is another term for proud.

You do not develop pride overnight. It is a process that grows like a cancer within a person. It may begin with a puffed-up self image, a little success, a little more of a puffed-up attitude, then arrogance, then haughtiness, and finally pride. And then the rug will get pulled out and there is destruction. It definitely is a weight that gets heavier day by day. Finally, the proud person is a broken person—possibly mentally, physically, spiritually, and maybe even emotionally.

Let's look again at I Peter 5:6, which states, *"Humble yourselves therefore under the mighty hand of God, that He may exalt you in due time."* You see, to be exalted is what one wants in the first place. And there is only one way exaltation will have any meaning, and that is when God is exalting us. Please take note of the fact that it was Peter who wrote this scripture. He had been humbled under the mighty hand of God, and he knew what it was like to have the weight of pride lifted from him.

419

Peter also knew what it was to be exalted by God. There is no better and enjoyable feeling than to be exalted by God. You know when you have His approval, His "well done, good and faithful servant" feeling encompass you. No one else needs to see or know it—just you and Jesus—and the two of you can be so happy and excited. You do not need man's approval. It will not last anyway. Someone will become jealous and bring you down with one disapproving look, but when God exalts you, it is a lasting fact.

PRAYER: Heavenly Father, I do not want to fall into the trap of pride, since it is such a destructive weight. Yet I do not want to live like I am ashamed of who I am either. In Romans 1:16, Paul says he was *"not ashamed of the Gospel of Christ, for it is the power of God unto salvation to every one that believeth."* So, I will take pride in who you say that I am. I am a child of God, bought and paid for by the life, death, and resurrection of Jesus Christ. I was wonderfully made in my mother's womb, the Bible says. You are in the exalting business and I put my trust in you. Personal, fleshly pride can go away, as it is a weight I do not need, nor want. Satan, with all his tricks and plans for my destruction, can just go back to the hole he crawled out from. I am planning to walk the life God has set before me, and I will keep my eye on you, Lord. In Jesus' name, Amen.

OCTOBER 13th

 Before we talk about survival tools, I would like to clarify a misconception you might have, as I did at one time. Temptation itself is not a sin. *Giving in to temptation* is the sin. If temptation were a sin, then Jesus would not have been sinless. He was tempted severely in the wilderness, and again in the Garden of Gethsemane just before His crucifixion, yet He was sinless.

Temptation is Satan's tactic to make us choose to disobey God. So, when you realize you are being tempted, you have the privilege to choose to rebuke it in the name of Jesus and gain a victory over your old nature one more time. Thank God for the temptation and your ability to recognize what Satan is up to, and for the Godly desire to rebuke it rather than succumb to it.

God wants us to live the good life, to make the right choices daily. God's survival tools will help you put this into practice. But, if you thought that the temptation itself was the sin, then you would be trying to resist something you did not need to waste your time on, and it could develop into another weight—that of unnecessary guilt. This was a burden on my heart for several years, until I finally figured it out. What a relief! You see, *"The truth shall make you free"* (John 8:32).

Now, we need to talk about survival tools. In every one of us there is instilled a will to survive! Nurses and doctors will often tell of some infant seriously ill at birth with a will to live that is astonishing. Babies soon learn what works, too. If they are hungry, they cry. And if crying loud works better, then they cry louder. It becomes a survival tool in their minds.

Unfortunately, most of the survival tools we pack in our tool chest as we grow up are designed to protect our old nature, also called the "flesh." Those are tools we need to learn to discard when we are born again, when we want our new nature to survive and not the old.

You don't need to teach a child to be jealous, angry, fretful, selfish, or deceitful. Children learn to use these tools to survive, to control their environment, and to manipulate those in authority around them. But, later in life, those tools will have to go. But to unlearn something is a whole lot harder than learning something.

God has better survival tools, and as we delve into this subject, I hope that you will be able to learn to use them.

PRAYER: Heavenly Father, I never thought about things like anger, jealousy, selfishness, etc., as survival tools, but when I look at how they work to protect our old nature, it is as clear as crystal. I look forward to learning about your survival tools that can take the place of the old ones I have learned to use. I want my old nature to decrease and my new nature increases. Open my mind so that I can grasp the whole truth of both excess baggage and survival tools. In Jesus' name, Amen.

OCTOBER 14th

When you are afraid, what survival tools did you used to use? Did you call on someone to come to your side to stand with you? Did you cry, shudder, and faint, or become filled with even more fear? Let's turn to some verses to see what advice we can find there. Mark 5:35-42 reads: *"While He yet spake, there came the ruler of the synagogue's house certain which said, 'Thy daughter is dead: why troublest thou the Master any further?' As soon as Jesus heard the word that was spoken, He saith unto the ruler of the synagogue, 'Be not afraid, only believe.' And He suffered no man to follow Him, save Peter, and James, and John the brother of James. And He cometh to the house of the ruler of the synagogue, and seeth the turnult, and them that wept and wailed greatly. And when He was come in, He saith unto them, 'Why make ye this ado, and weep? The damsel is not dead, but sleepeth.' And they laughed Him to scorn . But when He had put them all out, He taketh the father and the mother of the damsel, and them that were with Him, and entereth in where the damsel was lying. And He took the damsel by the hand, and said unto her, 'Talitha cumi;' which is, being interpreted, 'Damsel, I say unto thee, arise.' And straightway the damsel arose, and walked; for she was of the age of twelve years. And they were astonished with a great astonishment."*

Jesus' Word to them was to "be not afraid." Why could He say that and why should they do what He said to them? He could say that because He is in charge of both life and death. Fear of that kind does not come from God, but rather it is from the devil. Satan wants to cripple us with fear, but Jesus is more powerful than any fear we might have, and the moment we give that fear to Him, He will take it away and show us His power to save, heal, and be there for us through thick or thin. We will look at some more scriptures tomorrow about this.

PRAYER: Heavenly Father, it sounds way too easy to just "be not afraid!" I suspect it is a bit more than that. To not be afraid, I will have to really know you and your power to be able to put that into practice. So, help me start with the small things in life and work up to the big things. I see it as a learning process, and it will take some practice to perfect that kind of response. I will look to you for help to do that. In Jesus' name, Amen.

OCTOBER 15th

In Mark, when Jesus was walking on the water toward the disciples in the boat, they thought He was a ghost. But Jesus spoke to them, as we read in Mark 6:50, *"For they all saw Him and were troubled. And immediately He talked with them, and saith unto them, 'Be of good cheer: it is I; be not afraid.'"*

We also see a reference to fear in Deuteronomy 20:1, which states: *"When thou goest out to battle against thine enemies, and seest horses, and chariots, and a people more than thou, be not afraid of them: for the Lord thy God is with thee, which brought thee up out of the land of Egypt."*

When we find ourselves filled with fear, we typically are caught up with the circumstances surrounding us. Jesus is telling us to take our eyes off the circumstances and deliberately place our eyes on Him. That is one of our survival tools.

It is hard to learn to not dwell on the circumstances that surround us, and turn our eyes to Jesus for His help instead. I believe it is one of the hardest lessons to learn. The old nature wants us to look at the circumstance. Remember how Lot's wife looked back to the city they were leaving? She just could not keep her eyes off the circumstances, and she did not survive either.

Begin to practice turning your eyes away from the ugly circumstances, and instead looking at the One who is all powerful, everywhere present, and all knowing, God the Son, who has won the victory over sin, death, and the power of the devil. That is where your fear will be set aside. God is always good and He can be trusted!

PRAYER: Dear Lord Jesus, I come to you for the help I will need when my circumstances overwhelm me, when fear tries to take over my body, mind, and emotions, and when it threatens to destroy my peace and my trust in you. I know you will be there for me, because you have promised to never leave me nor forsake me. That is my assurance of victory over fear. In Jesus' name, Amen.

OCTOBER 16th

I believe we all find ourselves in some kind of trouble or affliction from time to time. What do you do when that happens? Do you depend on your own wits to figure your way out of the trouble? What is God's way to deal with affliction or trouble? James 5:13-16 reads: *"Is any among you afflicted* (suffering)*? Let him pray. Is any merry? Let him sing praises. Is any sick among you? Let him call for the elders of the church: and let them pray over him, anointing him with oil in the name of the Lord: And the prayer of faith shall save the sick, and the Lord shall raise him up and if he have committed sins, they shall be forgiven him."*

Another one of God's survival tools is prayer. Too many people pray only when all else fails. We ought to pray at the very first sign of trouble. In fact, it is also wise to sing praises at the time of trouble. Music moves God's heart and it defeats the devil.

Psalm 119:71 says, *"It is good for me that I have been afflicted; that I might learn thy statutes."* What are we to make of this verse? It is *good* to be afflicted? Through affliction, the Psalmist learned about God's laws. For example, there is the law of sowing and reaping. You always reap more than what you sowed. Maybe your affliction was the result of sowing the wrong attitude, the wrong kind of talk to someone, and then you

424

had to reap what you sowed. That is when you acknowledge that it was good to learn the lesson and then move on.

I Thessalonians 5:18 also states, *"In every thing give thanks: for this is the will of God in Christ Jesus concerning you."* A real good survival tool is to offer up thanksgiving to God in the midst of affliction and trouble. God calls that kind of thanksgiving a *sacrifice* of thanksgiving. You will not *want* to give thanks, and your old nature will just scream at you in rebellion. But God's Spirit will be blessed when you do that because God will know that *you* know that He is in charge, and that His way is always good and best in your life.

Prayer and thanksgiving are part of your new survival tools. Be quick to use them. An old survival tool was to bellyache and complain to anyone who would be willing to listen to our tale of woe. That tool will not bring much of a victory in your life, so use God's survival tools instead.

Romans 8:28 reads, *"And we know that all things work together for good to them that love God, to them who are the called according to His purpose."* This speaks of the right kind of attitude toward the troubles in our lives. God wants to bring gold out of ashes, and He is able to do that when *your attitude is right*, which is an attitude that He is in charge and that no matter what the devil throws at us, God will be there to bring out the best of a bad situation for us.

I know someone who lost his job, and he was just devastated. But he ended up getting a much better job with better pay and better benefits, and better working conditions too. In fact, I have seen situations turn for the better in so many different cases, I am thoroughly convince that a bad situation is God's way of moving us upward and forward, not downward and backward.

So, our survival tool is to never lose hope, but instead hope in the future God has for us. He will turn evil into good. When you have that attitude, it is not so hard to give thanks for everything. I have used God's survival tools many, many times in my life, and, believe me, they can work wonders.

PRAYER: Heavenly Father, I thank you for the survival tools I am learning about. I pray that I will be able to remember to use them when affliction and troubles come my way. I have come to the conclusion that you do not want your children to be a defeated lot, but to live a life of victory. I also see that making use of the survival tools you have given me is a step in the right direction to live that life of victory. Thank you, Father, for showing me this truth. In Jesus' mighty name, Amen.

OCTOBER 17th

When we live according to the flesh (letting the old nature be in control), then most often anger becomes the natural survival tool. People have learned that they can manipulate others with their anger. That manipulation is a learned behavior. People learn that they can use it to get what they want or think they need. Then, when they are going to begin to live a life acceptable to God, they have to *unlearn* using anger as a survival tool.

Here is where we come face to face with that word, "choice," again and again. We have already talked about how important it is to make the right choices in life, because we live with the results of our choices for years to come. I want to take you to some verses in which you will hopefully see what survival tools you need to use instead of anger and malice. Ephesians 4:17-20 states: ***"This I say therefore, and testify in the Lord, that ye henceforth walk not as other Gentiles walk, in the vanity of their mind. Having their understanding darkened, being alienated from the life of God through the ignorance that is in them, because of the blindness of their heart. Who being past feeling have given themselves over unto lasciviousness*** (immorality)***, to work all uncleanness with greediness. But ye have not so learned Christ."***

The Apostle Paul is beginning to talk to the people at this church about their lives *before* and *after* knowing Christ. Before, their minds were blind and full of darkness, and their lives showed others that was true. But they did not learn that from Christ. Their lives were to be a shining example of who was the boss in their lives.

Ephesians 4:21 continues, *"If so be that ye have heard Him, and have been taught by Him, as the truth is in Jesus."* If you have Jesus in your heart, then your life will not be the same as it was before you accepted Him. How can such a change take place? It will require one choice after another, day after day. What you will find is that the old survival tools (those you used to use to live and protect your old nature) will have to go, and you will need to *choose* to use Godly survival tools and depend on God to fight your battles. We will continue on in Ephesians tomorrow. I hope it will help you see how much better God's tools are then the ones you are used to using.

Prayer: Heavenly Father, I remember growing up thinking anger was just something that happened to people. It never occurred to me that it was a choice. But, then again, I also grew up thinking happiness was something that just happened to people too—as if those who had enough money, friends, security, etc., would just naturally be happy. Then I had to learn that happiness, too, was a choice. I am so thankful that I learned that truth because it sure made a difference in the way I looked at life. I pray that all who read this devotional will also learn that truth. I pray that it will help all to understand that our attitudes determine the spiritual victories in our lives. I also thank you, Father, for the gift of the Holy Spirit within us to help us make the right choices, and to live according to that choice. In Jesus' name, Amen.

OCTOBER 18th

Today, we will look at Ephesians 4:22-23, which reads, *"That ye put off concerning the former conversation (manner of life) the old man, which is corrupt according to the deceitful lusts; and be renewed in the spirit of your mind."*

It is plain to be seen that Paul is working into a comparison of the old and new nature at war within every believer in Jesus Christ. We are told to "put off" our former way of life. That is a flat out choice, is it not? That way of life is corrupt, the Bible says, and the reason it is corrupt is because of deceitful lusts of our old nature.

Who, may I ask, is the master of deceit? That is the devil's number one trump card. He is able to work deceit in us because our old nature is his strong ally. In fact, our old nature and the devil are bedfellows. Our old nature will scream, "I want, I must have, I need, I will get my way no matter what," etc. Is it any wonder that it was so easy to use anger as a survival tool? It came naturally, through the deceit of lust.

The survival tool God wants us to use is the renewing of the spirit of our minds. How is that done? You can renew the spirit of your mind by such things as daily reading God's Word, studying daily devotions and books written by good authors about the things of God, and singing hymns and gospel songs. Listening to radio or TV programs that feed you spiritually is also a good way to renew the spirit of your mind.

Ephesians 4:24 continues, *"And that ye put on the new man, which after God is created in righteousness and true holiness* (holiness of truth). *"* To "put on the new man" is also a choice, but did you notice you must "put off the old man" before you can "put on the new man"?

You need to realize that when you turn your life over to Christ, you have chosen to put off the old man and to put on the new man. This is not the same as getting yourself cleaned up before coming to Jesus. You come to Him just as you are. You cannot clean yourself up. But God is at work to woo you to Himself. That is the work of the Holy Spirit.

When you finally make the choice to ask Jesus into your heart, you have a "double nature." Before that, you did not have a new nature, and there was nothing for your old nature to fight. Have you examined what it was that made you decide to live a different life? What circumstance pushed you over the edge for you to try Jesus? Once you made that decision, you invited a new member into your heart, and Satan would not stand still. He will fight it with all his might.

This, then, is when you begin the process of putting off the old man and putting on the new man. The Spirit of Christ Jesus lives within you now to give you the power to make the right choices in life. He is there to help you use your new survival tools so that you can live a life of victory.

We will look at some more of those old and new survival tools tomorrow, but I want to draw your attention to one more thing. Notice that your new man is created in righteousness and true holiness, which is what Jesus is. You now have a new nature of righteousness and holiness and that is what your life is supposed to reflect.

PRAYER: Heavenly Father, I am beginning to see the warfare that has gone on in my life before I knew the truth about your survival tools. I am so thankful that your word is here to teach me to use your way to a joyful, peaceful life. I am thankful to *know* that Satan is out to disrupt my joy and happiness, and to steal it away actually, but I have learned that he can not do that without first getting my permission. And, in ignorance, I have given it to him time and again. I am thankful I now have a new way of putting him to flight, and to having you in control of my anger, malice, bitterness, and so on. I can feel my heart is already lighter, and I thank you. In Jesus' name, Amen.

OCTOBER 19th

Ephesians 4:25-28 reads: *"Wherefore putting away lying, speak every man truth with his neighbor: for we are members one of another. Be ye angry, and sin not: let not the sun go down upon your wrath: Neither give place to the devil. Let him who stole, steal no more: but rather let him labor, working with his hands the thing which is good, that he may have to give to him that needeth."*

Lying used to be a survival tool. It never works, but people will still use it over and over again, thinking that it will. The reason it never works is that our old nature is in tune with the devil, who is the father of lies. How easy it is for him to convince the old nature that, "Just this one little lie won't hurt. It will get you off the hook for now anyhow." So you fall for it.

Now, however, you must put lying aside. You can no longer use it as a survival tool. Instead, we need to speak the truth. At times, speaking the truth may seem to get you into even more trouble, and that is exactly what the devil is working to accomplish. But stick with the truth and, in time, God will exalt you.

Remember that Jesus said, *"I am the truth, the life, and the way"*(John 14:6). You just can't go wrong in telling the truth. However, if you were in the practice of lying, it will be a really big struggle to switch survival tools, but I strongly advice you to make the right choice.

In our scripture for today, we read, *"...let not the sun go down upon your wrath"* (Ephesians 4:26). In other words, do not go to bed with wrath. Wrath is not the same as anger. Wrath is a notch higher, and it will eat on you all night long. You will wake up with it in the morning and spoil your day before it has even begun.

Give your wrath to Jesus, and ask Him to take it away and to renew the spirit of your mind. What does it mean to not give place to the devil (verse 27 of today's reading)? The devil can only accomplish through us what we allow him to. We hold the key to his activity in and through us. So, do not give him the green light. Do not use his old survival tools to get to where you want to go.

For the person who has survived by stealing, do not steal anymore, but rather have a desire to find a job and be able to help others who have a need like you used to have. I see a repay-blessing attitude here. Someone might use stealing as a survival tool before Christ comes into his life. After accepting Jesus, though, he is asked to work and be a giver. That is a whole 180-degree turn, which is what our life in Christ is supposed to look like to God.

I hope as you are reading this that you are becoming aware of the survival tools you used to apply to get through life, and how you have switched to God's type of tools to be a shining witness to the goodness of the Lord in your life.

PRAYER: Heavenly Father, again I thank you for opening my eyes to the truth. I am becoming aware of things I never even thought about as survival tools in my life. I was not aware that there were so many new survival tools available to the believer, so I ask for your help to remind me to use those tools and which one to use for each situation I find myself in. In Jesus' name, Amen.

OCTOBER 20th

Ephesians 4:29-30 reads: *"Let no corrupt communication (speech) proceed out of your mouth, but that which is good to the use of edifying, that it may minister grace unto the hearers. And grieve not the Holy Spirit of God, whereby ye are sealed unto the day of redemption."*

I am always amazed at how much God can get said in just a few words. There is so much power and truth in these two verses, and I hope I can do them justice. That word, "let," which we have seen in verse 28 also, implies that we are to stop allowing corrupt speech to issue forth from our mouths. The ability to use corrupt speech is present in our thoughts and mind, but we can put a stop to that by not allowing it to come out of our mouths. Instead, we are to use our ability to speak to edify God and to minister to others.

I don't think we have any idea how important our influence can be no matter where we are. The Bible says that we are *"the salt of the earth"* (Matthew 5:13).

What does salt do? It is a preservative. And, like salt, *we* can preserve peace, friendly relationships, family unity, and so on. Salt is also a coolant that is used to freeze ice cream and make ice water even colder. *We* too can cool down a heated situation by using God's survival tools. Interestingly, salt also has a warming property. It will melt ice, and *we* can warm up a cold situation. Salt is also used to flavor foods, and *we* can be a sprinkle of joy in a sad situation—a sprinkle of love in an angry, hateful situation, or a flavor of cooperation in an uncooperative situation. You may think of more ways we are like salt to add to this.

The Bible does not say, "You *will become* the salt of the earth," but that we *are*. And since you live on this earth, no matter where you live, you are salt.

Matthew 5:13 states: *"Ye are the salt of the earth: but if the salt have lost his savor, wherewith shall it be salted? It is thenceforth good for nothing, but to be cast out and to be trodden down under foot of men."*

I hope you notice the warning about losing saltiness—the ability to preserve, cool, warm, and flavor. I believe that salt is also a survival tool, and you already have it. Remember, Ephesians 4:30 says, *"Grieve not the Holy Spirit of God."* How do we grieve the Holy Spirit of God? When we deliberately choose to do wrong things, we deliberate disobey the Word of God. In other words, these choices, these *put on*s and *put off*s are so obvious that they should not be hard to obey, should they?

But, we will slip off into our old ways of living, using our old survival tools. This grieves the Holy Spirit, because He is at work with our new nature to get us to choose the right rather than the wrong. The Holy Spirit is the ally of our new nature, and when it comes to authority, the Holy Spirit has much more power and authority than the devil and all his demons, so it should be a no-brainer when we need to decide what to do. Every time we choose the wrong, we will also have to live through the fruit of that choice. Remember sowing and reaping?

Notice that this verse says also we are *"sealed unto the day of redemption"* by the Holy Spirit. When God sent His Holy Spirit to live within you forever, that was God's seal on you to preserve you to Himself. For women who preserve food by canning, you know that once that jar is sealed properly, it will stay preserved until the day you open it and use it.

And so it is with the Holy Spirit. God has sealed you until the day you are presented to Jesus as a bride (the Church). The Holy Spirit has such a magnificent job—to present the bride to Christ without spot or wrinkle, pure and holy. When we disobey God's Word, we grieve the Holy Spirit. The Holy Spirit stands ready to give you the power to make the right

432

choices and to carry out that choice. So, what do you have to lose to make the right choice? You have absolutely nothing to lose and everything to gain, including a "Well done, thou good and faithful servant" from God.

PRAYER: Heavenly Father, so, I am sealed, huh? That sounds almost too good to be true. I have canned and preserved many jars of fruits and vegetables, and I know how well they are kept until I need to use them, and now I realize just how kept I am also by your Holy Spirit. What a word of assurance that is! Thank you, Father, for such love, mercy, and grace, with which you have blessed me this day. In Jesus' name, Amen.

OCTOBER 21st

Ephesians 4:31-32 reads: *"Let all bitterness, and wrath, and anger, and clamor, and evil speaking be put away from you with all malice* (evil intent)*: And be ye kind one to another, tender hearted, forgiving one another, even as God for Christ's sake hath forgiven you."*

You can see two kinds of behavior in these verses, and you are asked to make a choice to put away the old way of doing things and take on a new way. I see that, again, as using different survival tools to get through life. Bitterness, wrath, anger, clamor (a noisy demand), evil speaking, and all malice were once your ways to survive life.

But these old survival tools have all got to go, or be put away. Can you do that? Yes, with the help of God, you can be kind to one another and forgive as God forgave you for Christ's sake. Kindness and forgiveness become your new survival tools. Once you have put them into practice, you will find how wonderfully they work.

I can remember my mother saying, "If you can't say something nice about someone, don't say anything at all." It is easier said then done, right? But if you begin to check yourself, you will find you can do it. Can you decide to have a tender heart? Yes, you can! It doesn't just happen, but rather you *decide* to have a tender heart. You will need to recognize

433

your hard heart in order to do that. The devil does not want you to see that you have a hard heart. Satan can not use a tender heart, because Jesus rules a tender heart.

Many people have developed a hard heart because it was the only way they could survive as children. It became a survival tool for them, which they carried with them into their adult lives, and even into their Christian lives. But, once Jesus has come in to stay, those survival tools have got to go.

Those people will feel like they have left their vulnerable heart stark naked when they decide to have a tender heart. But God is able to protect a tender heart, so you will need to ask Him to protect your heart from harm and from torment and hurt.

A tender heart is God's first choice for you, and that is for your own good. It is a better survival tool than a hard heart. God's abundant love is able to penetrate a tender heart a whole lot better than a hard heart. And nothing is more wonderful than to know and feel God's tender love.

Matthew 5:43-45 explains: *"You have heard that it hath been said, 'Thou shalt love thy neighbor, and hate thine enemy.' But I say unto you, 'Love your enemies, bless (pray for) them that curse (persecute) you, do good to them that hate you, and pray for them which despitefully use you, and persecute you; THAT ye may be the children of your Father which is in heaven: for He maketh His sun to rise on the evil and on the good, and sendeth rain on the just and on the unjust.' "*

God gives you survival tools aplenty. Practice love instead of hate. Bless, pray for, and do good towards others instead of cursing, plotting revenge, and being filled with hatred. You will feel better, and you will turn God's attention, in a positive way, toward those who have been mistreating you. It will help them to see their wicked ways and to *want* to change. They will also see your ability to be an overcomer.

PRAYER: Heavenly Father, I see survival tools as ammunition to fight the spiritual enemy in my life. Satan does not care who he uses to get to me, and when a friend whom I trusted betrays me, it is so hard to have kind feelings toward them. But kindness is exactly what you, Lord, are prepared to give me, to help me fight the urge to curse instead of pray. All I have to do is *decide* beforehand that I will depend on your help when the time comes to pray instead of criticize or curse. Then, you will be there for me, at that moment. That proves to me, once again, that all of life is "all of God and none of self." I cannot do anything to add to what you have already done on my behalf, to ensure a life of victory over the evil one. I thank you, Father, for all that you have done on my behalf. In Jesus' name, Amen.

OCTOBER 22nd

 God has a word of advice in regard to the company we keep, since that will affect our walk with Him. In Romans 16:17-18, Paul says: *"Now I beseech you, brethren, mark them which cause divisions and offenses (occasions of stumbling) contrary to the doctrine which we have learned; and avoid them. For they that are such serve not our Lord Jesus Christ, but their own belly; and by good words and fair speeches deceive (beguile) the hearts of the simple (innocent)."*

Paul is talking here about those who are teaching a different doctrine that is not in tune with who God is, and are subsequently causing divisions and offenses. We may do that in our everyday lives as well. We need to be careful who we choose to have as friends, simply because they can be a large influence in our lives.

There are people who lift you up, but there are others who tear you down. If you are spiritually strong enough to be the good influence in the lives of those who tear you down, then maybe God has put them in your life to be the answer to someone's prayer for that person. But be aware that such a negative influence is easily rubbed off on you.

You will need to use survival tools from God to be that positive influence to the offensive person. It *can* be done, but it won't be easy. You just might become the offensive person to them by trying too hard to do God's job, and instead that person's wicked tongue can paint you as the evil one. It will take a lot of prayer, a lot of patience, and maybe even fasting to get the job done.

Christians are being watched and scrutinized by others to see if their talk and their walk are in harmony. If you say one thing and do another, your witness is out the window. So, just be careful with whom you choose to be friends. By "friends," I mean those with whom you fellowship intimately, sharing feelings, hurts, hopes, dreams, hates, dislikes, and so on. Our scripture today is sharing spiritual things, but I also see, from experience in my life, how important it is to have the right fellowship in other areas as well.

Look at II John 10-11, which says: *"If there come any unto you, and bring not this doctrine (teaching), receive him not into your house, neither bid him God speed; For he that biddeth him God speed, is partaker of his evil deeds."*

Although this refers to a doctrine or teaching, I also believe we need to watch the influence certain people can have on us as Christians. We need to practice making good choices. It is like the saying, "An ounce of prevention is worth a pound of cure."

PRAYER: Heavenly Father, I can plainly see that a person with the gift of mercy would be hard pressed to not go rushing into the life of someone they think they can "fix." It is hard to not help in time of need. However, I also know that the desire to help and befriend can also be one's own ruin. I have seen it happen. I believe, Lord, that I will have to depend on you to direct my path, my choices, and my desires, so that I will not rush in where angels fear to tread. Help me watch for your open doors, and closed doors, and then depend on your hand to guide me. Help me to know and understand my own limitations, so that I do not bite off a bigger chunk than I can chew. In Jesus' name, Amen.

OCTOBER 23rd

 We have talked about wisdom before, but I believe it is

important to see wisdom as a survival tool also. James 3:13-17 states:
"Who is a wise man and endued with knowledge among you? Let him show out of a good conversation (by his good life) his works with meekness of wisdom. But if ye have bitter envying (jealousy) and strife in your heart, glory not, and lie not against the truth. This wisdom descendeth NOT from above, but is earthly, sensual, devilish (demonic). For where envying and strife is, there is confusion and every evil work. But the wisdom that is from above is first pure, then peaceable, gentle, and easy to be intreated (sensible), *full of mercy and good fruits, without partiality* (variance), *and without hypocrisy."*

In these verses, we see that there are four sources of wisdom— wisdom from above, and wisdom that is earthly, sensual, and devilish (i.e. from the demonic realm of activity).

What kind of wisdom does the world (earthly wisdom) try to feed us? The world says that the only road to happiness is one in which you have a three-car garage, a big house, and lots of vacation time. If you have that, then you will be happy. That is completely false according to God's wisdom. He will tell you that the road to happiness is found in Matthew 6:33, which reads, *"Seek ye first the kingdom of God and His righteousness, and all these things shall be added unto you."* Get your priorities in order, and you will have peace, joy, and happiness that you never knew was possible.

What kind of wisdom is sensual? I believe this wisdom says, "If it feels good, just do it," regardless of what "it" is. The fruit of that wisdom will only bring sadness, harm to others and yourself, and maybe even death. What kind of wisdom is that? God's wisdom is seen in James 1:2-4, which states:
"My brethren, count it all joy when ye fall into divers (manifold) temptations; Knowing this, that the trying of your faith worketh patience. But let patience have her perfect work, that ye may be perfect and entire wanting nothing."

To the world, this is ridiculous and is far from wisdom. But, this is God's kind of wisdom. Satan wants us to fuss and worry, and try to figure out what to do when multiple temptations come at us. But you will not accomplish a thing by following the world's way of reacting, except putting a bigger burden on yourself. Turn it all over to God to handle. He will amaze you with His way of handling the people who are against you.

Let me also remind you of Proverbs 16:7, which reads, *"When a man's ways please the Lord, He maketh even his enemies to be at peace with him."* If you count it all joy, knowing that God can step in and do a number on those who are against you, then to fall into many temptations is not the dreaded thing Satan intends it to be, and God has a legal right to work a number on those who are making it hard for you. So, a survival tool here is to keep a level head and focus your eyes on what God is going to do on your behalf. He will be there for you, without a doubt!

I believe it is also important to look at James 3:16, which states, *"For where envying and strife is, there is confusion and every evil work."* That ought to be a warning to not let envy and strife occupy a place in our homes. In some homes, those are their survival tools, or learned behaviors. These take a long time to unlearn and are never addressed, so the family members grow up and take it right along with them into the homes they set up. Take a check on your home.

PRAYER: Heavenly Father, I want to subscribe to this new way of reacting when trouble comes knocking on my door, but I know I will need your presence and help when it comes. Help me to keep my eyes on you and on your answer to this prayer. I thank you beforehand for the help you plan to give me for support in my time of need. In Jesus' name, Amen.

OCTOBER 24th

Today we will look at wisdom that is "from above."

Remember, James 3:17-18 reads: *"But the wisdom that is from above is first pure, then peaceable* (the opposite from strife)*, gentle, and easy to be intreated, full of mercy and good fruits, without partiality (variance), and without hypocrisy. And the fruit of righteousness is sown in peace of them that make peace."*

The CEV translates these verses as, *"But the wisdom that comes from above leads us to be pure, friendly, gentle, sensible, kind, helpful, genuine, and sincere. When peace-makers plant seeds of peace, they will harvest justice."*

The fourth source of wisdom is "from above," which means it comes from God the Father. His kind of wisdom brings the fruit of purity, friendship, gentleness, sensibility, kindness, and helpfulness. It is genuine and sincere, not fake. You reap what you sow, and the fruit of this wisdom is justice.

The choice is yours. Which wisdom you are going to practice? I have lived many places in my life, from Michigan and Iowa to Minnesota, and I have been able to step inside the door of a home and feel the atmosphere of the character of that home right away, especially as a child. If the spirit of gentleness is there, you just know it. The same is true of peace and kindness. If it was genuine, there was the sense of a spirit in the air that made you feel safe and welcome. That is the result of wisdom from above that dwells there. Invite that spirit of wisdom to dominate your home. It will be one of your best survival tools, and it will serve you well.

PRAYER: Heavenly Father, I do invite the spirit of wisdom to come in and dominate my home. I see that it is one survival tool I will need to use a lot, and I pray that you will put on a red light when I slip into false types of wisdom to solve a problem. I do not care for the fruit of that type of wisdom—strife and envying. There is enough confusion in the world without inviting it into my home by using the wrong kind of wisdom. I thank you, Father, for bringing this truth to my attention, and I look to you for the help I will need to put this all into practice. In Jesus' name, Amen.

OCTOBER 25th

Ephesians 5:14-18 reads: *"Wherefore he saith, 'Awake thou that sleepest, and arise from the dead, and Christ shall give thee light (shine upon thee).' See then that ye walk circumspectly* (cautiously), *not as fools (the unwise), but as wise. Redeeming the time, because the days are evil. Wherefore be ye not unwise but understanding what the will of the Lord is. And be not drunk with wine, where in is excess; (riot) but be filled with the Spirit.* "

We are admonished not to be a sleeping Christian, but to let Christ's light shine in and through us, live cautiously, and never forget that the devil roams about like a roaring lion seeking whom he may devour. Live wisely, not like an unwise person who is a fool.

Understand what the will of the Lord is for you. You find this out by being in an attitude of prayer, and giving God the praise and honor He rightfully deserves. Do not be drunk with wine. If wine, or alcohol, has been a survival tool, then it must go. God has a better tool ready to be used, which is to be filled with the Holy Spirit instead. Then you won't need wine to help you get through life's bumps.

To be filled with the Holy Spirit, all you have to do is ask God to fill you. Jesus prayed to His Father to send the Holy Spirit to support you and help you grow into a full-grown Christian. God would be only too glad to *fill* you with the Holy Spirit. Your whole outlook on life will change and you will be amazed at the power you will have to stand, and to withstand. Try it. You will find that you like it .

PRAYER: Heavenly Father, I am surrounded with new survival tools. What amazes me is that there are so many wrong kinds of survival tool out there that the world tries to tell us we need in order to get through life. No wonder Satan is called "the god of this world!" And, without thinking, we give him our worship by using his tools. Father, I really need your help in recognizing his tools and choosing not to use them. I need your help to choose instead to come to you in prayer and songs of praise, have the right kind of friends around me to help me when I feel down, expect the Holy Spirit to encourage, me and to practice forgiveness. I have only listed some of the survival tools available, but with such an arsenal, I should not fail, and I am encouraged! Thank you, Father, for supplying me with so much help. In Jesus' name, Amen.

OCTOBER 26th

I hope you have been encouraged by our study of excess baggage and survival tools. God wants us to grow up a little more each day. It is a process, a progression.

God Himself works in progression. The whole Bible attests to that. He created the heavens and earth in progression. Seedtime and harvest is progression, as is birth, life, and death. Our spiritual growth is no different. Like our spiritual growth, our association with those around us must grow and mature.

Marriage is also a progression. Some don't like the way it progresses for them, and they opt for a divorce. But, guess what, the next marriage must also progress.

The one common denominator in your life is you! If you are at war with yourself, how can you live in peace with someone else? I don't think it can be done. First, you must make peace between yourself and God, and then you can practice peace with others. To love your neighbor as you love yourself means you cannot be at war with yourself. You must be satisfied with what God created, which is *you.*

When that is settled, then you can reach out and love others. The only way to peace with God is to have Jesus (the One who brought peace into the world) in your heart and in your life. Romans 5:1 states, *"Therefore being justified by faith, we have peace with God through our Lord Jesus Christ."* Can it be any more plain? Have a happy, fulfilled life!

PRAYER: Heavenly Father, I do want to grow in grace and holiness, and I can see progress as I read these devotions each day. I find it easier to come to you more quickly when each hurdle comes along in my life. I do not try to fix it by myself so much as I used to. I thank you for that progress, but I still need a lot of help to do a better job of fleeing to you in my time of need. Old habits die hard, but I am encouraged as I see signs of the old survival tools being thrown away to be replaced by the new ones. Walking close to you is an adventure, and I am enjoying the trip. Thank you, Father, Son, and Holy Spirit, for being in my life to stay. In Jesus' name, Amen.

OCTOBER 27ᵗʰ

We are going to take a sharp turn and look back in the Old Testament at some profound questions in Job for a while. Many consider the book of Job the oldest in the Bible. There are some who believe that it was lived out while Moses was in Egypt, but, in all honesty, no one knows for sure to what date in history the book of Job belongs. I like to leave this type of debate to the experts, and suffice it for now that it is an old book.

I find it interesting that the questions Job asked are almost identical to questions that are asked today. In addressing those questions now, hopefully you and I can learn a little more about the character of God.

For some background, Job was a very rich man, with many servants, cattle, and possessions. He also had seven sons and three daughters. In one day, he lost everything. Satan had gone up before God and accused Him of treating Job as His pet, blessing Job above all others. Job was an upright, faithful person and worshipped God. Why should he not be blessed by God? But Satan almost demanded an opportunity at tempting Job to deny God.

Satan predicted that Job would deny God in Job 1:11, which reads, *"But put forth thine hand now, and touch all that he hath, and he will curse thee to thy face. "* God gave Satan permission to go so far, but no further in Job 1:12, which states, *"And the Lord said unto Satan, 'Behold, all that he hath is in thy power, only upon himself put not forth thine hand. ' So Satan went forth from the presence of the Lord."*

In this reference, we can see the *permissive will* of God. It was not God's *directive will* to have such destruction fall on Job. We also see the temptation/test scenario here. To me, it looks like Satan challenged God to test Job's faith, to see if he would curse God to His face. Satan did indeed lay hold of all that Job had, and, in one day, Job lost his oxen, sheep, camels, servants, and all his children.

We see Job's reaction to this news in Job 1:20-22: *"Then Job arose, and rent his mantle, and shaved his head, and fell down upon the ground, and <u>worshipped</u>, And said, 'Naked came I out of my mother's* *womb, and naked shall I return thither: The Lord gave, and the Lord hath taken away; blessed be the name of the Lord.' In all this Job sinned not, nor charged God foolishly.*"

Job withstood the temptation to curse God to His face, and he passed the test of his faith in God, but Satan did not give up easily. In chapter 2, Satan was right back in God's face, but we will look at that tomorrow.

If Satan accused Job before God this way, how does he accuse us before God? The bible says that he does just that in Revelation 12:10, which reads: *"I heard a loud voice saying in heaven, 'Now is come (authority) salvation, and strength, and the kingdom of our God, and the power of His Christ: for the accuser of our brethren is cast down, which accused them before our God day and night.'* "

But we, in this age of grace, have an advantage that Job did not have. I John 2:1 says, *"My little children, these things write I unto you, that ye sin not. And if any man sin, we have an advocate with the Father, Jesus Christ the righteous."*

PRAYER: Heavenly Father, I am learning something very important about Satan, the enemy of my soul. He really wants to separate me from you, and does not care what he does to accomplish that. I must keep my eye on you, who is far more powerful than Satan, and I need to put my faith and trust in you and none other . Thank you, Father, for planning my salvation, carrying it out, and then giving it to me as a free gift. How blessed I am to have such a God to worship. I claim my space in the shadow of your presence as my place of safety. I know my advocate, Jesus, is pleading for me. In Jesus' name, Amen.

OCTOBER 28th

God asked Satan a question in Job 2:3: *"Hast thou considered my servant Job, that there is none like him in the earth, a perfect and an upright man, one that feareth God, and escheweth evil? And still he holdeth fast his integrity, although thou movest me against him, to destroy him without cause."*

Just think about that. Satan moved God to move against Job *without cause*! The CEV translation of this verse reads, *"...and he hasn't changed even though you persuaded me to destroy him for no reason."*

I need to remind you that Job lived in an era before a Savior had come to take away our sins and defeat the devil and all his power over the human race. We live in a time when we can be under the umbrella of God's safety because we are *in Christ Jesus*. However, Satan still tries his best to accuse us.

Satan has not been cast down to earth completely yet. That is a future event, so he is still accusing us before God day and night. And every time we disobey God, we give Satan license to accuse us, and he will try to go the limit to bring us down. We desperately need God's survival tools to withstand such an enemy.

Satan wants us dead, but our lives are in God's hands, not Satan's. I firmly believe that every Christian's life is in the hands of God, and He picks the time of our death, not Satan. God says, "There is a time to be born and a time to die."

I believe His Word, and my faith is firmly planted on His Word. I hope yours is too. It will bring the fruit of peace into your heart and mind. Satan still has his eye on Job, as we see in Job 2:4-7, which reads: *"And Satan answered the Lord, and said, 'Skin for skin, yea, all that a man hath will he give for his life. But put forth thine hand now, and touch his bone and his flesh, and he will curse (renounce) thee to thy face.' And the Lord said unto Satan, 'Behold he is in thine hand; but save his life.' So went Satan forth from the presence of the Lord, and smote Job with sore boils from the sole of his foot unto his crown."*

Job is completely oblivious to what is going on behind the scenes between God and Satan. He does not know that there is a battle for his integrity. Will Job be able to stand up to the temptation that is coming at him with horrifying force? I believe we need to realize just what kind of a spiritual battle there is in the unseen world regarding our lives and how we live them.

PRAYER: Heavenly Father, I had no idea Satan was this active against me, and I am grateful for this insight into how we are the object of your love—and at the same time, the object of Satan's hate. Your blessings on us when we are obedient must be like a bitter pill in Satan's stomach. And oh, how we like to receive your blessings! I pray that my faith in your Word will always be there to sustain me in the trials of life. I keep remembering that your Word to us is to "Fear not!" Satan is a defeated enemy, and your Word also says in Roman 8:37, *"Nay, in all these things we are more than conquerors through Him that loved us."* I lay claim to the truth of these words, and I will walk with my head high and my shoulders square, taking my stand on the Word of God. In Jesus' name, Amen.

OCTOBER 29th

I am sure Job did not feel much like a conqueror when his body was full of boils. He must have been miserable. Can you put yourself in his place? I know it is a stretch, but just try. He lost all his income, his cattle and servants, all his family except his wife, and then he got boils all over his body. Can it get any worse?

Well, yes, it can. Job 2:8-9 continues: *"And he took a potsherd* (a broken piece of pottery) *to scrape himself withal; and he sat down among the ashes. Then said his wife unto him, 'Dost thou still retain thine integrity? Curse (renounce) God and die.' "*

How would you like to have her for your wife? She would rather have a dead husband who would be willing to curse the God who had blessed them than have to live with a sick husband who believed in and followed a faithful God. We see Job's response in Job 2:10, *"But he said unto her, 'Thou speakest as one of the foolish women speaketh. What?*

Shall we receive good at the hand of God, and shall we not receive evil?'
In all this did not Job sin with his lips."

Job asked his wife a profound question, one we need to ask ourselves. Do we expect only good in this life, and never any setbacks? That is an unreal expectation. God is interested in our reactions to the setbacks in life.

So far, Job was up to the temptation and test. I can just see Satan pulling his hair out, wondering what is holding this man together. Satan even used Job's wife to thrust a dagger into his heart. Job's own beloved wife told him to curse the God he loved and then die.

As you look at the trials in your life, do they look small compared to Job's? I know mine do. And Job's faith in God would be tested beyond compare before he was through with this trial.

Let's not be too hard on his wife, however. She had given birth to ten children who all died in one day. How would you have reacted to that? Then her husband became totally disabled! She too had a full plate of sorrow and discomfort.

PRAYER: Heavenly Father, I can hardly believe a person could go through such a harsh trial and come out standing on his feet. He must have had an intimate relationship with you, Father, to be able to have such a strong faith. I am thankful that this book is in the Bible. It helps those of us who read it to see an example of what real faith is like. I am growing, but I have no desire to be tested to that degree. I don't think anyone would. I will rely on your promise to not give us more to bear then we can stand. You are still God—a God who loves us and has promised to never leave us or forsake us, and who loves us with a sacrificial love. You gave your only Son so we might live. Like Job, I will stick with a God like that. In Jesus' name, Amen.

OCTOBER 30th

Job 2:11-13 reads: *"Now when Job's three friends heard of all this evil that was come upon him, they came every one from his own place; Eliphaz the Temanite, and Bildad the Shuhite, and*

446

*Zophar the Naamathite: for <u>they had made an appointment together to</u>
<u>come to mourn with him and to comfort him.</u> And when they lifted up*
their eyes afar off, and knew him not, they lifted up their voice, and wept;
and they rent every one his mantle, and sprinkled dust upon their heads
toward heaven. So they sat down with him upon the ground seven days
and seven nights, and none spake a word unto him: they saw that his
grief was very great."

One can only wonder what kind of friends these three were. They
had agreed together to go visit Job, but he looked so awful, they did not
even recognize him. They did all the right things—displayed deep
mourning and grief, rent their clothes and sprinkled dust on their heads.
These were customary signs of great repentance, grief, and mourning.

But, if they had really come to comfort him, they had a very odd
way of showing that. To sit and stare at a sick person for seven days and
seven nights without a word of comfort is unthinkable. Do you have words
of comfort for the sick, a word of hope from the Bible perhaps? Surely you
don't give those in pain around you the silent treatment.

Job was about the richest man for miles around, and perhaps these
three men were business acquaintances who just might have been jealous of
him. But they did come to see him. We have to give them that.

PRAYER: Heavenly Father, I pray that I will have at least a few words of
hope to give to those who are sick and hurting. I pray that this lesson will
stay with me and help me remember what it means to be a friend. I thank
you, too, for giving us a "behind the scene" look at what can happen in the
spiritual realm, so that when we are sorely tested, we can have an idea that
it is not so much about us as it is about the devil's desire to do us harm, and
his right to stick it to us. As I study your Word, and as I see how the devil
tempted Jesus, it is obvious that he has a certain amount of authority and
power, even though he is a defeated enemy. I am thankful, Lord God, for
this knowledge. It helps me to see the whole picture and gives me a motive
to persevere, and I know you will help me to do that. In Jesus' name,
Amen.

OCTOBER 31st

For the next 30 chapters or more of Job, the three friends finally talk, but they did not comfort Job at all. They accused him of being a terrible sinner who needed to repent. They also indicated that when a person loses all that he has, as Job had, it is God who is punishing him because of sin. Therefore, if Job would only repent, it would all be okay again.

Job insisted on his integrity, that he had not sinned as they accused him of doing. You can read these chapters on your own, it will give you an idea of how harsh they were on Job.

Finally, in chapter 32, a fourth friend spoke up. Elihu had come and listened to the first three speak and debate with Job. He defended Job to a small degree and criticized the three friends for not answering Job's questions. Elihu debated with Job for several more chapters.

During the long discourse from chapters 3 through 37, several profound questions are asked. We will begin with 3:1-3, where Job is the first to break the silence, *"After this opened Job his mouth, and cursed his day* (the day of his birth). *And Job spake and said, 'Let the day perish wherein I was born, and the night in which it was said, There is a man child conceived.' "* And in Job 3:11, he continues, *"Why died I not from the womb? Why did I not give up the ghost when I came out of the belly?"*

Job questioned why he had been allowed to live, if this was the way his life was to go. That is not the profound question, but it sets the stage for it. Toward the end of chapter, Job 3:20-26, he pours out his anguish: *"Wherefore is light given to him that is in misery, and life unto the bitter in soul, Which long for death, but it cometh not; and dig for it more than for hid treasures; Which rejoice exceedingly, and are glad, when they can find the grave? Why is light given to a man whose way is hid, and whom God hath hedged in? For my sighing cometh before I eat, and my roarings are poured out like the waters. For the thing I greatly feared is come upon me, and that which I was afraid of is come unto me.*

I was not in safety, neither had I rest, neither was I quiet; yet trouble came."

Job is asking, "Why do those who trust in God suffer?" But notice that he states that what he had greatly feared had come upon him. Satan is the one who brings fear. This sickness that he had, no doubt, was something that he had feared, but that was not the problem here. Job did not know about the conversation between the devil and God and that he, Job, was the object of that conversation. Neither did his four friends know that. They were all wrestling with deep spiritual questions, and with only a thimbleful of knowledge of the spiritual battle behind the scenes. You see, Satan could not force death on Job, but don't think for a moment Satan did not think that he could convince Job to take his own life.

Why do bad things happen to good people? It is simple. Satan is the evil one who is at work, day and night, trying to get us to agree with him and sin to our hearts content. He expects us to then complain when the bad things happen to us, and blame God for it. Death, sickness, accidents, and nature's rages (tornadoes, hurricanes, fires, and floods) all contribute to our woes. All are a result of the fallen nature and sinfulness that is in the world. Is that God's fault? I don't think so. Put the blame where it belongs.

PRAYER: Heavenly Father, I am reminded of what King David said in Psalm 23:5, *"Thou preparest a table before me in the presence of mine enemies."* And it is no different today! The enemy is all around us. Why, Lord, do we want to blame you for all the bad things that happen around us? One day we will all have to acknowledge that you are *good.* You do not devise evil, not ever. We all need to take responsibility for our actions. I thank you for the suffering that Job went through and that it was recorded for us to read and learn by it. Help us all get a better handle on your character through the questions that are asked in this book. If we ever see you any different than complete love, mercy, and grace, give us a good shaking to wake us up to the real truth. Without you, we would be nothing; and hatred and evil would rule this earth. Forgive us, Lord, for even wanting to lay the blame for all the wrongs in the world at your feet.

Forgive me for complaining about it and not doing anything to put a stop to it. In Jesus' name, Amen.

NOVEMBER 1st

✝ The next profound question is found in Job 7:17-21, where Job asks: *"What is man, that thou shouldest magnify him? And that thou shouldest set thine heart upon him? And that thou shouldest visit him every morning, and try him every moment? How long wilt thou not depart from me, nor let me alone till I swallow down my spitle? If I have sinned; what shall I do unto thee, O thou preserver* (watcher) *of men? Why hast thou set me as a mark against thee, so that I am a burden to myself? And why dost thou not pardon my transgression, and take away mine iniquity? For now shall I sleep in the dust; and thou shalt seek me in the morning but I shall not be."*

The question is, "What is man that God should magnify him?". or "Why does God pay attention to mankind at all?" Well, man was God's crowning glory of creation, because we were created in His image. .There is a God-shaped hole in our heart that only He can fill. God will always be on the prowl for His own creation. He will seek after us until there is no more use for Him to try. God forbid that should ever happen to any of us.

God is at work wooing us to Himself. Job's problem was that he had no clue as to what or why he was suffering the tragedies he had endured. And we would not know what was happening to us if we did not have Job's account in the Bible.

If we could ever get a glimpse of how important each one of us is to God, we would have a much better understanding of how much God loves and cares for us. God knew all along that Job's end would be even better than his beginning. We need to know that too.

Never minimize your importance in God's eyes. That is an insult to the God, who created you just the way you are. Job was in pain. He had suffered the loss of his children and his finances. He also suffered mentally (all hell was out to get him), physically (his body was under siege), spiritually (his wife told him to curse God and die), and socially (his friends were not for him). Even God seemed far away. But Job did not curse God. Imagine that!

PRAYER: Heavenly Father, I better take another look at myself in the mirror. You are pretty interested in me, according to your Word. The CEV translation of Psalm 139:13-17 says: *"You are the one who put me together in my mother's body. And I praise you because of the wonderful way you created me. Everything you do is marvelous! Of this I have no doubt. Nothing about me is hidden from you! I was secretly woven together deep in the earth below, but with your own eyes you saw my body being formed. Even before I was born you had written in your book everything I would do. Your thoughts are far beyond my understanding, much more than I could ever imagine."*

I thank you, Lord, for who and what I am, and for the attention you pay to me. I also thank you for my children, who you so graciously have given to me. They, too, were created by your hand and are precious in your sight. Help me to not lose sight of how precise you have created me, and help me to have a greater appreciation for that. In Jesus' name, Amen.

NOVEMBER 2nd

Let's turn to Job 9:1-4, which reads: *"Then Job answered and said, 'I know it is so of a truth, but how should man be just with God? If he contend with Him, He cannot answer him one of a thousand. He is wise in heart, and mighty in strength: who hath hardened himself against Him, and hath prospered?' "*

I want to urge you to read these verses in your own Bible as well. Job and his friends were in a head-to-head debate over heavy issues concerning God, whom they couldn't see or talk to face to face.

The question Job asked is, "How can a man be just with God?" Mankind and God are poles apart. Sin separated mankind from God, and man is helpless to do anything about it. It is a fact of life that we all die as a result of sin. It is a law as sure as gravity.

451

Only God could figure out a solution to that problem, and only God could carry it out. His solution is none other than His own Son, Jesus Christ. Is that so hard to understand? Job knew in his heart that He was separated from God, yet he worshipped Him with all his strength and with the knowledge that he had of God at that time.

The CEV translates Job 9:3-4 as, *"Not once in a thousand times could we win our case if we took Him to court. God is wise and powerful—who could possibly oppose Him and win?"* Job had a good perspective of God. How did he learn all that? He communed with God daily and wanted to please God and to serve Him. God was well aware of Job's spiritual condition, or God would never have allowed Satan to attack him like that.

Job knew that in order for mankind to have a relationship with God, there would have to be an intermediary. We know Him as Jesus Christ. Before He came, there was no one to go between mankind and God, no one to make peace, give power to overcome, bring joy in the midst of sorrow, and so on. Do you realize what a blessed time we live in? We, of all people, should be almost jumping up and down, proclaiming, "This is the day of grace. Don't miss out on what it means!"

Job knew he needed an intermediary, but there was none. He couldn't bring his case to a court trial. He knew he would lose anyway. And, day after day, he was scraping his body while he sat in a pile of ashes, and his friends insisted that he was guilty of some horrendous sin or none of this would have happened to him. And you think you have trouble?

How long would this go on for Job? God often comes on us suddenly. Suddenly, God will put a stop to all this debating, and set the record straight.

PRAYER: Heavenly Father, I thank you that we have an intermediary who has lived like we do and has suffered, been rejected, betrayed, and even died like we do. He knows what it is to live here on this sinful earth. He can identify fully with our life. Lord, you reached down and brought us up closer to you, so that we can converse with you and expect an answer. I feel so blessed to live in this time, the age of grace. I give you all the praise

452

and thanksgiving for such wonderful blessings in my life. In Jesus' wonderful name, Amen.

NOVEMBER 3rd

✝ Job asks another profound question in Job 14:7-14, which reads: *"For there is hope of a tree, if it be cut down, that it will sprout again, and that the tender branch thereof will not cease. Though the root thereof wax old in the earth, and the stock thereof die in the ground; Yet through the secret of water it will bud, and bring forth boughs like a plant. But man dieth, and wasteth away: yea man giveth up the ghost, and where is he? As the waters fail from the sea, and the flood decayeth and drieth up: so man lieth down, and riseth not: till the heavens be no more, they shall not awake, nor be raised out of their sleep. O that thou wouldest hide me in the grave (Shoel), that thou wouldest keep me secret, until thy wrath be past, that thou wouldest appoint me a set time, and remember me! If a man die, shall he live again? All the days of my appointed time will I wait, till my charge (release should) come."*

Job had reasoned that when a tree is cut down, it can come back to life, sprout a new branch and live. But what about man? Does he live again?

Job had just asked shortly before, "What is man that thou art mindful of him?" If mankind was so important, why would people not live again? If a tree can live again after it is cut down, then why not mankind? Even today, there is a debate as to whether there is really life after death. It is an age-old question. Today we have accounts of those who have died and seen the other side, and then lived to tell about it.

Job had come to that conclusion in a small way. People who are willing to delve into this topic will consider making a choice to see to it that their eternal security is made sure. Accepting Jesus as Lord and Savior is

453

the only way to make sure your eternal life will be lived in union with your Creator, and not in union with the enemy, Satan himself.

PRAYER: Heavenly Father, I know many people do not even think about where they will spend eternity, but I am convinced there is life after death. I also believe that we choose where we will spend eternity now, while we are living our lives on this earth. I have decided to live with you, Lord, in union with my Creator. I look forward to that time in my life, a part of the eternity I am already living, because you have said that I have passed from death to life (John 5:24). In Jesus' name, Amen.

NOVEMBER 4th

Picking up where we left off yesterday, let's look at John 5:24, which reads: *"Verily, verily, I say unto you, 'He that heareth my word, and believeth on Him that sent me, hath everlasting life, and shall not come into condemnation (judgment); but is passed from death unto life.' "*

Please notice the verbs in this verse. Jesus uses the present tense and the past tense. When He says, *"hath everlasting life,"* He means right now. You don't wait until to die to find out whether you have everlasting life. When He says, *"shall not come into condemnation,"* He is referring to a future time. There will be a judgment, but it is *not* for you. You are excluded by this verse, and there is no higher authority than Jesus, who is speaking here.

Also notice that He says, *"but is passed from death unto life,"* with "is," making it the present tense. *Today* you are living in eternal life or eternal death. The moment you have Jesus in your heart, you have crossed over the line and are under the umbrella of *life*.

If this is a hard concept to grasp, then ask God to make it understandable to you. He will be glad to answer that prayer. Your eternal life is sealed when Jesus is in you and you are in Him. I have to admit this

454

was a very hard concept for me to believe I could subscribe to. I was convinced that no one could *know* they were going to live eternally with God. To me, it was the height of arrogance. Who was I to twist God's arm and declare that I will live eternally with Him in paradise?

You see, I had it all backwards. It was God who made it available to me, and no matter how hard I had tried, I could never arrange a way to be saved from the penalty of my sins. God did it all and then handed the gift package to me. All I had to do was to accept His Son as my Savior. He had died for me, paid the price and penalty for sin, and declared me fit for heaven when He entered my heart.

The burden for me was to accept what God had done. Once I realized it was that simple, it all made sense to me, and I was so grateful to be able to know that I would go to heaven when I died. In fact, I had eternal life within me *right then*! It was a matter of just stepping over the line (death) for it to be a reality.

Job wrestled with this deep question. He did not know what we know, and he did not live in the age of grace like we do. But He knew his God, and he knew that it would be in the character of God to provide such a blessing for those who are faithful to Him.

PRAYER: Heavenly Father, how I thank you for the blessing of the assurance of eternal life, right here and now. It boggles the mind to think of how much you loved the people of the whole world, that you were willing to send your only begotten Son to be the substitute for us all. There is no way we could ever repay you for such love. And all you want from us in return is our faithfulness and obedience. What a small part we are asked to pay, and yet many rebel even at that. Forgive us, Lord, when we want our way so much that we think we can do a better job of handling our lives. May the Holy Spirit prompt our ability to choose wisely. In Jesus' name, Amen.

NOVEMBER 5th

✝ In Job 21:7-15, we read: *"__Wherefore do the wicked live,__ __become old, yea are mighty in power?__ Their seed is established in their sight with them, and their offspring before their eyes. Their houses are safe from fear, neither is the rod of God upon them. Their bull gendereeth, and faileth not; their cow calveth, and casteth not her calf. They send forth their little ones like a flock, and their children dance. They spend their days in wealth, and in a moment go down to the grave. Therefore they say unto God, 'Depart from us; for we desire not the knowledge of thy ways. What is the Almighty, that we should serve Him? and what profit should we have if we pray unto Him?' "*

Job is really pleading with God for answers to some deep questions. He wanted to know why wicked people seem to be blessed in every way—they lived to be old while enjoying power and wealth, their houses were safe from fear, God's rod of discipline was not upon them, their cattle bred, their children played and danced, and they did not die slowly, but just up and die.

So, why would they want a God in their lives? Their attitude was, "Who needs God anyway? We do just fine with out Him." Job concluded by reasoning, "What profit should we have if we pray to Him?" Job must be thinking of all the prayers and worship he had given to God, and wondered what he had gained.

Here he sat, having lost everything, with even his body wasting away to nothing but skin and bones. He had no hope of ever getting any better. His three friends accuse him of gross sin, and offer no comfort or hope. So, can anyone tell Job why the wicked prosper and live?

It is a question that is asked even today. But the day will come when all the wicked people's wealth will not be able to give their souls peace. Their wealth cannot assure them of good health, safety from accidents, and so on.

The question of what life is all about is at the bottom of all this. Life here is a preparation for life in heaven. Those who have lived just for their own pleasure won't have anything stored up in heaven for their eternal life. However, you can see why Job is thinking like this. He tried to live the right kind of life, and here he is, stuck in a rut he cannot escape.

Remember, Job does not know the behind-the-scenes battle—how Satan challenged God regarding Job's faith. But now that we know that this sort of thing can happen, we need to look at our circumstances with renewed wisdom. Job has a big lesson to learn, and he will learn it.

Another thing we need to know about God is that He wants us to grow in grace and holiness. If we don't allow Him to grow us up, then God will have to use hurtful measures to do it. Our growth is way more important to God than our comfort, simply because He is preparing us for eternity. He wants His best for us in eternity.

PRAYER: Heavenly Father, I see that we grow in grace and holiness as we meditate on your Word, study it, and learn from it. I pray I will never turn away from reading and meditating on your Word. Give me the wisdom and discernment to put this Word into practice in my day-by-day life. I want to join hands with you to bring this Word to the world around me. In Jesus' name, Amen.

NOVEMBER 6th

Job 28:12 reads, *"But where shall wisdom be found? And where is the place of understanding?"* Job goes on to indicate that wisdom is elusive—no matter where you look, you can not find wisdom. I strongly urge you to read the whole book of Job, especially this chapter about wisdom.

Let's look at a couple more verses from this chapter. In Job 28:20, Job asks, *"Whence then cometh wisdom? And where is the place of understanding?"* And in Job 28:28, we see the answer, *"And unto man he said, 'Behold, the fear of the Lord, that is wisdom; and to depart from evil is understanding.' "*

I marvel that Job could figure that out way back then when God was not revealed to mankind like He is today. Do you remember that we talked at length about knowledge, understanding, and wisdom earlier in the year? God is full of knowledge, understanding, and wisdom. He also wants us to possess these three attributes, and even Job recognized their importance.

In chapters 29 through 31, Job has an "I, me, my, and mine" problem. If you read through those chapters and circle those words in a color so they stand out, you will be amazed at what it looks like. Job did not see his nature, which was sinful. He had not willfully practiced sin. He *had* practiced prayer and sacrifice, but in the eyes of God, all mankind *is* sinful, and that is what Job did not understand.

God is going to show Job that fact pretty soon, and it will change Job's view. Have you ever stopped to think about how often you say, "I," "me," "my," and "mine"? It could be an eye-opener. Let me remind you of that verse I have quoted so many times, *"Humble yourself therefore, under the mighty hand of God that He may exalt you in due time"* (I Peter 5:6).

When you do your own humbling, then God does not have to do it for you. When you do it, it is a private thing. When God does it, it is a public thing. God does not want to embarrass us, not ever. But, if that is what it is going to take to shape us up, He will resort to that kind of thing.

Can you think back to a time when God had to humble you? You could have been willing to change on your own and not become embarrassed. Our pride can get in the way of us changing and growing into the people God wants us to be. If you had wisdom, then you would have changed.

God wants our character to be like His—full of love, patience, kindness, gentleness, etc. If we insist on being unkind, impatient, rough, and hateful, then God will step in and do the job of humbling.

PRAYER: Heavenly Father, I hope I have learned a good lesson today. I do not want you to have to humble me. I hope I can see when I need to change, and become the person you want me to be, and be willing to change sooner rather than later. One of the things I am learning is that you, Father, will have your way no matter how often we put a barrier or stumbling block in the way with our disobedience or rebellion. You will have your will done, so we better decide to cooperate, and the sooner the better. Help me, Lord, to follow through with my desire to be an obedient, faithful follower of the Lord Jesus Christ. In Jesus' name, Amen.

NOVEMBER 7ᵗʰ

✝ In Job 31:14, we read, *"What then shall I do when God riseth up? And when He visiteth, what shall I answer Him?"* This is the last question of Job's we will address.

What can any of us say when God asks us to make an account of ourselves and our lives? All His knowledge of us is more than we even know about ourselves. He knows our every motive, even every intention of our words. Without a mediator, an advocate, we would stand naked before God.

But, thankfully, we will not stand before God. Instead, we will be examined by Jesus, who knew what it was to live on this earth as a human being. Job knew he was no match for God, yet he had complained to the high heaven about his plight. After all, he had worshipped God faithfully.

In Job 32, Elihu finally spoke up with more sense than the other three friends. As I see it, Elihu was there to turn Job and his three friends' attention back to the true God, and prepare Job to hear from God.

Job 32:1-3 reads: *"So these three men ceased to answer Job, because he was righteous in his own eyes. Then was kindled the wrath of Elihu the son of Barachel the Buzite, of the kindred of Ram: against Job was his wrath kindled, because he justified himself rather than God. Also against his three friends was his wrath kindled, because they had found no answer, and yet had condemned Job."*

Elihu saw that Job was justifying himself, and he also saw that the three friends did not show any compassion for Job. Instead of offering words of comfort, they continued to condemn Job. You can read all of what Elihu had to say in Job 32 through 37.

PRAYER: Heavenly Father, I see that you will not leave us or forsake us, you provided a man to stand in the gap for Job. It shows me you will do the same for me, and that is a comforting thought. If we keep our eyes on your character, we will have the confidence we need to stand the trials of life. How will Job come out in the end? Will he be able to see what he needs to change in his life? I think the question I need to ask is, "Am I able to make the changes that are necessary in my life?" I ask for your help to examine myself, to look deep into my own soul, and give me the strength to make the changes you want me to make so that I will reflect your love, mercy, and grace. In Jesus' name, Amen.

NOVEMBER 8th

God begins to ask Job some questions in Job 38:1-5, which reads: *"Then the Lord answered Job out of the whirlwind, and said, 'Who is this that darkeneth counsel by words without knowledge? Gird up now thy loins like a man, for I will demand of thee and answer thou me. Where wast thou when I laid the foundation of the earth? Declare, if thou hast understanding. Who hath laid the measure thereof, if thou knowest? Or who hath stretched the line upon it?' "*

God is essentially saying to Job, "You wanted to talk to me? Well here is your chance. I will ask the questions and you can answer them." In Job 38:21-23, God continues: *"Knowest thou it, because thou wast then born? Or because the number of thy days is great? Hast thou entered into the treasures of the snow? Or hast thou seen the treasures of the hail, which I have reserved against the time of trouble, against the day of battle and war?"*

In order to fully understand the depth of this verse, we need to look at a verse from Revelation that refers to the great tribulation that will come upon the earth. Revelation 16:21 reads: *"And there fell upon man a great hail out of heaven, every stone about the weight of a talent* (about a hundred pounds): *and men blasphemed God because of the plague of the hail; for the plague thereof was exceeding great."*

God has indeed reserved a hail storm for a battle. We also need to look at Job 38:24, where God asks, *"By what way is the light parted, which scattereth the east wind upon the earth?"* Every time you look at a prism and see the different colors dancing on the wall, you see light that has been parted. How did the writer of Job know that? But this is God speaking here. God continued questioning Job, and, in chapter 40, Job finally answers. We will look at that tomorrow.

PRAYER: Heavenly Father, How could we ever answer the questions you ask? Isaiah 55:8-9 states *"'For my thoughts are not your thoughts, neither are your ways my ways,' saith the Lord. 'For as the heavens are higher than the earth, so are my ways higher than your ways, and my thoughts higher than your thoughts.' "* I see by this scripture that the gap between us proves we need a man to stand in the gap for us to communicate with you. Thank you for sending Jesus to be that man. We can talk to Him at any time, and He will understand our difficulty in relating to the glory and majesty of a Holy God. Job did not have someone to stand in the gap for him, but he had the knowledge of your goodness that had sustained him. You knew he would stand the test and come out a better man. That should encourage me and all others to not succumb to defeat when similar tests come our way, but instead to stand strong in our faith in your Word. Fill me with the courage I need to not run away in defeat. In Jesus' name, Amen.

NOVEMBER 9th

A conversation between God and Job finally begins to take place in Job 40:1-5, which reads: *"Moreover the Lord answered Job, and said, 'Shall he that contendeth with the Almighty instruct Him? He that reproveth* (argues with) *God, let him answer it.' Then Job answered the Lord, and said, 'Behold I am vile* (of small account)*; what shall I answer thee? I will lay mine hand upon my mouth. Once have I spoken; but I will not answer: yea, twice; but I will proceed no further.' "*

Once God rose up and answered Job, Job did not know what to say. He did admit his condition however, "I am of small account." Personally, I believe our biggest problem is that we think of God as too small to take care of our big problems, and too big to be concerned about our little problems. Either way, we lose.

God wants us to go to Him with everything, big or small, and to see Him as being ready and willing to help us in our times need, with any need we might have. Job 40:6-9 continues: *"Then answered the Lord unto Job out of the whirlwind, and said, 'Gird up thy loins now like a man: I will demand of thee and declare thou unto me. Wilt thou also disannul my judgment? Wilt thou condemn me, that thou mayest be righteous* (justified)*? Hast thou an arm like God? Or canst thou thunder with a voice like Him?' "*

God is pointing out to Job that mankind is no match for Him. He said "gird up thy loins *like a man*." Job is a man, and surely he cannot judge God, or justify himself before God.

When God asked Job if he had an arm like God, I believe that is referring to a power like God's. God wrote the Ten Commandments, with his finger, and brought Israel out of Egypt with a strong arm. He also talks about the hand of God, and each one has a certain amount of power—the finger, the hand, the arm, and the strong arm.

So God asked Job if he had an arm like His. I am sure Job knew what God was talking about. And can Job annul God's judgments? By no means! The Lord God went on for the rest of chapter 40 and all of chapter 41 discussing His abilities, His creation, and so on. Finally, in chapter 42, Job got it! We will address that tomorrow.

PRAYER: Heavenly Father, I often wonder what you think when you look down on this earth and watch us sinful, faltering human beings struggle with life. If only we would know, beyond a shadow of a doubt, your love and care for us first, we would avoid so much anxiety and worry. How do we shift gears and live like we ought to live, in full rest in your finished work of salvation and the work of the Holy Spirit in our lives right now? We have so much more help today than Job did in his day. But I see so much hurt, anxiety, disappointments, sorrow, and a hundred other things plaguing believers, and their lives are far from victorious. Holy Spirit, sweep across our land and fill your people with your power. Help us to run our race with confidence. Heavenly Father, I am thankful that I can bring both my small and big problems to you, and you are well able to help me with solutions. I cease from trying to make a solution of my own, and I pray that your Holy Spirit will help me to look for your answers to my every trial and temptation that arises. I am thankful for the book of Job to help me see the character of Satan, of God, of so-called friends, and of Job himself. It is a very good character study for me, and I set as a goal to stand strong in the faith as Job did. In Jesus' name, Amen.

NOVEMBER 10th

Job 42:1-6 reads: *"Then Job answered the Lord, and said, 'I know that thou canst do every thing, and that no thought can be withholden from thee. Who is he that hideth counsel without knowledge? Therefore have I uttered that I understood not; things too wonderful for me, which I knew not. Hear, I beseech thee, and I will speak: I will demand of thee, and declare thou unto me. I have heard of thee by the hearing of the ear: but now mine eye seeth thee. Wherefore I abhor myself, and repent in dust and ashes.' "*

Job finally saw himself. All the words of his friends did not open up the revelation of his true nature. But, when God showed Job His majesty, strength, knowledge, understanding, and wisdom, then Job was able to see his own lowliness compared to God.

Have you ever measured your own stature with God's? Try it sometime, and it will surely humble you. I am sometimes amazed at how we try to boss God around. We pray and pray and tell God how to fix our problems, but do we listen to what God is telling us about Himself through His Word?

463

Job did not hesitate to do the right thing when such a revelation came to him. He confessed how he felt about himself compared to God. He abhorred himself! Then he repented.

Do we hear much about repentance today? I don't think so. Repentance is an important part of changing our way of thinking, of doing and of living. It means to turn around, or turn away from, and take a new direction in life. In other words, it is putting off the old self and putting on the new self. Job repented in dust and ashes. He repented openly and without shame.

Job had heard about God, but he had not really *seen* (that is, perceived) God. God wanted Job to know Him in a deeper way than to just have heard about Him.

Now, can you see what God's goals were in and through all this suffering and those debates with the Job's friends? God allowed Satan to rob Job of his children, his sustenance, the support of his wife and friends, and even his health, until there was nothing left but his faith in God. Then God showed up and gave Job a lesson on humility. God showed Job who *He* was and who Job was in His eyes.

What is your concept of God? How big is He to you? How significant are you to Him? Does God really care about you and your every-day life? Will you only understand that sort of thing after going through some tough time and the experience of God's provisions and help?

Now that we see how Job was humbled, we need to look at what it means by, "God will exalt you in *due time*" (I Peter 5:6). The due season came after Job humbled himself and admitted he must be little in his own eyes, but big in God's eyes. How can we count it all joy when we fall into a multitude of temptations and trials? We can do that because God is counting you worthy of His time and effort to be with you through those times, and He has a great blessing in store for you once you have gone through it. Satan is a thief, but we can ask God to give back to us everything that Satan has stolen. That is the exaltation part of the equation, which is promised to us by our Heavenly Father.

PRAYER: Dear Heavenly Father, this ongoing battle we are in is sometimes more that we can take. Yet you are there to go through it with us, and you won't let it get to be more than we can bear. Is the blessing on the other side in direct relationship to the depth of the struggle? It would appear to be so. Help me to be prepared for anything of this nature that comes into my life, so that I, too, can come out of it with my faith in God still as strong as Job's, and receive the blessing in store for me. In Jesus' precious name, Amen.

NOVEMBER 11th

Job 42:7-9 reads: *"And it was so, that after the Lord had spoken these words to Job, the Lord said to Eliphaz the Temanite, 'My wrath is kindled against thee and against thy two friends: for ye have not spoken of me the thing that is right, as my servant Job hath. Therefore take unto you now seven bullocks and seven rams, and go to my servant Job, and offer up for yourselves a burnt offering; and my servant Job shall pray for you: for him will I accept: lest I deal with you after your folly, in that ye have not spoken of me the thing which is right, like my servant Job.' So Eliphaz the Temanite, and Bildad the Shuhite and Zophar the Naamathite went, and did according as the Lord commanded them: the Lord also accepted Job."*

Wow, what a turn about! These three friends had railed on Job, up one side and down the other. But God justified Job's witness, even in the midst of his misery, which the three friends had used to condemn him. They had indicated that if he were good and righteous, then he would not be suffering as he was, but since he was in such a condition of loss and suffering, then surely there was sin in his life that needed confessing and repentance.

Job did not willingly sin, and he had willingly turned to God for every thing. The three friends had no business condemning Job when God had not condemned him. Remember, no law had yet been written whereby sin could be measured, such as the Ten Commandments. And where there is no law, sin cannot be computed or measured. If there are no speeding laws, how can an officer say you are speeding, or write you a ticket?

These three friends had made themselves judge and jury, but only God can hold that position. God's wrath had been kindled against them. This is a good lesson for us. Be careful how you paint a picture of God to others by your words. We do not want God's wrath to be kindled against us either, do we?

PRAYER: Heavenly Father, I see that when you step in, things change in a hurry. In fact, I have seen that over and over again in the Bible's accounts of people's lives. It happened to Joseph in jail, and suddenly he was standing in front of Pharaoh, and then promoted to second highest in the Kingdom of Egypt. I also see that before exaltation there was a humbling experience, which the subject had to suffer through to the end. I also see that is a lesson we need to learn while we are not in a situation of turmoil, so that we can hold up under it when it happens to us. Both Joseph and Job completed their tests. They hung onto their integrity and faith in you. They also withstood their temptations. They did not succumb to grumbling and murmuring against you. Job did not do what Satan had told God he would do, that is "curse God to His face." Satan has plans against me, but, Father, you also have plans for me to have the opportunity to bring you honor and glory. My prayer today is that I will be as faithful and obedient as Job was—to not falter or fail, but instead stand strong and confident in your willingness and ability to defend and protect me through life. In Jesus' name, Amen.

NOVEMBER 12th

✝ Job 42:10-11 reads: *"And the Lord turned the captivity of Job, when he prayed for his friends: also the Lord gave Job twice as much, as he had before. Then came there unto him all is brethren, and all his sisters, and all they that had been of his acquaintance before, and they bemoaned him, and comforted him over all the evil that the Lord had*

466

brought upon him: Every man also gave him a piece of money, and every one an earring of gold."

Job's captivity (he had been "held captive" by his illness) was finished when he prayed for his friends. This is a strange lesson, but it is a lesson we need to learn. God had been using Job through this whole ordeal to touch the hearts of those three who the Bible called "friends."

Job might have been the only person on the earth through whom those friends could see the heart of God. God is good, all the time, and only Job could prove that to these three men.

If Job had rebelled, saying he just could not pray for these men after all the hateful things they had said about him, then he would have failed to show God's goodness to them, and God could not have used him to the fullest. But, instead, Job obeyed God.

The Bible does not tell us how he felt, but we need to be careful to not go by our feelings. We, too, must obey God no matter what. A lot of people have a hard time receiving gifts, getting something for nothing. All Job's family and friends, who had been conspicuously absent through his whole ordeal, are now coming back to him once his suffering is over and God had exalted him. How many of you have families and friends just like that? Sad to say, that is often the case, and it should not be.

Job had learned to receive goodness from God, and he realized it was a free gift. Then he was able to receive from others as well. He could have been insulted when they came bearing gifts *after* he was healed and blessed by God. Satan could have been tempting him to say, "Now that I am in a position to take care of myself, and even to be able to give to others, now they come and try to bless me? Where were they when I really needed them? They can have their gifts. I don't want them."

This is the way people often feel. But just maybe God had prompted Job's brothers, sisters, and friends to bless him with gifts at this time. At any rate, Job accepted their gifts.

Jesus has come with free gifts for us also. And how do we receive them? Are we picky, choosing only those gifts that we are comfortable with and rejecting those that would cause us to stand out in a crowd?

There are so many lessons to learn from the life of Job. We see how to suffer unjustly, withstand the criticism of a spouse and friends, and endure the absence of family support. We also learn how to trust God, no matter what Satan throws at us, and how to be humble gracefully. Job shows us how to pray for those who have not been kind to us, and how to be obedient to God in our compassion towards others.

God has lessons for each one of us to learn. Can we learn them through Job's experience, or does God need to humble us to the point of humiliation in order to get us to humble ourselves? Remember, I Peter 5:6 says, *"Humble <u>YOURSELF</u> therefore under the mighty hand of God that <u>He</u> may <u>exalt you</u> in due time."* When you suffer humbly as Job did, then God does not need to do the humbling.

PRAYER: Heavenly Father, I thank you for the lessons given to me in the book of Job. I pray that I will learn them without being put to a test to have to learn them the hard way. But, if that is what it is going to take, then I pray that we can go through it together, because I never want to walk that path by myself. I lay claim to that verse that says you will never leave me or forsake me. I put my hand in yours and I won't let go. You bring a peace into my life that I cannot find anywhere else. My heart overflows with gratitude for your loving kindness and longsuffering, your mercy, and grace. In Jesus' name, Amen.

NOVEMBER 13th

Job 42:12-17 reads: *"So the Lord blessed the latter end of Job more than his beginning: for he had fourteen thousand sheep, and six thousand camels, and a thousand yoke of oxen and a thousand she asses. He had also seven sons and three daughters. And he called the name of the first Jemima; and the name of the second Kezia; and the name of the third Kerenhapuch. And in all the land were no women found so fair as the daughters of Job: and their father gave them inheritance among their brethren. After this lived Job an hundred and forty years, and saw his sons, and his sons' sons, even four generations. So Job died being old and full of days."*

Job's possessions were returned to him double. His children were also returned to him. He had ten who had lived (and died and he would see them again in heaven), and his ten children who had been added to the family would also be with him in eternity.

It is interesting that his life had been *"full of days,"* as the Bible says. Look at what Job had said in Job 7:3-4: *"So am I made to possess months of vanity, and wearisome nights are appointed to me. When I lie down, I say, 'When shall I arise, and the night be gone?' And I am full of tossings to and fro unto the dawning of the day."*

Once the suffering had passed and Job had been blessed, God could say of him that his life had been full of days. Is your life full of days? How long the nights are when you are in pain, or troubled of mind and spirit. One would think the night will never end.

Oh, how we long for the fullness of days. And God says it is our heritage. We are to inherit the good things now and forever, not just when we die and go to heaven. God wants us to have an abundant life right now.

As we learn the tough lessons of life, we gain more and more of the abundant life. There is a song that goes, "O, what peace we often forfeit. O, what needless pain we bear, all because we do not carry everything to God in prayer." Do not forfeit peace. God is there to provide it for each and every one of us.

PRAYER: Heavenly Father, thank you for these lessons. I can see that many of them I have already learned. I am so thankful for learning that I can claim peace in the midst of turmoil. You have taught me to rely on you when the whole world looks like it has turned upside down. What peace that has brought into my life! I pray that all who read this will experience that same peace when they go to you, God, in prayer, and claim it as their own. Turmoil is only too happy to fill our hearts and bring us strife instead of peace, uneasiness instead of rest, and anger instead of joy. I pray that we

469

will try being more than conquerors. We can do it because, God, you will help us. In Jesus' name, Amen.

NOVEMBER 14th

There are a couple of words in the Bible I want to examine. The first one is "come." God the Father invites us to come in Isaiah 1:18 which reads, " *'Come now, and let us reason together,' saith the Lord: 'though your sins be as scarlet, they shall be white as snow; though they be red like crimson, they shall be as wool.' "*

We have talked about this verse before, but I want you to look at it from the point of view that it is an invitation from God. He invites us into His presence for the precise purpose to discuss, debate, and reason with Him. I believe God is filled with joy when we want to search out a truth in His Word and let Him know that we are searching for a certain truth.

In fact, the Holy Spirit is called the Spirit of truth. In John 16:13, we read, *"Howbeit when He, the Spirit of truth is come, He will guide you into all truth; for He shall not speak of Himself; but whatsoever He shall hear, that shall He speak, and He will show you things to come."*

God is way more anxious for us to know the truth than we are to even ask for it. His invitation is not just a "drop in for a little talk" type of invitation. God means business here. He wants us to consider our sins, which are crimson, but God announced that they shall be white like snow. That may sound impossible, but God knew that the color red will wipe out red and make it look white. That is exactly how Jesus' red blood of redemption will turn our red sins white before God's eyes.

The verbs are in the future tense, because this was not accomplished until Jesus came and shed His blood for our sins and died our death. Then our red sins were turned to white in the eyes of God. Accept God's invitation to come and reason together with Him.

PRAYER: Heavenly Father, thank you for such an invitation. I accept it and I will come to you when I have a question about anything that has to do with my salvation, sanctification, and struggles in this world while walking your narrow road. Help me with compromise, so I do not toy with that idea as a way to live this life on earth. Knowing the truth is the way to victory. Thank you for showing me how to accomplish that. In Jesus' name, Amen.

NOVEMBER 15th

Jesus issued us a different invitation that also includes the word "come." In Matthew 11:28, He says, *"Come unto me all ye that labor and are heavy laden, and I will give you rest."* Outside of Jesus, there is turmoil, sweat and tears, worry and anxiety, and no rest at all. But Jesus knows that when you come to Him, and give your burdens over to Him, you will experience true rest and peace.

Jesus explains how it is all accomplished as He continues in Matthew 11:29-30, *"Take my yoke upon you, and learn of me; for I am meek and lowly in heart: and ye shall find rest unto your souls . For my yoke is easy, and my burden is light."* Jesus is our example. He said, "Learn of me." He is meek and lowly of heart. He will put your soul at rest.

I also want to draw your attention to the fact that, for both the Father and Son, the burden of success is *not* up to you. The invitation has been issued, and your choice is to accept or to ignore it. To come to God the Father and God the Son is to have the benefits that accompany the believer through this life on earth.

God does not send out that invitation, "to come", lightly. It is a serious invitation, with a serious purpose, and a serious outcome if it is ignored. Ask God to show you all there is to know about forgiveness, and then get a concordance and look up the word "forgiveness" and make a journal on what the Word says to you. You will learn more than you can imagine. Before you start such a search, be sure to pray to have the Holy Spirit enlighten your mind to the truth. Remember, He is the guide to the truth.

PRAYER: Heavenly Father, yes, I do want to learn the truth, and I do want the Holy Spirit of truth to guide me into all the truth. I am so thankful that I can ask for, and expect to have, the truth from your Word. I have heard it said, "We are not supposed to know all that," and now I am being told I may know that truth. It is a hard hurdle to get over the old word that said I was not supposed to know all that. But, Lord, you must have had this Bible written for a purpose, and since I can read it from cover to cover, I should be able to extract the truth from the pages of this Book. I remember you saying, *"You shall know the truth and the truth shall make you free"* (John 8:32). So, there I have it—I can search the Word for the truth. You have invited me to do so. Thank you, Father, for that assurance. In Jesus' name, Amen.

NOVEMBER 16th

There are several reasons why Jesus came into the world. We will look at a few of those reasons today. John 5:43 reads, *"I am come in my Father's name, and ye received me not; if another shall come in his own name, him ye will receive."*

For Jesus to come in His Father's name means that all His Father's power is available to Him. Jesus came with power and with authority because He came in the name of His Heavenly Father, the Creator of the universe, God Almighty. That is how Jesus was equipped to come.

We see another reason for His coming in John 9:39, which reads, *"And Jesus said, 'For judgment I am come into this world; that they which see not, might see, and that they which see might be made blind.' "* The very fact that Jesus came to earth creates a judgment. It means that everyone who has heard of Him has to make a choice, and that choice judges them as a believer if they accept Him and as a non-believer if they reject Him. Those who really *see* Him as Savior from their sins have become spiritually awake and are spiritually seeing. Those who *see* Him as

Savior of their sins but reject Him are rebels, and God is saying they deserve to become spiritually blind.

This is a severe judgment, but God cannot wink at sin. It must be dealt with. Jesus dealt with it when He shed His blood as a sacrifice for sin, and died the penalty of sin. You are either for Him or you are against Him.

John 10:10 states, *"The thief cometh not but for to steal, and to kill, and to destroy: I am come that they might have life, and that they might have it more abundantly."* Jesus came to bring a new kind of life to earth, a born-again life that only believers in Jesus can have.

So, we see by these verses that Jesus came to administer God's power and authority on earth, to be a standard for judgment, and to bring life eternal (beginning the day you invite Jesus into your heart) to the people of this world.

Also look at John 12:46, which reads, *"I am come a light into the world, that whosoever believeth on me should not abide in darkness."* People are either walking around in spiritual light or spiritual darkness. It is one or the other. What is your choice? That is a part of the judgment we read about in John 9:39.

Jesus came once, as a babe in a manger, to bring with Him all of these things. He will come again, and the Bible is not silent on that subject. Why will He come again, and when? We will explore that in a few days!

PRAYER: Heavenly Father, again I thank you for showing me the truths of your Word. As I think about your Book, the Bible, I am amazed at how it has stood the test of time, and how it has been preserved throughout the ages. There are those who have died to make sure it was passed on from generation to generation. I pray that I will be among those who have been willing to pass on the truths of your Word, and to live a life that displays those truths. Help me, Lord, to be a pleasing vessel for you. Give me the will to stand the tests that come my way and to persevere. In Jesus' name, Amen.

NOVEMBER 17th

Do you remember when we addressed God's perfect timing? There is a "come" to God's perfect timing also.

With that in mind, let's look again at the account of Jesus at the wedding feast that ran out of wine. Jesus' mother had told Him about the problem, and He reminded her that He was on a time schedule, as we see in John 2:4, which reads, *"Jesus saith unto her, 'Woman, what have I to do with thee? Mine hour is not yet come.' "* And in John 7:7-8, Jesus continues, *"The world cannot hate you; but me it hateth, because I testify of it, that the works thereof are evil. Go ye up unto the feast: I go not up yet unto this feast; for my time is not yet full come."*

Jesus' brothers had encouraged him to attend a feast in Jerusalem and to make Himself known by a miracle. But Jesus made sure that He did everything according to God's timetable. There was a right time for every small detail in the life of Jesus, and He was obligated to live a life that was in complete harmony with the will of the Father.

I always say, "God is not a minute early, nor is He a minute late." That is so true, and you find it out loud and clear as you read and meditate on the Word of God.

PRAYER: Heavenly Father, I am happy to see your perfect timing in my life. The better I know you through your Word, the more I see your perfect timing, and how helpful it is. I also know that you know what is in store for me daily as well. Forgive me, Lord, for not trusting in your goodness and mercy. It seems to be so easy to become anxious and filled with stress, and I know it is a ploy of the devil, but he seems to sneak in the back door every now and then. I thank you for giving the Holy Spirit to step up to the plate and help me to recognize what is going on. Thank you for the promise to never leave me nor forsake me. In Jesus' name, Amen.

NOVEMBER 18th

✝ Let's look at another place where Jesus says "come" in John 11:43, which reads, *"And when He thus had spoken, He cried with a loud voice, 'Lazarus, come forth.' "* This was a call for Lazarus to come back to life, back into the lives of his sisters. Jesus simply said, "Come forth!"

Jesus' words had authority, and since he had waited two more days to come to Lazarus' grave, it had to be the perfect timing to use His authority. Jesus' command to "come forth" defied all natural forces. It split the bonds of death and set Lazarus free from the power of the grave. This was the Father's will.

In John 6:38, Jesus says, *"For I came down from heaven, not to do mine own will, but the will of Him that sent me."* Jesus is not finished doing the Father's will yet. He will come again. He promised that to us in John 14:1-3, which reads: *"Let not your heart be troubled: .ye believe in God, believe also in me. In my Father's house are many mansions: if it were not so, I would have told you. I go to prepare a place for you. And if I go and prepare a place for you, I will come again, and receive you unto myself, that where I am, there you may be also."*

That is a promise from Jesus Himself. He will *come* and get us to take us to that mansion He prepared for us.

PRAYER: Heavenly Father, I believe that when you come to get us that will be the biggest day of our lives. It is so reassuring to know that you are expecting us. If you can come to earth as a babe, vulnerable and needy, it should be no stretch of the imagination that you can come as a thief in the night or as a man of authority in power and great glory. Yes, Lord, we love your appearing as you have promised. In Jesus' name, Amen.

NOVEMBER 19th

✝ Isaiah 48:16 reads, *"Come ye near unto me, hear ye this: I have not spoken in secret from the beginning; from the time that it was, there am I: and now the Lord God, and His Spirit, hath sent me."* Throughout the Bible, there is this invitation to come to God. The burden of responsibility in that invitation is on us. Like receiving a wedding invitation, the next step is for you to either accept it or reject it and send a refusal, an "I am sorry, but …" God has acted, and we need to react.

At some appointed time in the future, all the nations of the earth will come to worship God. Psalms 86:9 reads, *"All nations whom thou hast made shall come and worship before thee, O Lord; and shall glorify thy name."* And Isaiah 66:23 states, *" 'And it shall come to pass that from one new moon to another, and from one Sabbath to another, shall all flesh come to worship before me,' saith the Lord."*

What we have here is a future event when the whole world will acknowledge God Almighty as worthy of worship and will *come* to Him to worship. Are you ready to come to God willingly to offer up your worship?

Each Sunday, when the church bells ring, it is an invitation to come there to worship the Lord of lords and the King of kings. We should not only think about it on Sunday, but we ought to also pray during the week that our hearts will be ready to receive the message prepared for us, to ask God to help us be in tune with His Spirit that day, and to sing with all our hearts to offer up praises to God, who has cared for us all week.

God created you with the purpose to worship Him, and He invited you to come to His house to worship, to offer up your voice in song and in praise to Him for His goodness, mercy, and grace. The Bible makes it clear that you have been invited. What is your response to that?

PRAYER: Heavenly Father, yes, I desire to offer up my praise and worship to you, and I look forward to being in your presence at worship. I pray that I don't just listen and then not put into practice what your Word has said to me. Help me to be a witness of your grace to those around me.

Forgive me for murmuring or complaining, Lord. I have been so blessed by you. Help me to be a blessing to others. In Jesus' name, Amen.

NOVEMBER 20th

In the last book of the Bible, Revelation, one of the last verses still resounds with the invitation to come, but this invitation is issued *to* Jesus to come back for us. Let us look at what is said about Jesus' coming. Revelation 22:17reads: *"And the Spirit and the Bride* (the church) *say, 'Come.' And let him that heareth say, 'Come.' And let him that is athrist come. And whosoever will, let him take of the water of life freely."*

The cry of the Spirit of God and the Bride of Christ (which is the Church), in harmony, say *"Come,"* to the Lord Jesus Christ. They together yearn for Jesus to *come* and set up His kingdom rule on this earth, to put an end to evil and to usher in a rule governed by love, mercy and grace. The thirsty are invited to *come* and drink freely of the water of life, which flows from Jesus.

Then we go to the last two verses in the Bible, Revelation 22:20-21, which state: *"He which testifieth these things* (Jesus is speaking here), *saith, 'Surely I* come *quickly.' Amen. Even so, come, Lord Jesus. The grace of our Lord Jesus Christ be with you al (The Saints)l. Amen."*

We hear very little about the second coming of Jesus, and that is a sad fact. He *will* come again, and we are supposed to look forward to that with great joy and excitement. Even if we die before that happens, we need to live in that expectancy with great joy.

Is there a fear surrounding that event to prevent you from having it before you on the horizon as a joyous event? Do you instead view it as a dreaded event? If so, then you are lacking some assurance from the Word of God. It *is* a joyous event for believers. It will be like going to the county fair to see if the article you brought won a blue ribbon. It will be rewards day. Jesus will be very happy that day. It will be one of the most glorious days in His life. May that also be so for you.

PRAYER: Heavenly Father, one day my body will die. Are you saying that Jesus will *come* and receive me, according to your Word? I am very glad to hear that, and I want to keep it in my heart as a very positive event in my future. I do not want Jesus' return to be a dread in my heart. I pray that I may know you so well that I will look forward to that meeting. In Jesus' name, Amen.

NOVEMBER 21st

We have looked at the word "come" in the Bible, and now we want to look at (and to grow by) the word "go." Matthew 28:18-20 reads: *"And Jesus came and spake unto them, saying, 'All power (authority) is given unto me in heaven and earth. <u>GO ye therefore,</u> and teach (make disciples of) all nations, baptizing them in the name of the Father, Son, and Holy Ghost: Teaching them to observe all things whatsoever I have commanded you: and lo, I am with you always, even unto the end of the world. Amen.' "*

When Jesus *comes* to us, the next step is for us to *go* where He wants us to go. We have a job to do for the kingdom of God here on earth. That job may be to go to your next door neighbor, or to people you work with, or your boss, relatives, friends, etc.

Think of the people you rub shoulders with on a day-to-day basis. They are a part of the "world" Jesus is talking about in Revelation. Why do we think of far-off places when we read, *"Go into all the world"*? I believe it is the devil's ploy to blind you to the fact that you have people all around you that are also a part of that world. But, since you are not in a far-off land, you think you are excused from teaching or making disciples.

We are always a witness to the goodness and faithfulness of God. You cannot excuse yourself because you are at home and not in a far-off

478

land. Are you prepared to be a witness with a word in due season when you *go* shopping? What about when you *go* to a party? If not, why not?

We are to teach others to observe all things, to be sensitive to what is happening around in families, neighborhoods, states, the nation, and the world. Never forget how important prayer is in the life of a believer. Before you go, pray for an open door, and that you are able to see that open door (spiritually, I mean). And ask that you will be not only willing, but also able to step through that open door to be the witness God is calling you to be. We will look more at this when we talk about the next big word, which will be "sent."

PRAYER: Heavenly Father, are you telling me that whenever I am in a relationship with anyone, I am under your employment with a job description? That is what I see is happening here. I sense you are nodding your head in the affirmative. I will need the help of the Holy Spirit to make me ready for anything and everything at a moment's notice. You know what I know, and what I don't know. So please, Lord, do not give me an order that is too big for me, but rather one that I can witness to from the pool of experiences I have had and the right scripture to back it up. I want to be a blessing to you, and to bring you honor, not disgrace. In Jesus' name, Amen.

NOVEMBER 22nd

✝ Deuteronomy 31:8 says, *"And the Lord, He it is that doth GO before thee; He will be with thee, He will not fail thee, neither forsake thee: fear not, neither be dismayed."* These words were spoken by Moses to Joshua as he was leading the people right up to the Promised Land. God is the same yesterday, today, and tomorrow. He never changes. So, if God was going *before* them then, you can be sure He is going *before* you now.

You do not go in your own power ever. Instead, you go in the mighty power of Jesus' name. We learned yesterday that, since Jesus had all authority in heaven and earth, you can go and teach, lead, and whatever God asks you to do. Can you think of a greater authority than that which you have through Jesus? You have the best and most at your disposal.

The Lord is there, even before you are there. God prepares the way ahead of you. So, when He opens a door before you to witness to someone because they have asked you a question about your faith or a verse in the Bible, then you know there is an open door set before you by God Himself. That is the beginning of a spiritual adventure as exciting as any adventure in this world. So, the bottom line is this: God won't send you anywhere that He has not gone ahead of you to prepare. You can rest your faith on this truth.

PRAYER: Heavenly Father, I am thankful that you prepare the way before me. With that, I can know that you are in the midst of each opportunity, and I do not stand alone. It is not hard to be the teacher or witness when it has been prearranged by you. I believe you have also prepared the heart of the one to whom I am speaking. And, if it does not look like they have received it, I can still be assured that this was a part of your overall plan. If I just give it time, I will see the fruit of my labor, right? I know that as true because in I Corinthians 3:6, Paul says, *"I have planted, Apollos watered, but GOD GAVE THE INCREASE."* If there is to be any fruit (the increase), it will *not* have to come from me anyway, so I am only responsible for being obedient and faithful, (planting and watering). I am thankful for this truth. It makes it simple for me to read such a job description. In Jesus' name, Amen.

NOVEMBER 23rd

John 14:2 reads, *"In my Father's house are many mansions: if it were not so, I would have told you, I GO to prepare a place for you."* Jesus has even gone ahead of us to heaven to prepare a place for us. He is always a step ahead of us, and nothing takes Him by surprise.

I think one of the hardest truths for us to comprehend is that God is for us *all the time*. He will search for us when we drift away, just as a shepherd searches for his sheep when the count is off by one. God wanted us with Him so much that He was willing to sacrifice His own Son to assure us the opportunity to live with Him throughout all eternity.

Then Jesus came to assure us that He was in total agreement with God's plan of salvation—so much so, in fact, that He was willing to *be* the sacrifice to pave the way for us to simply accept that gift of love from God. And then, to top it all off, Jesus went ahead to paradise to prepare a place for us there! Can you grasp the enormity of what has been done for you? What have you done that could top all that? Not a thing. In fact, we could do nothing to save ourselves, but God has done it *all* because He loved us so much.

Have you ever wondered what kind of a place is prepared for you there? I believe it will be individually prepared to fit who we are in God's eyes. He knows what He created when He created us, and He has wanted us to reach the potential He put in us. I believe our heavenly home will reflect all that.

PRAYER: Heavenly Father, I look forward to that heavenly home. It is a comforting thought that you have prepared it for me. I also thank you for the assurance of salvation, and that I can know beyond a shadow of a doubt that I will be welcomed by you there. I thank you for this Word that gives me the truth upon which I can rest my faith, and by which I can stand the storms of life that Satan sends my way to try to defeat me. Your love for me is awesome, and for that I am thankful also. In Jesus' name, Amen.

NOVEMBER 24th

Deuteronomy 28:14 reads, *"And thou shalt not GO aside from any of the words which I command thee this day, to the right hand, or to the left, to GO after other gods to serve them."* In this chapter, Moses is giving the children of Israel the words of God in regard to how they are to act as His children. There were stipulations in detail as to what the blessings would be if they followed Him, and what the curses would be if they did not.

They could never say, "No one told me." So, if there was disobedience, it would not be God's fault, now would it? They were told not to *go* after other gods to serve them. Did they obey that command? No! And they had to suffer the consequences of their choices.

The Israelites worshipped the false gods of the land they were invading, which God had told them many times not to do. Well, guess what? We have false gods today too, and people follow and serve them. The god of money and the god of success can come between you and God. Anything that becomes more important than our Heavenly Father, and our Lord and Savior, Jesus Christ, will become a false god in our lives. I believe sex has become a god to many people, as well. Even possessions, or "toys," can come between you and God.

You may be aware of many other false gods crying out to you to worship them. I just want you to be aware that it is no different today than it was back in Moses' day. That table that is prepared, according to Psalm 23, is always in the presence of our enemy. The enemy is close at hand and wants us to worship *him*, not the God of the universe. We are going to *go* somewhere, and it will either be toward God our Father or toward other gods, but *go* we will.

PRAYER: Heavenly Father, I will need your help to travel through this life avoiding the false gods that vie for a place in my life. Help me to recognize the false gods around me, and give me the faith to put them behind me. Help me to keep my eyes on you, Lord Jesus, so my path to heaven is not full of detours, but a straight path. In Jesus' name, Amen.

NOVEMBER 25th

John 6:65-69 reads: *"And He said, 'Therefore said I unto you, that no man can come unto me, except it were given unto him*

of my Father.' From that time many of His disciples went back, and walked no more with Him. Then said Jesus unto the twelve, 'Will ye also GO away?' Then Simon Peter answered Him, 'Lord, to whom shall we GO? Thou hast the words of eternal life. And we believe and are sure that thou art that Christ, the Son of the living God.(The Holy One of God)' "

Peter had come to realize that there is nowhere else to *go* to for eternal life. No other god in the whole world was able to give the gift of eternal life to sinful mankind. If you have been hunting for the truth, know and believe that there is nowhere else to *go* to find truth except in the Bible, the eternal Word of God.

PRAYER: Heavenly Father, I am glad for the assurance, like Peter had, to know beyond a shadow of a doubt that there is no other place to go to find truth. Thank you for that gift. I pray that I will be able to pass on that truth to others who do not yet know it. I also pray that the truth will set me free from all fears, like your Word promises in John 8:32, *"You shall know the truth and the truth shall make you free."* May your Holy Spirit minister more truths to me as I read and study your Word. In Jesus' name, Amen.

NOVEMBER 26th

Luke 9:59-60 reads, *"And He said unto another, 'Follow me.' But he said, 'Lord, suffer me first to GO and bury my father.' Jesus said unto him, 'Let the dead bury their dead: but GO thou and preach the kingdom of God.' "* In other words, nothing is more important than to tell the old, old story of Jesus and His love. This man wanted to stay at home until his father had died, and then he would go and serve the Lord. We are either *in* the will of God and *doing* what He wants us to do, or we are *outside* the will of God and *not doing* what He wants us to do.

The moment you give your life to Jesus and ask Him into your heart, you are a full-time employee of God the Father, Son, and Holy Spirit.

There is no middle ground. Our attitude toward God is either dead or alive. Which is it for you?

If the man in this scripture wanted to stay at home and live there until his father had died, then his attitude toward God was already dead. That is why Jesus said, "Let the dead bury the dead." It is not that God wants us to neglect our parents, but when our parents become more important to us than God, they become a stumbling block to our growth and usefulness.

If this man's father was sick and needed his son to care for him, I doubt God would have called him into active service. God wants us to honor our father and our mother. That, in fact, is one of the Ten Commandments. But God wants us to be ready to follow Him, and that means to be able to *go*.

Every day, we have the opportunity to *go* be a servant in the kingdom of God, to witness to the truth of His Word that is within us.

PRAYER: Heavenly Father, for some reason, I always felt that to *go* meant to actually go to some far off place. I see now, however, that it means to be ready to go right where I live and be a witness right in my back or front yard, in my neighborhood, in my church, in my place of work, or school, even with my friends. In fact, these may be the hardest of all places to be a witness, because they all know me so well. I think it may also be that just being the person you want me to be, showing my peace and my love for the Word of God and so on, that in itself will be a witness or manifestation of your presence in my life. So help me, Lord, to live a life that will reflect who you are. If there are to be words spoken, I will wait for your open door proving to me that you are present and in charge of this divine appointment. In Jesus' name, Amen.

NOVEMBER 27th

Now that we have looked at "come" and "go," we will spend the next few days looking at the word "send." I believe it is important to see how "sending" fits into the picture from God's point of view. Is God in the sending business? If so, who does He send and to do what or where?

As I look at a concordance, I see that the first reference of "send" is found in Genesis 24:7. For some background, Abraham had a son named Isaac who needed a wife . Abraham did not want him to have a Canaanite wife, so Abraham employed his eldest servant, who ruled over all he had, to go to the people from whom Abraham had come to find a wife for Isaac.

We see that the servant's name is Eliezer in Genesis 15:2, which reads, *"And Abram* (whose name was changed to Abraham) *said, 'Lord God, what wilt thou give me, seeing I go childless, and the steward of my home is this Eliezer of Damascus?' "* The name Eliezer means "mighty divine helper." Many scholars feel that he is a type, or picture, of the Holy Spirit, like a foreshadowing of the Holy Spirit to come.

Genesis 24:2-7 reads: *"And Abraham said unto his eldest servant of his house, that ruled over all that he had, 'Put, I pray thee, thy hand under my thigh; And I will make thee swear by the Lord, the God of heaven, and the God of the earth, that thou shalt not take a wife unto my son of the daughters of the Canaanites, among whom I dwell. But thou shalt go unto my country, and to my kindred, and take a wife unto my son Isaac.' And the servant said unto him, 'Peradventure the woman will not be willing to follow me unto this land, must I needs bring thy son again unto the land from whence thou camest?' And Abraham said unto him, 'Beware thou that thou bring not my son thither again. The Lord God of heaven, which took me from my father's house, and from the land of my kindred, and which spake unto me, and that sware unto me, saying, "Unto thy seed will I give this land:" He shall* SEND *His angel before thee, and thou shalt take a wife unto my son from thence.' "*

Abraham was so sure of God, that he just knew Eliezer would find a wife for Isaac. In fact, Abraham expected God to *"send* His angel before" Eliezer. Many people believe that when the Bible refers to "His angel" or "the Lord's angel," that it is a reference to Jesus before He was born of the virgin Mary. However, what we are looking at today is the word "send." If

485

we had the time to follow this story through, you would see how thoroughly Eliezer is directed in every step of his journey, as if by the Holy Spirit.

When Eliezer found her, she willingly came to marry Isaac, the son of Abraham, sight unseen. If God could send a heavenly personage during the Old Testament times, He can certainly send such a personage to help us do His will now. It is a part of the character of God!

PRAYER: Heavenly Father, it is surprising how you pave the way before us to make sure your will is accomplished in your timing. How impatient we often get, jumping the gun and doing something foolish to try to accomplish what only you can do. Eliezer's account makes it clear, once again, that you are in control. The sooner I recognize that, the better off I will be, and the fewer mistakes I will make. You are an awesome God— bigger than I can even imagine, and yet small enough to squeeze into the slightest crack in my nature to let me know I am drifting off to the left or right. Thank you for caring that much. In Jesus' name, Amen.

NOVEMBER 28th

✝ Today we will jump ahead to the time when the children of Israel were traveling out of bondage from Egypt toward the Promised Land. In Exodus 23:20-23, God says: ***"Behold, I SEND an Angel before thee, to keep thee in the way, and to bring thee into the place which I have prepared. Beware of Him, and obey His voice, provoke Him not; for He will not pardon your transgressions: for my name is in Him. But if thou shalt indeed obey His voice, and do all that I speak; then I will be an enemy unto thine enemies, and an adversary unto thine adversaries. For mine Angel shall go before thee, and bring thee in unto the Amorites, and the Hittities, and the Perizzites, and the Canaanites, the Hivites, and the Jebusites: and I will cut them off."***

There were six nations that God wanted off the land He had promised to Abraham and his descendants. Therefore, God sent His Angel to go before them. Yes, indeed, God is in the *sending* business.

This is a special angel again. His voice must be obeyed to the letter. They are advised to not provoke Him, "for He will not pardon your transgressions!" That's a pretty serious warning, I would say. That is the kind of angel God sent to go before them.

The Angel had a big job—to bring the Israelites to the place that God had prepared. There is a place prepared for us also. And did someone go before to prepare that for us?

Let's look at something else God sent before the Israelites. Exodus 23:27-28 reads: *"I will SEND fear before thee, and will destroy (discomfort) all the people to whom thou shalt come, and I will make all thine enemies turn their backs unto thee. And I will SEND hornets before thee, which shall drive out the Hivite, the Canaanite, and the Hittite, from before thee."*

God is not limited like we humans are. He is able to turn nature upside down, and use it to drive out the enemy of His people. He is also able to send a spirit of fear to the people who do not worship Him.

But what is God's word to those who believe in and worship Him? II Timothy 1:7 states, *"For God hath not given us the spirit of fear (fearfulness); but of power, and of love, and of a sound mind (discipline)"* Even Rahab testified to the spirit of fear in Joshua 2:9-11, which reads: *"And she said unto the men, 'I know that the Lord hath given you the land, and that your terror is fallen upon us and that all the inhabitants of the land faint because of you. For we have heard how the Lord dried up the water of the Red Sea for you, when ye came out of Egypt; and what ye did unto the two kings of the Amorites, that were on the other side Jordan, Sihon and Og, whom ye utterly destroyed. And as soon as we had heard these things, our hearts did melt, neither did there remain any more courage in any man, because of you: for the Lord your God, He is God in heaven above and in earth beneath.' "*

You can see how the spirit of fear from God had filled the hearts of the inhabitants of Canaan. When God stands up to fight for a nation, He has many ways to do that. Let's hope America never does anything to turn God's favor away from her. I fear that there are signs of that happening all

487

around us. Pray for our country, for the rulers of our country to have wisdom from God to pass laws in harmony with God's ethics and morality. God can *send* hornets, fear, earthquakes, famine, tidal waves, volcanoes, diseases, plagues, or war from another nation, to completely destroy America. It has happened to Israel, and it can happen to us.

PRAYER: Heavenly Father, it is a fearful thing to stir up your wrath, and I learn in your Word that willfully committing sin will stir up your wrath quicker than anything else. I want to lift up our country, America. Forgive us our sins. They are many. Raise up men and women throughout our land who believe in you to raise up a standard against all that is evil in your sight and point the way back to you. Let the spirit of God that filled our land when it was being birthed spread again throughout our land. Create in the hearts of men women and children a desire to live a life that glorifies you. Let us put people in office that will not fold under the pressure to become more and more worldly. Hear our hearts' cry, Lord. In Jesus' name, Amen.

NOVEMBER 29th

Today we will look at some verses from Isaiah, where he describes a vision of the Lord in heaven. Isaiah saw the Lord high and lifted up, and His train filled the temple. Heavenly, six-winged, flaming creatures flew around, and as they shouted, *"Holy, Holy, Holy, Lord All-Powerful! The earth is filled with your glory"* (Isaiah 6:3), the door posts of the temple shook and the temple was filled with smoke.

The CEV translates Isaiah 6:5-8 as: *"Then I cried out, 'I'm doomed! Everything I say is sinful, and so are the words of everyone around me. Yet I have seen the King, the Lord All Powerful. One of the flaming creatures flew over to me with a burning coal that it had taken from the altar with a pair of metal tongs. It touched my lips with the hot coal and said, "This has touched your lips. Your sins are forgiven, and you are no longer guilty." After this, I heard the Lord ask, "Is there*

anyone I can SEND ? Will someone go for us?" I'll go, I answered.
"Send me!"""

God was asking for someone that He could send on a mission. I have the notion that in reality we all have been called for something, even if it seems very small and insignificant. I firmly believe that every one of us who believes in God the Father, Son, and Holy Spirit has a mission on this earth.

It has been said that you are either a mission field or a missionary. The choice is yours! Maybe God is asking you to be an influence in the life of just one person. Do you want to miss that opportunity to be the person God created you to be?

Tomorrow we will talk about the message Isaiah was to deliver. I want to point out that in today's verse, God asked, *"Will someone go for us?"* Many scholars believe that refers to the Trinity, since it is in the plural, personal pronoun. Just like in Genesis 1:26 says, *"And God said, "Let us make man in our image, after our likeness."* Again, this uses plural, personal pronouns. Like God the Father is speaking to God the Son and God the Holy Spirit.

PRAYER: Heavenly Father, just as Isaiah was ready to answer the call to be sent, I hope I will be as willing to go. I have learned that you do not ask more of me than I am able to give, and that you will go with me wherever you send me. I also see that if I am in need of *receiving* a message, you have in mind to send to someone through me, you will fill that need also. The road goes both ways, right? There would be no object to send someone unless there was a need that had to be met, and when I had that need, there was someone sent by you to fill that need for me spiritually. How well I recall those times of need and how there was someone with just the right words to help me see the truth. I want to thank you for those messengers who answered your call to be there for me when I needed it. In Jesus' name, Amen.

NOVEMBER 30th

✝ We see the message that Isaiah was to carry in Isaiah 6:9-13 (again, from CEV): *"Then the Lord told me to go and speak this message to the people. 'You will listen and listen, but never understand. You will look and look, but never see.' The Lord also said, 'Make these people stubborn! Make them stop up their ears, cover their eyes, and fail to understand. Don't let them turn to me and be healed.' Then I asked the Lord, 'How long will this last?' The Lord answered: 'Until their towns are destroyed and their houses are deserted, until their fields are empty, and I have sent them far away, leaving their land in ruins. If only a tenth of the people are left, even they will be destroyed. But just as stumps remain after trees have been cut down, some of my chosen ones will be left.' "*

Isaiah has a hard message to deliver to the nation of Israel. It also looks like it won't even do any good to bring that message, because they won't listen. But, they can never accuse God of not warning them of the consequences they would endure for not turning from their wicked ways.

Even today, there are people who hear the Word of God over and over again, and that Word has no effect in their lives. The result of that is a hardening of the heart. Their conscience becomes seared to the point that they can no longer hear or see what God is saying to them or what He is doing in their lives.

It is a serious condition, and one that could have been avoided. Israel was forever turning a deaf ear to the prophets God was sending to them. God wanted that His word be obeyed. Instead, Israel killed many of the prophets because they did not like the message he was bringing.

And they even killed the Son of God, who brought a message of salvation that all may be saved! It would cost them nothing more than to, by faith, accept God's blood sacrifice to have peace with God, and sin and death would have been defeated for them. But they would not accept it.

The message God gave Isaiah is more or less a picture of the future of the nation of Israel. God said it would last until there was only a remnant left, like the stump of a tree. After World War II, there were very few Jews left in the world, especially when you consider how many came out of Egypt so many years ago. Their country and towns were not in their own hands, but in the hands of Gentiles . The land was pretty much in ruins too.

After Israel became a nation and they began to rebuild the cities and reclaim the land, the land flourished. But, as yet, the nation has not accepted Jesus as their Messiah. That is a future event, and it will happen, because God's will, *will be done*. It is his determinate will. It is a date set in stone for the future, and it will happen with or without Israel's cooperation. In the meantime, God will *send* messengers to Israel with the message of Jesus, whom God *sent* to tell them about His love for them.

PRAYER: Heavenly Father, I pray that I will not ever close my ears to your message, but that I will have a willingness to hear your Word, and open my eyes so that I can see your works for your people, both in the Nation of Israel and in the Church I pray for pastors to bring the true message of salvation and sanctification to help us to grow up into the full stature of Christ, as your Word encourages us to do. Forgive my lazy spirit, which neglects the reading and study of your Word. Help me not to just read your Word, but to meditate on it after I have read it. How quickly a year can pass by, with so many things left undone because time has slipped through my fingers. But you encourage us to redeem the time in Ephesians 5:16, which says, *"Redeeming the time, for the days are evil."* In Jesus' name, Amen.

DECEMBER 1st

I want to continue with the word "send" for a few days. Luke 10:1-3 reads: *"After these things the Lord appointed other seventy also, and SENT them two and two before His face into every city and place, whither He Himself would come. Therefore said He unto them, 'The harvest truly is great, but the laborers are few: pray ye therefore the Lord of the harvest, that He would send forth laborers into His harvest. Go your ways: behold, I SEND you forth as lambs among wolves.' "*

Is it any different today? To a certain extent, I believe it is. At that time, Jesus had not defeated the devil. Now Jesus has given us His name as a weapon against the "wolves" of our day.

I also believe the opposition we face today is different. We are exposed to so much more opposition than they were in Jesus' day. We are being fed a constant diet of worldly garbage. It comes to us via the radio, television, magazines, and other people. The population of the world has also increased mightily.

Compare your own childhood to the childhood of your children or grandchildren. I believe the exposure to temptation of our day was minimal compared to the temptations the young people have to withstand today. However, God is still in the sending business now, every bit as much as He was when this was written in the Bible.

But we can't say He did not warn us what it would be like. We are as lambs among wolves, and wolves love to devour lambs. If we are not aware of it, we could be so naïve when we go into the world as a light in a dark place. We make one mistake after another because we don't think there are any wolves out there to attack us.

Wolves sneak around watching their prey. And when there is an opportunity, they pounce on the prey and kill it. A lamb is a very easy prey, because it drifts away from the flock as it eats its fill, and has very little defenses. Nothing about a lamb, even its voice, is loud, or demanding.

I have often wondered how Jesus felt when He knew He was going to soon die on the cross, and would not rise for three days. How did He feel knowing the Holy Spirit would not come to fill the disciples with power for ten days after He had ascended into heaven? It would be up to the disciples to stand like lambs among wolves, holding the only Words of eternal salvation.

Was God taking a chance, or what? It was from that little beginning that the gospel of good news has spread over the whole world, and it is still going forth today. Lambs among wolves carry that same gospel into the world.

What is your part in that program? Do you dare to be a lamb among wolves? Yes, we can be. We have the powerful name of Jesus in our arsenal!

PRAYER: Heavenly Father, I find you often give us a warning in your Word, and I think we often read right past it without stopping to make ourselves aware of just what that warning should mean to us. Give me the discernment we need, to see the wolves in our day, and to look ahead, like in a game of chess or checkers, to see what the enemy's next move might be. Help us to be prepared ahead of time to avoid the wolves, outsmart them, or destroy them before they destroy us. I believe the Holy Spirit was given for just such a purpose as this, to help us to always be an overcomer. We lay hold of the promise in your Word found in I John 4:4, which reads, *"Ye are of God little children, and have overcome them: because greater is He that is IN you, than he that is IN the world."* (The "them" in this verse refers to evil spirits in the world, and the Holy Spirit is He who dwells within you that is greater). Lord Jesus, we lay claim to this verse in our life, and we plan on being an overcomer in every situation we encounter. I know your kind of help will be there for me when the situation arrives, and I depend on that. I refuse to allow Satan to steal my joy or my rest as I live each day for your glory. In Jesus' name, Amen .

DECEMBER 2nd

Today we will look at some verses from John 17, which contains "Jesus' High Priestly prayer." It is the prayer that Jesus poured out to His Heavenly Father shortly before He was crucified. Jesus was concerned about His disciples, who would be left alone and vulnerable. They would not only be vulnerable to the world and satanic attacks, but vulnerable to their peers and religious leaders who orchestrated Jesus' crucifixion.

Read the whole prayer and get inside Jesus' heart as He pours out Himself to His Heavenly Father. In John 17:8, Jesus prays, *"For I have given unto them the words which thou gavest me: and they have received them, and have known surely that I came out from thee, and they have believed that thou didst SEND me."*

If it was important for the disciples to know that God the Father had *sent* Jesus into the world, it must surely be important for us to really know that truth also. The disciples lived when some who had witnessed the events of Jesus' birth were still alive. We live in a day when all we have are the accounts of His birth more than 2,000 years ago.

Think about Jesus' prayer. Do you think it is only for the disciples? By no means! It is for us today as well. John 17:20-21 continues: *"Neither pray I for these alone, but for them also which shall* (future tense)*, believe on me through their word: That they may be one; as thou, Father, art in me, and I in thee, that they also may be one in us: that the world may believe that thou hast SENT me."*

This prayer was extended down through the ages, and will be in effect right up to the time when Jesus comes to receive us to Himself. Also, please notice that when we all know that one truth—that God the Father *sent* Jesus into the world—then we all become one in both the Father and in Christ Jesus. Then that shall result in the world also coming to the belief that God *sent* Jesus into the world.

Jesus was with the Father before the world was created. He has always been with the Father. But, one day in history, Jesus and the Father agreed to a plan to give everyone in world an opportunity to have a restored fellowship with their Creator.

Jesus agreed to be *sent* into the world as a babe, to be a second Adam, and do things right so we, who could not avoid sin and its devastating consequences, could choose the right way back to God and be saved from those consequences. Yes, indeed, Jesus was *sent* by His Father into this world. Read all of John 17, and notice how many times the word "world" is written in there. We are *in* the world, but not *of* the world. So don't let the world crush you in any way.

494

PRAYER: Heavenly Father, I am so grateful that you sent Jesus into the world to rescue me. And I am grateful that Jesus came to do what was needed to purchase eternal life for me. My life with you cannot compare to anything the world can offer. I pray, dear Father, that I will be the witness to this truth in such a way that those around me may believe the truth also. In Jesus' precious name, Amen

DECEMBER 3rd

 Yesterday we talked about God the Father sending Jesus into the world. Today we will look at another side of that type of *sending*. In John 14, Jesus had been teaching the disciples about His leaving them. He explained that He is the only way to the Father—He is the way, the truth, and the life—and that He would send another Comforter when He left. In John 14:25-26, Jesus says: *"These things have I spoken unto you, being yet present with you. But the Comforter, which is the Holy Ghost, whom the Father will SEND in my name, He shall teach you all things, and bring all things to your remembrance, whatsoever I have said unto you."*

In verse 26, you see the Trinity, the Father, Son, and Holy Spirit. In John 14:16, Jesus had told them, *"I will pray the <u>Father</u>, and He shall give you another <u>Comforter</u>, that He may abide with you <u>for ever</u>."* Then, in verse 26, Jesus says it as a fact, *"But the Comforter, which is the <u>Holy Ghost</u>, whom the <u>Father</u> will SEND in <u>my name</u>* (notice the Trinity in those words), *He shall teach you all things, and bring all things to your remembrance, whatsoever I have said unto you."*

Jesus prayed for the Comforter (the third person in the God-head) to come and abide forever with believers. Then God the Father *sent* the Comforter, the Holy Ghost, to us in Jesus' name.

Everything that God does has to be perfect and precise. It is a step by step process, and everything has its reasons and purposes. We can't always grasp what all those reasons are, but just know that they are important or they would not have been recorded in that order. Jesus was *sent* by God the Father, and Jesus had a special job to do for God the Father. Then, God the Father *sent* the Holy Ghost with a special job to do.

Let's look back to Acts 1:1, which reads, ***"The former treatise have I made, O Theophilus, of all that Jesus began both to do and teach."*** The books of Acts and Luke are both written by Luke, and they are both addressed to Theophilus. In Luke, he is called, ***"most excellant Theophilus,"*** which would indicate that he is a man of high position. Otherwise, not much is known of him regarding whom he was or where he came from. Some speculate that he and Luke are both from Antioch of Syria.

In both Luke and Acts, Luke is writing about Jesus' life, in Acts Luke recounted the beginning of the church and the history of the believers after the resurrection. It is here we learn that Jesus ascended into heaven 40 days after the resurrection. We continue with Acts 1:5, where Luke writes: ***"Until the day in which He was taken up, after that He through the Holy Ghost had given commandments unto the apostles whom He had chosen. To whom also He shewed himself alive after His passion by many infallible proofs, being seen of them forty days, and speaking of the things pertaining to the kingdom of God. And, being assembled together with them, commanded them that they should not depart from Jerusalem, but wait for the promise of the Father, which, saith He, ye have heard of me. For John truly baptized with water; but ye shall be baptized with the Holy Ghost not many days hence."***

The promise of the Father is the Comforter Jesus spoke about, whom God would *send* in Jesus' name. We will see how the Apostles and believers were baptized in the Holy Ghost in just a few days.

PRAYER: Heavenly Father, thank you for those who were prompted to write the accounts of the life of Jesus and those of the early church. We are so privileged to be able to read those accounts today and know and understand the character of God the Father, Son, and Holy Ghost. There is such unity in the Trinity, and, Father, you expect that kind of unity to be visible in the church today too. Forgive us for our part in creating disunity among the brethren. Help me be a witness to the truth of your Word, and help me to be faithful to being the witness you have called me to be. With the help of the Spirit of Truth within me, it should not be a problem to be that kind of witness, but my old nature, Lord, gets in the way. Help me put that old nature down and allow the new nature, that divine nature I have from you, rise up and take control. In Jesus' name, Amen.

DECEMBER 4th

 Today, we will continue in Acts. I don't want to leave any loose ends regarding the Comforter whom God *sent* in Jesus' name.

In Acts 1:6-7, there is a little discussion as to when Jesus would establish the Nation of Israel on the earth. Jesus said it was not for us to know the times and seasons that God has power and authority over. Acts 1:8-12 continues, first with Jesus speaking: " *'But ye shall receive power, after that the Holy Ghost is come upon you: and ye shall be witnesses unto me both in Jerusalem, and in all Judea, and in Samaria, and unto the uttermost parts of the earth.' And when He had spolen these things, while they beheld, He was taken up; and a cloud received Him out of their sight." And while they looked steadfast toward heaven as He went up, behold, two men stood by them in white apparel; Which also said, 'Ye men of Galilee, why stand ye gazing up into heaven? This same Jesus, which is taken up from you into heaven, shall so come in like manner as ye have seen Him go into heaven.' Then returned they unto Jerusalem from the mount called Olivet, which is from Jerusalem a Sabbath day's journey."*

We find out in verse 3, **"To whom also he showed himself alive after his passion by many infallible proofs, being seen of them forty days, and speaking of the things pertaining to the Kingdome of God"**, that Jesus ascended into heaven 40 days after the resurrection. File this away in your mind for future reference. We also learn that Jesus ascended to heaven in a cloud and will come back just like He went away, in a cloud. Then the disciples returned to Jerusalem as they had been told to do, to wait for the promise from the Father, which was that the Comforter should come. Did you notice the "as" and "so" in the reference above?

PRAYER: Heavenly Father, I know that you keep every promise you make, and you have kept the promise of sending the Comforter also. I thank you for the gift of the Holy Ghost, the Holy Spirit, who lives within each of us who have Jesus as our Savior. I thank you for the guidance of the truth, and for the comfort the Holy Spirit ministers to me day after day. I also thank you for the power He gives me to live out this life in a victorious mindset. He ministers to me the power to overcome my old nature and to be a witness at a moment's notice. I thank you, Father, for sending the Holy Spirit to my heart, and to the hearts of the believers all over the world. In Jesus' name, Amen.

DECEMBER 5th

 Today, we will turn to Acts 2:1, which reads, *"And when the day of Pentecost was fully come, they were all with one accord in one place."* I want to stop here and explain something. The day of Pentecost was much like the Day of Passover and Unleavened bread. It was one of the great feasts designated by God back in Leviticus 23. These feasts foreshadowed events to come, and they were to be observed among the people of Israel no matter what.

Jesus rose from the dead on the Feast of First Fruits, which was a foreshadowing of Jesus' own resurrection, because He was called the "first fruits" of the resurrection. Fifty days after the Feast of First Fruits was to be the day of Pentecost. We know that Pentecost took place 50 days after Jesus rose from the dead, and we already saw that He ascended 40 days after resurrection, so Pentecost was 10 days later.

So, in Acts 2, they were all together and ready to celebrate the Feast of Pentecost. According to verse 13, they were in an upper room. Remember, they were told to wait in Jerusalem until the Comforter had come. Oftentimes, God stretches our patience to the breaking point. They had waited first 40 days and then 10 more days. That is almost two months. Acts 2:2-5 continues: *"And suddenly there came a sound from heaven as of a rushing mighty wind, and it filled all the house where they were sitting. And there appeared unto them cloven tongues like as of fire, and it sat upon each of them. And they were all filled with the Holy Ghost, and began to speak with other tongues, as the Spirit gave them utterance."*

This is often called the "birthday of the church." It was from this experience that the believers, who were filled with a heavenly power, went out boldly to proclaim the truth about their risen Lord and Savior. They became unstoppable, and they went in every direction radiating out from Jerusalem. Remember, Jesus said they were to be witnesses *"both in Jerusalem, then in Judea, in Samaria, and the uttermost parts of the earth"* (Acts 1:8). This was the fulfillment of the promised Comforter that God would *send* to the earth.

PRAYER: Heavenly Father, I am so glad you saw fit to *send* the Holy Spirit to dwell in our hearts and to be here with mighty power to assure us of victory in Jesus' name at all times. You even defeated the power of death for our lives, and removed the fear of death for us. You took away Satan's power, and instead gave us your own divine power to become a higher power over the devil. And we can use that gift at any time of the day or night, any day of the week. I don't know how to tell you how grateful I am for that privilege. You are so kind and patient, and all you ask in return is that I believe and trust in you. Help me to get back on track when the cares of this world pull me away from you. I never want to drift from you, but sometimes it just happens and I am not aware of it. Keep me steadfast in your love. In Jesus' name, Amen.

DECEMBER 6th

 I feel we would not have a complete picture of God's *sending* plan if we did not look at the commission given

499

to the Apostle Paul. (His name was originally Saul, but he changed his name to Paul later on.) In Acts 26, Paul was standing trial before King Agrippa, and he was recounting his conversion experience, when Jesus, the risen Lord, had appeared to him.

Paul had been a devout Jew who had not believed in Jesus and was trying to stamp out the message of a risen Lord Jesus Christ. Paul had seen Jesus as an impostor, so he was persecuting Christians. He was on his way to the city of Damascus to arrest Christians and bring them to Jerusalem for trial where they could be punished by death.

But Jesus met Paul face to face on his way to Damascus, and he was converted right then and there. He became such a powerful witness that the leaders of the Jews wanted *him* put to death, so they had him arrested. Paul was a Roman citizen and had appealed for a hearing before a Roman court, and that was how he came to be standing before King Agrippa in a Roman court of law.

Paul was recounting his experience to the King in Acts 26:13-19, where he says: *"At midday, O king, I saw in the way a light from heaven, above the brightness of the sun, shining round about me and them which journeyed with me. And when we were all fallen to the earth, I heard a voice speaking unto me, and saying in the Hebrew tongue, 'Saul, Saul, why persecutest thou me? It is hard for thee to kick against the pricks* (goad).*' And I said, 'Who art thou, Lord?' And He said, 'I am Jesus whom thou persecutest. But rise, and stand upon thy feet: for I have appeared unto thee for this purpose, to make thee a minister and a witness both of these things which thou hast seen, and of those things in the which I will appear unto thee. Delivering thee from the people, and from the Gentiles, unto whom now I SEND thee. To open their eyes, and to turn them from darkness to light, and from the power of Satan unto God, that they may receive forgiveness of sin, and inheritance among them which are sanctified by faith that is in me.' Whereupon O king Agrippa, I was not disobedient unto the heavenly vision."*

God needed just the right person to take the gospel to the Gentiles, and Paul, who wrote 13 Epistles, was that man. Paul was just as zealous to carry the message of Jesus to the gentile world as he had been to persecute the Christians before he knew the truth about Jesus.

The question that we need to answer is, "Are we ready to be *sent* by God to do the work that is needed in the harvest fields?" Only you can answer for yourself, and I must answer for me. Can we all say "yes" together?

PRAYER: Heavenly Father, I know we need to see our life as a place to be a witness for you right where we are, right now. I believe you will give me the Holy Spirit's power to speak out your words when the time is right, and I also believe you will give me the spirit of discernment so that I will know how much to say and when to keep quiet. I trust you, Lord, to be right there beside me when I need you. I thank you for the years of preparation you have been giving me to know your Word and how it applies to my life and those to whom I am a witness. You come alive to me, Lord, in the pages of the Bible, and I thank you for the Holy Spirit who is able to accomplish making you alive within my heart. In Jesus' name, Amen.

DECEMBER 7th

 I want to spend a few days addressing the work of the Holy Spirit, which is sanctification. Each member of the Trinity has a certain job ascribed to Him. God the Father is known as the Creator, God the Son is known as the Savior/Redeemer, and God the Holy Spirit is known as the Sanctifier.

Sanctification means to grow spiritually by God's grace, so that the believer will become more holy day by day—more separated from sin, the world, and the devil. This is accomplished by the Word of God, *"Sanctify them through thy truth, thy Word is truth."* (John 17:17) and by the Holy Spirit, as we read in Romans 8:3-5: *"For what the law could not do, in that it was weak through the flesh, God sending His own Son in the likeness of sinful flesh, and for sin, condemned sin in the flesh: That the righteousness of the law might be fulfilled in us, who walk not after the*

501

flesh, but after the Spirit (Holy Spirit). *For they that are after the flesh do mind the things of the flesh; but they that are after the Spirit* (Holy Spirit) *mind the things of the Spirit."*

Sanctification is ongoing, meant to bring us into the full-grown man or woman. Ephesians 4:13 reads, *"Till we all come in the unity of the faith, and of the knowledge of the Son of God, unto a perfect* (full-grown) *man unto the measure of the stature of Christ."* This, in a nut shell, is what sanctification is, and the Holy Spirit is at work in the life of every believer to bring us all into unity and full growth.

PRAYER: Heavenly Father, we do not usually hear much about the Holy Spirit's work in our lives. I thank you for what your Word says that He does in the life of a believer. I pray that I will be sensitive to His work on my behalf, and help me to listen to Him who leads, suggests, and guides me into the truth of the Word of God. In Jesus' name, Amen.

DECEMBER 8th

 I want you to see what Jesus said about the Spirit of Truth (another name for the Holy Spirit) in John 16:13-15, which reads: *"Howbeit when He, the Spirit of truth, is come, He will guide you into all the truth: for He shall not speak of Himself; but whatsoever He shall hear, that shall He speak and He will shew you things to come. He shall glorify me: for He shall receive of mine, and shall shew it unto you. All things that the Father hath are mine: therefore said I, that He shall take of mine, and shall shew it unto you."*

The Holy Spirit guides us into the truth of the Word of God. What you learn through these daily devotions has nothing to do with me, but rather it is the Holy Spirit who is guiding you into truth as you read God's Word. The Word will convict you of sin, bring you comfort and minister forgiveness to your soul. And it is the Holy Spirit who is active in your mind and heart to cause you to lay hold of the truth and make it your own.

This produces within you a process called sanctification. Just as we want our children to grow into well-balanced adults, so too does God want Christians to grow up into spiritually well-balanced adults. The Holy Spirit creates within us a desire to know the Word of God. Do not quench that work of the Spirit by turning a deaf ear when your soul cries out to know God better. Join a Bible study group and just listen to what God's Word says to you. The Holy Spirit has been given to us, the believers, to help us do that.

PRAYER: Heavenly Father, I thank you for the Holy Spirit who helps me to grow in grace and holiness. I realize that your Word is my necessary food, and my day is not complete unless I read some of your Word. I believe there is much more to the Bible that I can lay hold of, so I ask that the Holy Spirit will open my eyes and ears to glean all I can from each scripture reference I read. In Jesus' name, Amen.

DECEMBER 9th

 We need to look at a few more references regarding the Holy Spirit. In John 14:16, Jesus says, *"I will pray the Father, and He shall give you another Comforter, that He may abide with you for ever."* I want you to see that the Holy Spirit will live with you forever.

Also look at I Corinthians 6:19, which reads, *"What? Know ye not that your body is the temple of the Holy Ghost which is in you, which ye have of God, and ye are not your own?"* Your body, soul, and spirit are like a temple where God dwells, and God the Holy Spirit lives within you. The Bible says it is forever! This should be a very comforting thought to us all.

Turn to Ephesians 1:19-20, which states: *"And what is the exceeding greatness of His power to us-ward who believe, according to the working of His mighty power, which He wrought in Christ, when He raised Him from the dead, and set Him at His own right hand in the heavenly places."*

The same power that raised Jesus from the dead is also available to us. And it is through that power that the Holy Spirit works for our spiritual growth, to develop us into spiritually full-grown men and women.

I believe there is a day in the future when the Holy Spirit will be called back into heaven, just as Jesus ascended back to heaven from where He came. I also believe that, since the Holy Spirit has been given to us forever, when He is called back, we will go with Him.

In the Christian Church, that event is called the rapture of the Church. In the Old Testament, the Spirit of the Lord would descend upon a particular believer for a time to cause him or her to say or write a word on God's behalf. But I don't think the Spirit dwelt on earth as He does now in the lives of the believers. *We* need to learn how to listen to the Spirit of God within us, to be led by that Spirit.

Begin to ask the Holy Spirit to enlighten you as you read God's Word, to help you discern the truth from error, right from wrong, what is good for you from what is bad. Then the Holy Spirit will become very active in your everyday life. Your intimacy with God will grow by leaps and bounds. It will also help you to enter into God's rest. That is a place where peace that passes all understanding permeates your whole body, soul, and spirit.

PRAYER: Heavenly Father, I want to be able to hear the Holy Spirit speak to me, but I am not so used to doing that. I ask you to help me to have ears to hear the Spirit nudging me to get my attention. Give me discernment, Lord, so I may know how to obey the Spirit also. I see this whole process as something that will take practice, so I ask that you lead me as I begin. In Jesus' name, Amen.

DECEMBER 10th

 I believe it is a good idea to look at the book of Acts and see what the Holy Spirit began to do through the believers. This was a brand new experience for the early apostles. The whole responsibility of getting the message of the gospel (the plan of salvation) out to the world rested on their shoulders. Never forget they were told, *"Go ye therefore, and make disciples of all nations, baptizing them in the name of the Father, and of the Son, and of the Holy Ghost"* (Matthew 28:19).

Let's look at Acts 1:8, which reads, *"But ye shall receive power, after that the Holy Ghost is come upon you: and ye shall be witnesses unto me both in Jerusalem, and in all Judea , and in Samaria, and unto the uttermost part of the earth."* Can you comprehend the scope of the job description the disciples had been given? And it was to take effect as soon as they had been given the power of the baptism of the Holy Ghost.

As we look at some of the work the disciples did, you will begin to see that they believed the Word of Jesus, and they were willing to give their lives for the task before them. Much like soldiers going off to war, each was willing to give his life if need be. For a few days, we will follow the work of the Holy Spirit in the life of the early church.

PRAYER: Heavenly Father, is this where the rubber hits the road? I am beginning to see that this does not begin and end with the original disciples, but it also reaches down the ages to my day, to our day. I am beginning to really see that to accept Jesus as Lord and Savior means that I am in full-time employment for my Heavenly Father. I am either in the light, with the Word of God in my heart and mind, or I am walking in darkness—either a missionary or a mission field. How I need the power of the Holy Spirit in my life! Fill me and use me, Lord, according to your gracious will. In Jesus' name, Amen.

DECEMBER 11th

 The early church began to live a communal life. They pooled their assets and lived together. I am not sure just why they did this. It might have been a way of feeling safe, or of having strength in numbers. Acts 4:33-35 describes this: *"And with great power gave the apostles witness of the resurrection of the Lord Jesus: and great grace was upon them all. Neither was there any among them that lacked : for as many as were possessors of lands or houses sold them, and brought the prices of the things that were sold. And laid them down at the apostles' feet: and distribution was made unto every man according as he had need."*

One couple, however, had conspired to sell their property and give only part of it to the church, as we see in Acts 5:1-5, which reads: *"But a certain man named Ananias, with Sapphira his wife, sold a possession, And kept back part of the price, his wife also being privy to it, and brought a certain part, and laid it at the apostles' feet. But Peter said, 'Ananias, why hath Satan filled thine heart to lie to the Holy Ghost, and to keep back part of the price of the land? Whiles it remained, was it not thine own? And after it was sold, was it not in thine own power? Why hast thou conceived this thing in thine heart? Thou hast not lied unto men, but unto God.' And Ananias hearing these words fell down, and gave up the ghost: and great fear came on all them that heard these things."*

Some men there buried Ananias, and three hours later his wife came and they asked her the same question. She lied, like her husband, since they had planned the whole thing together, and she died also.

Let's ask ourselves a few questions. How did Peter know they were lying? Who gave Peter the wisdom to show Ananias how the land and the money was all his and he did not need to lie about it? Who was Ananias trying to impress? What sin brought on this act of lying?

I believe it was the sin of pride. Ananias wanted to impress the people that he, as a solid believer, was as fully committed as everyone else. I also believe that the Holy Spirit gave Peter discernment, so he just knew Ananias had sold it for more than he was saying. Remember, the Holy Spirit is also called the Spirit of Truth. I believe all this happened in the early stages of the development of the church so that it would start out on the right foot, the foundation of truth!

PRAYER: Heavenly Father, I realize by these verses that when I lie, it is to the Holy Spirit. When a lie is told, I can almost see Satan laughing in the face of the Holy Spirit. By lying, we give the devil permission to use us to grieve the Holy Spirit, since Satan is the father of lies! Oh, Lord, forgive me when I yield to the temptation to lie, and help me to put a guard on my desire and choice to lie. I see what destruction lying can bring into the picture. All sin will lead eventually to death. I am reminded of Proverbs 18:21, which says, *"Death and life are in the power of the tongue: and they that love it shall eat the fruit thereof."* It looks to me, Lord, that I can lie myself right into hell! Does lying become a habit also, Lord? It is a heavy thought, and I cannot deny what the Scripture says to me in these references. I desire not to lie, therefore, Lord, put a stop to lies before they even come out of my mouth, or before they take root in my mind. The Bible says that you know my words before they are even spoken, so I believe I can ask you to guard me and nudge me even before the words are ever spoken. With that, the habit, even the desire, to lie will eventually die. Psalm 139:4 also says, *"For there is not a word in my tongue but, lo, O Lord, thou knowest it altogether."* Help me, Lord, to be an overcomer in this area of lying. In Jesus' name, Amen.

DECEMBER 12th

 The early church had many obstacles to overcome and a lot of opposition to push past. It began right after Jesus was raised from the dead and the Holy Spirit had been poured out on the believers.

The apostles had been teaching and performing miracle healings right and left. The religious leaders were furious, and had some apostles put in jail and told them not to preach or teach in that name anymore. Then an angel let them out of prison by night, and the next day they were back in the temple teaching as before. In fact, the angel had told them to do that.

Again, the captain and officers of Israel brought the disciples to the council over which the High Priest presided. Acts 5:27-33 explains: *"And when they had brought them, they set them before the council: and the high priest asked them, saying, 'Did not we straitly command you that ye should not teach in this name? And, behold, ye have filled Jerusalem with your doctrine* (teaching), *and <u>intend to bring this man's blood upon us</u>.' Then Peter and the other apostles answered and said, 'We ought to obey God rather than men. The God of our fathers raised up Jesus, whom ye slew and hanged on a tree. Him hath God exalted with His right hand to be a Prince and a Savior, for to give repentance to Israel, and forgiveness of sins. And we are His witnesses of these things; and so is also the Holy Ghost, whom God hath given to them that obey Him.' When they heard that, they were cut to the heart, and took counsel to slay them."*

Take note of the apostles' boldness. They listened to the Holy Spirit and not to the religious leaders who were mere men. They spoke out loud and clear about what had happened and who was in charge when they said that God had exalted Jesus to be a Prince and Savior, and to bring forgiveness to Israel. The apostles gave the main points of the message of salvation: repentance, forgiveness, and acknowledging Jesus as Prince and Savior.

There is one more thing to take note of, however. After hearing what Peter had to say, the religious leaders were convicted of sin, "cut to the heart." Any time you hear that, it means that the Holy Spirit had convicted them of their sin. Their reaction to that, however, was to kill the messengers because they did not like their message.

To believe enough to be convicted, and still not repent is a serious thing. First comes belief, then the choice to repent or reject the message. When one repents and is convicted of sin, then he must ask for forgiveness and receive it. The recipients of this message knew it was the truth, but did not accept it. Instead, they chose to entertain murderous thoughts against the apostles.

The Holy Spirit had convicted them of their sin, but unless the listener takes the steps to believe, repent, and ask for forgiveness, his belief will work against him. To believe a message is the truth, have the Holy Spirit convict one of sin, and to *reject* the conviction is to reject the work of the Holy Spirit. Please do not ever do that. Instead, humble yourself and ask for forgiveness. God is a good God, patient and kind, and full of mercy and grace.

PRAYER: Heavenly Father, as Christians, it would be hard to function at all without the work of the Holy Spirit. I want to thank you for the gift of the Holy Spirit. Help me to expect His help more than I do. I think I miss a lot of things you do in my life simply because I am not aware that it is the Spirit at work on my behalf. Help me be more sensitive to the fact that the Holy Spirit lives within me and wants to be the ally to my new nature, to aid me in living an overcoming life. In Jesus' name, Amen.

DECEMBER 13th

 We will spend a couple more days addressing the Holy Spirit. If you are wondering why I use the word "Holy Ghost" sometimes and "Holy Spirit" other times, it is because I quote from King James translation, which uses "Holy Ghost." More modern translations use "Holy Spirit." They are one and the same, the third person of the God-head.

As time went on, so many people were joining the Church that the apostles needed help. They were taking care of widows, as we see in Acts 6:1-4, which reads: ***"And in those days, when the number of the disciples was multiplied, there arose a murmuring of the Grecian Jews against the Hebrews, because their widows were neglected in the daily ministration.*** (The people who joined and followed the apostles were called disciples. A disciple is a follower and an apostle is a "sent" one) ***Then the twelve*** (apostles) ***called the multitude of the disciples unto them, and said, 'It is not reason that we should leave the word of God, and serve tables. Wherefore, brethren, look ye out among you seven men of honest report, full of the Holy Ghost and wisdom, whom we may appoint over this***

509

business. But we will give ourselves continually to prayer, and to the ministry of the word.' "

They picked seven men, one of whom was a man named Stephen. We will look at his life today, beginning with Acts 6:6-8, which reads: *"Whom they set before the apostles: and when they had prayed, they laid their hands on them. And the word of God increased; and the number of the disciples multiplied in Jerusalem greatly; and a company of priests were obedient to the faith. And Stephen, full of faith* (grace) *and power, did great wonders and miracles among the people."*

We see that Stephen was full of Holy Spirit, faith, power, and grace. He also performed great miracles. Have you wondered where Satan was all this time as the church is growing? Well, he was close by. His playing field was getting smaller, and I'm sure he felt he had to put a stop to that. But we will look at that tomorrow.

PRAYER: Heavenly Father, I am amazed at how the disciples, turned apostles, functioned after Jesus died, rose again, appeared to them, and ascended to heaven, and after the Holy Spirit was poured out on them. They became a "take charge" group. Is that what you want your Church to look and act like? Let us not disappoint you, Lord. Help us all to fit into your plan for your Church on earth. Give us the knowledge, understanding, and wisdom when changes are necessary. We do not want to be so stuck in a rut that we cannot change our ways of thinking or the ways we do the work of the Church. If the early church could push ahead and add to their numbers, then, Lord, it should not be so hard for us to push forward also. Help me be the person you can count on to do what you have planned for me to do just where I am. In Jesus' name, Amen.

DECEMBER 14th

In order to fully understand what is going on in the book of Acts, you need to have some background, so today we will look at some verses about the synagogue of several different people groups. Acts 6:9-15 states: *"Then there arose certain of the synagogue, which is called, The synagogue of the Libertines, and Cyrenians, and Alexandrians and of them of Cilicia and of Asia disputing with Stephan. And they were not able to resist the wisdom and the spirit by which he spoke. Then they suborned men, which said, 'We have heard him speak blasphemous words against Moses, and against God.' And they stirred up the people, and the elders, and the scribes, and came upon him, and caught him, and brought him to the council. And set up false witnesses, which said, 'This man ceaseth not to speak blasphemous words against this holy place, and the law: For we have heard him say that this Jesus of Nazareth shall destroy this place, and shall change the customs which Moses delivered us.' And all that sat in the council, looking steadfastly on him, saw his face as it had been the face of an angel."*

The synagogue is not the same as the temple. There was only one temple, but each city could have its own synagogue. Also, people from other nations could have their own synagogue in Jerusalem.

The synagogue was where people learned about the laws of the Bible, called the laws of Moses, and to worship or have a social gathering. The temple was the place where the priests ministered the sacrifices. Only the priest was permitted to enter the temple, but there were also courts surrounding the temple where the people could gather.

At this time, the number of Christians was growing by leaps and bound. In these verses, we can see there were several synagogues in Jerusalem. We can also see even in yesterday's reference (Acts 6:1) the spirit of jealousy began to rear its ugly head.

Satan finally got his licks in. You just know you will see him show up when the church begins to grow in any significant way. It is the same today. But the Christian is never to be defeated. We are to be the overcomers in every situation, to be more than conquerors, as the Bible says.

I can just imagine what a bold, powerful man Stephen was. And I'll just bet he influenced others to be bold too. Yes, Satan would try to eliminate him. Also be aware that the same people who had been involved with the death of Jesus are using the same tactic in Stephen's case. They accused him of blasphemy and to speaking against Moses and the law. That was the same law the leaders broke right and left, but no one called them on it because they had such power in the synagogue that no one would be safe to come against the leaders. Jesus called them hypocrites and vipers to their face, and they *crucified Him.*

By the way, did you notice in yesterday's scripture that the leaders said the apostles were trying to bring Jesus' blood on them? Do you recall that the crowd had yelled, *"His blood be upon us and our children"* (Matthew 27:25)? Is it any wonder they were feeling guilty of being involved in shedding innocent blood? But, a short time later, they are at it again—this time accusing Stephen.

PRAYER: Heavenly Father, is there such a spirit of resistance to your truth even today? I realize that toward the end of the age the spirit of the anti-Christ and anti-God gain more momentum, right along until the earth will be covered with it. I recall that your Word says in Matthew 16:18, *"and upon this rock I will build my church; and the gates of hell shall not prevail against it."* I lay hold of that promise and take my stand on your side. There is no other place of safety from the enemy and his fiery darts. Thank you, Father, for that place of safety in your Son, Jesus Christ. In Jesus' name, Amen.

DECEMBER 15th

 In Acts 7, the High priest asked Stephen if the accusations against him were true. Then Stephen recounts the history of the nation of Israel, from the call God gave to Abram to leave his country to go to a land God would show him, and on through the promises God gave to Abram of a people, land, and a blessing. Stephen recounted Israel's time in Egypt, deliverance from Egypt, conquering the Promised Land, and on and on through their rebellion against God and killing of the prophets.

To give you an idea of the scope of the depth of Stephen's account of Israel's history, look at Acts 7:9, which reads, *"And the patriarchs, moved with envy, sold Joseph into Egypt: but God was with him."* And Acts 7:35 says, *"This Moses whom they refused, saying, 'Who made thee ruler and a judge?' The same did God send to be a ruler and a deliverer by the hand of the angel which appeared to him in the bush."* Also turn to Acts 7:37, which states, *"This is THAT Moses, which said unto the children of Israel, 'A prophet shall the Lord your God raise up unto you of your brethren, like unto me; Him shall ye hear.' "*

This last verse definitely points to Jesus, and the religious leaders should have recognized Him as the fulfillment of Moses' own prophecy when Jesus came on the scene. Acts 7:41-42 also reads: *"And they made a calf in those days, and offered sacrifice unto the idol, and rejoiced in the works of their own hands. THEN God turned, and gave them up to worship the host of heaven; as it is written in the book of the prophets, O ye house of Israel, have ye offered to me slain beasts and sacrifices by the space of forty years in the wilderness?"*

Let's also look at Acts 7:51-52, which reads: *"Ye stiff necked and uncircumcised in heart and ears, ye do ALWAYS resist the Holy Ghost: as your fathers did, so do ye. Which of the prophets have not your fathers persecuted? And they have slain them which shewed before of the coming of the Just,* (Righteous) *One; of whom ye have been NOW the betrayers and murderers."*

Stephen poured it out on them, pointing to their history of *always* resisting God and practicing evil, right up through the crucifixion of the Messiah! Everything Stephen said was painfully true, and the council members heard it for themselves. *They* had brought Stephen there, and *they* had asked him to answer for himself.

Think about it! Stephen made good use of the opportunity and privilege to answer for the hope that was within him. We will look at the result of all this tomorrow. I recommend that you read all 60 verses of Acts 7. Ask God to show you the truth of the verses that you should especially look at.

513

Is Israel as a nation any different today? When will they accept Jesus as their Messiah and be saved? The Bible *teaches* that one day they will accept Him and be saved. I wonder how long until they do. Pray for the nation of Israel and the peace of Jerusalem.

PRAYER: Heavenly Father, as I read your Word in Acts 7, I see that you are a God with patience beyond any human kind, and I marvel at your control of anger. How it must grieve your heart to love a people, like your chosen people, who have rejected your plans for them, who flat-out disobey you in many ways, and even called down the guilt of the blood of Jesus upon themselves and their children. You have displayed great patience with me also, and as I see your patience and long suffering at work, it makes me want to live a life that brings joy and honor to your holy name. Help me to answer your call, accept your truths, and be quickly willing to be a "sent one," not hesitating and deliberating while I drag my feet and do nothing. In Jesus' name, Amen.

DECEMBER 16th

 Acts 7:54-58 reads: *"When they heard these things, they were cut to the heart, and they gnashed on him with their teeth* (they were furious)*. But he, <u>being full of the Holy Ghost</u>, looked up steadfastly into heaven, and saw the glory of God, and Jesus standing on the right hand of God. Then they cried out with a loud voice, and stopped their ears, and ran upon him with one accord. And cast him out of the city, and stoned him; and the witnesses laid down their clothes at a young man's feet whose name was Saul."*

The young man, Saul, is none other than the Apostle Paul. Remember, after his conversion he changed his name to Paul. At first, Paul was set on stamping out Christianity. He killed Christians until Jesus met him face to face on the road to Damascus.

Acts 7:59-60 continues: *"And they stoned Stephen, calling upon God, and saying, 'Lord Jesus receive my spirit.' And he kneeled down, and cried with a loud voice, 'Lord, lay not this sin to their charge.' And when he had said this, he fell asleep* (which means he died). "

Did you notice that after Stephen's speech of defense, the members of the council were convicted of their sin? But instead of repenting and asking for forgiveness, they put to death the voice of truth. That was their way of living with themselves.

The moment the Holy Spirit convicts you of something you say or do that displeases God, do not hesitate, but rather immediately confess it as a sin and name it before God. Then ask for forgiveness, and receive it gladly.

The sooner you do this the better. Sin that is left to ferment will, like yeast, only increase and increase. If I have said something that I later realize was wrong, I also ask for a crop failure because what you sow you also reap. I can't take back what I said, so I ask God to not let those seeds germinate, or grow, or be watered and fertilized.

Satan loves it when he can take those kinds of seeds and multiply them. Intercept that plan with a prayer to God asking Him to create a crop failure. God is always *for* us and we tend to forget that. He will step in, on our behalf, especially if we are humble enough to admit our wrong and ask for forgiveness.

Did you also notice Stephen *prayed* for the accusers who killed him? Jesus did the same thing by saying, *"Father, forgive them for they know not what they do…,"* as He was crucified the on cross (Luke 23:34).

PRAYER: Heavenly Father, thank you for showing me your patience with stubborn, disobedient mankind. Thank you, too, for giving me a front-row seat to see how a man filled with the Holy Spirit faces death—without fear, but with an inner peace and thanksgiving in his heart. I believe that the Holy Spirit gave him that kind of peace and power when he needed it, and that the Holy Spirit will give it to me also, when I have need of it. I can depend on that truth, because I recall the Word that said the Holy Spirit was given to me forever! Help me, Lord, to never let go of these truths. I want to make them a part of my very being. In Jesus' precious name, Amen.

DECEMBER 17th

 Today I want to talk to you about praying in Jesus' name. I think I touched on this before, but I believe it needs to be reinforced again before this year is over.

In John 16, Jesus speaks of a day when He would no longer be walking this earth, and the disciples (turned apostles) could no longer go to Him personally to ask for anything. They would be at the mercy of the elements, their own human frailties, the opposing religious leaders, and, yes, Satan himself. In John 16:23-24, Jesus told them: *"And in that day ye shall ask me nothing. Verily, verily, I say unto you, what-so-ever ye shall ask the Father in my name, He will give it you. Hitherto have ye asked nothing in my name: ask, and ye shall receive, that your joy may be full."*

After Jesus paid for our sins by dying on the cross, He had done all that was necessary in God's eyes for each of us to be able to live a victorious life. But there was one more thing we needed to know, and that was how to pray to our Heavenly Father under a new set of terms.

When we pray in Jesus' name to God the Father, we present to God our supplications under the umbrella of all that Jesus is to the Father, and all that He is to us. What does that mean? Jesus is the fullness of truth, grace, wisdom, mercy, authority, and power. He is even the fullness of God's glory. All that the Father is, so too is Jesus.

Jesus, Himself, has told us to ask the Father in His name. It is not just something we tack on at the end of prayer. You need to know that. It is going to the Father with a power and authority beyond description. It is tapping into the love, mercy, and grace of God, because we have the right to do that.

This was a hard lesson for me to learn. It seemed so wrong to go to God in that kind of assurance and boldness. But it is that very thing that brings glory to God, who provided this way for us to pray. To see us actually take advantage of that gift proves to God that we got the message.

516

PRAYER: Heavenly Father, every truth you reveal to me in your Word helps me to know you better, and enriches my confidence in you. It is great to become better acquainted with your ways, your hopes and desires for me, and your power to help me to be an overcomer in this sin-ridden world. I often wonder how I ever survived before I knew and trusted your love for me. I am so grateful for just owning a Bible, which others have died to preserve, and for those who have painstakingly translated your Word so that I can read it in my own language. We have a tendency to overlook those who have gone before us and laid down a foundation of belief and faith for us to build upon. Yes, Lord, I want to offer up a prayer of thanksgiving for all of that. In Jesus' name, Amen.

DECEMBER 18th

The last few days we have seen how Stephen, who was filled with the Holy Ghost, lived his life. He witnessed to his faith in God the Father, and we saw how he was willing to die for his faith in God the Son.

If we are going to live victorious lives, then we too need to be filled with the Holy Ghost. James 4:2 says, *"...Ye have not because ye ask not."* I believe Christians need to ask God to fill them with the Holy Spirit. If you have never done that, be sure you do not neglect doing it.

The Holy Spirit is so powerfully kind, gentle, prudent, wise, and gracious. You will never find a better friend. He helps you to understand the Words of the Bible and gives you the desire to believe and follow them.

Ephesians 4:30 reads, *"And grieve not the Holy Spirit of God, whereby ye are sealed unto the day of redemption."* We can actually cause the Holy Spirit to grieve. He has feelings, just as the God the Father and Son do.

The Holy Spirit is not just a power, like electricity. He is a person, the third person of the God-head. Notice that Ephesians 4:30 says that we are *"sealed by the Holy Spirit unto the day of redemption."* We have been preserved, kept safe from all things.

Think of a can of soda. It is sealed up and kept safe until you open it to drink it. Also consider canned vegetables on the shelf in the grocery store. They too are sealed, kept safe from spoilage, until they are opened for eating. The Holy Spirit has His seal on you, to preserve you until the day of redemption. That is when you will see Jesus face to face and your journey to your heavenly home is complete.

We are also admonished in I Thessalonians 5:19 to *"quench not the Spirit."* When you refuse to listen to the Spirit, then you begin to quench the Spirit in your life. Have you ever been on your way to the car to go shopping and then remembered you left something behind? Maybe you left your grocery list, or something to be returned that you were to bring along? Who do you think reminded you of that? It was the Spirit of God, His Holy Spirit! Satan would love to have you forget those things, and ruin your day. He would love to make you go back to town another day and waste all that gas, time, and money.

Have you ever called someone on the phone and they tell you how wonderful it was that you called at just the right time? Who urged you to make the call? You got it—it was the Holy Spirit. Begin to listen to Him.

Remember, too, that Satan is also at work trying to have you listen to him, so beware. You will need to discern who is speaking to you. Reflect on it and analyze, who would get the glory or praise for your actions. If you would get the glory, then for sure Satan is the one speaking to you.

PRAYER: Heavenly Father, here I am again, asking for your help. Help me to discern who is speaking to me. I do not want to do the will of Satan, but I do want to do your will. I am excited about hearing from you in my day-to-day life, and I want to put into practice what I am learning today. Give me ears to hear from your Spirit, and then give me the willingness to obey Him. In Jesus' precious name, Amen.

DECEMBER 19th

 Romans 5:5 reads, *"And hope maketh not ashamed; because the love of God is shed abroad in our hearts by the Holy Spirit which is given unto us."* And Romans 5:8 continues, *"But God commanded His love toward us, in that, while we were yet sinners, Christ died for us."*

I hope I can help you to see the sequence of events here. In these two verses, you see the Trinity again; *"love of <u>God</u> ... by the <u>Holy Spirit</u>"* and *"<u>Christ</u> died for us."* How was God going to bring His love down to earth, reveal it to us, and then leave it here to permeate our very being? I don't think the people in the Old Testament times really knew that kind of love. How could they?

Think about it. God commanded His love to come to earth, and it was Jesus who brought it here. He revealed God's love for us by living a sinless life, and then taking our sins upon Himself to die the death we all should have died. With that, He made it possible for God and mankind to be reconciled.

Then, when Jesus had finished His work on earth, He prayed to the Father to send the Comforter, the Holy Ghost, to be with us forever. It is through the Holy Ghost that God's own love is shed in our hearts. We now have the capacity to love as God the Father and Jesus the Son loved, because the Holy Spirit takes what the Father had given to Jesus and brings it to us.

PRAYER: Heavenly Father, I see how the Trinity works together for a common purpose, and it is comforting to know that the Trinity is at work on my behalf. I thank you, Father, for such love displayed through Jesus on my behalf. Thank you, too, for the Holy Spirit, who makes it possible for me to know your love. Thank you for making me a vessel through whom your love can flow out to others. This way, we can make a good team. There are those I name in my heart before you that I want to also experience, first hand, your love for them. Put people in their paths to show them your love, kindness, and patience. In Jesus' name, Amen.

DECEMBER 20ᵗʰ

Let's look again at John 16:12-15, where Jesus says: *"I have yet many things to say unto you, but ye cannot hear them now.* (I believe they could not understand them until the Holy Spirit filled them, and it would be sometime later before the Holy Spirit would come.) *Howbeit when He, the Spirit of truth, is come, He will guide you into all truth: for He shall not speak of Himself; but whatsoever He shall hear, that shall He speak: and He will show you things to come. He shall glorify me* (Jesus): *for He shall receive of mine, and shall show it unto you. All things that the Father hath are mine: therefore said I, that He shall take of mine, and shall show it unto you."*

Could it be any clearer? God had given everything to Jesus, and the Holy Spirit would take what the Son had and administer that to us, the believers. I firmly believe that people who do not know Jesus, or do not have Him in their hearts, can not really know what it is to love.

Let me share one more reference with you. I John 4:6-8 reads: *"We are of God: he that knoweth God heareth us; he that is not of God heareth not us. Hereby know we the Spirit of truth* (the same "Spirit of truth" as in the reference above)*, and the spirit of error* (Satan)*. Beloved, let us love one another: for love is of God; and every one that loveth is born* (begotten) *of God, and knoweth God. He that loveth not knoweth not God; for God is love."*

Did you get that? God *is* love. God cannot be hate and love at the same time. He *is* love. He cannot think or act evil, because He is love. So, let me go back to the first reference of today. Jesus said that everything of the Father's was His. And all that is His (Jesus') would be given to the Holy Spirit, and the Holy Spirit would share it with us.

I will use three points to describe the process of how God's love becomes ours to share. First, Jesus brought God's kind of love (sacrificial

520

and unconditional) to earth and demonstrated what it was, how it works, and its results through His life. Second, the Holy Spirit takes God's love, now known to the world through Jesus, and gives it to us to effect a change in our lives. Third, we cannot give away what we do not have. So it is as we allow God's love to reshape our lives that we become ready to go out and demonstrate His love to those around us.

Now look again at I John 4:6-8. Love came from God, and Jesus was chosen to bring it to earth to show us how it is lived out. The Holy Spirit is the one who actually gives it to us to live our lives while continuing to demonstrate it to the world. Get acquainted with the Holy Spirit in your Christian walk. Be open to His whispers and nudges in your conscience and mind.

PRAYER: Heavenly Father, thank you for your love, which you sent to earth to dwell within me. I pray that I will be quick to display that love in my life. Help me to be as generous as you are with your love. Satan has only hate and evil on his mind, and he tries to invade my way of thinking, so I pray that I will be quick to recognize those kinds of thoughts that want to take root in my mind. They push your love right out of the way, and I know your love can't come through when bitterness, jealousy, envy, hate, and anger grow in my mind and try to take over. I am going to be of the opinion, Lord, that love is much stronger than evil thoughts, and your love will win out in this battle of the mind. Thank you, Father, for your love! In Jesus' name, Amen.

DECEMBER 21st

 For a few days, I would like to talk about Christian maturity. Just as we want our children to grow in a well-balanced way and to show signs of maturity, so too does God want His children to grow and show signs of spiritual maturity.

I believe that Ephesians is a good place to see what God has in mind in regard to our maturity and what He has done to help us achieve it.

To begin, let me remind you that before anything could happen to us in regard to growth, Jesus had to come and do His job. When His job was completed on earth, and in hell, He ascended into heaven and sat down in a position of authority, at the right hand of God.

Now, let's turn to Ephesians 1:20-23, which reads: *"Which He (God) wrought in Christ when He raised Him from the dead, and set Him at His own right hand in the heavenly places, Far above all principality, and power, and might, and dominion, and every name that is named, not only in this world, but also in that which is to come: And hath put all things under His (Jesus') feet, and gave Him to be the head over all things to the church, Which is His body, the fulness of Him that filleth all in all."*

Once this was all accomplished, Jesus administered gifts to the Church for its growth and maturity. Ephesians 4:7 states, *"But unto every one of us is given grace according to the measure of the gift of Christ."* Look at that verse for a moment. Every believer has been gifted with a measure of grace.

Remember, *justice* is getting what you deserve, *mercy* is *not* getting what you deserve, and *grace* is getting what you don't deserve. We do not deserve pardon and forgiveness, but it has been given to us on the basis of what Christ has done for us. We also do not deserve to be made the righteousness of God but, in Christ we are.

In II Corinthians 5:21, we read, *"For He (God) hath made Him (Jesus) to be sin for us, who knew no sin, that we might be made the righteousness of God in Him (Jesus)."* You had nothing to do with it except to accept Jesus as Lord and Savior. God did all the rest, including making you righteous, as righteous as Christ. At this point, then, you are ready to grow in your spiritual life, to grow more Christ-like every day. We will continue in Ephesians tomorrow.

PRAYER: Heavenly Father, I can remember when I did not think about my spiritual life as something that needed to grow, but it surely made sense to me once I realized it. If I can be born again, there has to be a life that will either die of neglect or grow by being fed. I am glad you have provided a way that will help me to be fed regularly. I want to grow in a well-balanced way—not with a diet of soda and sweets, but rather a diet of meat and potatoes. I look forward, Lord, to being fed something more than milk and toast. In Jesus' name, Amen.

DECEMBER 22nd

 Ephesians 4:8-10 reads: *"Wherefore* (that points back to verse 7 of yesterday) *He saith, 'When He ascended up on high, He led captivity captive, and gave gifts unto men.' (Now that He ascended, what is it but that He also descended first into the lower parts of the earth? He that descended is the same also that ascended up far above all heavens, that He might fill all things.)"*

Verses 9 and 10 are in parenthesis in the King James Bible. I believe they are filling in a detail about leading captivity captive. Continuing with the idea of gifts Ephesians 4:11 states, *"And He gave some to be apostles; and some, prophets; and some, evangelists; and some, pastors and teachers."* These were all the gifts from Christ that were given to the church, the body of believers, of whom Christ is the head.

What are the functions of apostles, prophets, evangelists, pastors, and teachers? They are to teach the Word of God, help others understand His Word, encourage, exhort, offer help in times of need, and correct problems when needed. Ephesians 4:12-13 explains that these gifts are: *"For the perfecting of the saints* (the believers, the body of Christ), *for unto the work of the ministry, for the edifying, building up, of the body of Christ: Till we all come in the unity of the faith, and of the knowledge of the Son of God, unto a perfect full-grown man, unto the measure of the stature of the fullness of Christ.."*

Can it be more plainly written? God's desire is for His Church to grow up into a mature body. The Head, which is Christ Jesus, is fully mature. Is it not His right to expect His body, the Church, to grow up into a mature body also? He has given us the gift of people with the ability to feed us the proper spiritual food so that we may grow. This, then, is the road to maturity. How far are you on that journey?

PRAYER: Heavenly Father, thank you for the people in my life who have helped me to see the light, to understand the Word of God, and to grow in my faith, trust, and knowledge of you. I want to continue to grow, and I know that the Holy Spirit is at work within me to assist me. I thank you for that also. If I am to speak a word of encouragement to anyone else, to encourage them as I have been encouraged, then give me the right words, attitude, and timing to do that for your name's sake. In Jesus' name, Amen.

DECEMBER 23rd

 In I Peter 2:1-3, we read: *"Wherefore laying aside all malice (wickedness), and all guile, and hypocrisies, and envies, and all evil speaking, As newborn babes, desire (long for) the sincere milk of the word (the spiritual milk, which is without guile), that ye may grow thereby unto salvation: If so be that ye have tasted that the Lord is gracious."*

There are two steps you must choose to take to grow. You need to *lay aside* things of your old nature—malice, guile, envies, evil speaking, etc.—and *desire*, *long for*, and *crave* words of truth. The Word of God is the "sincere milk" or "spiritual milk," and nourishes us to "grow unto salvation."

These two steps can be taken simultaneously, but often the laying aside is a longer process. Satan is at work in our old nature, urging us to resist breaking our bad habits. The Holy Spirit is at work in our new nature, helping us to lay hold of new and better habits.

I believe that when people are introduced to God's Word in such a way they can see and hear that He is speaking to them individually, they develop a strong desire to know more and more, and thereby begin to drink the spiritual milk of the Word. Many times it is not until after that experience, when the Holy Spirit begins to reveal the old, bad habits and, one by one, they are dropped by the wayside.

We cannot clean ourselves up. If we could, Jesus would not have had to die for us. It is the work of the Holy Spirit to help us to grow, and clean us up in the meantime. That whole process is called "sanctification." Sanctification however, is needed for you to desire that sincere spiritual milk. If you do not have such a desire, but would like it, then ask God and He will give it to you.

Many people wait until God has put them flat on their backs, where they have to look at the ceiling and don't know where to turn. Why not *choose* to desire to read and learn more about God's Word, and avoid the burden ignorance can be. God is at work all the time wooing people through the Holy Spirit to come to Him, learn of Him, and grow.

PRAYER: Heavenly Father, this admonition to set aside my old ways and to desire more of your Word reminds me of the verse in Hebrews 12:1, which says *"...Lay aside every weight and sin, and run with patience, the race set before us."* Here we see step one and step two. To me, it is very evident that we cannot have it both ways. It is either one or the other. There is no way we can do all this on our own. We need the help of the Holy Spirit to accomplish our mission here. Therefore, Lord, I do ask that you fill me with your Holy Spirit and help me not to become weary or faint hearted, but instead to persevere and determine to be more than a conqueror. I desire to be a victorious Christian over every situation that comes my way. I don't desire this, Lord, to bring glory to my name, but rather to bring glory to *your* name. Jesus, you have done everything on my behalf so that I can walk in victory, and I do not want to diminish you in any way by being a weak Christian. You have said, "Ask and you shall receive," (John 16:24) so, Lord, I am asking. In Jesus' name, Amen.

DECEMBER 24th

Today is Christmas Eve, a most blessed time in the life of the church, when we pause and dwell of the birth of our Savior. God gave promises to the Old Testament saints, and I believe it would do us well to look at some of those promises and realize how they were fulfilled to the letter.

To me, things like that verify the credibility of God's Word. Isaiah 7:14 reads, *"Therefore the Lord himself shall give you a sign; Behold, a virgin shall conceive, and bear a son, and shall call his name Immanuel."* Immanuel means "God is with us."

Also look at Luke 1:26-27, which states: *"And in the sixth month the angel Gabriel was sent from God unto a city of Galilee, named Nazareth, To a virgin espoused to a man whose name was Joseph, of the house of David and the virgin's name was Mary."*

Luke 1:30-33 continues: *"And the angel said unto her, 'Fear not, Mary: for thou hast found favor with God. And, behold, thou shalt conceive in thy womb, and bring forth a son, and shalt call his name JESUS. He shall be great, and shall be called the Son of the Highest: and the Lord God shall give unto Him the throne of His father David: And He shall reign over the house of Jacob for ever; and of His kingdom there shall be no end.' "*

In these verses, we see that Jesus was to be a descendent of David, who was from Judah, a specific tribe of Jacob. When Jacob was old and near death, he pronounced a blessing on each one of his sons, and Judah was the one through whom the Messiah would come. Genesis 49:10 reads: *The sceptre* (the official staff of a ruler, symbolizing his authority and power) *shall not depart from Judah, nor a lawgiver from between his feet, until Shiloh come, and unto him shall the gathering of the people be."*

Jesus is described as a lion in Genesis 49:9 it reads: *"Judah is a lion's whelp: from the prey, my son, thou art gone up: he stooped down, he crouched as a lion, and as an old lion as a lioness: who shall rouse him up?* And in Revelation 5:5, which states, *"And one of the elders saith unto me, 'Weep not: behold, the Lion of the tribe of Judah, the Root of*

David, hath prevailed to open the book, and to loose the seven seals thereof.' "

When you study God's Word, all these fine details are important, and you don't want to miss a one of them. Jesus' birthplace was named in Micah 5:2, which was about 700 years before He was born and states: *"But thou, Bethlehem Ephratah, though thou be little among the thousands of Judah, yet out of thee shall he come forth unto me that is to be <u>ruler in Israel</u>; whose going forth have been from of old, from everlasting."*

It is interesting that it was prophesied that Jesus would be born in Bethlehem. His parents lived in Nazareth in Galilee, 94 miles north of Bethlehem—88 miles from Nazareth to Jerusalem, and 6 miles from Jerusalem to Bethlehem. Imagine Mary riding a donkey or walking that far just before giving birth. But God knew, and Micah, inspired by the Spirit of God, wrote it down.

You see, Caesar Agustus called for a tax, and they had to go back to the place of their ancestors to pay it. Luke 2:4 explains, *"And Joseph also went up from Galilee, out of the city of Nazareth, into Judaea, unto the city of David, which is called Bethlehem; because he was of the house and lineage of David."*

With that, Jesus was born just exactly where God's Word said He would be born. That day, God stepped into our history in a way never before heard of. He would, from that time on, dwell among men.

We live in a fantastic time of history. The Church calls this the age of grace, and so it is. God's grace is being offered to the whole world. And His grace is not only offered, but it is free to all. Give thanks to God this night as you think about the angels singing praises, and the shepherds as they left their sheep to see this event that had come to pass. Allow yourself to get caught up in the majesty of it all—God among men, women, and children forever. Worship the Giver and the Gift, God the Father and God the Son!

PRAYER: Heavenly Father, how I thank you for seeing it fit to send your Son to live among us sinners. How you must have trusted Mary and Joseph to tend and care for this little boy. I marvel even today that you can trust your precious Word to me, a sinner, saved by grace, who must disappoint you again and again by my neglect and disobedience. Forgive me, Lord, for that. Help me to make a new commitment to my devotion to you, and to put you first in my life at all times. In Jesus' name, Amen.

DECEMBER 25th

A blessed Christmas to you who are reading these devotions. In the midst of all the family activity, let us not forget whose we are and why. God sent His Son to earth, not to judge us, but to seek us out and to save the lost. Never in history had such good news been brought to earth.

It is good that we take some time in the year to stop, celebrate, remember from where we came, where we are going, and why. All because God, out of His great love for us, stooped down to earth in the form of a child to offer us the free gift of salvation.

Are the gifts we give each other without strings? Do you have a giving attitude all year long, or only at Christmas time? John 3:16 is the crux of Jesus' whole life, and it says, *"For God so loved the world, that He gave His only begotten Son, that whosoever believeth in Him, shall NOT perish but have eternal LIFE."* Today is a day to celebrate that great gift with family.

PRAYER: Heavenly Father, I often wonder what you think as you look down on our planet as we celebrate the birth of your Son, Jesus. Sometimes it is hard to find Jesus among all the worldly trappings that crowd our Christian celebration of Jesus' birthday. Forgive us, Lord, for not having you as our centerpiece this day. Right now, I stop and worship you for your patience and your hopes for me, for the life you have given me—and not just physical life, but my spiritual and eternal life. Those are gifts that cannot be bought with money, no matter how much money I have. They are priceless. And Jesus, you shouldered the burden of our salvation willingly so that we could have a living relationship with you, Father. How blessed we are for that. What gifts we have from you today and forever. Thank you! In Jesus' name, Amen.

DECEMBER 26th

 I can imagine you are all in a holiday mood yet. It seems to linger around awhile every year. Things began to heat up for Mary and Joseph, however. We do not know for sure how long it was after Jesus' birth before Herod wanted all boy babies killed from the age two and under. Matthew 2:16-18 says: *"Then Herod, when he saw that he was mocked of the wise men, was exceeding wroth, and sent forth, and slew all the male children that were in Bethlehem, and in all the coasts thereof, from two years old and under, according to the time which he had diligently enquired of the wise men. Then was fulfilled that which was spoken by Jeremiah* (31:15) *the prophet, saying. 'In Rama was there a voice heard, lamentation, and weeping, and great mourning, Rachel weeping for her children, and would not be comforted, because they are not* (meaning they were dead).' "

Satan is already at work to disrupt God's plan for this earth and the people on it. But God is a step ahead of Satan. The wise men had come. God had warned them not to go back to Herod and tell him about Jesus, but instead to depart and go back to their own country by another way.

This infuriated Herod, and in anger he made a decree to have that new King (Jesus) killed. In a rage, he ordered that every boy child from age two and under should be killed. But God protected His Son. In Matthew 2:13-14, we read: *"And when they* (the wise men) *departed, behold, the angel of the Lord appeareth to Joseph in a dream, saying, 'Arise, and take the young child and his mother, and flee to Egypt, and be thou there until I bring thee word: for Herod will seek the young child to destroy him.' When he arose, he took the young child and his mother by night, and departed into Egypt:"* This fulfilled a prophecy in Hosea 11:1 *"Out of Egypt have I called my son."*

529

When you become aware of the battle that is going on between God and Satan, the Bible become much easier to understand. That battle is even taking place in the lives of each of us. All through Jesus' life, you can see that battle also. It began before he was two years old, and maybe before that.

Did Satan know that Mary carried the Son of God, and did he nudge Caesar Agustus to have the people go to pay a tax back in the home of their ancestors just at the time that Mary was to deliver her baby. Did Satan arrange for the place to be so full there was no room for the birth except in a stable? If the long trip didn't kill the baby, maybe Satan hoped the child would get sick and die. But that didn't work, so he killed hundreds, maybe even thousands, of innocent children in the hope that one of them would be Jesus, the King of the Jews.

Can you imagine the weeping that resulted from that decree issued from a frightened Caesar? As you read the gospels, notice how Satan attacks Jesus again and again.

I would like to put forth a challenge before you. Read the gospel of Matthew, and everywhere that it refers to the fulfillment of a prophecy, highlight it and note what the prophecy is. I also numbered them, and in my Bible there are 14 such references. Matthew is trying to prove to the nation of Israel that Jesus is the fulfillment of all the prophecies about the Messiah.

PRAYER: Heavenly Father, I wonder why Satan thinks he can outwit you. Why does he try, and try again, to bring your people and your plan down to destruction? He must think that someplace along the line he will be able to thwart your plan, even if it is just a little bit. I see how diligent I need to be in my life to keep him from invading my life with his devious temptations and plots against me. Help me to see him coming so I can prepare for his tactics and firmly defeat him. Give me the spirit of discernment in good measure, and also wisdom to make wise use of what I know and understand. In Jesus' name, Amen.

DECEMBER 27th

 Let's see how Jesus gets back in the Holy Land to do the work God sent Him to do. Matthew 2:19-23 reads: *"But when Herod was dead, behold, an angel of the Lord appeareth in a dream to Joseph in Egypt, saying, 'Arise, and take the young child and his mother, and go into the land of Israel: for they are dead which sought the young child's life.' And he arose, and took the young child and his mother, and came into the land of Israel. But when he heard that Archelaus did reign in Judaea in the room* (place) *of his father Herod, he was afraid to go thither: notwithstanding, being warned of God in a dream, he turned aside into the parts of Galilee. And he came and dwelt in a city called Nazareth: that it might be fulfilled which was spoken by the prophets, 'He shall be called a Nazarene.' "*

In the Amplified Bible, Matthew 2:23 is translated, *"He went and dwelt in a town called Nazareth, so that what was spoken through the prophets might be fulfilled, 'He shall be called a Nazarene.' "* Nazarene means "branch," or "separated one." When you begin to pay attention to the small details that are recorded in the Bible, it is amazing how thorough God is. Everything is done with precision, without one small thing omitted or forgotten.

That is His attitude about your life also. He is in the midst of your life, even if you are not aware of it. Even if you did not care, God cares. But He will not invade your freedom of choice. Don't blame God when He allows hardships to cause you to make a choice *for* God instead of *against* Him.

Just think, Mary gave birth to Jesus, but Joseph was responsible for His protection. God gave the dream to Joseph, and told him what to do and when. As they stayed in Egypt, I doubt that God spoke to them. It became a test of faith. They might have wondered, "Are we to stay here any longer? Should we go back now or just sit here and wait?"

Can't you see how it would test your faith? And when the angel told them to go back, and they learned that a son of Herod was ruling, did they wonder whether they really heard from God? But, you see, an angel told them to go to Galilee, which is much farther north of Judea.

Can you learn to depend on God that much in your life? That is what God really wants from us—complete and total dependence. At any rate, Jesus was back in the land that had been promised to Abraham, Isaac, and Jacob. And Jesus *is that blessing* promised to those patriarchs.

PRAYER: Heavenly Father, I marvel at how you trusted mere sinful mankind to raise your Son and to watch over Him. And I wonder at how you must trust me as well with your Word, the only thing we have on earth that will tell us of your love and your sacrifice on our behalf. I am beginning to really realize just how much power you have bestowed on us Christians to spread this message throughout the whole world. This is your earth, and these are your people. It is your Word of salvation, and your power to accomplish a task so big it would stagger us if we did not totally depend on you and your power to accomplish it. I am reminded of Isaiah 55:11, which says, *"So shall my word be that goeth forth out of my mouth: it shall not return unto me void, but it shall accomplish that which I please, and it shall prosper in the thing whereto I sent it."* I notice, Lord, that you say "so shall" and "it shall," and I take it that means it is your directive and determinate wills at work in and through sinful mankind as we share your Word with others. I am glad to know how the book ends, that you and I win! I give you all the praise and glory for that sure victory. In Jesus' name, Amen.

(Just in passing, the "as" that belongs to the "so" in V11 can be found in V10. Look it up and discover its meaning yourself)

DECEMBER 28th

 We have only four days left of this year, and it has been a glorious year. God is good! I want to talk again about the mature Christian. The mature Christian will display an inner calm and assurance, which should be noticeable to the nonbeliever.

Our calm is to provoke them into jealousy, so they want what we have, which is a solid relationship with the Lord. Paul had learned to be content, and he explains it as a learning experience. In fact, we never get completely out of the learning stage of our Christian lives. But although a mature Christian has learned to be content, that doesn't mean there won't be more things to learn.

Let's look at Phillipians 4:11-13, which reads: *"Not that I speak in respect of want: for I have learned, in whatsoever state I am, therewith to be content. I know both how to be abased, and I know how to abound: every where and in all things I am instructed both to be full and to be hungry, both to abound and to suffer need. I can do all things through Christ which strengeneth me."*

Paul found his ability to stand, and withstand, was in the power of Christ. Every thing in Paul's life was identified with his place *in* Christ. We, too, must see ourselves as *in* Christ, in a place of power, safety, assurance, and victory. That is the place of a mature Christian, and it is a glorious place. Once you try it you will never want to be any place else.

PRAYER: Heavenly Father, I come before you to ask for your peace to fill me as I step into that place of complete trust in Jesus. This is new ground for me to stand on, but if Paul could suffer untold hardships and still claim victory in Christ, then surely I can do that also. I want to praise you Lord, for your goodness. I have been given new views of who you are through the year. And with a God like you who is faithful, able, patient, and kind, I should have no fears of failure. All you require of me is to be faithful and obedient. I stand before you and ask for your help to keep me on the straight and narrow path, so my eyes would not rove to greener pastures or look back to lost opportunities. I give myself to you to shape and mold into the character of Christ Jesus. In Jesus' name, Amen.

DECEMBER 29th

 Another sign of a mature Christian is how he or she suffers. In I Peter 2:20-21, we read: *"For what glory is it, if, when ye be buffeted for your faults, ye shall take it patiently? But if, when ye do well, and suffer for it, ye take it patiently, this is acceptable with God. For even hereunto were ye called: because Christ also suffered for us, leaving us an example, that ye should follow His steps."*

Here we see that God is interested in the way Christians react to trials and suffering. If we did something for which we ought to hurt a little, and then take that patiently, well, we ought to since it was our fault in the first place. But when we suffer patiently for something that was not our own doing, that is also acceptable to God.

Jesus, who was without sin, suffered for us, so shouldn't we suffer and experience some hardships or criticism for bearing His name? Is it any wonder that we also see such references as James 1:2-4, which says: *"My brethren, count it all joy when ye fall into divers* (various) *temptations: Knowing this, that the trying of your faith worketh patience. But let patience have her perfect work, that ye maybe perfect and entire, wanting nothing."*

You can see the steps of maturity in those verses. Our Christian reaction to trials and tests work patience in our character, and brings us into perfection or maturity. Ask God to help you endure patiently, to react in a godly way to the things that befall you in life. Maintain that inner peace in the midst of storms.

It is not easy, but it is doable. You just have to practice it awhile, and even that will mature your Christian character. Do you know why? It will prove God to you in your life, because He will be right there to help you do it. Lay hold of the truth in Philippians 4:6-7, which reads: *"Be careful for nothing* (in nothing be anxious); *but in every thing by prayer and supplication with thanksgiving let your requests be made known unto God. And the peace of God which passeth all understanding, shall keep* (guard) *your hearts and minds* (thoughts) *through Christ Jesus."*

534

God wants to hear from you when you are going through the tough times. He invites you to pray and tell Him how you feel and what you want. Make your requests known to Him. Then you will have that peace beyond description!

PRAYER: Heavenly Father, I know I will need you to stand beside me as I train myself to react in the way you want me to, as I weather the storms of life. I thank you for the promise of that special kind of peace, and I claim it for myself right now. Even if I am not now going through a tough time, I still claim it so that when a storm arises, it will be there for me and I can just remind myself that I have already claimed it. Thank you for being such a kind Father to me. In Jesus' name, Amen.

DECEMBER 30th

 Let's look at one more great reference in regard to suffering and maturity. In I Peter 4:14-16, we read: *"Yet if ye be reproached for the name of Christ, happy* (blessed) *are ye; for the spirit of glory and of God resteth upon you: on their part he is evil spoken of, but on your part he is glorified. But let none of you suffer as a murderer, or as a thief, or as an evil doer, or as a busybody in other men's matters. Yet if any man suffer <u>as a Christian</u>, let him not be ashamed; but let him gloryify God on this behalf* (in this name). *"*

There are two ways to suffer: as an evildoer or as a Christian. The choice is yours to make. Your maturity as a Christian will make a difference in which path you chose. Anything that is alive must grow. Nothing stands still, but is either growing a little or dying some each day. The same is true of our faith in God. That growth will result in maturity.

There are people who have a mature body, but they have neglected to nourish their minds to grow. There are Christians who have allowed their knowledge of God to grow, but have neglected nourishing their spirits to grow. Your spirit grows as you step out in faith and obedience to God's Word, which will help you find out first hand just how much God wants to

535

bless and encourage you on your way. That is how your spirit grows, which in turn brings about Christian maturity.

There is an intimacy with God that awaits the Christian who wants to grow in both knowledge and obedience to the Word of God. It is my prayer that this daily devotional will help you attain that.

PRAYER: Heavenly Father, after all you have done for me, I need to tell you how grateful I am to be able to say I am a Christian and that I belong to you through your Son Jesus Christ. When I suffer or am criticized for my faith in you, help me to show your love for that person through me. I want to react in a way that will bring glory to your holy name. I pray that I will never be ashamed of the name of Jesus. I do not want to wave it like a red flag before an animal in a provoking manner, like a matador, but neither do I want to hide the fact that I wear your name. Help me to strike that balance in my witness for you. In Jesus' name, Amen.

DECEMBER 31st

 We will close out the year with a few more references to what makes a mature Christian. When you plant a fruit tree, you patiently wait for the tree to grow and bear fruit. The tree is watered, fertilized, staked up to grow straight, and finally the days come when you find fruit on it. The fruit is delicious, and the tree grows and grows. But it will also need to be pruned.

As we read through the Bible, we see that we, like a fruit tree, are to be fruit-bearing Christians. Matthew 7:15-20 reads: *"Beware of false prophets, which come to you in sheep's clothing, but inwardly they are ravening wolves. Ye shall know them by their fruits. Do men gather grapes of thorns, or figs of thistles? Even so every good tree bringeth forth good fruit; but a corrupt tree bringeth forth evil fruit. A good tree cannot bring forth evil fruit, neither can a corrupt tree bring forth good*

536

fruit. Every tree that bringeth not forth good fruit is hewn down, and cast into the fire. Wherefore by their fruits ye shall know them. "

We are told in this scripture that we are to be fruit inspectors, not judges. Just as a tree's fruit will tell you what kind of tree it is, so too will a person's fruit tell you what kind of a person he or she is: good or corrupt.

So, what kind of fruit can be expected from a Christian? Since the Holy Spirit lives within us, we should bear fruit that reflect the character of the Holy Spirit. Galatians 5:22 explains, *"But the fruit of the Spirit is love, joy, peace, long-suffering, gentleness* (**kindness**), *goodness, faith* (**faithfulness**), *meekness, temperance: against such there is no law.* "

Consider each one of these types of fruit in relation to your life, and decide what is missing. God wants us to display each and every one of these kinds of fruit, since the Holy Spirit lives within us and is able to show that kind of fruit through us on a daily basis.

I want to remind you that there is no law against this kind of fruit. No law says you can love just so much, or have so much joy in your heart or else you will be arrested! There is no limit to love, joy, peace, and so on! Ask God to help you live a life that is full with the fruit of the Spirit.

Take a look at John 15:5, where Jesus says, *"I am the vine and ye are the branches: He that abideth in me, and I in him, the same bringeth forth much fruit: for without me ye can do nothing."* We must at all times abide in Christ Jesus. He is the source of our very existence.

Now let's also see what Jesus says in John 15:1-2: *"I am the true vine, and my Father is the husbandman* (vine grower). *Every branch in me that beareth not fruit He taketh away: and every branch that beareth fruit, He purgeth it, that it may bring forth more fruit."*

Purging, or pruning, is painful. Good parts of the branch are cut away, but the purpose is to bring forth *more* fruit. If you bear good fruit, God will want more of the same kind of fruit from you. Are you able to withstand the pruning process and come out standing with a smile on your face? I believe that is a real sign of a mature Christian.

I feel led to add one more reference that will show the work of a mature Christian. In II Corinthians 1:3-4, we read: *"Blessed be God, even the Father of our Lord Jesus Christ, the Father of mercies, and the God of all comfort; Who comforteth us in all our tribulation* (affliction), *that we may be able to comfort them which are in any trouble, by the comfort wherewith we ourselves are comforted of God."*

When you have had a tough time, whether it was a financial failure, job loss, rejection, or the death of a loved one, and you went to God in prayer and were comforted, then that prepared you to help others who need to be comforted in their time of need. You do not go rushing in as a fixer-upper, but allow God to lead you to the person He wants you to be a comforter.

You will know that you know you are called to reach out to that person in time of need. Pray that God will give you the right words of comfort, and He will.

Have a happy New Year, bear much fruit, live life to the fullest, and praise God through it all.

PRAYER: Heavenly Father, it would appear that we will bear fruit of one kind or the other. It is up to us, with our free will, to choose to bear fruit that reflects the character of the Holy Spirit. I know how Satan wants to steal my love, joy, peace, patience, kindness, goodness, faithfulness, meekness, and temperance, but I can choose to display those characteristics in spite of my circumstances and how I feel. It is a bit frightening to realize that the world is watching to see how Christians act and react to the trials and tribulations of life, so, Lord, I ask you to help me be the witness you want me to be. I will not need to give it another thought, since you are able to prompt me as you see Satan set up his agenda against me. With your help, I will be aware of what is happening, so I can make the right choices at a moment's notice. Thank you for this past year. I ask that you usher me into the New Year with a determination to be the person you created me to be. In Jesus' name, Amen.